The Making of the English Literary C
From the Middle Ages to the Late Eigl

It is widely accepted among literary scholars that canon-formation began in the eighteenth century when scholarly editions and critical treatments of older works, designed to educate readers about the national literary heritage, appeared for the first time. In *The Making of the English Literary Canon* Trevor Ross challenges this assumption, arguing that canon-formation was going on well before the eighteenth century but was based on a very different set of literary and cultural values. Covering a period that extends from the Middle Ages to the institutionalization of literature in the eighteenth century, Ross's comprehensive history traces the evolution of cultural attitudes towards literature in English society, highlighting the diverse interests and assumptions that defined and shaped the literary canon.

An indigenous canon of letters, Ross argues, had been both the hope and the aim of English authors since the Middle Ages. Early authors believed that promoting the idea of a national literature would help publicize their work and favour literary production in the vernacular. Ross places these early gestures toward canon-making in the context of the highly rhetorical habits of thought that dominated medieval and Renaissance culture, habits that were gradually displaced by an emergent rationalist understanding of literary value. He shows that, beginning in the late seventeenth century, canon-makers became less concerned with how English literature was produced than with how it was read and received.

By showing that canon-formation has served different functions in the past, *The Making of the English Literary Canon* is relevant not only to current debates over the canon but also as an important corrective to prevailing views of early modern English literature and of how it was first evaluated, promoted, and preserved.

TREVOR ROSS is associate professor of English, Dalhousie University.

The Making of the English Literary Canon

From the Middle Ages to
the Late Eighteenth Century

T R E V O R   R O S S

McGill-Queen's University Press
Montreal & Kingston • London • Ithaca

© McGill-Queen's University Press 1998
ISBN 0-7735-1683-2 (cloth)
ISBN 0-7735-2080-5 (paper)

Legal deposit second quarter 1998
Bibliothèque nationale du Québec

Printed in Canada on acid-free paper
First paperback edition 2000

This book was first published with the help of a grant from the Humanities
and Social Sciences Federation of Canada, using funds provided by the
Social Sciences and Humanities Research Council of Canada.

McGill-Queen's University Press acknowledges the financial support
of the Government of Canada through the Book Publishing Industry
Development Program (BPIDP) for its publishing activities. We also
acknowledge the support of the Canada Council for the Arts for our
publishing program.

Canadian Cataloguing in Publication Data

Ross, Trevor Thornton, 1961–
    The making of the English literary canon: from the Middle Ages to the
    late eighteenth century
    Includes bibliographical references and index.
    ISBN 0-7735-1683-2 (bnd)
    ISBN 0-7735-2080-5 (pbk)
    1. English poetry – History and criticism. 2. Canon (Literature). I. Title.
    PR161.R68 1998   821.009   C97-901156-6

Typeset in New Baskerville 10/12
by Caractéra inc., Quebec City

For my parents,
Alistair and Thérèse

Contents

Acknowledgments

Material from several chapters has previously appeared in *ELH, Modern Language Quarterly*, and *Renaissance and Reformation*. I thank these publications for permission to reprint work here.

This project began as a doctoral dissertation, which I defended at the University of Toronto. I thank the department of English at Toronto for providing me with financial aid that enabled me to conduct research at the Folger Shakespeare Library, and the Social Science and Humanities Research Council of Canada for granting me a generous fellowship. Lawrence Lipking, John Baird, Ruth Harvey, William Halewood, and Nancy Lindheim all provided thoughtful and welcome comments on various aspects of the work, and Kyp Harness assisted me in producing the original typescript of the dissertation.

The current work represents a thorough rethinking and revision of the dissertation. It began renewed life at a workshop organized by the Center for 17th- and 18th-Century Studies at UCLA and the Clark Library. I thank the Center for having invited me, and the workshop's participants for their helpful remarks. I have greatly benefited at various stages of the revision from the support of friends and colleagues, especially John Baxter, JoAnna Dutka, Anne Higgins, and Ronald Huebert. I am grateful to Marshall Brown for his warm words of encouragement, and to Lyn Bennett for her invaluable assistance in helping me to prepare the final typescript. I also wish to thank Philip J. Cercone and the editorial staff at McGill-Queen's University Press, and Curtis Fahey for his care and attention in copy-editing the work.

I am indebted to Brian Corman and Laura Hopkins, without whose unfailing judgment and grace I would never have been able to complete this work.

Introduction

I begin by comparing two images of English poets. The first is a frontispiece that appeared before two collections of John Skelton's verse from the late 1520s, *Agaynste a Comely Coystrowne* and *Dyvers Balettys and Dyties Solacyous*. The woodcut offers no reliable sense of the poet's physical features, nor is it the first pictorial representation of an English poet – the likenesses of Chaucer in the *Troilus* frontispiece, and in Hoccleve's *Regiment of Princes* (*c.* 1412), are likely the earliest such portraits. The Skelton frontispiece is nonetheless remarkable, since it is the first to honour an English poet with the classical symbols of the poetic profession: "Skelton" wears a laurel crown, holds before him an open book and what appears to be another book or a pen, and is seated at a large cathedra structure, in the manner of Virgil and other subjects of early literary portraiture.[1] Such symbolism would have pleased the original Skelton, who was widely recognized in his lifetime and after as "poet laureate." As the accompanying Latin caption taken from the poet's earlier *Garlande of Laurell* (1523) announces, "all species of trees yield to the laurel."

My second image bears many of these same conventional symbols, but the story it tells seems more modern for the image is the now familiar one of a young author working in the humbling presence of his canonical fathers. The ephebe in this case is Christopher Smart, as he is depicted in the frontispiece to his short-lived periodical miscellany *The Universal Visiter, and Memorialist* (1756).[2] Smart is shown seated at a writing desk, at work on the next issue of his paper. He is gazing up at a row of five busts, raised on a mantel and surrounded by an oversized laurel wreath. The busts bear representations of Chaucer, Spenser, Shakespeare, Waller, and Dryden. Each bust has a verse legend inscribed on its base. These verses are reprinted below the frontispiece:

> To CHAUCER! who the English Tongue design'd:
> To SPENCER! who improv'd it, and refin'd:
> To Muse-fir'd SHAKESPEAR! who increas'd its Praise,
> Rich in bold Compounds, & strong-painted Phrase,
> To WALLER! Sweet'ner of its manly Sound:
> To DRYDEN! who its full Perfection found.

Behind the busts are bookshelves containing a number of folios, including the works of Gower, Sidney, Milton, and eighteen other English authors (Skelton not among them.) Above these bookshelves is a Latin inscription that tells us this is Apollo's Temple of the English.

The history I relate here is essentially contained in these two images, in their differences as much as their common symbolism. Both are representations of canon-formation, of poetic identities being sanctified with laurel crowns and preserved in printed editions. Both images suggest an element of cultural belatedness, more prominent in the later frontispiece yet implicit in the conventionality of the earlier woodcut. Above all, for my purposes, both images would be unthinkable or risible within an English culture that did not already think highly of its own literature. How that culture thought and felt about its literature, and how those perceptions changed from Skelton's time to Smart's, are the subjects of this history. The differences between the images tell of this change. In the earlier woodcut, the enthroned poet is an authoritative symbol, visual certification of Skelton's authorial profession and laureate status, and rhetorical assurance to the reader of the canonical value of the poetry. In the later image, the seated Smart, though canonized for his poetry in our century, derives whatever authority he may possess from the canonic masters before him. For Smart in this image is probably not writing verse, as Skelton is in his portrait, but rather essaying a historical commentary on the older English poets; this would have been in keeping with the declared "memorializing" aims of *The Universal Visiter*, whose fare included essays on Chaucer, Spenser, Shakespeare, and Pope.[3] Skelton is seen producing English poetry, Smart receiving and *re*producing it for a modern audience, rendering it accessible through commentary, certifying its canonicity, consecrating it within its own hallowed temple.[4]

It is with these later functions that we associate the formation of literary canons. At present, canons are made and preserved within critical and academic institutions as well as cultural establishments such as public libraries, publishing houses, repertory theatres, and so on. Modern canon-formation, in this way, is an aspect of reception, of introducing readers to the literature of the near or distant past, and of preserving that literature in the hope of maintaining the culture that helped to produce it. This process, a complicated one and one that has received intense scrutiny of late, can be rightly said to have begun, in England at least, during the eighteenth century. But the portrait of Skelton suggests that the idea of an English canon predates the eighteenth century, and that a version of canon-formation, one largely non-institutional and hence unfamiliar to us now, informed the production and reception of English literature well before the eighteenth century. My aim is to provide a sense of this earlier version of canon-formation and to trace its history and eventual displacement in early modernity.

Whether it is at root a material or ideological change, something happens in the eighteenth century to the way in which works of art and literature are valued. No longer considered rhetorical or didactic instruments, they become prized as autonomous creations. In Northrop Frye's formulation, "nearly every work of art in the past had a social function in its own time, a function which was often not primarily an aesthetic function at all. The whole conception of 'works of art' as a classification for all pictures, statues, poems, and musical compositions is a relatively modern one." Frye does not attempt to explain the change he is describing, yet such an explanation can be derived from something Frye says in his preceding paragraph. Defending the study of the humanities, Frye writes that it is "the consumer, not the producer, who benefits by culture, the consumer who becomes humanized and liberally educated."[5] Arguably, it is this assumption that is the "relatively modern" conception, the one that led to the ascendancy of such concepts as literature and the aesthetic, and the one that defined the modern process of canon-formation. I would suggest that the differences between Skelton the enthroned laureate and Smart the memorialist of dead laureates reflect such a change in how literary value is perceived, a change from production to consumption, invention to reception, writing to reading.

This change, in its broadest outlines, has been described as a movement from aristocratic to bourgeois concepts of art and literature,[6] as a rupture, in Foucauldian terminology, between an earlier *épistemé* of similitude and a later *épistemé* of the rationalist human sciences,[7] and, for some who lived through it, as the triumph of the moderns over the ancients. In the terms I wish to borrow here, the change is one more round in the age-old quarrel between rhetoric and philosophy. In particular, the change marks a cognitive restructuring or "epistemological shift" from a rhetorical to a modern "objectivist" culture.[8] Its salient feature with respect to literary canonicity is the difference between how either culture hopes to achieve a sense of community or solidarity, conceived of as either ultimate value or ultimate truth.[9] A rhetorical culture seeks solidarity through the power of words, a verbal power that is designed to contain or defeat divisions within or among the culture's subjects. An objectivist culture searches for transcendence through the power of knowledge, the acquisition of which is supposed eventually to help its subjects understand and so overcome conflicts within themselves or between themselves and the objects that surround them. Whereas a rhetorical culture seeks transcendence in the Word, in the atemporal, eternal utterance of essence, an objectivist culture moves gradually and progressively towards essence, or at least towards a harmonious understanding of social and cultural differences.

I use this opposition not as an explanatory mechanism for identifying the various causes of the change I am describing, but only as an historical model for heightening the central contrast I am proposing between canonicity based on production and canonicity based on consumption. Yet my categories of "rhetorical" and "objectivist" are not entirely heuristic either, since they do refer to divergent ways of understanding and organizing experience. No actual culture is ever purely one or the other, just as both forms of transcendence are impossible idealizations that involve a radical denial of the limits of representation: verbal power can never escape the agonistic, divisive structures of rhetoric upon which it relies, just as there exists no transparent language to communicate knowledge objectively since language is forever coloured by belief and desire, including the desire for transcendence. And to the degree that its structures of thought are made operative by belief and ideology, knowledge always involves an element of persuasion – by proof if not by verbal seduction – while rhetoric can never be utterly distinguished from knowledge since verbal power cannot long obtain assent without demonstrating some reference to the phenomenal.[10] Yet, however elusive the goal of transcendence, both modes of thought, in the minds of those who abide by them, do promise at least moments of mastery. A rhetorical culture is empowered by speakers who utilize their oratorical skills in the service of the community; an objectivist culture is empowered by interpreters who seek to better their community by continually contributing to a body of knowledge about experience. A rhetorical culture thus prizes invention, eloquence, and verbal production, whereas an objectivist culture invokes methods of empirical observation and analysis, reading and research, interpretation and judgment, criticism, and other "forms of attention."[11]

A fuller sense of this distinction as it relates specifically to the history of canon-formation is available from a description Richard McKeon has provided of an historic change in the understanding of Christian dogma: "In the course of the development of canon law, the art of rhetoric, which takes into account the character and authority of speakers, the circumstances and sensibilities of audiences, and the modes and styles of communications, was transformed into an art of interpretation by which apparent contradictions of conflicting canons might be removed or justified by consideration of differences of audiences, circumstances, and intentions as they determine differences of meaning in what is said."[12] By analogy, when early English writers want to praise a work, they merely assert its value. They make claims for it, often with reference to a standard derived from classical rhetoric such as "eloquence." They assume, rightly or not, that the tastes and sensibilities of their readers are much like their own; they will, in any event, use their verbal power to induce such conformity of response. Inconsistencies inevitably appear, as early writers often make identical claims about divergent works or conflicting prescriptive standards, though these inconsistencies are not terribly disquieting in a rhetorical culture where the contingency of verbal power is to some degree assumed: one persuasive opinion gives way to another more persuasive opinion, and so on. But to a culture shifting towards the rigours of objectivism, inconsistencies are embarrassments, signs of confusion and divisions that need to be overcome through knowledge.[13] A solution is to relax the absoluteness of standards or, more precisely, to replace prescriptive standards with an absoluteness of method and factual certainty by using historicist arguments such as "times change," "tastes change," or "the aims and styles of writing change." As a rhetorical culture gives way to a seemingly more diversified objectivist culture, so interpretations of changing values replace or supplement declarations of value. In other words, it is the objectivist desire of resolving contradictions in the definition of the English canon that leads to the rise of interpretation, literary history, and other related critical practices in the eighteenth century.

A sketch of early literary values may clarify the point. Before "literature" in its modern sense emerged in the later eighteenth century, there was the rhetorical category of "poetry" or "poesy," a term that had at its root an idea of "making." For critics from antiquity to the Renaissance, from Aristotle to Jonson, poetry designated the "skill, or Crafte of Making ... the habit, or the Art."[14] Poetry is at once the activity and the ability of the begetter of fictions and verses. It has to do with production. This does not necessarily mean that the value of poetry is tied to the particular needs of the poet. Rather, the social function and truth-value of poetry are defined in terms of utility and instrumentality. Thus, the immortality topos, until recently the prime operative trope behind all poetic production, makes the patron not the consumer of verse but its subject. The poet is welcome because he ensures fame for his client and his community; they value the poet's continued output, and whether they feel engaged in a particular way by a work is beside the point, only a by-product, as it were. Utility is equally foregrounded in other early notions of poetry's function. Until well into the eighteenth century, the highest praise that could be awarded a poet held that he had refined his community's or his age's language, in the sense that he had tapped new sources and varieties of eloquence and so had proven the language's beauty and versatility. Chaucer is the father of English poetry because he opens the way for more poets by proving that English is a poetic, productive language, a source of verbal power.

Even the didactic tradition is largely understood from the point of view of the poet's contribution to the state or community as a whole. The poet teaches as he delights; he is prophet, guide, and singer. The audience may experience catharsis, find its moral beliefs reinforced, or may even learn something, but early defences of poetry's utility rarely detail the nature of these effects on individual listeners or readers. Rather, these effects are benefits to the community at large. Consumption, in effect, is not readily distinguished from production. The culture, the totality of poet and audience, is the consumer and the producer, and there is felt to be no problem as to the question of where value resides, in the poetic activity, the poetic utterance, or its reception. It is the same value that circulates all around; or, at a minimum, the poetic activity is felt to operate within a system of roughly equal exchange. Whatever immortalizing, expressive, educative, or exhortative effects poetry is felt to produce are ascribed to the verbal powers of the poet who, in turn, is at one with the interests of the community. The poet is not a maker of commodities for an autonomous audience, or even a creator of autonomous works of art, but an agent of production working on behalf of established social relations. Certainly this is what early poets assert time and again in their own defence. Perhaps the most prevalent foundational myth of rhetorical culture holds that civil society is itself the offspring of the poets and orators. In Cicero's much-cited version, no other force approaches the power of poetic eloquence in helping "to gather scattered humanity into one place, or to lead it out of its brutish existence in the wilderness up to our present condition of civilization as men and as citizens, or, after the establishment of social communities, to give shape to laws, tribunals, and civic rights."[15] In short, verbal power serves to bridge divisions.

Then there are all the occasional and pragmatic uses of poetry, its indispensability in centuries past as an eloquent tool for the aspiring courtier who wished to get ahead, make friends, and make love. At his disposal were a multiplicity of compositional aids, from the several "artes" of poetry that were thinly disguised guidebooks on courtly manners, to the many commonplace books that cut and paste together verse snippets, rhetorical figures, and metrical models, all designed to help the courtier to mount Parnassus or whatever. To later anthologists, these textbooks seemed shockingly arbitrary and appallingly short on editorial apparatus. Exclaimed one eighteenth-century editor, looking over an early miscellany, "There is ... so abrupt and sudden a hurry from one idea to another in every chapter ... that the sentences slip through the reader's apprehension as quicksilver through the fingers."[16] Then again, these anthologies were neither prepared for easy consumption by a reader nor designed necessarily to render a fixed and inimitable canon unto posterity. The purpose of consulting these collections or of reading any canonical poetry was to enable you to compose some poetry yourself or to sharpen your communicative and suasive skills. With such powers, you could feel, however provisionally and however circumscribed by rhetorical conventions, that you controlled value itself – the happy *homo rhetoricus* lately reawakened in neopragmatist imaginings.[17] Of course, the audience could simply experience pleasure or emotive transport from listening to the poet's craft. Yet even then, Longinus could conceive of the sublime as a technique that could be outlined in a handbook for young authors and, above all, as an experience that could inspire listeners to feel like producers themselves: elevated by true sublimity, "we come to believe we have created what we have only heard."[18]

Classical aesthetics did not often take into account the specific responses or requirements of audiences.[19] Rather, the norms of classical rhetoric were designed in accordance with the immediate needs of speakers and "makers." By extension, early evaluative standards were keyed explicitly to each new generation's requirements for cultural and ideological production. This recalls Frye's claim, in the passage I quoted above, that the work of art in the past had a social function *in its own time.* Canon-formation in its older conception is unfamiliar to us now largely because it is a severely restricted conception, restricted precisely by the presentism Frye identifies. Works from the distant past could be deemed canonical only if they could be shown to contribute to the productivity and stature of the present age and to the circulation of contemporary values. The classical canon stood as a pedagogical model of rhetorical eloquence and as an ideological model of poetry-making in the service of empire-building. As to the status and utility of the indigenous canon, Defoe's rehearsal of contemporary opinion in *A Vindication of the Press* (1718) is typical of two centuries' worth of English criticism in the way it itemizes the palpable benefits of literary production: "How much the World is oblig'd ... to the famous Writings of *Milton* for the Foundation of Divine Poetry; Poetry in general is improv'd from the Writings of *Chaucer, Spencer,* and others; Dramatick Entertainments perfected by *Shakespear,* our Language and Poetry refin'd by *Dryden;* the Passions rais'd by *Otway;* the Inclination mov'd by *Cowley;* and the World diverted by *Hudibras,* (not to mention the Perfections of Mr. *Addison,* and several others of this Age) I leave to the determination of every impartial Reader."[20] Defoe's catalogue is also typical in the way it projects ultimate evaluative authority onto a rhetorical fiction, in this case the "impartial reader." The narrow prescriptions of the earliest professional critics – Rymer, Dennis, Gildon – were merely an extreme version of this presentist thinking, insofar as they presumed the possibility of literary "perfection" or correctness being achieved in "this Age" (though in emphasizing critical method, these critics were beginning to measure value objectively). On the margins of this canon, then, were a vast diversity of works once esteemed by previous generations of English readers – including, at one time or another, the works of Chaucer, Spenser, and Shakespeare – yet whose utility and value in relation to the present could no longer be readily affirmed. The canon was something to be produced, not *reproduced.*

Today, canon-formation is almost exclusively associated with the mechanisms of cultural reproduction, and in particular with the establishment of university curricula and syllabi. In an objectivist culture, literary production is at the service of consumption, in particular the acquiring and systematizing of knowledge about experience. Invention is still prized, as the modern cults of genius and originality may attest, but the social function of written art is no longer understood in relation to the practical requirements of either the author or the immediate occasions such art is designed to address. Nor is verbal production necessarily valued, as it once was, as a means to enable further production. If anything, the assumption in post-Romantic aesthetics is that the true genius will exhaust human knowledge and literary expression by encapsulating the whole truth of experience. The poet-genius may be valued as the master interpreter, one who sheds new light on our world or who makes us perceive experience from the point of view of another, but in either case it is the acquisition of knowledge by the subject that is foremost. Such efforts of the human imagination may, in theory, lead to solidarity insofar as they encourage an understanding of personal and cultural differences, but the advancement of society depends on the capacity and willingness of readers to engage in such efforts, as well as on the work of critical and pedagogical authorities to encourage readers into making such efforts.

To borrow one of Pierre Bourdieu's key distinctions in his sociology of aesthetics, we could say that modern authors may, as in a rhetorical culture, garner *symbolic capital* – prestige, fame, honour, and the like, which can be deployed to influence any form of social exchange – yet the true test of a work's canonicity for an objectivist culture occurs when it is put to the service of *cultural capital*, which is a form of capital peculiar to the relatively autonomous field of cultural production, and which can be used to compete with other modes of capital (economic, political, religious) in the perennial contest for social power. Cultural capital, according to Bourdieu, represents the measure of accredited intellectual competence that is required to interpret the meaning and to appreciate the value of cultural goods and relations. In an objectivist culture, canonical texts are treated as a sort of code which can be fully deciphered only by those who are recognized to possess the necessary disposition, learning, and skill. Cultural capital, as it is unequally distributed among social agents and institutions, thus becomes the locus of contestation in a struggle for distinction and legitimacy.[21] (Bourdieu uses "cultural" in its restricted sense as referring to artistic activity rather than its broad sense in denoting an entire mode of life and thought. Risking confusion, I use the term both in its broad sense, when contrasting a rhetorical to an objectivist culture, and in its restricted sense, when applying Bourdieu's sociology of aesthetics to the autonomization of the cultural field that marked the passage to objectivist thinking. "Culture," Raymond Williams once remarked, "is one of the two or three most complicated words in the English language."[22])

Hence canon-formation in an objectivist culture is an aspect of reception and cultural reproduction. Literature is valued by and for its consumers, by educated readers who enjoy its affects, by teachers like Frye who uphold its liberalizing potentialities, and by theorists like the New Critics who value it for *itself*, as if it involved a non-instrumental, imaginative act of reading. Each is involved, to a greater or lesser degree, in keeping canonical works alive in times of change and making clear their modernity for every new generation of readers. This is usually accomplished through a variety of hermeneutic or historicist practices, or some interplay between them. "Commentary,"

Frye writes, "is allegoralization,"[23] and so, like the old Christian allegorizations of the classics, modern interpretive practices seek to provide readers with knowledge or insight into a canonical work's thematic resonances. Awareness of such resonances, it is hoped, will diminish the work's forbidding alterity and so make it seem enduring or relevant to contemporary concerns. The canonical work is brought as much as possible into the reader's horizon of expectations; hence, modern interpretations differ from the old allegories by replacing the latter's instrumentalist assumptions with a paradoxical account of how the value of a work may remain constant and intrinsic even as its meaning is subject to continual reinterpretation. Historicist inquiries, such as philology, biography, and literary history, aim at the reverse, at broadening this horizon of expectations by providing readers with packages of historical information that will enable them to overcome the work's alterity. Readers, it is hoped, are transported intellectually as much as possible into the work's context of origin and encouraged to partake in a dialogue with the meanings and horizons of earlier cultures. The assumption in either case is that knowledge, however lengthy the process of accumulating and methodizing it, serves to bridge divisions.

The process of systematizing knowledge, however, requires that the respective spheres of the reader, the text, the author, and the social context be continually distinguished; the art of interpretation, as McKeon suggests, emphasizes differences between audiences, cultures, texts, and so on. Thus, literary value is no longer understood, as it was in a rhetorical culture, to circulate endlessly in a system of roughly equal exchange. Instead, the activities of writing and reading are seen as more or less separate and of divergent utility or significance. In a rhetorical culture, there exists a structure of conviction that posits the apparent commensurability of author, reader, and text: all function within a productive economy on behalf of established social relations, and so their value is felt to be similar and freely exchangeable. In an objectivist culture, that value is no longer seen as commensurable since it is felt to be intrinsic rather than circulating, residing in the text itself or in either of the distinct activities of writing or reading. Literary theorists since the mid-eighteenth century have been much preoccupied with identifying the discrete values for each of these spheres or activities: the autonomy or organic integrity of the work of art, the nature of poetic creativity and originality, the special character of the aesthetic experience, and so on. Each of these values has in turn been represented by its own canon, the Romantic cult of the poet-genius, say, or the New Critical tradition of autotelic "verbal icons." All these canons may be seen as ultimately enabling the goal of acquiring knowledge, but the tendency in modern thinking is to allow for a plurality of values, whether centred on the text or oriented towards the author or reader. It is nonetheless a limited plurality: if conflicts in rhetoricist canons tend to arise from having the same claim being made about dissimilar works, conflicts in objectivist canons tend to occur as a result of markedly dissimilar claims being made on behalf of the same work.

Given this plurality of values, there emerges the difficulty of establishing the "source" of value and evaluative certainty. In modern aesthetic discourse, reader and text occupy the irreconcilable grounds of subject and object, and therefore the question of value and canonicity continually reaches an "aporia of judgment," an undecidability as to where value resides, in the text or its affects, in the reader's innate judgment, or in what he or she has learned from reading works of intrinsic merit.[24] This aporia is equally reached in a rhetorical culture, but there it is continually deferred through verbal power: if all readers learn to be "impartial" or "learned," as Defoe and other early writers repeatedly insist, then all could agree and the community would thrive. A similar, if much less vocal, deferral occurs in modern culture: if only all readers would know all there is to know about literature, or would perceive and interpret it in like fashion, then all could agree and each could thrive. The contrast in reasoning nonetheless suggests that a rhetorical culture tends to operate as though value is conferred by a real or fictive community of verbally adept "learned readers" who are themselves producers, whereas an objectivist culture tends to assume that value is inherent (or at least potentially so) within aesthetic objects and simply experienced by sensitive readers – for a culture to be consumed, it must first be made into commodities.[25] Yet, just as no culture is ever purely rhetorical or objectivist, so the question of value is never definitively resolved. This is so because of the limitations of either culture: a rhetorical culture relies on language at the cost of understanding how language alone can never help one to arrive at truth, while an objectivist culture prizes truth at the cost of understanding how truth is always mediated through language.

Since its economy does not rely on verbal power among its subjects, an objectivist culture can afford to be less vocal in how it defines literary value or where it locates it. In a rhetorical culture, the function and utility of literature, of producing and consuming it, are always clearly and forthrightly proclaimed. The vast bulk of early English criticism is pragmatic, prescriptive, and sharply evaluative. Whatever the ultimate source of evaluative authority, be it a patron, monarch, or God, certainty must be always asserted so that the culture's operative universe of belief be continually maintained and that English subjects remain constantly aware of the productive role they are to play within their culture's moral economy. In an objectivist culture, certainty is always *assumed* but, perhaps to avoid conflict or to defer the question of evaluative authority, the functions of literature and of consuming it are not quite so loudly proclaimed. Humanists like Frye believe that literature serves the formation of the self, but this emphasis on the self does not provide much sense of how value may circulate within a larger economy. In an objectivist culture, the systematizing of knowledge requires that the workings of an economy be measured often down to the last variable and contingency, but value is not made to appear widely circulating since consumption, the acquisition of knowledge, is prized above production.[26] The literary system of readers and their texts is made to seem depoliticized and "disinterested" because readers are considered consumers who are not expected to contribute productively to a larger social and moral economy. The perception is that literature serves no productive function within the economy – it operates, Bourdieu would suggest, within the relatively autonomous field of cultural production, whose self-definition depends upon a collective disavowal of economic or other interests. Readers, it seems, serve no productive function other than, potentially, the supreme function of contributing to human knowledge and of helping to overcome social divisions. Literature is valuable only insofar as it helps to fashion and educate more and better readers, receivers of ever more refined sensibility, consumers of ever greater disinterestedness. "The task of the moral technology of Literature," Terry Eagleton writes, "is to produce an historically peculiar form of human subject who is sensitive, receptive, imaginative and so on ... *about nothing in particular.*"[27]

There is, as Eagleton recognizes, a rich history of aesthetic philosophy, or "aesthetic ideology," contained within his catch-all tag "and so on."[28] Within the limited, autonomous economy of aesthetics, value is understood to circulate a great deal and in a highly complicated manner among works of art and their audience. In a sense, where canonicity in the past was informed by a restrictive presentism, modern objectivist theories of value are restricted by an intense localism in their dual emphases on self-formation and the autonomy of aesthetic experience. But my narrative ends before the refinements of aesthetic philosophy come to be widely appropriated in English thought. It records the gradual exclusion of pragmatic, instrumentalist notions of canonicity from critical discourse, the eventual supersession of reception over production as the focus of such discourse, and the slow processes of depoliticization and autonomization, of getting used to the idea that reading or writing literary works may not necessarily empower you to accomplish anything in particular. My subject, in other words, is not aesthetic theory in early modern England, but the practical ramifications of this epistemological shift, as I have outlined it, for the way in which the English valued and canonized their own literature.

Previous scholarship on canon-making in early modern England has tended to fall into five broad categories: reception histories of particular author's works, such as Shakespeare's; case studies of seminal events in the formation of English literature, such as the publication of self-canonizing gestures like Spenser's *The Shepheardes Calender* (1579) or Jonson's folio *Workes* (1616); surveys of changing tastes or habits of literary "appreciation"; histories of literary theory and particular critical practices; and literary histories such as Lawrence Lipking's *The Ordering of the Arts in Eighteenth-Century England* (1970) or Howard Weinbrot's *Britannia's Issue: The Rise of British Literature from Dryden to Ossian* (1993) that focus on canon-making efforts within specific periods.[29] My narrative is intended both as a synthesis of these studies and as a corrective to some of their assumptions. No previous work has ever examined the changing reputation of English literature as a whole prior to the nineteenth century. Yet, to the extent that "English literature" is an idea whose history can be traced, my narrative is closer in nature to a history of an idea than to a conventional reception history, even though I have restricted myself in my selection of evidence to early authors' own statements on previous English writers, on norms of literary value, and on the canonical status of their own work. By surveying such authorial statements, I aim to provide a sense of the changing values that have been associated with canonical works, of the diverse interests that have informed the making of the canon, and of the several functions that the canon has been made to serve. Since its approach is analytical and discursive, my narrative also considers a number of case histories, including Jonson's folio, though its emphasis is sociological rather than strictly literary or biographical; these case studies are provided to illustrate larger changing patterns in prevailing conditions for cultural production and reception. My narrative is not intended as a history of taste, since it is concerned more with how the function of literature was variously understood by a changing English society than with how particular conventions, styles, or genres may have become dominant at different periods. Moreover, the notion of "taste," I suggest, can be applied to literary evaluation before the eighteenth century only with a great deal of anachronistic reduction, since it bespeaks an ideology of aesthetic consumption that was crystallized only very late in the period I examine. A similar objection can be raised against works like René Wellek's *The Rise of English Literary History* (1941), which surveys early forms of critical activity in search of a historicist approach to literature. This approach, as I suggest in my final chapter, began to be pursued by critics only with the ascendancy of what I call objectivist thinking.

Though I deal with literary criticism in several chapters, my narrative is not a study of aesthetic theory or poetics but rather, as I have been emphasizing, of cultural practices and assumptions about valuing literary work.[30] These practices may include critical evaluation in its broadest sense yet may equally involve other phenomena, notably authors' self-advertisements, modes of dissemination and publication, censorship and the dispersal of library collections, the teaching of literature, authors' attitudes toward their audiences, the editing of older works, among many others. I have examined several of these phenomena, though some (patronage, literacy rates, class considerations, and so on) I have referred to only in passing.[31] A preliminary study like this one has necessarily to be selective: an exhaustive study of all the material, social, and ideological conditions that made possible the emergence of a literary canon in England would have required several volumes. It might have also required describing some of the decisive breaks and developments that histories of criticism and English literature routinely rehearse, such as the rise of humanist learning or the paradigmatic shift from Elizabethan aureation to the epigrammatic compression of later verse. These historic signposts have been largely ignored in this study, in part because they have been thoroughly discussed elsewhere, and in part because they are only broadly related to the multiple contingencies and interests that have impelled authors to propose a canon of English literature. Canons are, in Wendell V. Harris's phrase, "selections with purposes," and these purposes can be quite numerous and varied: legitimizing the writing activity or particular literary movements, defining a literary system, asserting evaluative authority, setting authoritative models or common frames of reference, transmitting a cultural heritage, and so on.[32] Many such purposes are operative during the period I cover, yet most fall outside the purview of standard histories of criticism and English literature.

Likewise, what has usually been identified as the chief impetus for canon-making, the rise of nationalism, can be related only in a general sense to the diverse hopes and concerns that have motivated authors to propose canons. Lipking and Weinbrot both suggest that the canon of indigenous letters was "ordered" only in the eighteenth century as a direct result of "a growing individual and national confidence."[33] Yet, from the beginnings of English literature, authors have been engaged in canonizing gestures on behalf of an imagined community, though one whose self-definition has undergone continual transformation. In one form or another, local or nativist sentiment has always been a potential cause of literary canon-formation, but not a sufficient one. Certainly, as I note when discussing the catalogues of John Leland and John Bale, the heightened national self-consciousness that followed in the immediate aftermath of the English Reformation did not stop people from destroying thousands of rare English manuscripts. As much as nationalist sentiment has been an incentive to celebrate a heritage of letters, so the making of canons has frequently served to inspire a sense of communal identification on behalf of particular interests: nationalism during the Elizabethan period, for example, may have spurred some writers and critics to call for the enshrinement of a vernacular canon, though it is equally the case that English poets exploited prevailing sentiments in order to promote their activity. Authors have invoked nationalist feelings in a variety of ways and on behalf of divergent practices (for example, both for and against neo-classicist refinement). Accordingly, it is difficult to measure the influence of such feelings upon how the value of English literature was perceived, especially in earlier periods.

Expressions of communal self-identification have to be seen as operating in conjunction with other powerful ideologies that have helped to determine conceptions of canonicity; among these ideologies, I consider in particular the contrasting value-systems of civic and commercial humanism.[34] Perhaps more consequential are the many social and material changes that have altered the nature of literary production, notably the coming of print and the subsequent professionalization of authorship. And overriding all, I suggest, is the central cognitive shift from a rhetorical to an objectivist culture. Faced with this enormously complex interplay of contingencies, interests, and circumstances that have occasioned the making of canons, I have had to forego a detailed analysis of specific historical changes and to concentrate more on how the canon was formed than on why it was formed, more on the repercussions of historical change than on its causes. All the same, my reservations with arguments like Lipking's or Weinbrot's have to do with more than recognizing that the process of canon-making in England began well before the eighteenth century or that it may have been motivated by numerous considerations in addition to an intensified nationalism. Arguably, the increased national "affection" for English letters which they see as occurring over the course of the eighteenth century did not in fact represent a deepening of this affection so much as its broadening out (in more readers, more critics, more books, and so on). This change, in turn, reflected a new way of valuing literary writings whereby the consumption of literature had displaced its production as the primary concern of critical discourse. Thus, whereas Lipking treats Johnson's *Lives of the English Poets* (1779–81) as inaugurating a modern ordering of the canon, Johnson's criticism serves as a terminus within my narrative because its essential tenets are those of an older, residual understanding of canonical value, the final sustained expression of rhetoricist thinking at a historical moment when most of its operative beliefs had given way to modern empirical and rationalist presuppositions. Rhetorical valorization and the drive to harmonize the canon do not at all disappear with Johnson, of course. They have merely now to compete with the knowledge of how cultures differ and values change.

Rhetorical assertiveness has characterized much of the recent warring over the canon that has preoccupied university departments of literature for the past decade.[35] Though this study does not deal directly with current controversies, it offers an implicit critique of how these debates often sorely lack historical perspective on the issues they address. Many of these issues have been of long standing. I consider several. First, an indigenous canon of letters has been the hope and purpose of English authors from early on. Yet, just as prevailing concepts of canonicity have been redefined as a result of the shift in critical emphasis from production to consumption, so the canon has been the subject of continual revision and updating on behalf of contemporary desires and interests. This study might, in this sense, be more appropriately entitled "the makings of English literary canons." However, authors and critics have not always acknowledged or endorsed this process of revision, since they have routinely invoked the ideal of a literary tradition in order to derive a sense of legitimacy, inspiration, and evaluative certainty. The canon has often seemed to them as much a burden to be overturned as a standard to be upheld.

Secondly, the notion that the canon is primarily a hierarchical construct is a relatively recent assumption, one that is, paradoxically, consequent upon a pluralization of the canon that reflects both the differentiating forces of the marketplace and an objectivist discourse of discrimination and systematization. In contrast, early canon-makers tended to assume that communal solidarity could be best achieved by proposing harmonious canons that were more authoritative the more they demonstrated amplitude or even completeness of record. For all canon-makers, then, the practical task of assessing the quality of literary works has often been as important as the symbolic one of defining how literary value ought to be distributed within a culture: as something to be either shared as part of a collective cultural achievement or identified particularly with the fruits of genius, the intrinsic worth of the text, or the isolate rewards of reading.

Thirdly, the relation of authorship and canonicity to forms of social power has been a persistent concern among English writers. Although the ways in which they have negotiated a legitimate space for their activity within English society have varied considerably, many have espoused a version of disinterestedness in order to make their practice seem distinctive and their assertions credible. And although the ideals of disinterestedness and aesthetic autonomy received formal theoretical articulation only within Enlightenment and Romantic philosophy, they were already implicit in the attempts by professional authors to declare their relative independence from powerful political and economic interests. The gradual autonomization of the cultural field, certified by the objectivist separation of spheres of human activity, was thus in the first instance a response to how the conditions for literary production were altered following the advent of a commercial print trade.

Fourthly, the modern belief that canonical texts are inherently rich and various in meaning develops from the need among professional critics and educators to justify their supervision of reading practices. Within a rhetorical culture, the meaning of a work was thought to be more or less fixed yet open to reformulation. Though a number of early English authors were keen to ensure that their writings were disseminated in their original or corrected versions, they were motivated by a desire less to exercise proprietary control than to enhance the effectivity of their verbal power in helping to circulate value dynamically within the moral economy of English society. Textual authenticity in relation to older English texts became a major concern of critics and editors only later, once the activity of reading literature had come to seem vital to the acculturation of the self and to the acquisition of cultural capital. To establish their authority over cultural consumption, critics increasingly attempted to demonstrate their competence by searching for "latent beauties" within canonical English writings, beauties which, they believed, could be reliably discovered only within authentic versions of those texts.

Finally, from the earliest attempts to canonize themselves or their predecessors, English authors have been struggling with a central paradox within canon-formation, the paradox of whether canonical value is absolute or relative, its standards enduring or contingent. All authors in the period I survey believed that all human activity was ultimately sanctioned by an absolute source of value, whether identified with God or his temporal sovereign, evinced in a consensual structure of conviction sustained by verbal power, located in some aspect of objective reality, or made manifest in the fullness of time. The difficulty for authors, however, was to reconcile this sense of absolute value with an equally compelling desire to acknowledge change and difference, whether in the distinctiveness of an English tradition, the renewing modernity of their own work, the alterity of older writings, or the vicissitudes of experience. This paradox, so often overlooked in current debates, has occasioned some of the most compelling episodes and critical thinking within the history of the English literary canon.

Since these interrelated topics have informed various episodes in this history, I develop my discussion of them at several points in my narrative. If I have refrained from attempting to indicate precisely when the English began to think highly of their literature, I hope that I have provided some sense of the lengthy and complicated changes in the way English literature was valued, from the earliest signs of poetic self-consciousness to the beginnings of its institutionalization in the later eighteenth century.

PART ONE

Versions of Canonic Harmony

1 Early Gestures

An ancient Greek word, "canon" originally meant either of two things, a measuring rod or, later, a list. From the first is derived the idea of a standard that can be applied as a law or principle. From the second comes the concept of canonization, the Catholic practice of admitting someone to the list of saints. Modern critics often assume that only the oldest definition, a canon as rule, is relevant to considerations of literary canonicity. This may be the result of analogizing the literary canon to the hegemonic rigidity of the biblical canon, since the usage of "canon" as a term for a body of writings first developed in relation to the Bible, in the fourth century C.E., as an attempt by Church authorities to distinguish "authentic" Scripture from competing canons that mixed scriptural writings with apocrypha; as McKeon notes, the "Greek word 'heresy' is derived from election or selection: everyone elects what seems to him best."[1] Yet, in its fourth-century usage, "canon" designated a catalogue of authors and not a rule or measure. It may therefore be useful to consider literary canons as lists as much as standards of excellence. Among the earliest forms of writing, lists are the simplest of texts, held together by the most arbitrary of syntaxes, the page they are written on; as such, they imply a degree of self-consciousness about the written medium.[2] Canons are similarly the products and signs of literate cultures, texts of texts in effect, and they are often advanced by authors eager to call attention to their profession. Above all, canons are wholly arbitrary as syntactical units. Curtius, in his pioneering discussion of the subject, suggests that the "formation of a canon serves to safeguard a tradition" but that such a tradition is only ever "artificially preserved" by canon-making. His point is not simply that literary canons are open to revision, but that they are fictions, symbolic conveniences that link together often highly disparate works, disparate in their meaning, language, culture of origin, and even values. These imaginary packagings may shroud works in a mystificatory aura, but they remain no more than packages.[3]

So arbitrary are canons that they encourage two contrasting ways of ordering the items they contain. The first is the practice of hierarchization, of ranking items according to an evaluative scheme that discriminates between major and minor authors and excludes undesirable works. This process of selection has been the subject of much recent controversy: we have heard about how canons are formed by powerful identity politics that privilege certain values over others and create margins where neglected works – women writers, "minority" literatures, among many others – have been left to fade away without institutional preservation. Yet the second, much less scrutinized habit of thought can be equally exclusionary. Because they bring together any number of items without making clear their interrelations, lists can bespeak a levelling syntax, and the longer the list, the more likely its items will be treated as an amorphous, potentially uniform mass – the aim, for example, of much satiric catalogue-making. In this way, a literary canon may achieve unity by harmonizing any possible differences or competing values among the works it celebrates. There is little room for otherness in such a canon. Monolithic rather than gradational, such a canon serves to represent less a scale of excellence than an imagined consensual identity, the homogeneity of its culture of origin rather than the range of that culture's achievements.

In general, a modern objectivist culture observes the relative diversity of a hierarchical canon. Evaluative rankings of authors, for example, only begin to appear in English critical discourse in the mid-eighteenth century. A hierarchical canon, rather than symbolizing the uniformity of human nature, holds out the promise of achieving universality through a constant striving towards knowledge and excellence, an up-hierarchy struggle, as it were. It allows critics to promote an elitist set of values for readers, yet at the same time to acknowledge diversity, alterity, and canonic revision. Of course, a truly plural canon is a contradiction in terms – or, rather, the apparent pluralism of a canon can always be accommodated within oppressive social structures. The values that shape a hierarchical canon can be quite exclusionary, as evidenced by the restrictions placed on literacy, publication, and institutional reproduction that have resulted in a preponderance of white men of property in the canon of European authors. Those values may be disputed and submitted to critical analysis but such revisionary scrutiny is itself thoroughly objectivist in its aims and methods. In contrast, a rhetorical culture seeks out the empowering certainty of a harmonious canon, which presents an image of thoroughgoing consensus. Lengthy, uncritical catalogues of authors are common in Elizabethan writings, where they serve to denote a fundamental concord among artists and English society. A harmonious canon serves writers in a rhetorical culture who wish to prescribe a fixed set of authoritative models, to impose closure on the evaluation of older works, or to make their culture as a whole observe a clearly defined totality of values. These writers may also observe certain hierarchies, such as a classical hierarchy of genres designed to reflect a social hierarchy. But privileging certain values over others may not necessarily check the homogenizing pressures of canon-formation, for one of the prime functions of canons is to smooth over the complex, often conflicted relations between works and their contexts of origin and use, and thereby to render such works serviceable to the exercise of authority.

This chapter deals with how an ideal of canonic harmony was upheld by the earliest English poets in relation to their own art, by the Reformation antiquaries John Leland and John Bale in relation to England's literary history, and by Renaissance authors in relation to their audience. My emphasis is not so much upon the actual conditions of production and reception during the period. Rather, I am concerned with the terms and gestures authors used to defend and promulgate their activity. (Gesturing, as Bourdieu and others have defined it, is a conventionalized mode of attitudinizing that enables a social practice to naturalize or "misrecognize" the arbitrariness of its working assumptions and interests; examples include the tacit rules of disciplinarity in academic discourse, and the common tactic among artists of denying economic self-interest in order to acquire the prestige of appearing to be purely devoted to one's art.[4]) Canon-making, I would suggest, frequently served the self-defining gestures of English writers eager to promote a literary system in England. Yet, as much as these authors were keen to publicize their practice, they were also concerned to legitimize it by rendering it serviceable to authority. This entailed situating their writing in relation to a harmonious canon, whose symbolic value as a sign of social order was felt to be far more desirable than the discriminatory force of closely assessing and ranking each author's achievement. The task for these authors, then, was one of determining how best to suggest this harmony while still asserting the distinctive value of their work.

TO THE COMING OF PRINT

Canon-making begins when authorship begins, in the first cries of poets eager to legitimize their practice, to lend aura to their tradition, and to affirm the power of their art in preserving a sense of the past. Poetry's memorializing and mnemonic functions make it the preeminent vehicle of fame and solidarity in most oral and early literate cultures, providing it with a productive role within a community's moral order. In more developed societies this immortalizing function has become so doubtful that the responsibility for preserving the past has shifted from poets to institutions, and poetry has become one among numerous artifacts transmitted through institutional mechanisms. Few of these mechanisms, at least in relation to secular poetry, are operative during the period before the coming of print. Poetry in earlier ages is expected to preserve itself and to canonize its subjects through its verbal beauty and ease of retention. Yet the romance of immortality may not enthrall all of the people all of the time, and poets are never assured of a welcome reception, a situation that seemingly worsens the more their literary system develops. It thus becomes incumbent upon poets to use their rhetorical skills in the defence of their activity, by continually asserting the staying power of their verse, by retransmitting the poetry of their predecessors to demonstrate the staying power of all verse, and by reminding their patrons of the inevitability of change and how it can best be defeated through poetry. For poets to canonize, they must first declare their own bids for permanence. They must first canonize themselves.

This section surveys a few such self-heralding gestures among the earliest British poets as a prologue to a fuller consideration of how canonicity was defined within a rhetorical culture. These poets' gestures, it must be stressed, reflected the values of widely divergent cultures of origin and may have been continuous less with later forms of canon-making than with older oral, patristic, or classical traditions. Nonetheless, the examples presented here may serve to illustrate two related themes that are central to much of my overall narrative. The first theme recalls Foucault's claim that it is only during the Renaissance that artists begin to canonize themselves: "The artist was able to emerge from the age-old anonymity of epic singers only by usurping the power and meaning of the same epic values. The heroic dimension passed from the hero to the one whose task it had been to represent him at a time when Western culture itself became a world of representations."[5] On the face of it, Foucault's claim seems indisputable. The vast majority of medieval poets, from the minstrels that appear in *Beowulf* to the later balladeers and romancers, remain anonymous to us, whereas changing conditions for authorship, notably the coming of print, make for ever more elaborate displays of self-assertion among poets of the English Renaissance. The intense rhetoricity of early modern culture, as well, may be one aspect of what Foucault calls the new "world of representations."

However, any act of writing involves a claim to cultural legitimacy, whether or not the author chooses to inscribe him or herself in the writing.[6] As a result, any such claim may invite conflict over the source of cultural legitimation, whether it is felt to reside with the author, the literary tradition, the king or, most pervasively in the medieval era, the Church. The dynamic Foucault identifies between poet and hero is arguably just one of many possible tensions that exist within all early poetry, and one that is inherent within the immortality bargain that poets negotiate with their patrons, since poets routinely feel compelled to assert their art's time-defying authority as energetically as they memorialize the exploits of their patrons. Ideally in a rhetorical culture, poet and patron are expected to share equally in the symbolic value of the immortalizing song and by their consensus confirm the absolute integrity of their community's moral order. Yet poets have never enjoyed a monopoly on producing symbolic capital – religion, for one, has perennially exerted a greater claim – while, as countless poets through the ages have complained, patrons have often erringly considered the prestige afforded by cultural artifacts to be less enabling of social power than economic capital, political influence, or the brute immediacies of force. In addition, for any poet's authority to be credible, it must be presented as being to some degree morally independent of the political and economic patronage that underwrites poetic production. Thus, the more poets feel their livelihood threatened by competition, or their integrity challenged by too powerful interests, the more likely they will self-consciously present themselves to be more deserving of renown than their heroic subjects, and the more they will implicitly acknowledge the relativity of heroism, poetic or political, as a value.

Widsith (seventh century?), which contains some of the oldest verses in the language, rehearses such an example of poetic self-apotheosis, in this case a mythic canonization of the vernacular minstrel tradition, idealized in the title-figure, a super-*scop* who travels far and wide to immortalize the Saxon kings in song. Though largely a catalogue of names and tribes, the poem's framing narrative is less about patrons than about poets, about the "wayfaring gleemen" and the favourable treatment they earned at various courts, and about how heroic song will be heard appreciatively "till all is fled, light and life together."[7] Minstrelsy is the gleemen's self-professed "destiny," a term which suggests that these poets feel pressed to mythologize their identities as the purveyors of the "glory" of medieval warriors. Perhaps a begging poem, *Widsith* reveals an almost elegiac self-awareness among the minstrels, as though the threat they faced was very much greater and insuperable than a loss of patronage. That threat was probably Christianity, and no epic celebration of the worldly *scop* could hope to challenge the absolute power and meaning of the Christian hero.[8]

My second theme is suggested by Walter Benjamin in his essay on mechanical reproduction: "The uniqueness of a work of art," Benjamin writes, "is inseparable from its being imbedded in the fabric of tradition."[9] A version of the paradox that at some level occupies all considerations of value, Benjamin's axiom has first to do with the relativity of originality, how the concept goes hand in hand with the notion of a canon, how all works are to some degree conventional and intertextual, and how it is impossible to determine the originality of a work without comparing it to other similar works. The axiom has also to do with the two ways of conceiving a canon, as either a homogeneous, closely stitched tradition where absolute evaluative certainty is held utmost and uniqueness little esteemed, or a hierarchical scale of achievements where relative differences between works are emphasized above their similarities. If there is always a potential for conflict between poets and patrons, there is equally a tension between poets and their traditions, a tension that may express itself as an anxiety of influence but, more importantly in this context, as a conflict of interest between the individual talent's desire to assert his heroic uniqueness and his equally compelling need to draw legitimacy from a sense of tradition. The self-canonizing gestures of working poets always involve the possibility of displacing established canonical fathers – parricide being the operative metaphor, since English women writers rarely indulged in such revisionary gestures prior to the eighteenth century. Revisionism is an inevitable aspect of canon-formation, yet the more forceful the parricidal gesture, the less harmonious the canon. The same is true for the reverse: the more harmony and absolute integrity is sought, as it is in a medieval culture, the less vocal the poet's self-presentation.

In *Widsith*, this tension is resolved through myth: the canon of fellow gleemen is both homogeneous and unique, fully embodied as it is within the lone ageless hero of the title. In another Old English catalogue poem, *Deor* (9th century?), the homogeneity of the minstrel tradition is negated by the anxious self-definition of the eponymous *scop*. Having been supplanted in his patron's favour by his rival Heorrenda, the poet feels compelled to assert his individuality: "Deor was my name."[10] Yet, because the assertion is meaningful only if it is made within the framework of a tradition, Deor must insert his story within another controlling fiction, a vaguely Christian narrative of consoling *exempla* telling of legendary figures who have survived misfortune. His poetic uniqueness eclipsed by his rival's, Deor preserves his identity by transferring its source of legitimacy from the tradition celebrated in *Widsith* to its rival, Christianity, whose greater harmony and incontestable value are ultimately attributable to God. Deor's troubled self-consciousness suggests that his poem, like *Widsith*, may have served as a begging poem; implicitly, both lyrics mourn the disintegration of a common heroic culture, the culture of *Beowulf*, that had recognized a well-defined role for the gleemen within its moral economy. It is nonetheless a sign of an overwhelming desire for harmony during the period that both poets, however personally distressed, sacrifice their sense of self to an absolute identity, either the figurehead Widsith or God the Creator.

Like *Widsith*, Christianity presented a thoroughly uniform canon whose originality was perceived to flow from a single, divinely monologic source.[11] This suggests a corollary to Benjamin's dictum: the vitality and modernity of any tradition are contingent upon the ability of its members to locate its distinctive, renewing source of value.[12] The Christian tradition accomplishes this by treating as meaningless any claim for worldly uniqueness and self-determination. Bede's account of Caedmon the unlettered cattle-herd (*fl.* 670) is the first record of an English poet at work, yet Bede's preservation of Caedmon's name and song is a canonization that serves primarily to honour Christianity, affirming as it does the miracle of divine inspiration. Bede may have been motivated by affection for Anglo-Saxon verse, since Caedmon's hymn imparts religious doctrine in the heroic diction of a bardic past, yet the uniqueness of Caedmon's spontaneous verse-making renders any ideal of a poetic lineage irrelevant: "It is true that after him other Englishmen attempted to compose religious poems, but none could compare with him."[13] Caedmon's defining tradition, his true source of value, is not an indigenous poetic culture but a religious community, an ecclesiastically unified England whose history Bede is writing and within which Caedmon's story is but one more example of God's universal harmony.[14]

Christianity's challenge to the world of the *scops* was spiritual and ideological, but it was also symbolic – significant within a rhetorical culture, whose moral order relied so heavily on symbolic exchanges. Its claim to absolute truth was objectified in a well-defined literate tradition, a *canon* or "catalogue of authors," whose authority was signified by its ostensibly seamless homogeneity. This canon included both Scripture and so-called *auctores*, patristic and sometimes classical writers who were considered worthy enough to be studied in medieval schools. The *auctores* were regarded as the founding fathers of their respective disciplines and, as such, they were chiefly authors from the distant past, though some British authors like Bede and Aldhelm, and select Old English texts, would occasionally be honoured by later clerics as deserving of inclusion in scholarly reading lists.[15] Contemporary writers could not pretend to a place in this canon because they lacked *auctoritas*, a claim to truth that could be sanctioned only by the Church.[16] In principle, the *auctores* had already said all that was worth saying, and modern authors could not expect to add to this store of truth: they could not be producers, for productivity was little valued within the closed economy of the auctorial system. Closed, but not static: if the system discouraged production, it was well designed to ensure the reproduction of auctorial writings through their preservation in commentaries that continually refined their language of religious signification in changing times. Thus, if living writers could not aspire to auctorial ranks, they could claim to be *lectors*, whose task it was to rescribe, "compile," or interpret the works of the dead fathers; in performing these tasks, the *lectors* aided the perpetuation not only of canonical material but of the auctorial system and the authority of the Church.[17] The *auctor* doctrine therefore helped to restrict the extent of canon change even as it ensured the continual reintroduction of ancient writings, and Christian culture as a whole, in new settings. Later, "original" writings could either be rejected as inauthentic and left to oblivion, or be attributed wrongly to an *auctor*, which would ensure their absorption within the fabric of the Christian tradition. In this way, the auctorial system helped to maintain a powerfully appealing image of canonic harmony and sacred value, Christian culture being presented as the only meaningful context within which to write and reproduce works.

Although the auctorial system could be accommodated to strong articulations of vernacular self-consciousness, as in the era of high Anglo-Saxon learning, it was a discourse designed to perpetuate the idea of a uniform Christian culture and, accordingly, it did not formally recognize geographical boundaries. It encouraged a sense of intertextuality, since the established canon of works was edited and reworked without high regard for the distinctiveness of a work's originating context. Above all, its canon was perceived to be suprahistorical, impervious to internal change as much as to changes in human affairs, and constructed with an eye oriented towards the afterlife rather than earthly posterity. Hence, the doctrine helped to devaluate poetry's memorializing function and denied poetry its utility in the understanding of human history. The *scops* in *Widsith* and *Beowulf* had been honoured because their epic narratives immortalized their communities, gave voice to their hopes, and inspired a productive martial economy of heroic conquest. With the ascendancy of an auctorial order, and the prevailing Christian view that fame was mere worldly vanity, meaningless in the light of fortune and eternity, working poets could no longer use the immortality *topos* to justify their activity. Even a patriotic poet like Layamon, though assertive enough to inscribe himself in his poem as well as to write in the vernacular despite the linguistic aftermath of the Norman Conquest, could be content to assume the impersonal roles of *lector* and compiler of auctorial material. Without any accepted cultural system under which the arbitrariness of the trope of fame could be misrecognized, most poets saw little point in canonizing themselves.

As the trope had little normative force, poetry had no clear productive role to play in society, and certainly no occasional role other than the very marginal one of supplying rhetorical models in the teaching of grammar, a role reserved almost exclusively for classical poetry.[18] The Horatian view that poetry mixed delight with instruction remained prevalent, yet few secular poets could utter the claim with conviction, didactic functions being the purview of the *auctores* and pleasure a suspect value. Those few poets who entertained profane thoughts of posterity were indulging largely in self-persuasion, and they asserted the eternalizing function of their verse without much sense of a broader economy wherein this function might be considered legitimate. Introducing his *Topographies of Ireland* (1187), the Anglo-Latin chronicler Giraldus Cambrensis defended his pursuit of patronage by idealizing the cultural renewal that would be brought about were the spur of fame once again recognized as a legitimate motive for writing: "For nothing can better tend to kindle the sparks of mental vigour, and fan the innate fire into a flame, than that, supported by so many and such great authorities, and borne, as it were, upon their shoulders, we may rise to eminence by the aid of their manifold grandeur, if only we have confidence in ourselves."[19] The commonplace of standing upon the shoulders of ancient authorities suggests that even a writer as vain as Giraldus could not avoid using auctorial categories. In addition to putting into practice a suspicion of earthly fame, the *auctor* doctrine restricted poetic self-determination by being fundamentally directed towards the literary past and wholly designed to ensure the perpetuation of that past in the present. As allegorizing commentary made it possible eventually to appropriate a number of classical figures, including Virgil and other pagan poets, for a Christian culture, the auctorial canon could in time seem like a long-standing and unified tradition that correlated a religious to a political absolutism, one empowered by an imperial consensus uniting ancient Rome with Christian Europe. Yet contemporary authors could not assume that this consensus extended to their work nor could they seriously entertain thoughts of fashioning a new cultural harmony to rival this imperial-auctorial order.

At once overshadowed by their canonical fathers and prevented from standing by their side, contemporary authors could feel themselves uniquely apocryphal. Giraldus's contemporary, the courtly poet Walter Map, was being only mildly ironic when he despaired of being compared to the great rival canon of classical poetry: "The results of the industry of the ancients are in our hands; they make the deeds which even in their times were past, present to ours, and we keep mum; and thus their memory lives in us, and we forget our own. A notable wonder! the dead live, and the living are buried in their stead! ... Our writers have no influence [*auctoritas*]." Map's anxiety was as rhetorical as Giraldus's boasting, yet at least one of his works, the *Dissuasio Valerii ad Rufinum* (late twelfth century), was so highly regarded that his authorship was seriously doubted, the work being eventually attributed to an "authentic" *auctor,* the first-century Roman historian, Valerius Maximus. Map maintained that he included the names of dead men in his title "for I knew that would be popular: had I not done so, my book, like myself, would have been thrown aside." The prejudice against living authors, Map added, was merely the most obvious symptom of a broader cultural self-loathing: "Every century has disliked its own modernity; every age, from the first onwards, has preferred the previous one to itself."[20] Whether Map's sophisticated courtly society actually affected a disdain for the present is unimportant, for in essence the point he was making was a tactical one. Bemoaning the burden of the past, like quarrelling over ancients and moderns, is a symbolic struggle for legitimacy, thoroughly rhetorical in its positing of an agon of cultures. Through such gestures the poets routinely define their activity, relying upon their verbal power to call attention to themselves, to extort sympathy from their audience, or to comfort themselves with the thought that their neglect is owing to a paucity of adequate patrons. Rhetorical self-valorization works by verbal contest, a highly codified performance that persuades through the coercive pathologizing of an Other.[21] The poet achieves mastery by winning over an audience's beliefs, but the triumph can never be absolute because the divisive structures of rhetoric require that an Other be continually identified in order that it be repudiated. Map, for one, had targets other than his age's ostensibly blind veneration of the past, and he ridiculed both his poetic rivals and popular forms when he lamented that, whereas the Caesars were immortalized by poet-statesmen, only a "troupe of buffoons keeps alive the divine fame of the Charlemagnes and Pepins in popular ballads."[22]

Yet, however deliberate the rhetoric, canonicity remained beyond the reach of the living. Modern poets could use their suasive skills to publicize their work but not to effect any revision of the auctorial system. The pervasive ideology of *auctoritas* related all human activity to a world-historical order explicable only in the terms set out in the authoritative books, and self-conscious writers like Giraldus and Map had to abide by its evaluative codes when crying up their talents. Those codes dictated that modern authors could distinguish themselves from their immediate rivals or from tasteless audiences, but that they ought never assail the honoured past of the canonical fathers or to assume the heroic dimensions of the king, who, as God's agent, was the only human figure for whom self-legitimation was possible. Sanctioned by the double authority of God and the laws set down by the *auctores*, this monarchical self-determination was simply too powerful an ideological representation for authors to usurp. The figure of the king provided the link between the harmony of the authoritative canon and the harmony of the world order: "By correlating the divine basis for his rule with auctorial precedents, the medieval ruler sanctioned the *auctores*' cultural authority. As the source, the beneficiary, and the agent of the culture's authoritative books, the monarch was the perfected cultural form of the *auctor.* His rule was his book, and his subjects were compelled to submit their world to the edicts of that book."[23] For a modern writer to challenge the hegemony of the *auctores* would be tantamount to an offence against God's estate, and would leave the writer with no absolute value by which to underwrite the relativizing gestures of his own agonistic rhetoric.

The modern writer was left to exercise verbal tyranny upon the manners of his age. Map's derision of popular balladry was a common gesture, one sanctioned by the classical hierarchy of genres, which set a higher value on the forms of representation than on a work's subject or eloquent properties. Popular songs and narratives invariably occupied the lowest rank in this hierarchy, though much of Map's own writing, consisting of satires and otherworldly tales, would not have been placed much higher, a fact that may explain why he was keen to distinguish himself from balladeers. At the top, tragedy and the epic reigned supreme until the late Renaissance, which indicates that the hierarchy tended to reflect aristocratic, heroic values and was thus neither perfectly aligned with the Christian curriculum of *auctores* nor prominently defended in medieval literary theory. Still, the idea of the hierarchy no doubt agreed with Map's aristocratic audience which, at this time, was beginning to seek its own cultural legitimacy, separate from that of the clergy who had for so long enjoyed total dominion over literacy and learning. Attempting to eschew the auctorial order of the Church, this new courtly culture appropriated, in writings like Map's, the vigorous narrative forms of folk traditions, and it would eventually patronize literacy in the vernacular; yet, at the same time, it would eventually define itself in opposition to these lower-class traditions in order to claim distinction as a vernacular High Culture that could rival the literate clergy. Map's jibes at balladeers were as tactical as his complaints of belatedness, for he was supplying his aristocratic audience with the popular entertainments they enjoyed while satisfying their need to perceive themselves at a civilized remove from the populace.

Though scarcely comparable in force to the auctorial order, the normative authority of the generic hierarchy remained considerable enough that it, too, helped to discourage poetic self-determination. By focusing attention on conventions and kinds rather than the authorship of works, the hierarchy accorded with an auctorial emphasis on intertextuality and self-effacement for modern writers. The hierarchy may have also restricted canon change by limiting the range of experimentation and generic "modulation," though poetic species were relatively fluid in the pre-humanistic Middle Ages.[24] More important, until the eighteenth century and to some degree beyond, the observance of a generic hierarchy had the effect of fixing evaluative criteria in accordance with established models and conventions. This made it impossible to think that works in different genres might be of equal worth and deserving of equal praise; that is to say, the hierarchy disallowed competing claims for canonicity by manifestly dissimilar works. Not only did this tend to discourage a heroic ambition among poets skilled in the lesser genres, it also had the effect of perpetuating an ahistorical, harmonious canon where no profound conflict of values was possible since each work was compared in relation only to other works of the same genre. The hierarchy and its many rules prescribed evaluative closure, making the canon seem like a cohesive totality where works were assessed according to an unchanging structure of norms akin to the prevailing social order (which, in some sense, the generic hierarchy was designed to reinforce ideologically). Works and genres may have been hierarchically ranked, but the canon as a whole, it was believed, was founded on a coherent, homogeneous set of values.

Since there was no disputing that genres were of unequal value, Map could mock popular balladry without considering it a serious threat to the established canon or to his own work – even though, for centuries, there existed no clear theoretical demarcation between courtly and popular aesthetics insofar as both insisted that poetry appeal to pleasure and moral interest. However divergent the values they expressed, folk genres were easily dismissed, and their energies contained, because they were not considered an alternative tradition but merely trivialized as the lowest possible forms. Folk literature may not have even seemed like a genuine tradition because it was largely oral and thoroughly intertextual, recognized no models for authorship, and survived without institutional support.[25] The tradition's uncontested centrality within the moral economy of its originary audience ensured its harmony and continual reproduction without the safeguard of an official canon. Its canon, such as it was, was indistinguishable from legend: "Men speken of romances of prys, / Of Horn child and of Ypotys, / Of Beves and sir Gy, / Of sir Lybeux and Pleyndamour."[26]

Prior to the fourteenth century, the ideal of an indigenous poetic canon had been rarely proposed but the idea of canonical writings was clearly a familiar one to English writers. Medieval scholars had for a long time acknowledged a variety of separable bodies of authoritative texts: the Scriptural canon, the catalogue of patristic *auctores*, and the works of the pagan poets and philosophers. Yet secular writers in England, faced with unfavourable attitudes to authorship, could not be assured of belonging to an established canon, no matter how urgently they expressed their aspirations. The efflorescence and promotion of English poetry in the later fourteenth century were then hardly spontaneous: Chaucer and Gower both knew well the conventions and importance of self-presentation. The preconditions for the efflorescence are many, but worth noting in this context are, at a social level, the growing political legitimacy of the primary audience for English letters, and, at an intellectual level, the gradual dismantling of the auctorial system. The former development, which saw Chaucer and others writing for Chamber knights and prominent civil servants, helped to install the vernacular as a polite language and hence worthy of an official canon.[27] Though perhaps not so well established as to patronize poetry for its immortalizing function, this new audience of literate laymen looked to poetry for its pragmatic utility, as a source of worldly pleasure and as the eloquent voice of civil society. Versed in ideals of civic humanism, these "new men" were an ascendant, politically aware group, and, like all such groups, they related their social mobility to the advancement of society as a whole.[28] Theirs was a dynamic moral economy to which working poets could make a contribution by writing verse, notably love poetry, that reproduced this dynamism. The function of poetry within this economy was thus not so much conventionally didactic as ethical, recreational, and mimetic, naturalizing in its representations of a developing, increasingly strati-fied English society.

The rise of these new men may have contributed to the second development, the redefinition of *auctoritas*, since their ideology of social and personal advancement was a direct challenge to the univer-salism of the auctorial order. Yet, as I shall argue, English poets before the sixteenth century continued to rely on auctorial codes to define their activity, even as the assumptions underlying these codes were no longer entirely operative. The process of dismantling had begun in Italy, with the successful self-canonizations of several living poets, Dante and Petrarch chief among them. The latter's coronation in Rome on Easter Sunday, 1341, has been called "the beginning of poetry in the modern western world," both for its symbolic renuncia-tion of the supremacy of dead *auctores* and for its decisive refurbishing of poetry's public image.[29] However conventional its pagan imagery, the event was manifestly the realization of Petrarch's self-determination and marked the birth of an important figure, the Petrarchan or "laureate" poet.[30] This figure is central to the moral economy of a rhetorical culture, since his self-assumed mission is to deploy and circulate symbolic capital, itself largely conceived in terms of the civic humanist values of honour, prestige, and devotion to the public realm.[31] The laureate poet uses his verbal power on behalf of the advancement of the state, and he thus re-assumes the ancient role of the refiner of the language not, as under the auctorial system, to ensure the religious signification of past writings but to enhance the rhetorical effectivity of the present political order. For his efforts, he is rewarded in his lifetime with official, institutional canonization or, in Petrarch's case, with a highly politicized coronation whose figurative power matches that of a royal anointing. The spectacle of laureation, in Foucault's terms, exposes the king's own investiture as mere repre-sentation and confers upon the poet a symbolic authority to rival and, potentially, to revise the king's auctorial hegemony. For the laureate to effect *improvement* within the state, he must be able to rewrite the king's book; he must be an *author*, a cultural producer who advances his society in the very act of advancing himself. The laureate is there-fore in league with the "new men," since their ideology of civic human-ism stressed a masculinist ideal of the self-governing, morally autonomous citizen who could debate the common good with his male peers.[32] As the first poet of such laureate ambitions, Petrarch may have been for a time treated as an *auctor*, but his self-determination was so undeniable that his uniqueness could never be fully accommodated within the uniformity of the auctorial canon. That self-determination he managed instead to draw in dramatic fashion from all possible sources of legitimation: the Church, the king, the classical literary tradition, and the now powerful figure of the author.

Petrarch's self-legitimation also presented an intellectual challenge to the auctorial system, one that helped to alter perceptions of the canon in at least two respects. First, Petrarch diminished the sense of the canon's monolithic impersonality by treating classical authorities as "friends" who shared high-minded ideals for literature yet on whose moral failings he could pass censure: "I am ashamed of your many, great shortcomings, and take compassion on them," he wrote of Cicero.[33] Petrarch's language of bonding and contest, of speaking to famous "men" only to chide them for their "shortcomings," channelled rhetoric's usual polemical energies into a chivalric, masculinizing ritual where the combatants were as familiar to one another as they were opposed.[34] Even as it suggested a transhistorical intimacy of values, Petrarch's personalizing of *auctores* implied the possibility of revision, which threatened the serene harmony of the auctorial order. Such personalizing also relocated the source of poetic uniqueness from a divine voice to a distinct human subject, whose authority, as the Creator's had been in an earlier era, was made to reside in the presumed harmony of his works.

Secondly, Petrarch defied conventional belief in the canon's imperviousness to time. In his study of celebrated men of the past, *De Viris Illustribus*, written at about the time of his laureation, Petrarch intensified the standard opposition of ancients and moderns into a stark diachrony of classical enlightenment and medieval obscurity. Petrarch's line of canonic masters ended before the historical appearance of Christianity; the period of the patristic *auctores* was for him the "Dark Ages."[35] Against the universalism of Christian culture, Petrarch opposed a historical periodicity that denied the canon its deathless homogeneity. In addition, by elevating the classics of imperial Rome above his culture's own *auctores*, Petrarch implied that the canon ought to recognize a new standard of literary distinction to replace auctorial norms, a standard to be based in a formal purification of poetic discourse ostensibly afforded by classicism. In this way, Petrarch championed his practice's autonomy from the auctorial order by positing a return to poetry's origins – such a claim for purification is always a powerful gesture among cultural producers, since it implies that poetic art may endure by virtue of an essence which, however occasionally obscured, is ultimately independent of external history and the material conditions for authorship.[36] Of course, the idea of a return to an originating essence has often served to legitimize cultural reformations and canonic revisions: by looking forward to a classicist rebirth in the wake of the "Dark Ages," Petrarch was engaging in what Hans

Robert Jauss has called modernity's "ever-renewed attempt at self-definition by rejection of a past."[37] In so doing, Petrarch substituted for the absolute authority of the auctorial canon a relativistic account of authorial value, but his campaigning on behalf of change and difference was so forceful that he effectively revised the canon in his own image.

Though no English poet before the sixteenth century can be said to have defined himself and his activity as emphatically as Petrarch, his example set the terms for how authors after him would assert their independence from the conformity of the auctorial order. Petrarch's self-canonizing gestures and rhetorical emphases on historical temporality and canon change, on poetry's high calling and the poet's worldly authority, would be repeated with increasing frequency by English authors over the next three centuries. Yet self-definition is always achieved at a cost, one that can be inferred from Benjamin's dictum on the interdependence of tradition and uniqueness: the more poets assert their independence from a discredited past, the more they alienate themselves from their own tradition (even as they rely ever more on that tradition to define their identity against[38]). Modernity's continual revisionism means that no harmonious canon is possible, and this thought is unsettling to many early poets, who, just as much as they wish to make room within the canon for their own works, equally look to the authority of an established cultural order for inspiration, recognition, and evaluative certainty. What stopped early English poets from fully imitating Petrarch's example was precisely the feeling that self-canonization invited relativity and disharmony. The hope among later poets, schooled in ideals of classical eloquence, was that verbal power would overcome this relativity, even if verbal power was itself highly contingent. The poets of the fourteenth and fifteenth centuries could not share this hope since the verbal power of the English language had yet to be demonstrated. In addition, the authority of their primary audience of "new men" was not yet so assured that it could seem a credible alternative to aristocratic or ecclesiastical tutelage as a source of cultural legitimation. There was, then, a certain reluctance among these poets to do away entirely with the defining codes of the auctorial system.

The desire for recognition and self-determination was nonetheless strong, as is evident from a remarkable passage from the great scholar-bishop Richard de Bury's treatise on the love of books, the *Philobiblon* (1345). Writing not five years after Petrarch's coronation, and in a time of rising patriotism fostered by the wars with France and Scotland, de Bury hailed England's transcendence: "The admirable Minerva seems to have traversed the nations of men from end to end of the world, bravely touching on each that she might give herself to all. Already do we see that she has passed away from the Indians, the Babylonians, the Egyptians and the Greeks, the Arabians and the Latins. Already has she forsaken Athens, departed from Rome, passed by Paris, and is happily come to Britain, the noblest of islands, nay, the very microcosm, that she may show herself debtor both to Greeks and Barbarians."[39] This is the *translatio studii*, the myth that learning moves westward. Certainly the myth itself moves west, de Bury likely appropriating it from earlier French sources. In its suggestion that England is destined to cultural supremacy, the myth reveals the relativity of canon-making, for England's transcendence is contingent upon the fall of empires in the immediate east. The logic of historical determinism likewise requires that learning eventually leave England as dramatically as it arrived – the suggestion in Pope's ironic use of the myth in *The Dunciad*. De Bury's version of the myth is not so quite deterministic as to deny all continuity: learning survives even as empires die, and England owes its eminence to what it has inherited from previous traditions. But the fact that de Bury embraced the myth is indication that, with the passing of the universalism of the *auctores*, canonicity could be forcefully asserted only within a new, more local context, one national rather than imperial, contemporary rather than timeless. Though British writers were not yet wearing laurels, a healthy level of verbal production in the present generation was seen as essential to the state's advancement. Now, as Gower proclaimed in the *Confessio Amantis* (1390), was the time for English authors to write "for Engelondes sake."[40]

Gower was the first poet to invoke a specifically English Muse, *Anglica Carmente*, though in his time he was celebrated for having addressed his works to an international audience.[41] His sumptuous tomb in Southwark Cathedral shows the poet in splendid effigy, his head resting on a pile of his three books, each of which Gower had written in a distinct language – English, French, and Latin. The tomb identifies Gower as a poet, then a notably honorific term, and surrounds his likeness with much Petrarchan pretension, the poet's arms fully emblazoned and his effigy prominently displaying the gold chain awarded the poet by the king.[42] To the extent that he was the first to use the techniques of publicity and self-canonization on behalf of poetry's high calling and of his own career, Gower was arguably England's first "laureate" poet. Certainly writing in three languages was a pretension, since Gower chanced that he would be remembered in whichever of those languages proved the most durable. In early versions of the *Confessio*, Gower assumed the self-effacing role of a "compiler" but in later revisions elevated himself to a full-fledged "composer," a term usually reserved for *auctores*.[43] Like Jonson and Pope after him, Gower made certain that his work was appreciated in its best possible format, preparing final corrected versions of his works and supervising the copying of manuscripts.[44] He even supplied posterity with a few hints as to how he might be remembered. Among the editorial apparatus to the "authorized" manuscripts were two sets of commendatory verses, the first ever written for an English poet, that went so far as to claim that Gower's output surpassed Virgil's because of the English poet's ease at writing in three languages.[45]

Yet Gower also affected more conventional postures. In almost the same breath as he invoked his English Muse, Gower could apologize in highly formulaic terms for his inadequacies: "Sluggishness, dullness of perception, little leisure, and scant application, all these plead extenuation for me, least of poets, for inditing somewhat slight themes."[46] Gower may have felt it necessary to rely on the modesty *topos* because the highly moral and philosophical purport of his work assumed a degree of *auctoritas* that Gower's contemporary audience might not have been prepared to allow a living poet. Yet Gower's affected humility did not accord well with his laureate pretension – he still referred to himself as "poet" and not *lector* – nor finally with a set of didactic intentions that were fundamentally auctorial in their universalist assumptions: his major English work was presented to its readers as wisdom literature, its "confession" narrative consisting of exemplary stories of love linked to the Seven Deadly Sins (though Gower's Latin commentary is decidedly more insistent on its moral authority than his Ovidian poem[47]). Despite the outward signs of Petrarchan self-presentation, Gower did not seem committed to a goal of cultural advancement nor did he welcome the rejection of a past such advancement entailed. Gower, it is said, wished to be honoured as a modern *auctor*,[48] which is perhaps another way of saying that Gower's loyalties were deeply divided between respecting the all-encompassing harmony of the old order and pursuing the personally satisfying and liberating dream of fame.

With Chaucer the equation seemed almost totally reversed: if Gower styled himself an *auctor* in Petrarchan vestments, Chaucer wrote as a modern in the guise of a *lector*. Chaucer rarely professed a laureate ambition, and he often obscured whatever hopes he entertained for himself behind conventional protestations of inadequacy and humility. In his writings, Chaucer often presented himself as a "lewd compilator" or "translator" of the works of his *auctores*.[49] He called himself a "maker" rather than a "poete," a term he reserved for the ancients as well as for near-contemporaries like Dante and Petrarch.[50] Yet, in discriminating between imaginative "poetry" of the first order and his ostensibly second-rate "making," Chaucer may have implied that, in his view, the intertextual impersonality of the auctorial system had rightly given way to a hierarchy of renowned artists. As has often been noted, Chaucer showed a persistent fascination with canons and with the lofty apostrophes of the Petrarchan poet, yet he was seemingly too modest or ironic to come out with a full endorsement of what he was doing.[51] After his death Chaucer would be apotheosized as the refiner of the English language, but he never entertained such a self-image in his work, preferring instead to identify himself with the "rude speech" of his narrative personae. Nonetheless, Chaucer's apparent modesty, like Gower's shifting authorial self-presentations, may have reflected a deeper uncertainty about the role of the poet in Ricardian England, or about the ascendent if not yet secure legitimacy of the poet's primary audience. Gower nowhere doubted that what he produced would be of moral benefit to his culture, but he appeared unsure as to what kind of cultural producer he could profess to be; for his part, Chaucer made few claims for his work, and he seemed to question both what kind of cultural product he might be expected to furnish as a poet and how such a product might advance his culture beyond offering occasional pleasure or "moralitee." Chaucer's doubts were most clearly expressed in his "Retraccions" but they were equally evident from the design of *The Canterbury Tales*, which, in their complex heteroglossia, might have appeared to frustrate the courtly goal of refining a literary language on behalf of an emergent vernacular high culture, as though neither Chaucer nor his audience could take seriously or see much symbolic value in upholding such a goal. If anything, Chaucer made light of conventional aspirations to rhetorical eminence by exposing the arbitrariness of Petrarchan self-presentations. His Franklin, a representative "new man," echoes Persius in abjuring rhetoric in favour of "bare and pleyn" language: "I sleep nevere on the Mount of Pernaso" (*Can. Tales* 5:720–2). But the Franklin's gesture of disavowal is revealed to be part of a self-conscious performance whose rhetorical expertise belies his claim to unadorned speech.[52]

Chaucer most thoroughly called into question the fictions of authorship in his comic juxtapositions in *The House of Fame*: the opening invocation to the "god of slepe" (69) followed by the overdrawn appeal to the authority of legendary dreamers, the poet Geffrey who writes of love yet trusts his *auctors* over his senses, the Goddess Fame arbitrarily dispensing her favours yet surrounded by a time-honored canon of poets and historians, the "man of gret auctorite" (2158) showing up in the chaotic House of Rumour. The juxtapositions play upon the usual appositional styles of poetic self-definition, but the poet does not resolve his antitheses or fashion a new mythology of the author, and so there is a great temptation to see in the poem's confusions a crisis of self-determination: "*The House of Fame* registers Chaucer's problem of his identity as a poet."[53] The aim of Chaucer's usurpations remains ambiguous, though the poem's lack of closure does suggest a certain detachment or embarrassment at having to create a poetic identity out of the relativities that the poem exposes, between truth and fiction, *auctor* and author. Chaucer may not have claimed for himself the heroic image of the Petrarchan poet, but he appeared in this poem to recognize that the apparent certainties of the auctorial order had not proven invulnerable to revaluation and in fact had given way to a world of representations, where the poet's image (or his patrons') was to be entirely self-created and maintained by the poet's own verbal power without benefit of the kind of institutional mechanisms that had enabled the old auctorial system. And for a supremely self-conscious poet like Chaucer, the business of objectifying that self in a symbolic representation, one as felicitous as any other, must have seemed arbitrary, and possibly alienating.

The lack of an acceptable poetic identity, or of a definable social function for poetry, does not make Chaucer's self-presentation in the poem any the less dependent on verbal power or on revisions of earlier representations. Geffrey's invocation to Apollo notwithstanding, the poem's narrative reads like a comic rendition of "I never slept on Parnassus": Geffrey finds only disappointment in Fame's mountain-top palace and opts instead to search for "love-tydynges" in the lowly place next door. (Geffrey's gesture may serve to deny both poetic ambition and economic interest, and while the House of Fame is not explicitly equated with any English court or household, fame and patronage are traditionally linked by the immortality bargain: Geffrey's disappointment may be financial.) He prefers not to remain among the innumerable storytellers that fill the castle, nor beside the columns of renowned poets and writers who bear upon their shoulders the fame of their civilizations. This last image of a canon and of poetry's eternalizing function may seem a positive one, the poets' metal pillars being made of more durable stuff than the ice on which Fame's palace stands. But even this canon is sustained, like any tradition that seeks to reproduce itself, by the self-serving claims of other old books, and thus the canon is disharmonious since self-interest makes for "a litil envye" among the great poets (1476). This canon, and the immortality *topos*, are not the traditions of literary value Geffrey chooses to follow: "I wot [know] myself best how y stonde," he declares (1878). Chaucer may have been here engaging only in his own subtle version of envy-driven parricide, where the rhetorical renunciation of fame served to veil a deeper hope of being rewarded with a column of one's own.

The gestures of modesty throughout Chaucer's work may have functioned, in this sense, as strategic disavowals that allowed the poet to claim the distinguishing power of disinterest. Yet, if the *House of Fame* was Chaucer's fable of renunciation, the gesture left the poet without an enabling source of value. Whether he conceived of it as an overcrowded Parnassus or pillared canon, Chaucer, as with any poet eager to establish his canonicity, required a tradition against which his integrity could be measured and his uniqueness affirmed.

Renunciation not being the same as revision, the gesture could not furnish Chaucer with an alternative tradition that could provide him with an order of belief as to what he was doing. This other tradition is the lacuna in *The House of Fame*, and it is embodied at the very end of the poem in the unknown "man of gret auctorite" who will furnish Geffrey with what he needs to be a true poet. The man might be a Christian *auctor*, in which case Geffrey's final silence is appropriately the response of the self-effacing *lector*. Then again, the man's ghostly presence on the margins of the poem may indicate a situation where authorship has largely displaced *auctoritas*, and where the laureate poet must now be left to stand to some degree alone, at a relative distance from patrons and other powerful interests in order to remain morally independent. In effect, just as in our age we have witnessed the death of the author, so Chaucer could not identify his man because his culture had experienced the death of the *auctor*.[54] The old auctorial functions were by now mere fictions for Chaucer while, regrettably, the revisionary contests with the literary giants of the past were only just beginning. Yet, if Chaucer was to keep writing, his ambivalence over his status as cultural producer could not ultimately impede his attempts to legitimize his art. When he revived his image of a classical canon in the "envoi" to *Troilus and Criseyde*, it was with a notable absence of self-serving rhetoric that he asked his little book

> no makyng thow n'envie,
> But subgit be to alle poesye;
> And kis the steppes where as thow seest pace
> Virgile, Ovide, Omer, Lucan, and Stace.   (5:1789–92)

In this passage, Chaucer still refers to himself as mere "maker" and his book's final bow before "alle poesye" scarcely approaches the fraternal embrace Dante receives in the fourth book of the *Inferno*. But he calls his book a tragedy and consigns it to follow in the path of the past masters, with whose works it is implicitly compared. The venerable poets of antiquity are neither consecrated as *auctores* nor entombed on pillars but walk about as Petrarchan familiars, alive for all time, each unique yet none envied, and subject to no outside influence other than the seemingly absolute sphere of "alle poesye." With this image of a living, plural, and heroically autonomous tradition, Chaucer, modestly and without any revisionary gesture of usurpation, canonizes himself.

Chaucer made it possible to think of a literary tradition in English. For this he was honoured, by poets from Hoccleve to Dryden, as the "father," a tribute that referred less to Chaucer's antiquity than to the productive role he had played in the creation of English poetry.[55] Chaucer had figuratively sired all subsequent generations of English poets by demonstrating how the vernacular could be an eloquent, worldly language – a significant accomplishment in a rhetorical culture, where language is not merely a distinguishing feature of a community but a source and vehicle of power. Rhetorical theory holds that it is through the persuasive use of language that public decisions are made, values disseminated, and solidarity achieved. Though Chaucer may not have himself endorsed an ideal of refining the vernacular, this ideal would be quickly established in subsequent generations, as the Lancastrian and Tudor courts sought to define themselves as centres of a vernacular high culture to rival other emergent European cultures. During this period, Chaucer's works carried considerable symbolic capital, most of it attributed to his unmatched efforts at opening up the English wordhoard. His narratives appeared verbally rich and diverse, filled with representations of the vernacular being used effectively in different social circumstances and for specific occasions. Chaucer's poetry was thus seen as public-spirited because it both illustrated the flexibility and creative force of the vernacular and depicted a large, diverse public, God's plenty, whose social intercourse and communal harmony developed from this productive linguistic resource.

The poets of the fifteenth century who acclaimed Chaucer at the head of an indigenous canon did so in order at once to legitimize their own efforts in the language and to maintain an ideal of public poetry. Chaucer was revered as a pioneer and held up as a symbol of poetry working its inventive power within an English context. If anything, these later poets wrote as if Chaucer had not publicized his rhetorical innovations enough, the implication being that the character of Chaucer's reputation had a direct bearing on how these poets presented themselves. Lydgate, among others, was keen to crown his dead father with the bays Chaucer never claimed for himself: "my master Chauceris nowe is grave / The noble rethor Poete of breteine /

That worthy was the laurer to haue."[56] The hyperbolic eulogizing reflected, not only a tradition made conscious of itself, but the flatterers' sense of liberation at being able to extol fellow poets as heroes of comparable majesty to kings. Within a few decades after Chaucer had bid his book to kiss the footsteps of the ancients, an actual sovereign, King James of Scotland, could place Chaucer and Gower on their own steps "of rethorike, quhill thai were lyvand here, / Superlative as poetis laureate" (*Kingis Quair* [*c.* 1425], 1374–6). For the anonymous poet of the *Court of Sapience* (*c.* 1460), Chaucer and Gower had ascended the steps to enjoy their own "soveraynte" as "erthly goddes two."[57] The extravagance of the flattery signalled an intense fascination with the newly elevated status of English poetry, a fascination likewise demonstrated in the poets' various attempts at "literariness" ("aureation," obscure metaphoric stylization, formal artificiality, and so on), in their broad array of critical terms to describe the poetic activity,[58] as well as in the several reworkings of Chaucer's *House of Fame*: Lydgate's *Temple of Glas* (*c.* 1405), Douglas's *Palice of Honour* (*c.* 1501), and Skelton's *Garlande of Laurell* (1523).

This fascination, however, did not usually translate into self-canonizing gestures. Most poets of the period expressed instead an intense insecurity about their work, typically introducing their works with tropes of inadequacy and complaints of literary exhaustion. After Gower and Chaucer, the poet of the *Book of Curtesye* (*c.* 1477) lamented, "ther is no more to saye / For of our tunge they were both lok & kaye."[59] This affected humility, like most self-defining gestures among public poets, was motivated by political interests. As David Lawton has explained, a "willed, self-conscious and ostensible dullness" was the appropriate mask for public poets in a politically turbulent century, for it enabled them to advocate a conservative ideology of political and ethical caution to their factious patrons. The period's most representative genres – regimen, *de casibus*, and courtesy book – were among the most explicitly didactic and prescriptive, and were meant to influence the conduct of the nobility and the setting of royal policy. Such presumption in verse, a challenge to the king's authority far more direct than any ceremony of laureation, required, as Lawton suggests, "delicate and diplomatic handling of patron by poet."[60] The modesty *topos* was one among many defensive gestures deployed by these poets to enable them to survive as cultural spokesmen in a highly charged political atmosphere. The trope of literary exhaustion, for example, often prefaced the claim that the poet, no matter how overshadowed by his precursors, still felt compelled to write. Of Chaucer and Gower, wrote John Walton, "I to theym in makying am unmete," yet, he added, "most I shewe it forth that is in me."[61] Walton's disclaimer prefaced his translation (*c.* 1410) of Boethius's *De Consola-tione Philosophiae,* one of the most popular works among the period's aristocratic readers, for whom the book's themes of mutability and fortune's malice spoke resonantly to their sense of their own insecurity. In professing a lack of oratorical skill, Walton hoped to protect himself from possible charges of breaching social decorum; at the same time, he could affirm the social utility of his art by heralding the canon as a standard of rhetorical productivity. His modesty about his own powers served as an oblique disavowal of political interest, a symbolic gesture meant to ensure that the strong political import of his verse would be misrecognized as a legitimate form of conventional moral speech.

The gesture required that the English canon be presented as a repository of moral knowledge, and this entailed adjustments to the reputations of the Ricardian poets. Much like a pagan poet allegorized into a Christian *auctor,* Chaucer was made "noble rhetor" in the fif-teenth century. Such accommodation of past literature is inevitable aspect of canon-formation: in later periods, Chaucer would be hailed as an anti-prelate reformer *avant la lettre,* as a coterie poet, as a man of wit and good sense, and so on. To his fifteenth-century canonizers, Chaucer had to be transformed into a "grave" poet who wrote for clear utilitarian ends. Lydgate, for one, produced "improved" versions of Chaucer's works that satisfied contemporary demand for a florid style and didactic sententiousness. Chaucer's name would be frequently set in tandem with "moral" Gower's and, later, "virtuous" Lydgate's, as though, save for his *Troilus* and a few of the more traditional *Tales,* Chaucer seemed too much the lightweight and needed to have his standing bolstered by association with his more conventionally didactic peers. While not quite treating Chaucer as an *auctor,* these poets were eager to fit him into a uniform pantheon of moral poets, one that agreed with their broader political aims of maintaining universal order in English society. Typical of postulators in a rhetorical culture, these so-called Chaucerians proposed a harmonious canon as an ideograph of social harmony.

The balance these poets attempted to achieve was similar to Gower's juxtaposing of laureate pretension with traditional auctorial thinking, but their efforts seemed less paradoxical than Gower's because they projected their Petrarchan ambitions onto their immediate predeces-sors.[62] Their hope was that the canonization of Chaucer and Gower as moral rhetoricians would help to preserve a symbolic authority for English poetry, yet one that posited the poet as an agent of social order rather than cultural advancement. The Chaucerians wanted not so much to be Chaucer as to be part of a well-defined tradition at whose head may have stood Chaucer but whose foremost attribute was its homogeneity of values. The emphasis was on collective achievement without originality, on poetic productivity without revision. Even the versatile Lydgate, whose services were much in demand, was happy to offer his major works as additional *Canterbury Tales*, epicyclic extensions of Chaucer's corpus. The limits on authorial self-determination these poets set for themselves served the larger didactic goal of discouraging self-determination in a political sphere, so that poetic collectivity could be an inspiration to political cohesion. In Lawton's formulation, "the impressively homogeneous public voice of fifteenth-century poetry" represented "a ceaseless attempt to create continuity and unity where in the actual center of power there is instability and 'dyuisioun.'"[63] In place of the epic values of heroism and immortal glory, the poets commended to their patrons, and personified in their "dull" self-presentations, the virtues of prudence, stability, and harmony.

The voice was monologic, but it was not without its source. By hailing Chaucer as the first refiner of the language, the Lancastrian poets were making clear that the goal of crafting a literary language out of the rude vernacular was not merely imaginable but of considerable symbolic value: English poets could now aspire to be masters of language's civilizing force, the highest office traditionally ascribed to poets. This definitive certification of poetry's legitimacy may have seemed at odds with the poets' claims of inadequacy but, again, they may have been responding to specific political concerns. According to John H. Fisher, circumstancial evidence exists to indicate that not only was there a general effort in the early fifteenth century towards establishing Chancery English as the vernacular standard, but equally that direct political patronage for English poets both living and dead (through the markedly increased copying and dissemination of their work) was conducted in order to confirm English as a literary language that could be objectified in a canon of native poetry. On the basis of this evidence, Fisher concludes that the increase in literary production after 1400 "was encouraged by Henry IV, and even more by Henry V, as a deliberate policy intended to engage the support of Parliament and the English citizenry for a questionable usurpation of the throne. The publication of Chaucer's poems and his enshrinement as the perfecter of rhetoric in English were central to this effort."[64] Not since Alfred's learning projects in the ninth century had the idea of literature in the vernacular received royal endorsement, yet even more remarkable was that the Lancastrian kings believed that their political legitimacy could be buttressed by appropriating the symbolic capital of an English poetic canon.

As words are power in a rhetorical culture, so the ideal of refinement is tied to political authority. The perfecting of the language was for early authors a palpable measure of a monarch's polite influence on his court and people – as late as 1672, Dryden could still make the equation explicit in his *Defence of the Epilogue*. The political appropriation of the canon was eagerly encouraged by poets, even if it entailed subordinating their authority to the monarch's, because it secured for poetry a social function and legitimacy, without which poetry could not long survive in a rhetorical culture. To the extent that poetry could then project a commensurate value, a linguistic authority, back onto the king, here was rhetorical canon-making being practised in an almost ideal form, as if the realms of the aesthetic and the political were one. As the effects of refinement spread out dynamically from the court, poet and king could share equally in the prestige of being producers of linguistic capital – the special code of eloquence – vital to the moral integrity of the state. A sense of this ideological prestige was implicit in many early encomiums to Chaucer, whose embellishing "of oure rude moders englisshe tonge" was said to have profound social repercussions in the common culture beyond opening the way for more English poetry.[65] In Dunbar's version, Chaucer inspired a national consciousness: having nurtured "in oure tong ane flour imperiall," the poet ensured that the English language would soon be "Surmounting ewiry tong terrestriall."[66]

Yet, since these representations of the poet emphasized his status as an author, as a figure for whom the advancement of the state was inseparable from his self-advancement, conflict remained between poet and patron over which field, the aesthetic or the political, was the ultimate source of value, the final determinant of how the state would advance. Even among self-consciously "dull" poets, the desire for self-determination was not easily reconciled with the respect due a kingly authority that was not universally regarded as absolute. In the image many of his successors hoped to promulgate, Chaucer had shown that the language could be used to illuminate moral, religious, and political truths. Hence, verbal "correction" was seen as corresponding to rectifying problems of state. Just as Lydgate invoked Chaucer to "amende and correcte / The wronge tracys of my rude penne," so elsewhere he claimed that by furnishing princes with tragic stories of "othres fallying," he might prompt these princes to "themsilff correcte."[67] In effect, the king became a representation of the poets' making, as the object of their moral counsel and verbal refining. His authority, though it legitimized their project of generating a literary language, was to be subordinated to the value of the poets' own didactically uniform canon and of their rhetorical "perfectings," the realization of which, they claimed, would ultimately help to defeat political division. Social harmony was the absolute value that, in principle, grounded this economy of symbolic exchange between poet and king. But, since this harmony was deferred to some future moment, the economy of the authorial order, as compared to the auctorial, remained open and dynamically risky, its sources of legitimacy never quite fully integrated.

Some English writers may have been genuinely embarrassed at the "rudeness" of their language. Even Chaucer the refiner had worried that his meaning might be lost amid the ever-changing "diversitie / In Englissh and in writyng of oure tonge" (*Troilus* 5:1793–4). Latin remained the language of legal, religious, and diplomatic affairs, and, in an increasingly humanistic age, the language of the European intellectual elite; its eloquence was beyond question. Lydgate's introduction of a magniloquent Latinized diction into English poetry was likely an anxious attempt to lend the vernacular a veneer of neoclassic respectability, or to please the Lancastrian court by self-consciously outdoing Chaucer at "embellishing" the language. Yet the poets' expressed anxieties were always to some degree gestural: embarrassed or not, they continued to write in English. For the vast majority of British people, English became a literary language when the Pater Noster and the Bible were made available in the vernacular. And while the exalting of Chaucer and others as refiners of English may have helped to sanction the later poets' own efforts in the vernacular as well as to legitimize a shaky claim to the throne, the gesture would not have made much sense had there not already existed a widespread belief that English authors like Chaucer were authoritatively eloquent enough to sanction either more vernacular poetry or a line of kings. Beseeching readers to excuse their rudeness while lamenting that they "dwellyd nevere wyth the fresh rethoryens, / Gower, Chauncers, ner with lytgate," English poets remained hopeful that they, too, would be honoured for their refinements to the language.[68]

Reforming the language of the tribe is, in a rhetorical culture, at once the canon's unique source of value and the poet's most potent strategy of self-legitimization, since it serves to define a present through a constructive rejection of a "rude" cultural past. So it is that, in the sixteenth century, when Europeans began to learn of the "barbarous" peoples of the New World, complaints were still heard about the poverty and "uncouth" character of the English tongue. Still later, in the next century, when Chaucer's diction had itself come to seem "barbarous," poets mourned with undiminished stridency the impermanence and inelegance of their chosen medium. In all these cases, the sentiments may have been genuine but their expression was tactical. The immediate occasions for the complaints differed, though the dominant motive was ideological, since the implicit aim was not so much to alter the language as to insist upon a single polite standard of usage, a homogeneous voice refined by the poets and enshrined in a harmonious canon.

For the poets of the fifteenth century, idealizing a canonic harmony was a crucial aspect of their self-definition and, what amounts to the same thing, their self-preservation. Yet, without institutional mechanisms of the type that had maintained an auctorial order, a "dull" tradition could not remain vital for very long. In discouraging gestures of poetic self-determination, and in being so tied to specific political interests, it denied itself a source of unique and enabling value. It was perhaps inevitable, then, that an independent-minded, risk-taking poet like Skelton would soon appear to assert his own modernity by rejecting this self-limiting tradition. Emphasizing linguistic decay and evaluating the divergent styles of previous poets, Skelton made a claim for his own modern uniqueness by being among the first English writers to record dissonances in the canon's once-homogeneous voice: "Gowers Englysh is olde / And of no value told," he declared, while Lydgate was so verbose that it was difficult "to fynde / The sentence of his mynde."[69] More generously, in *A Garlande of Laurell*, Skelton cast himself as a reluctant candidate for the bays whom the previous English laureates had literally to press into joining their canon, "Tyll at the last they forcyd me sore."[70] By 1523, the year of the poem, Skelton had regained the protection of the Howards and could no longer be silenced by his old enemy Cardinal Wolsey. *A Garlande of Laurell* was thus an exercise in Petrarchan self-determination, where Skelton awarded himself the laurels in a symbolic usurpation of the power of his former oppressor.[71]

Challenging the uniformity of the canon was for Skelton an oblique way of dissociating himself from the corrupt hegemony of the court. Exiled from the centre of power, Skelton styled himself the laureate of the people, "the famous bard of whom a thousand speak."[72] In accepting to join the established canon in the *Garlande*, Skelton none-theless understood that his struggle for distinction required not a foresaking of his poetic lineage but its adjustment, at once its contin-uation and its recension. In the terms Skelton attributed to his fic-tional "Gower," revisionism was essential to the culture's renewal "Because that ye encrease and amplyfy / The brutid Britons of Brutus Albion, / That welny was loste when that we were gone."[73] This open espousal of canon change risked exposing the relative nature of can-onicity and undermining the integrity of the still-emergent indigenous tradition. Yet self-authorizing gestures like Skelton's were necessary for verbal power to retain its symbolic value and sense of ongoing productive utility. Whatever Skelton's specific political allegiances, English poetry could not long endure were not its central function in helping to circulate symbolic capital in the moral economy of the state continually reasserted.

Revisionism would become a crucial aspect of canon-formation in the sixteenth century when, for the first time, there arose the problem not simply of how to glorify a harmonious canon but of how to preserve that harmony in times of change. On the one hand, the importance of maintaining a productive national literature would be openly proclaimed: "so longe (of lykelyhode) as letters shal endure and continue, this noble royalme shall be the better."[74] On the other hand, there was an equally urgent cultural need to define a present by rejecting a past. While the medieval poets continued to receive the homages of later poets, they were increasingly singled out from the "barbarous" circumstances in which they lived and wrote. In order to be brought into conformity with later values, the dead poets had to be seen as anomalies in their own age: in one typical version, it was "moche to be marveyled" that so great a poet as Chaucer should ever have arisen "in his tyme whan doutlesse all good letters were layde a slepe through out the worlde."[75] Those good letters would henceforth appear to stand a better chance of survival, though the change that allowed for this enhanced preservation also altered prevailing notions of canonicity and of poetry's function as the key of memory and immortality. English poets would no longer have to rely solely on their verbal power to canonize themselves but could look forward to a more objective enshrinement in posterity. As Stephen Hawes suggested in his *Passetyme of Pleasure* (*c.* 1509), the poet's "goodly name / In prynted bokes, doth remayne in fame."[76]

DISSOLUTION IN THE CATALOGUES OF LELAND AND BALE

The formation of literary canons involves acts of both valuation and preservation. This much was understood in the medieval period, both by the clerics who maintained an auctorial order by reproducing the works of the dead, and by the poets who sought to improve conditions for authorship by their gestures of self-assertion. The existence of written works in a manuscript period was nonetheless precarious. All authors were at the mercy of scribes and insecure networks of dissemination. Worse, all writings were vulnerable to random destruction: the accidents of survival, the wages of censorship, and the eruptions of iconoclasm and mass plundering of library holdings. Early scholars responded to this destruction with resignation: Alcuin saw the Viking raid on Lindisfarne and its great library in 793 as a sign of God's displeasure with a corrupt Northumbrian people.[77] Modern canon-formation arguably begins with the refusal of such resignation and with the first systematic efforts to bring neglected writings under the stewardship of an established authority. It begins, that is, with the efforts of those who take it upon themselves to ensure the adequate reception and preservation of writings that are neither their own nor obviously essential to a productive moral economy. Authors in a rhetorical culture, such as the medieval clerics and poets, are usually concerned to perpetuate past traditions in order to safeguard their own vocations and beliefs, to promote universal order, or to help poetry perform its immortalizing function. Canon-formation in an objectivist culture, in contrast, is veered toward reception, and while modern scholars have a professional interest in reproducing the literature of the past, their acts of preservation are not meant to benefit anyone in particular, other than future readers.

Modern canon-making, by this definition, is inaugurated in England during the period of most intense destruction, the dissolution of the monasteries in the first decades of the Reformation. The unlikely pioneers in this case were the antiquaries John Leland and John Bale, who, in massive bio-bibliographical catalogues they compiled in the 1540s and 1550s, produced the first comprehensive objectifications of the canon of British letters. "Unlikely," because Leland and Bale were hardly moderns; they were concerned to argue for the symbolic and instrumental value of literature from ages past. Sadly for them and for learning in England, the destruction was of such a scale that it overwhelmed their arguments, as well as the antiquarians themselves. Bale wrote that he was moved to tears at the sight of the destruction: "thys is highly to be lamented, of all them that hath a naturall love to their contrey ... That in turnynge over of ye superstycyouse monasteryes, so lytle respecte was had to theyr lybraryes for the savegarde of those noble & precyouse monumentes."[78] And Leland, who went mad before he could finish his work, lamented how English books were being stolen and their glory appropriated by foreign scholars: "the Germans perceiving our desidiousness and negligence, do send daily young scholars hither, that spoileth them, and cutteth them out of libraries, returning home and putting them abroad as monuments of their own country."[79]

The catalogues they ultimately assembled were haunted by the Dissolution. One of the chief functions of these works, and the source of their utility for later bibliographers, was to trace a map of dispersal, since the antiquaries tried to keep track of the many rare items they came across during their researches, as if by achieving completeness of record they could contain the ongoing catastrophe.[80] But the dissolution also haunted the catalogues as a noticeable absence. Nowhere in these works did Leland and Bale declare their regret over the destruction. The above laments appeared in the antiquaries' correspondence, or in Bale's preface to his edition of Leland's New Year's address of 1546/7 to Henry VIII.[81] The antiquaries' silence on the causes of the destruction was for them a difficult trade-off, since the authority to which they addressed their appeal was the same authority, the Tudor court, that had initiated the Dissolution.[82] That same authority had also for a time enlisted Bale as an anti-clerical propagandist and had granted Leland his famous commission "to make a search after England's antiquities."[83] The court, through its tightly organized network of patronage, exercised full control over the national culture. There was no other institution the antiquaries could turn to.

Both claimed they had been inspired by the work of the continental bibliographers Johannes Trithemius and Conrad Gesner, whose exhaustive indexes of classical and patristic *auctores* proved extremely valuable within Europe's nascent print culture.[84] But what Leland and Bale produced were more than booklists. Bale's catalogues, the 1548 *Summarium* and the greatly expanded second edition, the *Catalogus* of 1557–59, just as much as Leland's (assembled by the early 1540s, and referred to extensively by Bale, but not published until 1709), differed from earlier bibliographies in that the urgency of the situation impelled the antiquaries to magnify the aura of their canons with allegorizing commentary, which, they hoped, would signal the ideological importance of preserving the British literary canon in its entirety, as a harmonious whole.[85] The dispersal of the libraries was indication enough that, outside the cloisters, the reasons for having a learned tradition were not self-evident. What Leland and Bale produced, then, were polemics for British letters, bibliographies as much animated as enervated by the sense that the writings they recorded may have already been lost. These polemics are of interest as canonizing gestures because the reality of the destruction rendered acute the task of resolving the central problem in all canon-formation, that of defining how literary works could retain their value in change. In remaining silent on the troubling fact that the Dissolution involved the authorized actions of their contemporaries in rejecting their past, the antiquaries suppressed the temporality of their own endeavours. Consequentially, their claims for the productive utility of the endangered writings were uttered without any sure sense of an economy wherein such claims might be considered meaningful. The canons they constructed were therefore harmonious, expansive, and virtually without modernity.

Leland and Bale were both strong supporters of Henry's reformist policies. Bale, one of the period's most prominent controversialists, applauded "the moste lawfull overthrow of the sodometrouse Abbeyes and Fryeryes," while in a late unpublished tract, the *Antiphilarchia*, Leland affirmed his loyalty to the king, crediting him with inaugurating research into the "independent" origins of the English Church.[86] Reluctant to blame authorities for their recklessness in carrying out the suppression, the antiquaries shrouded their attempts at damage control in the de-politicized discourse of myth, framing their canons with elaborate fictions about England's origins, its imperial destiny, and its long history of reformist thought. Leland opened his catalogue with entries describing the civilizing influence of bards and druids, while Bale constructed an extravagant narrative of British colonization that extended from Adam to Samothes Gigas (Homer's brother, no less) to the Trojan Brutus who gave Britain its name.[87] The Tudor monarchs, particularly Henry VII, had been anxious to strengthen their claim to the throne by declaring direct descent from Arthur and other semi-legendary figures of the English past; in widening this royal genealogizing to include men of letters, Leland and Bale were trying to save the literary tradition by playing to Tudor insecurities and by persuading the court to recognize the legitimizing power of antiquities. Through the sheer massiveness of their catalogues, as well, the antiquaries were hoping to convince their patrons that their research could benefit England in making it appear a cultural empire, in reply to those abroad who looked upon the destruction as confirmation "that we are despysers of lernynge."[88] Bale, in attempting to include every figure who could conceivably have some connection with British letters, went well beyond his original aim of preservation, with the result that the final version of his catalogue contained some 1400 entries, many of which, like those for Merlin and Pope Joan, had little to do with saving old manuscripts and much to do with portraying England as an elect nation. At less than 600 entries, Leland's catalogue was shorter yet no less far-reaching, since Leland expended considerable energy trying to refute other nations' claims on writers, many of them legendary, who he believed were British. His catalogue of writers was originally intended as the first part of a vast survey of Britain's land, nobility, and history, a project whose ideological significance Leland eagerly proclaimed: just as Charlemagne had among his treasures silver engravings of Rome and Constantinople, he told Henry, "so shall your Maiestie have thys your worlde and impery of Englande so sett fourthe in a quadrate table of silver."[89]

The third set of myths represented the most forceful argument for preservation the antiquaries had to offer, and the point of deepest disagreement between the two. Both claimed that their research could demonstrate the persistence of reformist thought in England. The old writings were worth preserving, they maintained, because long-concealed verities of primitive Christianity could be yet found among them. Said Bale to his patrons, "ye might paraventure se many unknowne wonders."[90] Leland similarly assured Henry that his efforts would bring "full manye thynges to lyght, as concernynge the usurped autoryte of the Byshopp of Rome and hys complyces, to the manyfest and vyolent derogacyon of kyngely dygnyte."[91] The *Antiphilarchia* notwithstanding, however, Leland's commitment to reformist ideals was far less intense than Bale's and seemed motivated less by religious conviction than by devotion to his king. Revising Leland's catalogue, Bale expressed dismay at how his colleague had treated many works "with no discrimination" in matters of doctrine.[92] Aside from publicizing suppressed works of radical theology, Bale believed that his cataloguing would serve to legitimize the Reformation by retracing England's history so as to confirm its unique destiny as a continuator of the early Church.[93] Bale was among the first English exponents of a powerful Protestant eschatology that rejected the Augustinian separation of divine from worldly existence and that saw instead the possibility of human history coinciding at some future time with the re-emergence of a true Christianity. As J.G.A. Pocock has explained, radical reformers like Bale believed that spiritual renaissance could occur only if humanity studied the writings of a historical line of divinely inspired authors: "God has pronounced, through the mouths of prophets, certain words in time; the occasions of these pronouncements, together with other happenings to which they refer, constitute a series of divine acts in past time; we believe that these acts were performed by believing the authors and the words they have relayed to us ... All is *logos*, and *logos* is a system of communications through time."[94] The goal Bale set for himself in his catalogue was to identify this *logos* from among all the writings ever produced in England, and to write the narrative of its history: "what continuaunce, what darkeninges, what decayes, what falle, and what rayse againe."[95]

The antiquaries' differences on this matter translated into two distinct approaches to canon-making. Whereas Leland hoped to erect a pantheon to honour king and empire, Bale desired the enabling continuities of a tradition. And whereas Leland was apt to lavish praise indiscriminately, Bale styled himself a discerning judge of England's "elected heritage."[96] Yet both antiquaries were confronted with the same problem, one that must invariably be considered in any attempt to claim for the texts of the past the power to transcend their origins and to remain valuable in change. For Leland and Bale, this problem was not simply one of defending the old books in the face of their widespread destruction. It was equally a problem of how to represent the enduring modernity of writing while at the same time relating each work to a particular historical context, to the occasion of its pronouncement, and to the life and times of its author. The problem was one of reconciling literary history, with its emphasis on change and historical specificity, with the hoped-for transhistoricism of canon-formation. This paradox of permanence and change could be circum-vented by the medieval form of the biographical catalogue, which recognized individual achievements without situating them in a his-torical narrative. The antiquaries, for reasons that had to do with their divergent motives for preserving the old books, were nonetheless concerned to identify diachronic patterns in their catalogues, whether these patterns emphasized the role of human agency, a periodization of history, or a narrative of decline and rebirth. Yet to call attention to historical change in this way heightened the sense that the books belonged to the past and were irrelevant to an age of reform. It therefore became incumbent on the antiquaries to suggest how these writings had retained their value in altered circumstances, including the circumstances of Dissolution, the one context Leland and Bale felt compelled to suppress in their narratives.

In the often quoted opening to his "New Year's Gift," Leland assured Henry that he was hard at work delivering "the monumentes of auncyent wryters ... out of deadly darkenesse to lyvelye lyght."[97] To a humanist like Leland, light signified eloquence.[98] His task, as he saw it, was to enliven England's sense of its past by rescuing its chronicles from the "darkness" of medieval expression. The lives of English kings and poets, he maintained, had been "hitherto sore obscured ... because men of eloquence hath not enterprised, to set them fourth in a floryshynge style."[99] Leland's idealization of eloquence made for a catalogue much closer in spirit to Petrarch's biographies of famous men than to the old booklists of *auctores*. Any bibliographical interest was secondary to the Petrarchan goals of glorifying the worthies of the past and refining the language. Leland's use of luminary meta-phors differed in one respect from Petrarch's, however. The latter's contrasting of radiant eloquence versus medieval obscurity corre-sponded to a revisionist periodization of history, a symmetry of illustrious ancients and barbarous moderns. This periodization was at odds with Leland's purpose in writing his catalogue, which was supposed to exalt not the classics but the very medieval writings whose inelegant style he maligned. Leland nonetheless found the codes of renaissance light and medieval dark reassuring in their clarity, even if their use entailed periodizing away a large chunk of literary history. His researches, he told Henry, would "open this wyndow, that the lyght shal be seane, so long, ye is to say, by ye space of a whole thousand yeares stopped up."[100] Leland's heavy reliance on such verbal appositions reflected his immersion in rhetorical thinking and, as well, the degree to which such thinking could not help him to deal seriously with historical change. His evaluative certainties being largely emotional, Leland could not adequately account for what made the old writings valuable.

Leland's faith in their canonicity stemmed from his fervent patriotism but equally from a concern for his own poetry, which he wrote throughout his career. His love of antiquities carried with it a high personal investment, since he had to assert their lastingness to confirm the memorializing power of his own verse. Leland's self-service in this respect was no worse than earlier poets', though Bale regretted his colleague's quest for self-determination: "I muche do feare it that he was vaynegloryouse, and that he had a poetycall wytt, whyche I lament, for I judge it one of the chefest thynges that caused hym to fall besydes hys ryghte dyscernynges."[101] Leland's personal stake in the immortality *topos* determined the nature of his canon, a comprehensive Parnassus founded on the self-authorizing agency of the scholar-poet, and hence a canon founded on the conflicting principles of inclusion and revision. While celebrating all British bookmen, the catalogue proposed an operative mythology of the modern laureate whose fame sprang from his ability to displace the poetic achievements of the past. Leland had therefore to show how his canon remained integral in its fullness even as the writers he honoured continually strove to surpass their precursors. The resulting catalogue was a spectacle of inconsistency. A devotee of Chaucer, Leland included in his entry on the poet commendatory verses comparing him to Homer and Virgil yet which claimed that he failed to achieved true greatness because he happened not to live in an age as favourable to learning as the classical period.[102] At the same time, Leland declared that several of Chaucer's compositions would endure, being equal to the best of the Latins. Unable to specify why Chaucer's work endured, Leland repeated the commonplace that Chaucer had refined the language, but, as a would-be refiner himself, Leland believed the standard for excellence in the vernacular rested no longer with Chaucer but with Wyatt.[103] While Chaucer's standing in the canon remained unexplained, Leland could not afford to deny the poet his permanence. The difficulty Leland had created for himself was one of reconciling a desire both for an inclusive and imperishable canon of British letters and for meaningful criteria by which to identify each work's unique value and to persuade his patrons of the symbolic worth of his entire canon.

Negotiating between these conflicting impulses, Leland heaped on the *formulae*. In his entry on Gower, Leland played to contemporary prejudice about the poet's "semi-barbarous age" but added that his importance could yet be recognized by those prepared to make historical allowances: "we overlook certain infelicities in the poems of Gower, and we hold him up as the first refiner of our native language. For before that time the English language lay uncultivated and nearly wholly raw. Nor was there anyone who could write in the vernacular, works suitable for a discriminating reader. Thus the value of his works lies in their careful cultivation, that, the rude weeds stamped out, instead of thistles arise the pliant violet and purple narcissus."[104] Leland was trying hard to transform his Tudor patrons into reflections of himself: his discriminating reader could appreciate the desirability of an extensive canon, and his humanist discretion did not disallow him from enjoying works from England's uncultured past. The discriminating or learned reader, as I shall argue in the next section, was a figure well known from classical rhetoric and routinely appeared in early evaluations of English writings. Yet there was something peculiar about Leland's use of the figure. In accordance with the agonistic structures of rhetoric, a discriminating reader had to discriminate against something. Leland's discriminating reader lacked this Other; he was an unlikely figure who combined humanist sophistication with a favourable disposition towards the works of long-departed national authors. The only Other Leland could identify was history itself, as his reader was supposed to dissociate the works from their barbarous cultures of origin. Such canon-making, in Leland's narrative of rebirth, would benefit an already "so flourishing age" by helping it to emerge from the "clouds of ignorance." What Leland was finally saying was that the preservation of the literary past would help to defeat the pernicious influence of the past. Attempting to court his patrons, Leland was forced to flatter them in their superiority over the very period and literature he was making claims for. The trade-off deprived his canon of any claim to modernity, and it left Leland with little more than emotion to defend the literary tradition.

If Leland's canon was empowered by the antinomic energies of verbal power, Bale's was secured in the Word. Because his vision of history insisted on the role of worldly life in human spiritual development, he considered the English people responsible for the eventual re-establishment of a true Church. As an elect race, the English had to believe in the *logos* of prophecy contained in the writings of their ancestors in order to achieve salvation. And even if these writings did not contain long-buried divine pronouncements, they could offer vital information on the occasions to which the reformist prophets had referred. Hence, in Bale's view, the English had to save their literature to save themselves. In lamenting the destruction, Bale was thinking not merely of his nation's reputation but of its spiritual redemption: "To put our auncient Chronicles, our noble hystoryes, our learned commentaryes & homelyes upon ye scriptures, to so homely an office of subjeccyon & utter contempte we have both greatly dishonoured our nacyon, and also shewed our selves very wycked to our posteryte."[105] Given this belief in the continuity of British letters, Bale looked more favourably upon medieval writings than did Leland. His catalogue included entries on Caedmon and other Anglo-Saxon figures, and one on "Gildas Cambrius," whom Bale believed to be Britain's first poet. Organizing his history according to a principle of reductive periodization, Bale was predisposed to believing in the actuality of the first-century Gildas because it would have meant that a British writer had flourished during the period of the primitive church. He was likewise prepared to assume that the late-fourteenth-century English poets were sympathetic to reform because they happened to fall into the one "century" that also included Wyclif – "century" being Bale's term for the roughly chronological groups of one hundred lives that made up each of his chapters. Bale had in fact initially ascribed the authorship of *Piers Plowman* to Wyclif himself, but he later corrected his error in the *Catalogus*. He claimed, as well, that Chaucer, whose canon of works had by this time been enlarged to include the virulently anti-clerical *Plowman's Tale*, wrote many works "in which he showed his disapproval of that great multitude of mumblers, the monks, of their idleness, their unintelligible prayers, their relics, pilgrimages and ceremonies."[106]

Periodization served Bale in making the old texts seem relevant to his age. Reducing the later fourteenth century into the age of Wyclif, the "morning star" of the Reformation, Bale turned literary history into a mirror of his own times.[107] His reduction worked in the other direction, too, since he condemned Catholic authors to their benighted "centuries," but in a sense these authors were equally modernized for the conflict of the two churches dominated Bale's narrative as a transhistorical phenomenon. Hardly historicist-minded, Bale spoke emphatically of the judgment of history: "what thynge more clerely tryeth the doctrynes of men, what they are, than do their ages or times?"[108] Yet such radical prescriptiveness was finally too deterministic for Bale, who was concerned to show the courage of those like Wyclif who had defied the Roman Church by bringing the "light of truth" to their age.[109] Just as Protestants of the present age were responsible for ensuring their salvation, so individual acts of conscience had been instrumental in the past in bringing about reform. However destined, the Reformation was a historical break realized through human agency and, in particular, through the power of the written word. Accordingly, the theme of Bale's catalogue, much more so than Leland's, was the moral centrality of writing in human affairs. Though Bale was often unclear as to how particular works contributed to the larger history of Christianity, his theme required that he pay close attention to the historical specificity of authors and their works: "Their ages are as necessary to be knowne as their doctrynes, and the tytles of their bokes so wele as their manyfest actes, to them that wyl throughly judge things as they are, & not be deceived by colours."[110] As a result, his catalogues juxtaposed the seemingly irreconcilable narratives of historicism and providence, authorship and *auctoritas*.

Bale's desire to present "things as they are" prompted him to reject Leland's call to embellish the English chronicles. On the contrary, Bale argued, the writers of the past ought to speak in their own words because "undoubtedly, authoryte it woulde adde unto them, to apere fyrst of all in their owue [*sic*] simplycyte or native colours without bewtie of speche." Making the old writings available to all English readers, in Bale's view, was a much more productive aim than the patrician goal of refining the language; disseminating the canon, he believed, could exert a harmonizing influence upon the English people in facilitating religious conformity. "And," he added, "for that purpose (I thynke) God hath iu [*sic*] thys age geven the noble art of prentynge."[111] If for Leland "light" denoted eloquence, it symbolized for reformers the liberatory powers of print – as Bale's friend John Foxe famously declared, "through the light of printing the world beginneth now to have eyes to see, and heads to judge."[112] Darkness, according to this scheme, was not medieval inelegance but the widespread illiteracy of a manuscript age. Bale, who spent his final years lobbying for the publication of pre-Reformation manuscripts, including works antithetical to his own thinking, blamed this illiteracy on a papist conspiracy that "hath alwayes ben busied, seking contrary wyse to obscure all thynges, that contayned any veryte necessarye."[113] Unfortunately, the coming of the printed book may have added to the prejudice against the aging, tangibly *un*modern manuscripts during the period of their wholesale destruction.

The destruction pointed up what was missing from Bale's narrative, a coherent account of how literature survived in change. The absence was even more apparent from his commentary on Leland's "Gift," where he repeatedly insisted on the existence of "thynges lastyng & durable" while at the same time loudly deploring their loss.[114] Just as a historicist inquiry can never be accommodated to a providential design, so a rhetorical structure of belief can never fully acknowledge physical contingencies. Bale's transcendent *logos* was not an image of survival because it fixed the source of value outside change, beyond the historicity of authors and their works. Though Bale's pleading for political action placed him among the humanists as well as the reformers of his age, his vision of history was as absolutist as Alcuin's theodicy. And although his arguments for the continuing utility of past literature provided his canon with an evaluative certainty that Leland's lacked, his catalogues seemed far more susceptible to anachronism than his colleague's, very much the productions of a particular time and place. Without a sense of how its *auctoritas* could renew itself through the centuries, Bale's totalizing canon seemed even less modern than Leland's unfinished, conflicted pantheon of authors.

The antiquaries' failure to deal with the question of how writings could remain valuable in altered circumstances illustrates the limitations of rhetorical thinking in the face of historical change. These limitations may account for the antiquaries' profound anxiety about the temporality of their own endeavour. Insofar as they recorded for posterity's sake the lives and works of hundreds of disparate authors, their catalogues objectified the rhetorical belief that literature held the keys to memory and immortality, a *topos* that pervaded Leland's writing, if not Bale's. But the very act of recording these lives presumed the need for such a register. Were it not for the catalogues, it seemed, all of these long-dead authors would have been left to oblivion. Leland and Bale were responding to a crisis, the dispersal of the monastic collections, which they felt threatened to obliterate England's literary inheritance. Their chosen response, massive catalogues of authors, served two purposes: to supply important information on the whereabouts of the dispersed items, and to secure for British letters the protection of fame through the framing of a literary canon. If, as Curtius maintains, canon-formation serves to safeguard a tradition, then the motive behind canon-formation springs from the feeling that a tradition needs this safeguard, that the works of the past are not in themselves immortal, that they are frequently subject to neglect or censorship, that all literature, catalogues of authors included, cannot ultimately survive without the help of canon-makers. Though canon-formation may posit the transhistoricism of literature, it is itself a fundamentally historical act, an ideological or emotional response to what is perceived to be a situation detrimental to the survival or right appreciation of literary works, or of authorship itself. What Leland and Bale were anxious to preserve were the conditions for all writing, conditions that could ensure the continuance of British letters and, in particular, the safeguarding of the very works of Leland and Bale.

Another conclusion to be drawn from this episode is that nationalism may not be a sufficient cause of canon-formation. The Reformation had greatly intensified national self-awareness. As Benedict Anderson has argued, the fragmentation of Western Europe after the collapse of the Western Empire, along with the reformers' sponsorship of a "print-vernacular," were central contributing factors in the creation "of a new form of imagined community, which in its basic morphology set the stage for the modern nation."[115] For canon-making to be a function of nationalist aspirations, however, there has to exist a structure of conviction wherein a literary tradition is considered not simply worthy of affection, but essential to generating communal identification by virtue of its distinctiveness and accessibility. The Lancastrians attempted to inspire such conviction in order to exploit the linguistic authority of the poetic canon, just as the Elizabethans would undertake a sustained publicity campaign aimed at establishing a cultural order comparable to those emerging abroad. Yet, with social passions in the mid-sixteenth century consumed by religious upheaval, this structure of identification was so narrowly and intensely defined as to exclude anything from a discredited past, including artifacts that had held significance only for a small number of clerics and scholars.[116] Only later in the century, once conditions had stabilized sufficiently for this sense of an imagined community to be felt among a broad range of activities, could literary production be (again) recognized as circulating a symbolic capital vital to the definition of a culture. Although personally motivated by patriotic sentiment, Leland and Bale were working without any definable structure of feeling backing up their efforts. Their canons seemed utterly arbitrary because there as yet existed no moral economy wherein their efforts might be legitimized. No wonder they spoke largely from emotion. Without any confirmed opinion on their side, they could be assured of nothing, not even an end to the Dissolution. It was thus a sad conclusion to Bale's work that he should see his own library, made up of books salvaged from the Dissolution, sacked and dispersed within five years of the publication of his *Summarium.*[117]

Of course, Leland and Bale were trying desperately to rally support for their cause, but therein lay a dilemma. In effect, Leland and Bale had simultaneously to affirm and deny the destruction, its causes and its meaning. On the one hand, the antiquaries were attempting to convince their patrons and fellow reformers of the legitimizing power of traditions while at the same time being careful not to embarrass their audience by blaming them for the damage. Leland, who acted as Henry's scout in acquiring selected items for the Royal Library, barely mentioned the destruction in his "New Year's Gift" and avoided any suggestion that the king had been reckless in having sanctioned the Dissolution.[118] Addressing the English people rather than the court, Bale was more explicit than Leland in condemning "the malyce or els slouthfull neglygence of thys wycked age, whych is muche geven to the destruccyon of thynges memorable."[119] Yet, however sharply he admonished his contemporaries, he could not account for this outbreak of wickedness among a generation that had also brought about Reformation. The iconoclastic hostility that was being directed against letters may have been a direct repercussion of Reformation, but this was not something Bale was prepared to acknowledge.[120]

On the other hand, what gave these catalogues their urgency, if not their lasting value, was the Dissolution. The work of the antiquaries was worthwhile because the situation was so bad, the damage so deplorable. By extension, the worth of the old books was itself magnified by the threat of extinction. They were, it seemed, no more valuable than at the moment of their impending loss. Out of contrast with the spectre of oblivion, these long-forgotten texts had suddenly acquired an aura of irreplaceableness and rarity. Ultimately, the canons of Leland and Bale derived their force and seeming harmoniousness less from the antiquaries' rhetorical claims in their behalf than from the magnitude of the ongoing catastrophe: the greater the number of old writings that could conceivably be lost, the more significant the gesture of enshrining them in a canon. Once the plundering had subsided, however, it would become harder to dramatize the symbolic worth of the old texts or to see them as constituting a harmonious tradition. Gone were the powerful evaluative certainties that were tenable only in a crisis like the Dissolution. Only when the non-utilitarian value of past writings had become widely accepted would there be a history of literature in England that was not also strenuously insisting on the enduring relevance of texts sunk virtually without a trace. And only then, in the eighteenth century, would the catalogues of Leland and Bale begin to receive the serious attention of scholars and critics. An anonymous 1785 redaction of passages from Warton's *History of English Poetry* was among the first literary histories to see Leland's canon-making as a symbolic act of preservation and as an unlikely admonition against modern complacency: "When we look into the accounts of the British writers which have been given us by Leland and other biographers, and observe the multitude of persons whom these biographers have rescued from oblivion, together with the praises they have bestowed upon them ... we are ready to believe that the times preceding the Reformation were much more learned than has usually been imagined."[121]

EVALUATIVE COMMUNITIES AND PRINT AUDIENCES

The Anglo-Saxon poetic codices, or the manuscript anthologies owned by Sir John Paston, may be considered canonical collections, valuable as indexes of taste and, in some cases, the only extant sources of early English literature available to later readers.[122] Yet, whoever compiled these collections made their selections without declaring principles of inclusion or any indications as to why the selections were worth reading. With the advent of the print trade, there was a greater impetus to come up with critical advertisements. Caxton's prefaces come to mind, but a more definitive example is Richard Tottel's address to the reader at the beginning of his famous miscellany, the *Songes and Sonettes* (1557):

That to have wel written in verse, yea & in small parcelles, deserveth great praise, the workes of divers Latines, Italians, and other, doe prove sufficiently. That our tong is able in that kynde to do as praiseworthely as ye rest, the honorable stile of the noble earle of Surrey, and the weightinesse of the depewitted sir Thomas Wyat the elders verse, with severall graces in sondry good Englishe writers, doe show abundantly. It resteth nowe (gentle reder) that thou thinke it not evill doon, to publish, to the honor of the Englishe tong, and for profit of the studious of Englishe eloquence, those workes which the ungentle horders up of such treasure have hereto envied thee. And for this point (good reder) thine own profit and pleasure, in these presently, and in moe hereafter, shal answere for my defence. If parhappes some mislike the statelinesse of stile removed from the rude skill of common eares: I aske help of the learned to defend their learned frendes, the authors of this work: And I exhort the unlearned, by reding to learne to be more skilful, and to purge that swinelike grossenesse, that maketh the swete maierome not to smell to their delight.[123]

Tottel's preface typifies early criticism at its most practical. Beyond rehearsing the stock claim that readers will derive "profit and pleasure" from his selection, Tottel is not interested in detailing his appreciation for the poetry of Surrey, Wyatt, and the nameless others – the title-page to his miscellany tells the reader more about the precise nature of the selections than does his preface. The object of his preface is instead to assert the praiseworthiness of English lyric verse.

Tottel's interests are commercial but his preface is designed less to invite potential customers than to construct an audience for his book.[124] He writes as though the volume had already been purchased, the purpose of his preface being to defend his publishing the works of his betters and to secure a favourable reception for his new candidates for the canon. Tottel is devising the terms for that reception: all those who enjoy the poetry are learned friends of the authors, while any adverse criticism is merely the uncouth noise of the unlearned. Readers are caught in the agonistic structures of Tottel's rhetoric: either they commend the poetry as canonical, or they are swine.[125]

Every canon has its evaluative community, a real or imagined consensus whose values the canon is felt to express or objectify, often to the exclusion of other values.[126] The need to delimit an evaluative community was acutely felt in an early print culture, where it seemed increasingly difficult for writers to determine the actual constituency that informed the making of the national canon. Among the many changes that have been attributed to the ascendancy of print (commodification, democratization, spatialization, and so on), the one most immediately perceived was the alienation it interposed between author and audience. This alienation was especially disquieting in a rhetorical culture, where poets, from courtly amateurs like Sidney to civic-minded laureates like Spenser, wrote not for an autonomous audience but in the service of social relations. Though a distinct rhetorical category, poetry for the courtly writers was not an activity separate from other socio-political practices. Poetry was felt to operate in a larger, dynamic if tightly controlled moral economy, where the value of any activity was understood in terms of usage and productivity. Within this economy, it is said, "the final test of poetry is always in *praxis* – how it contributes to the moral improvement of its readers and to the wider society."[127] Even this formulation does not adequately suggest the dialogic energies of a rhetorical culture: the hope of early writers was rather that poetry would improve society by encouraging readers to become themselves producers, to become active contributors to a community whose vitality and cohesion depended upon the continual exchange of symbols and persuasions. In an economy where value was seen as instrumental rather than intrinsic, the circulation of value through verbal power was considered more enabling of solidarity than the canonization of unique works of art.

In accordance with this notion of art's social utility, writers routinely deployed their verbal power to manipulate their readers' responses with representations of a totalizing economy within which there circulated endlessly and productively a restrictive order of polite values. Tottel fashioned such an evaluative community when he called on the learned to defend the poetry of their friends from the cavils of "common ears." In actuality, the friends of Wyatt and Surrey were likely the same "ungentle horders up" of manuscripts whom Tottel complained about. As a commercial bookseller, Tottel had to contend with the courtly poets' aversion to seeing their work appear in the machine-made, depersonalized copies of print.[128] Their disdain for the medium, as well as their disclaimers about how their verses were but youthful indulgences, were reworkings of the self-effacing tactics of earlier poets, but, unlike their "dull" predecessors, the courtiers were not so much protecting themselves from charges of moral presumption as seeking to retain authority over the poetry written within their own circle. This authority was total, pertaining to both the production and the reception of poetry; in a rhetorical culture, the former subsumes the latter. Even Tottel, in his preface, equated the reception of his anthology with its instrumental effectivity, and he encouraged readers to improve themselves by being "studious of Englishe eloquence" and learning to be "more skilful" in both the appreciation and composition of poetry. Evidence suggests that Tottel selected many of his poems on the basis of how easily they could be imitated by aspiring poets. His miscellany was designed as a poetic handbook, the first in a series of Elizabethan anthologies compiled to provide courtiers with the verbal equipment needed for social and political advancement.[129]

By objectifying poems as commodities and all but denying their musical and performative aspects, print makes them appear less as instruments of social transaction than as timeless objects occupying the autonomous sphere of what is now called "literature." Above all, it makes much less palpable the reality of social relations, and much less appreciable the circulation of productive energies. It does this in at least two ways: it distances authors physically and imaginatively from their audiences, and it promotes a division of labour where the activities of writing and reading are seen as separate and of divergent value. In the first instance, print sharply accelerates the process whereby the task of assessing poetry passes from an author's immediate, primary audience to a larger, secondary audience that receives his works in contexts he cannot easily foresee. Before print, an author like Chaucer could have a reasonable sense of his primary audience's expectations. In oral performances, the poet could exercise some control over his audience's responses by adjusting his delivery, level of oratory, or the details of his material. The immediacy of oral performance also heightened the aura of the poetry, the sense of its ritualistic function as an instrument of communal solidarity.[130] Print invited an almost instant loss of aura and control. By shifting evaluative authority to a secondary audience, print made it problematic for authors to know whom they were writing for, to predict how their works would be received, or to measure their moral and political effectivity. Mindful of these uncertainties, the courtiers preferred to keep their poetic efforts for their primary audience, among whom they were copied and exchanged in commonplace books. Though their networks of dissemination would eventually become so extensive as to sustain a commercial industry by the later seventeenth century, the sense of intimacy provided by manuscript publication, with its "personalizing" features of scribal idiosyncracy, could at least help the courtiers to maintain the illusion of private ritual.[131] These writers were, in effect, willing to cede authorial control over the appearance of their texts in order to retain a semblance of social control and exclusivity over their reception.

More profoundly, the coming of print threatened to disrupt the close relationship between production and consumption. In a rhetorical culture, readers' expectations were not usually distinguished from authors'. Robert Darnton has noted how difficult it can be to analyse the habits of early readers since these were rarely a consideration before the eighteenth century: "The documents rarely show readers at work, fashioning meaning from texts ... Few of them are rich enough to provide even indirect access to the cognitive and affective elements of reading, and a few exceptional cases may not be enough for one to reconstruct the inner dimensions of that experience."[132] Not that readers were ignored. On the contrary, rhetoric was expressly taught as a social discourse for engaging audiences' responses. Yet, as the effectivity of rhetoric was posited on the belief that those responses were common to all humanity, the sensibilities of readers could not be seen as differing in any substantial way from those of producers. Hence, the few early treatises that discussed reading practices offered no more than extended versions of conventional instrumentalist and didacticist arguments found in most rhetorical handbooks and apologies for poetry.[133] Thomas Blundeville's *The true order and method of writing and reading hystories* (1574) was typical in the way it defined reading as a constructive act leading to further constructive acts: the purpose of reading, Blundeville claimed, was "to make our selves more wyse, aswell to direct our own actions, as also to counsell others, to sturre them to vertue, and to withdrawe them from vice, and to beautyfie our owne speache with grave examples, when we discourse of any matters, that therby it may have the more authoritie, waight, and credite."[134] The rules of writing were no different from those of reading; a critic like Puttenham could recommend his prescriptions as "not unnecessarie for all such as be willing themselves to become good makers in the vulgar, or to be able to judge of other mens making."[135] Within the moral economy of rhetorical culture, readers were not ideally differentiated from authors because it was felt more conducive to communal solidarity to insist on the energetic integrity of the totality than on the separate requirements of its agents.

Print seemed to threaten this integrity by heightening the distinctions, both material and intellectual, between the activities of producing and receiving literature.[136] Print meant more readers, readers who were not necessarily authors or patrons and who were therefore involved neither in the production of texts nor in the immediate occasions these texts were designed to address. Confronting texts in circumstances that could be greatly divergent from their original contexts of use, these readers could evaluate them with less sense of direct obligation to the author or patron, to the dictates of fashion and partisanship, or to the instrumentalist persuasions these texts may have presented. Aside from the financial transaction of purchasing a volume, consumers of printed texts were not required to consider themselves participants in a mode of social intercourse where the pleasures of reading could be bound up with expectations of reciprocity: the consumer did not have to repay the writer with pleasure in kind through patronage, formal praise, affirmations of friendship and indebtedness, or more literary production (as in the revisions and "answer" poems frequently exchanged among courtly writers[137]). It could be argued that, in weakening this sense of close exchange, print encouraged the separation of value from interest: readers could enjoy books for personal diversion and enrichment without having to abide by the demands of favour and deference, and they could draw on this education for ends that were not of direct benefit to any particular social formation. From the totalizing perspective of rhetorical thinking, however, such readerly autonomy seemed illegitimate, for it merely equated evaluative authority with the reader's self-interests. In this sense, print did not render the act of aesthetic reception more disinterested, since literature still operated within a system of socioeconomic exchange, though a system far more extensive and diversified than had previously been the case in a manuscript culture. Rather, print allowed for the perception that literature did not have to be prized for its symbolic capital as a mechanism of social transaction. Thus, by increasing the number and diversity of agents involved in the selection and usage of canonical writings, print pluralized the evaluative community, rendering the process of canon-making a matter less of peer evaluation than of cultural politics, with authors and booksellers trying to appeal to a wide diversity of readerly desires.[138]

Print seemed equally to empower authors with a greater autonomy. The ascendancy of print culture would, of course, eventually bring about the dismantling of courtly patronage and the thorough professionalization of letters. More immediately, it presented greater opportunities to aspiring laureates for histrionic displays of self-determination, and "few authors failed to give high priority to publicizing themselves. The art of puffery, the writing of blurbs and other familiar promotional devices were also exploited by early printers who worked aggressively to obtain public recognition for the authors and artists whose products they hoped to sell."[139] The name of the author became a major selling point of the book: "the authors name is sufficient to vent his worke," announced the preface to the 1622 quarto of *Othello*. This Machiavellian art of self-promotion gave impetus to the writing of commendatory verses, where fledgling poets would canonize their betters as a way of introducing themselves to the commonwealth of wit:

Chaucer by writing purchast fame,
And *Gower* got a worthie name:
Sweete *Surrey*, suckt *Pernassus* springs,
And *Wiat* wrote of wondrous things:
Olde *Rochfort* clambe the stately Throne,
Which *Muses* holde, in *Hellicone*.
Then thither let good *Gascoigne* go,
For sure his verse, deserveth so.[140]

Because one of the dominant conventions of commendatory verses was to market the author's name alongside his predecessors', public awareness of the canon probably owed something to puffery. Certainly, as the above example suggests, authorial self-advertisements intensified the mythologizing of the poet's calling and of a Parnassus far removed from print audiences. For, even as the commercial demands of the trade prompted them to write according to contemporary tastes, authors could believe that their art was not a mechanism of social transaction in which their interests coincided with their readers'. Print heightened authors' concern for their own personal and professional interests; at the same time, print authors could entertain only an abstract sense of how readers would use their texts, since these could be so broadly disseminated. Ultimately, as well, in promoting a change from the old emphasis on the fluid intertextuality of writing to modern notions of originality and intellectual property, the commercial market of letters helped to crystallize the modern sense of the author-function as a site of interpretive control. Authors were thus encouraged to perceive their art less as a mode of production within an economy of exchange than as a distinctive and self-directed activity.

This widening division between author and reader threatened to sever the tightly structured web of interdependencies that ensured a vibrant circulation of values. Ideally in a rhetorical culture, author and audience did not merely share a common civic-mindedness but were bound together in a public conversation – one of the chief functions of the poet, Puttenham declared, was "to call the people together by admiration, to a plausible and vertuous conversation"[141] – and a conversation that benefited both by benefiting a greater collectivity, be it the court, the state, or the Church. Moral order within this culture depended upon verbal and symbolic exchanges between agents whose responses were felt to be broadly similar, exchanges that, at their most vigorously productive, united the agents in a harmonious willed affiliation – a dialogical order leading to a transcendent structure of conviction. Rhetoric for the courtier, in particular, was equated not simply with psychological manipulation but with a mode of behaviour that determined in large measure the nature of his being. The courtier's identity was a reflection of public opinion, his self a nexus of social relations: in the wording of one influential guide to courtly life, Stefano Guazzo's *Civile Conversation* (trans. 1574), "the jugement which wee have to knowe our selves, is not ours, but wee borrow it of others."[142] For the courtier, the activities of composing and reading poetry were valuable only insofar as they were two inseparable elements of social discourse. The perfect courtier, in Sidney's words, aimed "not onely to read others *Poesies*, but to *poetise* for others reading."[143] Although the codes of civic humanism stressed that the virtuous citizen had to be self-governing and independent of economic necessity in order to devote himself to the common good, participation in the *polis* required that citizens recognize each other's autonomy according to a principle of equality wherein all "shared in the possession of a common, public personality."[144] The social conversation of the courtiers thus represented the appropriate discourse of this common, public personality.

Print undermined this reciprocity between agents by complicating the process of exchange and by increasing their diversity to the point where they no longer seemed to contribute equally to the collectivity. Profit in a symbolic economy was measured in terms of its circulation – "He that desires to *Print* a book," Donne urged in one of his sermons, "should much more desire, *to be* a book; to do some such exemplar things, as men might read, and relate, and profit by"[145] – yet print seemed to favour only the private desires of individual agents, from "greedy printers" who "so made prostitute" the art of poetry, to professional writers who wrote only for material gain, to readers who purchased books for nothing more than "idle" pleasure.[146] The charge of self-interest was the one print authors were most quick to deny. Edward Hake tried to assure his readers that money was never a major incentive in bringing out a second edition of his *Newes Out of Powles Churchyarde* (1579), not even for his bookseller: "What his gaine shalbe, I knowe not: and I am perswaded that gaine is not the onely, no nor the chiefest ende hee respecteth. But on the other part, what I shal gaine that am the Author of the booke, none can be so ignoraunt, but hee may easily ghesse. Once, money I gaine none at this time, either for writing altering or correcting of the same."[147] The stigma of print had as its inspiration a patrician contempt for public self-display, but it was not so much the dissemination of letters that offended the courtiers as the apparent displacement of communal solidarity by a new socio-economic order that stressed both material profit and specialization of interest. Their mode of manuscript circulation aided the courtier who wished to get ahead, but it also profited the collectivity by situating the courtiers in a network of social relations. In this way, the courtiers' gestures of dismissing their verse as youthful extravagance may have served to deflect a charge of self-interest. Yearning for the exclusivity of the coterie was equally an interest, but, since the coterie was felt to be the nation's most productive source of symbolic capital, the courtiers' self-interests were considered indistinguishable from the larger interests of the common good.

Beneath the gesturings, therefore, was a suspicion that the book trade was generating a new, less determinable economy to rival the aristocratic order: economic capital was threatening to displace symbolic and political capital as the source of legitimacy. Francis Davison, in the preface to his miscellany *A Poetical Rhapsody* (1602), scorned the opportunism of his printer in using the name value of canonical poets to market a collection of inferior verse: "If any except against the mixing (both at the beginning and ende of this booke) of diverse thinges written by great and learned personages, with our meane and worthles Scriblings, I utterly disclaime it, as being done by the Printer, either to grace the forefront with Sir *Ph. Sidneys*, and other names, or to make the booke grow to a competent volume."[148] The multiplying complexities of print culture portended a plurality of self-interested authors, printers, and readers, whose divergent values would be reflected in a disharmonious and hence illegitimate canon. To the courtiers, print rendered problematic the goal of social communion by making for overly distended social relations. It seemed to augur moral dissensus or, at least, conditions where canon-making would be a function no longer of interpersonal ritual but of the impersonal forces of the market place, no longer an act between men but one of many complex relations between persons and things. The pluralizing effects of print inhibited the courtly ideal of close intersubjectivity, of like-minded friends freely exchanging their similar opinions of one another. As John Lyly wrote to Thomas Watson in a letter that found its way into print, in the latter's *Hecatompathia* (1582): "seeing you have used mee so friendly, as to make me acquainted with your passions, I will shortly make you pryvie to mine, which I woulde be loth the printer should see."[149]

These gestures may have also reflected a certain ambivalence over how best to define the symbolic value of the courtly conversation: whether it should be perceived as benefiting the common good, as it had been since antiquity, or upraised by opposing it to a growing market for printed works. No doubt the courtiers' suspicions about print were exaggerated so as to magnify their coterie authority. The situation can be compared to the modern system of literary production, as anatomized by Pierre Bourdieu in his essay on "The Market of Symbolic Goods."[150] Bourdieu identifies within the literary market place two strata which operate as a defining opposition: the field of restricted production, a system of producers creating goods for like-minded producers, and the field of large-scale cultural production, where goods are produced for broad consumption. The latter field comprises the mass market of bestsellers produced to suit the demands of the public at large; the field of restricted production, in contrast, is the domain of literary "art," as defined by a network of artists, critics, and scholars, who insist on the relative autonomy of their field from the "vulgar demands of economics" as a means to enhance their work's symbolic value and the "(long-term) accumulation and gestation of symbolic capital" by the dominant class. Though in no sense can an established mass market be said to have existed in England before the eighteenth century, it is clear that the courtiers saw print as a potential field of large-scale production, one that they claimed was churning out "innumerable sortes of Englyshe Bookes, and infinite fardles of printed pamphlets, wherewith thys Countrey is pestered, all shoppes stuffed, and every study furnished."[151] Against this print market they defined their coterie as a restricted field, one limited to a close network of producers who were ostensibly less interested in seeking personal profit than in increasing the symbolic capital of the English community. If modern artists claim legitimacy by emphasizing the autonomy of the aesthetic experience from economic or political interests, the courtiers saw their coterie as central to the state's political and cultural economy, precisely because their verbal power supplied symbolic and ideological capital to the dominant class. The values of poetry seemed to them inseparable from their collective interests.

Yet, by opposing the symbolic capital of their poetry to the commercialism of the print trade, the courtiers were disavowing the economic nature of their own system of patronage – for the citizen to be able to contribute to the common good, he had to be appear free of economic preoccupations. Using symbolic capital to occlude naked economic self-interest is a familiar gesture in both pre-capitalist and capitalist economies – especially in the former, where, as Bourdieu notes, it is the dominant "logic of the pre-capitalist economy."[152] Symbolism in all such societies regularly serves to legitimize the interests of a dominant class by enabling it at once to mask and to misrecognize the source of its power in economic and social privilege. That is, aesthetics, which are defined by their relative autonomy from economic and political fields, provide the means to claim disinterest, the power to distinguish oneself by asserting an apparent independence from economic and political concerns, which nonetheless "always haunt the most 'disinterested' practices."[153] Though the doctrine of aesthetic disinterestedness received its first significant articulation only in the eighteenth century, the courtiers' derogation of print, as well as their system of private circulation, represented an early attempt to benefit from the distinguishing power of disinterest. A similar use of aesthetic indirection as a means to misrecognize the economics of patronage, and to distance its courtly beneficiaries from the stigma of interest, was apparent from the highly metaphoric codification of poet-patron relations in most dedications and love sonnets from the period.[154] At the same time as the value of verbal power in facilitating social harmony was being so strenuously asserted, then, the symbolic capital provided by the courtiers' own poetry was slowly being redefined, so that poetry's assumed centrality in the moral economy of the state was being eclipsed by its new symbolic value as a refuge from brusque economic realities. Then again, this ambivalence over the nature of poetry's symbolic value may have been another instance of the age-old tension between poet and patron, between, on the one hand, seeking legitimacy for cultural practices by insisting on their instrumental value within a larger moral economy, and, on the other, by affirming the poet's own moral independence from powerful influences.

If legitimacy is what producers hope will be granted them by the dominant class – John Collop, before his *Poesis Rediviva* (1656), asked his dedicatee, the Marquis of Dorchester, for "legitimation, the most piercing ray of your judgement"[155] – then distinction is the value they claim by demarcating their work from the activities of those below them on the social hierarchy. Print culture would not actually undermine the courtiers' evaluative authority for some time, but the commodification of literature that print entailed was a threat they could exaggerate to reinforce the binarism of high and low – "bookes be stale," wrote Lyly, "when they be printed, bicause they be common."[156] Given their prevalence and rhetorical force, then, these codes of distinction were inevitably deployed by print authors and booksellers eager to gain legitimacy. To justify his publication of courtly lyrics, Tottel had to appeal to this structure of conviction in requesting the aid of the "learned to defend their learned frendes." Tottel's learned reader was Leland's discriminating reader, a recycled version of the *auctor* in that "he" functioned as a patron of authority to whom authors could address their works and to whom all readers had to orient themselves. For the Renaissance author struggling with increased audience autonomy, the learned reader presented a comforting fiction of poets and audiences united by common ideals; he was a presentist precursor to the later notion of the test of time, which posits a consensus achieved over multiple generations that are otherwise distinguishable by cultural differences, differences that would have been unthinkable to an age empowered by rhetoric. Thus, Milton hoped for a "fit audience ... though few," while Ben Jonson, in the preface to *Catiline* (1611), could search London for the "Reader extraordinary" who stood apart from the mere "Reader in Ordinairie."[157] The purpose of these fictions was not simply to trivialize contrary opinion or to reduce the responses of diverse readers to a predictable set of reactions. The aim was to refuse judgment altogether, to create a situation where criticism was seen as unnecessary because all agents participated in a consensus of values. That the judgment of print audiences was redundant was a staple theme in addresses to the reader: "It shall be needlesse (gentle Reader)," writes John Bodenham before his canonical miscellany *Belvedére* (1600), "to make any Apologie for the defence of this labour, because the same being collected from so many singular mens workes; and the worth of them all having been so especially approoved, and past with no meane applause the censure of all in generall; doth both disburden me of that paines, and sets the better approbation on this excellent booke."

Foucault has observed that texts were assigned real authors "only when the author became subject to punishment and to the extent that his discourse was considered transgressive."[158] In much the same way, the use of learned reader as a critical commonplace was intensified when writers began to sense the alienation that print imposed between themselves and their audience. The commonplace served to guard against readerly transgressions, but, more than this, it obviated against any possible conflict of values by antagonizing the reader into joining the group to which the author already belonged: "I esteeme more the prayse of one learned Reader," declared Gascoigne, "than I regard the curious carping of ten thousande unlettered Tattlers."[159] It was a fictive antagonism, perhaps, but one that was aimed at precluding any possibility of an evaluative plurality among readers. Readers were coerced into a conversation with the author, where each praised the other in a constant exchange of assertions and persuasions. Readers read not merely to please themselves but to become learned and meritorious enough to earn the esteem of the authors they praised.[160] Autonomy was available to neither author nor reader in such a relationship, nor was there finally much difference in value between the activity either agent performed. The learned reader denied the "aporia of judgment," the undecidability as to where value resided, in the text, its invention or its reception: he was a representation of harmony, of an ongoing conversation where the same symbolic capital circulated all around. And insofar as the figure suggested that the value of texts, authors, and audiences was interchangeable, summoning the learned reader was a version of canon-formation.

The learned reader was a sign of verbal power at work, overcoming diversity by continually upholding a universe of belief – though, of course, self-legitimizing codes like the learned reader actually served to reinforce a class hierarchy and permitted the courtiers to misrecognize how they benefited politically from a system of widespread illiteracy. Yet the sign also revealed the limitations of verbal power. The oppositional codes of rhetoric required that the learned reader be always opposed to an unlearned other. As such, the fiction could not be truly comforting since it acknowledged the impossibility of having the same values all around. The positing of an unlearned reader allowed for the conflict and undecidability, even if *his* values were always dismissed, in Webbe's version, as "seldome true, and therefore not to be sought after."[161] This constant pathologizing of the unlearned was meant to create an illusory cultural coherence, of the civilized versus the barbarian, but it was also necessary to provide a sense that the author's verbal power was actually working and accomplishing something useful. The learned reader could be valued so long as he was busy mastering his enemies and helping to defeat social disunity. Sir John Harington's strenuous preface before his translation of *Orlando Furioso* (1591) illustrates the restlessness of rhetorical self-assertion in the way that judgment is said to be superfluous "among wise men" even as a horde of detractors is conjured up as justification for writing a defence of poetry:

Surely if learning in generall were of that account among us, as it ought to be among all men, and is among wise men, then should this my Apologie of Poesie (the verie first nurse and ancient grandmother of all learning) be as vaine and be aunswered, and truly answered, that no man disgraced it. But sith we live in such a time, in which nothing can escape the envious tooth, and backbiting tongue of an impure mouth ... therefore I thinke no man of judgement will judge this my labour needlesse, in seeking to remove away those slaunders that either the malice of those that love it not, or the folly of those that understand it not, hath devised against it.[162]

If the value of any activity was measured by how effectively it advanced society towards harmony, then harmony had to be continually deferred in order to allow for advancement, and for value itself. Likewise, the utility of any work was contingent upon the ability of its defenders to identify an other which the work would help to defeat. In short, the dynamism of rhetorical culture came at the cost of forever submitting to the bifurcating forces of language and never achieving a reassuring sense of complete solidarity. At the very moment when rhetoric was being most loudly productive, it was also being most furiously self-devouring.

The dynamism of a rhetorical economy proceeds from a verbal power that is always seeking to overcome divisions in the very act of perpetuating them. Given this dynamism, evaluative certainty in such an economy cannot be long obtained in the sense of being fixed in one object or agent (other than, in principle, God and king). In a modern culture, evaluative certainty is made to seem more stable and well defined by locating it in the intrinsic qualities of the work, the original genius of the author, or the innate faculties of the reader. Such fixing of value comes at the cost of understanding how value is exchanged between author, text and audience, and of making much less imperative the goal of social harmony. This can be seen in the later life of the learned reader, who, with the rise of the print trade in the seventeenth century, came to embody a distinct agent whose ontology preceded language and who struggled to overcome normative divisions through the power not of words but of his own wilful sensibility. In this later incarnation, the learned reader appeared as the "impartial reader" (as Defoe styled him), one who spoke for the independence of the cultural field from economic or other interests. More explicitly than the learned reader of traditional rhetoric, the impartial reader wielded the distinguishing power of disinterest. Alexander Brome, in the preface to his *Songs and other Poems* (1661), pleaded for such open-minded understanding from this new self-conscious being: "being taught by custome, to beg something of the *Reader*, it shall be this; that in *reading* and *judging* these *Poems*, he will consider his own frailty, and *fallibility*; and read with the same *temper* and *apprehension*, as if [he] himself had *written*, and I were to *judge*."[163] In this incarnation, the reader was seen as an autonomous subject, one who had the imaginative ability to recreate himself and to be a poet at one with Brome and so achieve a unity of response. This reader could also, implicitly, refuse such a consensus, and such a refusal would have been incontestable. If it was only a matter of the reader recreating himself "as if himself had written," then value was to be entirely *with* the reader. The idea would be made explicit in eighteenth-century versions of the fiction: all seems affect when, in *Tom Jones*, Fielding genially hands the reader a bill of fare.[164] A modern objectivist culture has thus the advantage of being able to specify the objects or agents of value with some degree of "knowledgeable" authority, but the advantage is gained at the notable cost of not having that authority seem effective and strongly felt. A rhetorical culture, incessantly agonistic and self-dramatizing though it may be, has at least the advantage of conviction, of the forceful sense that there exists a dynamic evaluative community wherein value emanates from all variety of human action and speech.

As the triumphs of verbal power are only ever provisional, that same power becomes a source of risk and irresolution within a rhetorical economy. In the same way that an evaluative community is routinely defined in opposition to a hostile other, the agonistic structures of rhetoric require that the canon be set against a discredited apocrypha. Almost as ubiquitous as the learned reader in early critical discourse were the imperious assaults on popular verses, romances, and the like, assaults invariably accompanied by the claim that a national canon of great books could not be established unless the literary system was purged of these forms. William Vaughan's version of the commonplace in his *Golden Grove* (1600) was comparatively succinct as these claims went: "Take away the abuse, which is meerely accidental, and let the substance of Poetrie stand still ... many of our English rimers and ballet-makers deserve for their baudy sonnets, and amorous allurements, to bee banished, or severely punished: and that Poetrie it selfe ought to bee honoured and made much of, as a precious Jewell, and a divine gift."[165] Most striking about assaults like these was their energetic reductiveness, their anxious searching after control. For Vaughan, there could exist no gradations of value other than the extreme polarization of divine poetry and profane balladry. Evaluative certainty had to be total and unequivocal, and the only canon he could envision was one of monolithic uniformity and stasis: "let the substance of Poetrie stand still."

Certainly poetry had its enemies, and Vaughan's housecleaning of the literary system was likely a concession to the moralists. Yet the concessions did not stop there but ran to the conservative Christian-Stoic terms about what was to be valued and what eliminated, the terms of stasis, constancy, and integrity as against those of change, variety, and "mixture."[166] Even a sophisticated apologist for poetry like Sidney could not conceive of an English canon without also blaming the "bastard Poets" who had turned the literary system into a "confused masse of words."[167] Sidney's phrase recalled his rebuke of the "Poet-haters" who "do prodigally spend a great many wandring words in quips and scoffes." Bad writing was the expense of words without order, unproductive and protean verbiage "which by sturring the spleene, may staie the brain from a th[o]rough beholding the worthinesse of the subject." Sidney was criticizing poetry's detractors for using rhetoric merely as a tool of psychological coercion and emptying it of all truth-claims. Yet perhaps what truly disturbed Sidney was that those truth-claims were indeterminate because they were subordinate to rhetoric's endless dualizing movement, the kind of inescapable verbal oscillations that occurred, for example, when Sidney dispraised "all that kind of people who seek a praise, by dispraising others."[168] Rhetoric served a society founded on the continual exchange of persuasions, but its divisive energies rendered impossible the categorical fixing of value, and the more forcefully fixity and harmony were proclaimed as absolute ideals, the more the assertions had to be reinforced with denigrations of an undesirable other. Or, in Sidney's version, the greater the reliance on verbal power, the less thorough the beholding of worthiness.

That rhetoric breeds itself is evident from the verbal overkill that Sidney found so deplorable in Puritan jeremiads against poetry. The Puritans' characteristic mode of attack, culminating in Prynne's colossal *Histriomastix* (1633), was plenitude of brute assertion, a lexical onslaught that in its performative excess mimicked the chaos of opinions that was said to follow upon the dissemination of immoral literature. Illicit works, claimed one censor, "maketh mens minds to be at variance one with another, and diversity of minds maketh seditions, seditions bring in tumults, tumults make insurrections and rebellions, insurrections make depopulations and bring in utter ruin and destruction of mens bodies, goods and lands."[169] The profusion of corrupting material unleashed by the printing presses could only be stemmed, it seemed, by an equally uncontrolled torrent of words: "*can then one*

Quarto *Tractate against Stage-playes be thought too large*," Prynne asked in his own defense, "*when as it must assault such ample Play-house* Volumes?"[170] The extravagance of the attacks demonstrated the diminishing returns of verbal power, the fact that the speaker could intensify his assault only by abandoning all sense of order and experience. Puritans like Prynne were of course a different class of rhetorical men from courtiers like Sidney; since value for them was fixed to a transcendent theology, they cared little for dialogue leading to solidarity, and they spurned the dynamic energies of verbal power even as their arguments were wholly fuelled by such energies. The result was a mode of complaint that seemed a grotesque parody of the ceaseless conversation of the courtiers – just as their visions of a world torn apart by print were the exact negative obverse of the poets' own age-old myth that they had been the original lawmakers of civilization. Plays, clamoured one censor, taught the arts of verbal seduction, yet to defeat these arts required listing them in a frantic nomenclative display, as if to fight fire with fire: "lascivious speches, idle and vaine scoffing, jeasting, and foolery, and cosenage, knavery, flattery, and what soever els, set forth in their coullors, phrases and tearmes, and the grace, elegancy, and lustre of the tongue."[171] In a sense, these exercises in verbal brutishness were extreme manifestations of the masculine competitiveness that rhetoric inspired among its practitioners.

Despite their alienation from language, the Puritan censors sought to control value by manipulating their print audience with extravagant fictive projections, save these were not of harmonious communities where no judgment was necessary but of dissensus where no judgment was possible. Their preferred vehicle for these projections was the blacklist, a catalogue of undesirable works that was designed to suggest in its heterogeneity the loss of order in a flood of printer's ink: "For in these daies in which there is so great licentiousness of printyng bookes, as in deede it maketh us all the worse ... We have gotten our Songes & Sonets, our Pallaces of pleasure, our unchaste Fables and Tragedies, and such lyke Sorceries, moe than any man may recken."[172] The practice of blacklisting, which included the Catholic indexes and the humanists' censures of popular romances, represented a negative form of canon-making, one that emanated from a fear of plurality, of the heresy of allowing everyone to choose what to read. In addition to proscribing books, blacklists functioned like canons in the way they magnified the value of good works by suggesting how these were in danger of being lost amid a torrent of worthless printed trash: "sundrie bookes, pamfletes, Poesies, ditties, songs, and other woorkes ... serving ... to let in a mayne Sea of wickednesse ... and to no small or sufferable wast of the treasure of this Realme which is thereby consumed and spent in paper."[173] Designed to inspire a longing for certainty, black-lists were effective only so long as they appeared as objectifications of change, variety, and uncontrolled growth. In this way they contrasted with early catalogues of authors, such as Puttenham's parading of learned English gentlemen who together formed a noble "crew of Courtly makers."[174] Lists like Puttenham's were projections of simili-tude, where the courtly poets were at once productive and non-competitive, enriching their community by their canonic harmony. Blacklists were tropes of amplification and multiformity that used the syntax of a list to suggest the opposite, an arbitrary piling up of evils. More so than extolments of the canon, then, blacklists derived their emotional force from the protean, self-begetting power of language, from a fear of words in motion.

What annoyed Sidney in Puritan attacks on poetry, their intermina-ble verbal assaults that stayed the brain from perceiving true value, was precisely what the Puritans themselves feared and what their blacklists were meant to express: "The swarming of lascivious, idle, and unprofitable bookes, Pamphletts, Playbookes, and Ballades; as namely, Ovid's Art of Love, the Parliament of Women ... Barns Poems, Parker's Ballades, in disgrace of Religion, &c. to the increase of all Vice, and withdrawing of the people from reading, studdying, and hearing the word of God."[175] Arguably, these blacklists were inspired by much the same anxiety over language that Sidney felt, for they emphasized the riskiness of a rhetorical economy, how its prolificity worked against letting values stand still. It was an anxiety that developed from the lurking sense that, under the bifurcating codes of rhetoric, there could be no dream of imaginary pantheons that was not at the same time a vision of hellish Dunciads. With the displacement of rhetorical think-ing in the later seventeenth century, blacklists became less indiscrim-inate, with the tendency among moralists like Collier to support their assaults with analyses of the literary evidence. But the image of the verbal deluge, of a promiscuous superabundance of works leading to the total breakdown of society, remained a powerful metaphor for reinforcing claims of absolute value precisely because of this sense that verbal power could itself be dangerously uncontainable: "Rhetoric is typically an overwhelming phenonemon, implemented by what the classical world and the Renaissance called *copia*, abundance, plenty, unstinted flow ... One can drown in rhetoric."[176]

This fear of a verbal flood reflected long-standing anxieties about change, which the coming of print did much to reanimate and, as well, to alter in their emphases. Ancient critics of mass culture deplored the degeneracy of the mob, the decline of moral standards, and the power of demagogues to delude human reason. These arguments did not disappear with the Renaissance but were rather modified with the recognition that printed material could produce effects not only on an uneducated mob but on isolated readers. The impersonality of the print medium ensured that the experience of literature would be an increasingly private affair between book and reader. This change in the character of literary education necessitated a crucial adjustment to the narratives of social disintegration caused by harmful literature. The former bestial irrationality of the crowd became instead a madness that came from within as much from without. In this version, the individual mind could not tolerate diversity because by nature, according to Stephen Gosson, it "is simple without mixture or composition, therefore those instructions that are given to the minde must bee simple without mingle mangle of fish & flesh, good & bad."[177] Harmony was the nature of being, it seemed. More to the point, it was not so much the propagandistic effects of books that were being warned against as the dangerous autonomy of the unguarded reader; within this reader, it was argued, the malign influence of reading entertainments such as romances insinuated itself until a point was reached when he could no longer be a productive contributor to his society:

What toyes, the dayly readyng of such a booke, may worke in the will of a yong jentleman, or a yong mayde, that liveth welthelie and idlelie, wise men can judge, and honest men do pitie. And yet ten *Morte Arthures* do not the tenth part so much harme, as one of these bookes, made in *Italie*, and translated in England. They open, not fond and common wayes to vice, but such sutle, cunnyng, new, and diverse shiftes, to cary yong willes to vanitie, and yong wittes to mischief ... Suffer these bookes to be read, and they shall soone displace all bookes of godly learnyng.[178]

Reading romances, it was said, had an isolating effect: evil values would circulate imperceptibly from book to reader, in the latter's idle and private moments, rather than being openly exchanged between like-minded agents.[179] At the same time, the verbal power of immoral writings was, if anything, considered far more potent and various than the instrumental persuasions of canonical literature, though the ultimate effect, as with the courtly conversation, was said to be the reader's total, monologic identification with the discourse to which he was exposed:

ROMANCE's or the *Bastard* sort of *Histories*, may be noted not for any great *uses* of them, but for manifold *abuses* by them, 1. In wasting *pretious time* which might be better *imployed*, 2. In stuffing the *Fancy* and *Memory* with ridiculous *Chimerah*'s, and wandering Imaginations, to the *excluding* or *stifling* of more serious and profitable meditations, 3. For *transporting* and *deluding* the *affec-tions*, with languishing *Love*, impossible *attempts* and *victories*, stupendious *inchantments*, wherewith the weake Reader is often so taken, that he makes himselfe (as it were) a *Party* to the businesse.[180]

Hence the rise of print stimulated fears both of a plethora of bad literature, and of an insidious evil that alienated readers from their society by turning them inward and forming in them a desire for imaginative self-determination. (Plays, being only secondarily a print genre, were subjected to all the traditional Platonic-Christian objec-tions, though their evil was also said to involve a subtle impairing of productive faculties. Comedy, Gosson contended, "locketh up [the] powres of the minde from doing their duetie, & like a kinde of drunkennes, maketh us stagger, very unfit, either to speake; or to walke as we shoulde in our vocation."[181])

The love of romances, wrote Vives in his influential *Instruction of a Christian Woman* (trans. 1540), was "a deedly sickenes," one that could not be described "lest hit hurte other with the smell, and defile them with the infection." Whatever else provoked attacks like these, there was clearly a distrust of print audiences, and particularly of the judg-ment of the autonomous reader. Like the invocations of the learned reader, these assaults were intended to retain in a public and govern-able sphere the activities of selecting and reading works of literature, activities that, according to Vives, were otherwise becoming "bothe commune and pryvate." Enumerating a sizable list of illicit titles, Vives advised that the woman who wished to read seek out the counsel of "wise and sad men," for "the woman ought nat to folowe her owne jugment, lest whan she hath but a lyght entryng in lernyng, she shuld take false for true, hurtful in stede of holsome, folishe and pevysh for sad and wise." Because women were not usually considered active contributors to society, educators like Vives had no difficulty denying them the authority to judge literature, or denying them more than reading if they abused the privilege: "It were better for them nat only to have no lernynge at all, but also to lese theyr eies, that they shulde nat rede: and theyr eares, that they shulde nat here."[182] Being poten-tially overwhelming, and possibly liberating, verbal power could long serve the maintenance of polite control without recourse to direct coercion.

It would be a simplification, however, to identify Vives's society of "wise and sad men" merely with his educated male peers. His learned men were one of a number of rhetorical gestures for signifying a harmonious evaluative community. While this community may have stood for the competitively masculinist virtues of productivity, utility, and persuasiveness, the prime function of these gestures was to make value seem dynamically circulated in a corporate economy where author and audience were seen as both interchangeable and free of self-interest. As such, they were available as persuasive models for anyone to use, including women writers.[183] By the same token, it would be simplistic to identify Vives's female reader with actual women, for she was equally a fiction, though not quite a version of the unlearned reader. Rather, the female reader represented the autonomous, unguarded consumer of print, the non-productive "common reader" as opposed to the authoritative "learned reader." It was an opposition that would be more widely invoked later, in the eighteenth century, when literature began to be itself treated as non-productive. Paradoxically, by the time that the phrase "common reader" had entered ordinary usage, readers and authors were no longer perceived as a uniform commonality.

From a modern point of view, the styles of rhetorical canon-making may seem reductive and emotional, little more than opinion-making or wordplay. In place of reasoned evaluations of specific works, they appear to offer only assertions, and assertions that are hard to take seriously because so often the same terms crop up inconsistently on both sides of an argument. Rhetoric seems to get its speakers no nearer to solidarity, because it is always creating more oppositions to overcome. Above all, it seems to offer its speakers the mastery of performance without the constative certainty of fact. Yet, in a rhetorical culture, mastery of performance was itself a way of knowing, one that was social, dramatic, contingent.[184] Rhetoric's restless drama made for a kind of verbal romance, where kings, authors, and readers fashioned themselves by communing in endless battle against the forces of diversity and "ignorance": "The names of Poets (all feare and dutie ascribed to her great and sacred Name) have beene placed with the names of the greatest Princes of the world, by the most autentique and worthiest judgements, without disparagement to their soveraigne titles: which if any man taking exception thereat, in ignorance [I] know not, I hold him unworthily to be placed by the meanest that is but graced with the title of a Poet. Thus gentle Reader I wish thee all happines."[185] The poets were here coming close to usurping the transcendent authority of the princes, but as long as conviction was maintained by pathologizing an unworthy opponent, the conflict between poet and patron could be deferred. Author and patron, poet and reader, remained essentially undifferentiated, and the literary system could be seen as both heroic and productive. This desire for stability and harmony may have reflected a troubled resistance to rhetoric, to its ceaseless oscillations that were at once its source of persuasive power and its severest limitations. Yet the claims for stasis and conformity may have been no more than oratorical strategies: in a rhetorical culture, the ability to argue with equal skill on either side of a question, including the question of rhetoric, was an ability that was taught and prized. The object of all these strategies was to create a social being, and whether he played the role of author or reader was much less important than that he gave profit, pleasure, and praise to others in the very act of seeking them for himself.

PART TWO

Consequences of Presentism

2 Albion's Parnassus and the Professional Author

Faustus, these bookes, thy wit, and our experience,
Shall make all Nations to Canonize us
                        Marlowe, *Doctor Faustus* I.i

In 1595 a Cambridge don by the name of William Covell proposed what he believed was a novel solution to England's problems during a time of economic inflation and political discontent. Addressing the English universities, Covell exhorted them, in his words, to "take the course to canonize your owne writers, that not every bald ballader to prejudice of Art, may passe current with a Poet's name."[1] By "your own writers," Covell meant any English poets who had a claim to a liberal education. Covell named several: Spenser, "Lucrecia Sweet Shakespeare," and "courte-deare-verse happie *Daniell*," among others. What Covell meant by "canonize" is less clear, though he seemed to be envisaging both direct university patronage of poets and a type of public ceremony, such as the bestowing of honorary degrees or Petrarchan laurels. However administered, canonization, Covell believed, would provide England with a pantheon of poetic heroes, whose examples might help to raise the nation's stature abroad and to quell dissent at home. Covell nowhere suggested that English poetry should be taught or studied. If poetry in any language was taught at all in the universities of Covell's time, it was only as a compositional aid, a model for student imitations. Covell's canon was purely a symbol of England's literary eminence. In other words, his act of canonization was a declaration of value, but a declaration unsupported by the mechanisms of reproduction and pedagogy. Other than ceaselessly to celebrate the names of the dead, to keep them "canonized in learnings catalogue," Covell's scholars had no means by which to keep the poetry of the past alive for later generations. Of course, Covell was interested neither in preserving old books nor in educating future students, but in saving an identity which he felt was being threatened. Awarding laurels to poets would serve the immediate needs of English society by bolstering its morale and reputation and harmonizing the contemporary literary system. Canonization would encourage more cultural production, and discourage literary in-fighting like the protracted dispute Covell cited between Gabriel Harvey and Thomas Nashe. Above all, according to Covell, canon-making would ensure that "every braineles toy should not usurpe the name of Poetrie."

Covell was evidently the first to call for a national canon of letters presided over by England's universities, though there was very little of an institutional nature about his canon. His pantheon was a monument of verbal power, contrived by scholars so that the English people might "be perswaded of this, that Fame shall be their servant, Honour shall be their subject, Glory shall be their crown, Eternitie their inheritance." As an instrument of persuasion, Covell's canon was designed to generate both production and social cohesion. It would inspire all English subjects with a sense of cultural empowerment, of fame and native glory being within their reach, and in so doing would help to allay social disaffection and to humiliate presumptuous poetasters. The many functions Covell's canon was to perform seemed altogether to conflict: it would stabilize the literary system even as it encouraged more wits to seek the laurels, and it would serve to induce social harmony among the English people even as it persuaded them of the rewards of cultural renewal. In his words, the social function of a literary system was to "control with the muses pen." In looking to his canon in this way, Covell was typical of canon-makers in a rhetorical culture, who clamoured for social order even as the instrumental nature of their own rhetoric required them to advocate change, productivity, and the ceaseless circulation of value. Such canon-making, from a modern point of view, is all emphatic gestures, more akin to boosterism or complaint than to anything like an adequate exercise of judgment. A project like Covell's, where a literary canon is proposed as an immediate cure for all of the English commonwealth's ills, may seem hopelessly naive in its evangelistic excess, and risibly incoherent in the way it promises both order and change. But in a rhetorical culture, it was the forcefulness, the sense of belief and certitude, that was the prime operative value of verbal power. All acts of rhetorical canon-making had to be emphatic in order to reinforce the structure of conviction, the circle of belief, upon which every such act depended for its legitimacy. In expressing himself in a way that abandoned coherence for certitude, Covell was no different from others of his culture for whom the sense of conviction that verbal power afforded was far more enabling than the precision that analysis provided. And in appearing to desire at once stability and change, he exerted no less conviction than a master rhetor like Donne, for whom change, however troubling, was also "the nursery / Of music, joy, life, and eternity" (*Elegy III*, 35–6).

In the late sixteenth and early seventeenth centuries, more people than ever before were convinced that a canon of English letters was both eminently desirable and possible, and it was this widespread sense of conviction, more than anything else, that encouraged more authors than ever before to aspire to such a canon. It was during this period that secular writers first began to hope for "canonization": apart from the examples of Covell and Faustus above, we can think of Donne's lovers whose legend will be "canonized for love" in the hymns and sonnets of later lovers.[2] The example of Donne's poem, just as much as Covell's tract, suggests that in these early usages "canonization" designated not merely an earthly, secular (or perhaps Protestant) form of apotheosis, but an act of consecration that was effective only so long as it was rehearsed again and again within a literary tradition it helped to authorize. The act of canonization was not conceived of as an isolated event, one that locked the author-hero in an imaginary museum, but as itself a productive gesture, one predicated on the value of that author's work in helping to foster more writing: "then live thou still, for still thy verse shall live / to unborne poets, which light and life will give."[3] The gesture, like Covell's canon, promised both stability and change: it presupposed that all subsequent literary production would be harmonized after the author-hero's own work, whose greatness necessitated this change, and yet the final measure of that greatness was the extent and vitality of the production it inspired.

The dual emphases on stability and renewal are necessarily a feature of all canons insofar as they enact the paradox of permanence and change; the authority of any tradition, as Benjamin suggested, is contingent upon the ability of its defenders to identify both its continuities and its unique, enabling sources of value. From a broader perspective yet, constraint and mobility are among the defining functions of all cultures, to the extent that each at once sets limits on behaviour and permits some measure of freedom, without which a culture could not reproduce itself.[4] In a rhetorical culture, these functions, besides being mediated through verbal power, were also what verbal power was all about, since rhetoric had long been assumed to furnish its speakers with the means both to move and control an audience: "Powre above powres, O heavenly Eloquence," apostrophized Samuel Daniel in *Musophilus* (1599), "[can] draw, divert, dispose, and fashion men /

Better then force or rigour can direct" (ll. 939, 947–8). Rhetorical canon-makers like Covell could believe so strongly in the ability of their pantheons to effect both order and change because that was precisely what any exercise of verbal power, their own included, was supposed to accomplish. What I wish to argue in this chapter, however, is that rhetorical canon-making had little to do with reproducing literature, in terms of either bringing old works into a contemporary horizon of understanding or transmitting new works to later genera-tions; as the key to memory, poetry in a rhetorical culture was believed to reproduce itself as well as its subjects, independent of any institu-tional mechanism.[5] Whether the expressed aim was to organize the literary system or to enrich its output or both, rhetorical canon-making, like much canon-making but more manifestly so, had to do with the politics of identity, and with the tasks of self-definition and of generating belief in the present. As in the example of Covell's canon, early English writings were irrelevant, and even contemporary works were significant only insofar as, by their numbers, they enhanced the effectiveness of canon-making as an ideological gesture in the here and now: "Our countrie breeds up Poets," Thomas Church-yard proudly declared in 1595, "As grasse springs from good ground."[6] Similarly, Donne could claim that his love would send erotic shock-waves throughout literary history, but all that truly concerned the poet was his persuasive triumph in the argumentative moment that was the poem. In Richard Lanham's phrase, rhetorical man was "present-centered."[7]

Canon-making in Renaissance critical discourse was almost always directed at a present community of cultural producers, and while such canon-making did not deal exclusively with contemporary writings, the literature of the past was usually recalled only to be used to heighten the sense of the present, to be invoked as a suitable past out of which the current tradition might be said to have emerged, or to be rejected as obsolescent out of a need for self-definition. Rhetorical canon-makers may likewise have made large promises about the utility of their canons in helping to circulate symbolic capital or to strengthen social relations, to inspire more production or to contain it, but these hopes and promises were, if not empty, part of the drama of assertion and so were meaningful only in the moments of their utterance and reception. This aspect of "presentism" may have reflected Renaissance anxieties about time, in that it was difficult for Covell and others like him to imagine audiences of the past or future being fundamentally different in character from those in the present. Verbal power was practised on a principle of universalism. The presentism may have equally been reinforced by the limited temporal focus of rhetoric, which was originally designed for verbal interaction in concrete social situations, designed to seduce, chasten, control, or effect change, all in an immediate context. To the extent that the past or the future remained topics of such interaction, they were merely examples, like Covell's vision of a well-ordered commonwealth, to be used in the act of persuasion, hypotheses to heighten conviction. And the more the gesture of canonization was to be emphatic – presented as all-powerful, as Covell's canon was – the less of an historical dimension it was likely to possess.

PROMOTING THE LITERARY SYSTEM: CLASSICISM AND THE PROBLEM OF MODERNITY

Canon-making during this period was primarily intended to enhance the value of literature in the vernacular and to help foster the English literary system. It is possible to argue that the "almost complete lack of historical outlook," or the "now mentality," which literary historians find so striking in Elizabethan critical discourse, was exacerbated by a reluctance to acknowledge the distressing realities of England's historicity, cultural isolation, and political marginality.[8] Embarrassment over the poverty of English culture was occasionally voiced, as in the mode of canon-boosting by complaint, a mode favoured by Gabriel Harvey:

What thoughe Italy, Spayne, and Fraunce, ravisshed with a certayne glorious and ambitious desier ... to sett oute and advance ther owne languages above the very Greake and Lattin, and ... do so highly and honorablely esteeme of ther countrye poets, reposing on greate parte of their sovraigne glory and reputation abroade in the worlde in the famous writings of their nobblist wittes? ... What, a goddes name, passe we what was dun in ruinous Athens or decayid Roome a thousand or twoe thousande yeares agoe? Doist thou not oversensibely perceive that the markett goith far otherwise in Inglande?[9]

It would not detract from the genuineness of Harvey's sentiments to say that the embarrassment here was being evoked strategically, even formulaically. Infrequent in early English criticism were those appreciative surveys of the indigenous poetic tradition that were not also either lamenting the paucity of canonical authors or expressing the hope that more would soon emerge. Most notorious was Sidney's dismay over "why England the Mother of excellent mindes should be growne so hard a step-mother to *Poets*, who certainly in wit ought to passe all others."[10] In 1580, with the literary system in a moribund state, such embarrassment would have been understandable. Because of the patronage of Sidney and others, by the end of the century the project of (once again) founding a national literature would be well under way, with the cornerstone of the canon, a national epic, substantially realized in *The Faerie Queene*. In Spenser's great work, declared Nashe, there was enough of the "miracle of wit, to bandie line for line for my life in the honor of *England*, gainst *Spaine*, *Fraunce*, *Italie*, and all the worlde."[11] Yet, even in the heady days of the late 1590s, Harvey could still feel compelled to lament that there were "all too few Aschams, Phaers, Sidneys, Spensers, Warners, Daniels, Silvesters, or Chapmans."[12]

In the absence of any institutional mechanism for reproducing literature, pronouncements and laments like Harvey's were the most effective means to keep literature centremost in the national culture, to plead for more patronage, and to promote more production. Many of these gestures were in fact little more than rhetorical exercises, such as Francis Meres's absurd 125-item matching of classic and English canons in his *Palladis Tamia* (1598), where the comparisons could turn on a mere play of words: "As *Anacreon* died by the pot: so *George Peele* by the pox."[13] At the same time these gestures implicitly served to control the literary system in emphasizing the particular social function of canon-formation. As in the case of the laments, optimistic evaluations of English poetry depended on a shared awareness of the temporal and cultural gulfs that separated the Moderns from the Ancients – "English verse," claimed Barnabe Googe in 1565, "is lyttle inferiour to the pleasaunt verses of the auncient Romaines" – or the developmental lag that set England behind its continental rivals – "I trust wee shall have Englishe Poetry at a higher price in short space," Webbe predicted in 1586, "and the rabble of balde Rymes shall be turned to famous workes, comparable (I suppose) with the best workes of Poetry in other tongues."[14] Within the familiar agonistic structures of rhetoric, these embarrassing cultural disparities were being put forward as an easily identifiable opposition to be overcome through verbal power; yet, even as predictions like Webbe's were designed to generate belief in the idea of an English literary system, their expressed goal of creating a system to compete with other canons set limits on productive freedom by making clear how and in what context literature was to be valued. All poetry, these predictions implied, had to contribute to the formation of an imagined English community that could be objectified in a vernacular high culture, one whose standards had long since been established in the humanist courts and schools of Europe. Some polemicists insisted that English authors not only write works to compare with the classics of antiquity, Italy, or France, but strive to work as an harmonious vernacular chorus. In one representative plea from 1606, imperial transcendence was said to be within the reach of the living if only they joined in a collective effort: "Let us therefore with cheerefull consent imitate those other great Empires, that our wits, learning, and inventions, by divine benefite equalling the best of theirs, our bookes and languages, with our men and marchandizes, may lovingly bee received and embraced amongst them also. Then shall this our puissant little Monarchie … bee more and more magnified … Encourage and gird your selves therefore with a pleasant equanimitie to this excellent service."[15] Such nationalist rallying of the troops was motivated as much by distress over cultural backwardness as by a desire to construct an English identity in the service of political absolutism.

To be sure, control over the literary system during this period was effected mainly through censorship, the patronage network, and to some degree the market. As ideological statements mediating the dictates of power, polemics like the above merely supplemented the extensive technologies of control deployed under feudal domination. The polemics were thus of service mostly to artists and intellectuals eager to make their mark within an emergent literary system. For them, polemics served as self-advertisements, even when they called for the regulation of literature. The ubiquitous critical attacks on popular forms, as I have noted, were in part reactions to print commercialism, reactions that also enabled the self-definition of aspiring courtly poets. This was perhaps even more the case with attacks launched by semi-professional authors, who, because of their education, considered themselves an intellectual cut above the audiences for whom they wrote. Of this type were Nashe's frequent verbal firestorms against middle-class tastes, notably in *The Anatomie of Absurditie* (1589), where he derided everything from moral tales to tavern songs: "our new found Songs and Sonets, which every rednose Fidler hath at his fingers end, and every ignorant Ale Knight will breath foorth over the potte, as soone as his braine waxeth hote."[16] A more curious example is John Lane's dedication before his unpublished version of *Guy of Warwick* (c. 1615), where Lane assailed all the usual rhetorical targets ("muse-traducinge, witt-abusinge, Poesie-missusinge Pieridistes") but also defended the value of romantic fiction against the moralists who, he claimed, were keen "to discourage the fertile wittes of our Englishe nation, which weare readie to comme into the deservinge ranck with the Greekes, Latines and Italienes … but for this odd fashion of presumed-sinceare wisdom, down strikinge with her lightned thunderbolt the deceased."[17] Attacks like these seemed designed less to exclude popular forms from an official canon than to appropriate their carnivalesque energies for a dominant culture.

More systematic in aiming to organize the canon were the various efforts at bringing English "into Art" through neoclassicist prescriptions, notably quantitative metre, the codification of generic conventions and hierarchies, and the ongoing Latinization of English grammar and vocabulary. As these prescriptions were initially promulgated by bilingual scholars like Ascham, they were slow to gain widespread approval, particularly among the courtiers, not all of whom had undergone a formal humanist education and who resisted this academic attempt at usurping their evaluative authority and at devaluing those medièval forms, such as the chivalric romance, for which Tudor aristocrats entertained a certain nostalgic attachment – courtly audiences, according to Puttenham, were often "desirous to heare of old adventures & valiaunces of noble knights in times past, as are those of king *Arthur* and his knights of the round table, Sir *Bevys* of *Southampton, Guy* of *Warwicke*, and others like."[18] Interestingly, the courtly amateurs spurned the quantitative movement in particular because its strict neoclassicism seemed to promise too much control and too little productive freedom, and yet the only way to lessen the undeniable authority of classical precedent was to set it on a par with the customary authority of indigenous practice. Quantitative verse, declared Puttenham, ought not to be "generally applauded at to the discredit of our forefathers maner of vulgar Poesie, or to the alteration or peradventure totall destruction of the same." Detractors of traditional metrics, he added, "do wrong, for they be sundry formes of poems and not all one."[19] The courtly advocacy of rhyme marked the only significant occasion in Renaissance critical discourse when an historical argument was used to defeat a too-limiting essentialism in favour of a canon open to both classical and medieval values. Its most sophisticated exponent was Samuel Daniel, who, in his *Defence of Ryme* (1603), came as close as anyone in his day to endorsing a far-reaching English canon as a challenge to presentist complacency: "What should I name *Walterus Mape, Gulielmus Nigellus, Gervasius Tilburiensis, Bracton, Bacon, Ockham*, and an infinite Catalogue of excellent men, most of them living about foure hundred yeeres since, and have left behinde them monuments of most profound judgement and learning in all sciences. So that it is but the cloudes gathered about our owne judgement that makes us thinke all other ages wrapt up in mistes, and the great distance betwixt us, that causes us to imagine men so farre off to bee so little in respect of our selves."[20] Yet even Daniel's apparent historicism was put in service of a revisionist argument that reconstructed

English literary history as a seemingly unified, organically developing "Gothic" tradition out of which rhyme could be said to have legitimately emerged.[21]

Neoclassicism was equally resisted by defenders of the vernacular, notably Richard Carew in his spirited essay on "The Excellency of the English Tongue" (1595): "Will you reade *Virgill*? take the Earle of Surrey, *Catullus*? *Shakespeare* and *Marlowes* fragment, *Ovid*? *Daniell*, *Lucan*? *Spencer*, *Martial*? Sir *John Davies* and others: will you have all in all for Prose and verse? take the miracle of our age Sir *Philip Sidney*."[22] Some of this resistance may have stemmed from a lingering reformist distrust of verbal embellishments, especially those derived from the official language of Catholic Europe, since the canon was frequently presented in these defences as an agent of linguistic conservatism, a repository of plain English. The vogue for Latinisms, complained John Jones in 1579, was an attempt by elites to mystify their own discourse and to occlude the source of their power, as though "truth cannot be delivered but in unknowen words and termes farfet, clean contrarie not onlye to the judgemente of our Elders, but also to the beste of our dayes, as in the skilfull workes of oure countrey menne, Chaucer, Gowre, Surrey, Cheeke, Chaloner, Recorde, Phaire, Wilson, Jewel, Dee, Digs, Fox, Holenshed &c. is apparante."[23] Jones may have not been far wrong: though canonical English writers could still represent a vernacular standard, few poets during this period were praised for "refining" their native language in the way that Chaucer was celebrated by his disciples in the fifteenth century.[24] Courtly nostalgia notwithstanding, the idea of refinement was being increasingly identified, especially under the Stuarts, with a classicist purification of poetic and rhetorical forms. Proving the vernacular's poetic versatility became less of a value than demonstrating "mastery" of eloquence according to specific norms for composition that were normally taught only to the sons of privilege – if English poetry was still centuries away from getting into the curriculum, the schools were, as ever, decisive in determining how the nation's poetry would be composed. As its opponents would long protest, neoclassicism's eventual ascendancy as the prevailing standard for literary "correctness" during much of the early modern period was primarily owing to the fact that it was an aesthetic practice designed to legitimize and reinforce polite control over literary evaluation. According to one frustrated popular author, neoclassic prescriptions were even being invoked to discourage literary expression among the lower orders: "such is the delicacie of our readers at this time, that there are none may be allowed of to write, but such as have bene trained at schoole with Pallas, or at the least have bene fostered up with the Muses."[25]

At the same time, neoclassicism exerted considerable appeal because it was also a convenient code for cultural self-persuasion and self-promotion. Like the "Renaissance" that nurtured it, neoclassicism presented an enabling revisionist narrative by which its proponents could misrecognize the relative marginality of their culture within the history of Western art. Emboldened by the idea of a renewed classical imperialism, Renaissance authors could believe that their age marked a return to the universalism of values authoritatively set out in the writings of the ancients; at the same time, they could believe their age distinctively civilized and refined in having shed its ignorant and barbarous medieval past (or, for Restoration neoclassicists, a rude and barbarous Elizabethan past). In their minds, their valuations of literary works were vastly more authoritative than those of medieval audiences but never at odds with the judgment of the ages. And since it posited a transhistorical human consensus yet equally a version of cultural history that elevated the present above an immediate past, neoclassicism could easily accord with a presentist mentality. Accordingly, quite apart from the exclusivity of the criteria it stipulated for literary excellence, neoclassicism's main utility for canon-makers was its ideological adaptability, in that it rendered antique prestige as well as, paradoxically, a narrative of achieved modernity accessible to the task of self-definition. In England, there would stand "a new Parnassus, and an other Helicon, nothinge inferiour to the olde," wrote Harvey, in *Pierces Supererogation* (1593), somewhat sardonically yet in keeping with the general tenor of a critical discourse that was everywhere deploying the paradigms and nomenclature of classicist canonicity. There were the anthologies *Englands Parnassus* and *Englands Helicon*, the three "Parnassus" comedies, and countless scraps of verse urging poets to "Transport *Pernassus* into *Britanie*." Neoclassicism could be used to sanction efforts intended as much to regulate the literary system as to expand it: "Then thus faire *Albion* flourish so / As *Thames* may nourish as did *Po*." Above all, the idea of a new classicism, of a *translatio studii* nonetheless still tethered to an essential *imperium* of values, offered Renaissance writers a useful cultural myth to answer how it was that artistic traditions could be both permanently valuable and productively changing. Parnassus and the universalism it symbolized could remain fundamentally unquestioned no matter how undeniable it was that languages and cultures had changed as the circumstances of production moved westward, and seemingly no matter how high nationalist sentiments ran: "Britayne soyle may bravely boast her state in fine, / That she a new Parnassus is, the Muses shrine."[26]

As the example of Daniel's *Defense* indicates, revisionist narratives could similarly, if less commonly, be extended to the English literary past. Within a mythology of Albion's Parnassus could be enshrined the image of the nativist bardic poet, from Colin Clout to "ancient Gower" in *Pericles*. Chaucer, in the frontispiece to Thomas Speght's 1598 edition of the *Works*, was given the royal treatment, his likeness surrounded by the heraldic shields of his purported "progenei." Poets' Corner in Westminster Abbey was established during this period, the bodies of Spenser, Beaumont, Drayton, and others being interred in the vicinity of a monument to Chaucer first erected in 1555. These gestures may have been acts of homage to a literary past, though the past was unlikely to be recalled without some sense of how its memorialization might contribute to the objective of cultural empowerment in the present. If early English authors were commemorated at all, they were usually extolled as part of an invented tradition of heroic patriots whose art had preserved the glories of England safely outside time. John Webster, following the model of the Chaucerian "House of Fame" from Jonson's *Masque of Queenes* (1609), turned England's canon into a device for holding up "London" in his Lord Mayor's pageant for 1624, the *Monuments of Honour*: "In the highest seate a Person representing *Troynovant* or the City, inthroned, in rich Habilaments; beneath her ... sit five famous Schollers and Poets of this our kingdome, as Sir *Jeffrey Chaucer*, the learned *Gower*, the excellent *John Lidgate*, the sharpe-witted Sr. *Thomas Moore*, and as last as worthy both Souldier and Scholler, Sir *Phillip Sidney*, these being Celebrators of honor, and the p[re]servers both of the names of men, and memories of Cities above, to posterity."[27] More impressively, the Scottish canon stood atop a gilded mound in the middle of an Edinburgh thoroughfare, in William Drummond's "Entertainment" for King Charles I's visit to the city in 1633: "In the midst of the streete, there was a Mountaine dressed up for *Parnassus*, where *Apollo* and the *Muses* appeared, and ancient Worthies of Scotland, for learning was represented; such as *Sedullius, Joannes Duns*, Bishop *Elphistoun* of *Aberdeen, Hector Boes, Joannes Major*, Bishop *Gawen Douglasse*, Sir *David Lindsay, Georges Buchananus*; the word over them was *Fama super aethera noti*."[28] The graphic anachronism of having the king confronted by impersonations of Duns Scotus and Gavin Douglas suggests how much a rhetorical culture valued its order of activities, literature included, in presentist terms. Duns Scotus and Gavin Douglas could appear before a Stuart king because all things thought worthy enough could live for an age that denied its historicity. "Nothing is more proper; Nothing more naturall," said Jonson, defending the mingling of the living and the dead in his *Masque of Queenes*, because "these all live; and together, in theyr Fame; and so I present them."[29]

Canon-makers eager to heighten poetry's legitimacy were quick to seize on its increased popularity at court – in masques, plays, and occasional verses – and on the fact that Elizabeth and James were known to have each tried their hand at versifying.[30] Catalogues of authors from the period routinely made mention of how many "great Princes, Earls, Lords and Knights for the Ornament and honour of learning, who for generall and particular causes and benefits have added their names to the society of writers."[31] Sidney, in his efforts on behalf of English literature and in the myths that accrued to his name following his spectacular death, provided poetry's apologists with a portrait of the artist as aristocratic hero, the learned soldier "deserving both the Lawrels and the Crowne to boote."[32] Something nonetheless remained of the old antagonisms between poet and patron over who had ultimate authority in the making and disseminating of values and representations. The print marketing of poets made for an intensified rhetoric of Petrarchan ennoblement, as Spenser, among others, was installed as "King of Poets."[33] This, too, was the age of the ever more sumptuous frontispiece portrait, but whereas authors from Caxton to Gascoigne had commonly been drawn kneeling before nobility, humbly presenting their books to their royal patrons, in literary portraits from about 1580 onwards – Harington for his Ariosto, Chapman for his Homer, Jonson for his 1616 folio, and so on – the subjects invariably dominated the spectral field and were routinely set amid a complex of mythological symbols whose meaning they ruled, from the laurels they commanded as poets to the gods and muses their works invoked.[34]

Besides this perennial contest between pen and crown, another conflict was beginning to make itself felt within the literary system, one that was potentially more disabling of the goal of canonic harmony because it set authors against one another. The conflict was a consequence in part of the rapid expansion of the literary system: eager to distinguish themselves above the growing pack of English inditers, authors engaged in bouts of warring self-promotion that inevitably undermined the goal of forming a harmonious canon. It was during this period that there first appeared in English writing the charges of plagiarism and of pandering to the public in exchange for instant celebrity.[35] This period also saw the eruption of the literary system's first major internal disputes on the proper conduct of the literary artist, the Harvey-Nashe controversy and the War of the Theatres (though the latter is assumed to have been a publicity stunt). Faced with increased competition for patronage and praise, authors aimed their rhetorical assaults at rivals in order to market their product. Previously it had been a standard practice in commendatory verses to welcome the rising poet among a fraternity of great literary figures. By the close of the sixteenth century, the conventions of puffery had begun to embrace a rhetoric of revision and exclusion:

> Foole that I was; I thought in younger time,
> That all the *Muses* had their graces sowne
> In *Chaucers*, *Spensers*, and sweet *Daniels* Rimes;
> (So, good seemes best, where better is unknowne)[36]

Critics perceived this competitiveness to be a direct result of the productive freedom afforded by the market, and accordingly they pleaded for more control within the literary system. Lodge, in *Wits Miserie* (1596), warned of the possible consequences of spurning the ideals of tradition and solidarity:

Lilly, the famous for facility in discourse: Spenser, best read in ancient poetry: Daniel, choise in word, and invention: Draiton, diligent and formall: Th. Nash, true English Aretine. All you unnamed professours, or friends of Poetry, (but by me inwardly honoured) knit your industries in private, to unite your fames in publicke: let the strong stay up the weake, & the weake march under conduct of the strong; ... But if besotted with foolish vain-glory, emulation, and contempt, you fall to neglect one another.[37]

Harvey was among the most vocal in complaining of the indecorous hostility, and of the self-service that lay behind it. Greene, he claimed, had "sought Fame by diffamation of other." Nashe, likewise, "disdaineth Thomas Delone, Philip Stubs, Robert Armin, and the common Pamfletters of London, even the painfullest Chroniclers tooe; bicause they stand in his way, hinder his scribling traffique, obscure his resplendishing Fame, or have not Chronicled him in their Catalogues of the renowned moderne autors."[38] However legitimate his accusations, Harvey, in dispraising the dispraisers, was merely perpetuating the cycle of bumptious and disharmonizing self-promotion, a fact recognized when both his works and Nashe's were suppressed in 1599.

Yet this conflict of authors may have reflected more than just the economic changes attendant upon the growth of a literary system. Arguably, the conflict also arose from the essential problem in canonformation of reconciling order with change. As the literary system expanded, it seemed increasingly difficult to assert the value of canonical uniformity while pointing out how the tradition was modern, alive, and productively changing. Ideally in a rhetorical culture, where the circulation of value was prized above its objectification, canonizing an author involved not so much attesting to his singular worth as proclaiming his enabling influence within a dynamic cultural economy. It seemed less important, in praises lavished on the poet, that Spenser had proven himself a unique poet in *The Faerie Queene* than that, by producing a national epic, he had led the way towards fostering a thriving literary culture. Spenser's influence was measured by how much his fellow pastoralists or even the state could use his work productively:

> Collyn was a mighty swaine,
> In his power all do flourish, ...
> By his toile we do nourish,
> And by him are inlarg'd.[39]

If authors were esteemed for how widely they stimulated the literary system, or how much they contributed to the maintenance of social relations, then the highest praise that could be given an author insisted less on the uniqueness of his work than on its lack of uniqueness, its harmonizing, communal power in being conducive of ongoing work. Exhaustive originality was not yet a value, and the myth of the solitary genius belonged to another, later period.

However, the emphases upon production and cultural advancement made for a strong sense of literary modernity, which translated, at the level of authorship, into a heightened awareness of the need to define how one's writings had effected productive changes within the literary tradition. While still affirming the value of a healthy literary system, authors were increasingly keen to demarcate their work from others' through acts of self-canonization that inevitably destabilized the system. Often these acts involved the rejection of a literary past; indeed, this was even true of acts of self-canonization which, as in the example of *The Shepheardes Calender* with its reverent nod to Chaucer's authority, seemed to use that past in order to sanction the modern poet's work. In Spenser's debut, and in E.K.'s commentary on the poem especially, there was a tension between recognizing the place of poetic forefathers and presenting Spenser as "our new Poete," one so self-assured as to eclipse all who went before him. E.K. relied on the conventional codes of distinction to champion his friend, including notoriously setting Spenser against "the rakehellye route of our ragged rymers." But asserting Spenser's modernity required that E.K. also use those codes to depreciate the work of Spenser's acknowledged precursors: "For what in most English wryters useth to be loose, and as it were ungyrt, in this Authour is well grounded, finely framed, and strongly trussed up together."[40] Later in the notes, Gascoigne was politely dismissed as a poet whose work had already become obsolescent: "a wittie gentleman, and the very chefe of our late rymers who, and if some partes of learning wanted not (albee it is well knowen he altogyther wanted not learning) no doubt would have attayned to the excellencye of those famous Poets."[41] By rejecting most English poetry produced within living memory, at a time when the English cultural elite was yearning for a canon "to keepe wing with the best," E.K. was making it impossible for Spenser not to seem like the only begetter of a new English tradition.[42]

E.K.'s epistle, the "arguments" of each eclogue, the annotations, the emblems and woodcuts, provided the book with an aura meant to recall humanist editions of classical texts. "The book's reflexive strategies," Louis Adrian Montrose has suggested, "are aimed at instituting it as the founding text of a new English literary canon."[43] Its brilliance as a canon-making gesture was recognized by contemporaries, for whom E.K.'s commentary was inspiration for the first arguments on behalf of treating English writings as classics worthy of reproduction: "they who will be pleas'd to credit our owne tongue, and age, may finde our present, and later Poets, capable of that commendation, which was given the antien[ts] among the Greekes: That if their writings were preserved, no part of Learning should wholy perish. *Spencer*, having as well delivered Morall, and Heroicall matter for use and action, as *Du Bartas* (now ours) Naturall and Divine, for study and meditation."[44] However, as a new canon could only be founded once, Spenser's gesture was essentially unrepeatable, in terms of keeping all of his work seemingly vital and modern throughout his career. Spenser, in his later writings, was faced with the old problem of authority, of finding new strategies to help promulgate his vision of English poetry. Feeling disappointed in his career, he defined his work increasingly through the rhetoric of control, occasionally invoking the sentiment of authorial collectivity – the brotherhood of fellow "shepheards" in *Colin Clouts Come Home Again* – but more frequently complaining of a literary system overrun by "Parasites and Sycophants" (*Tears of the Muses* 472). However much they appealed to a sense of canonic harmony, such reactive postures had scarce the productive force of a revisionist discourse of the "new poet," or, for that matter, the enabling authority of an achieved national epic. Having already proven that his work could revitalize England's literary culture, Spenser could not risk once again asserting his modernity without rendering his earlier work obsolescent.

The dilemma that confronted Spenser was a direct consequence of presentism. Unable or unwilling to recognize the prevalence of change in literary history, yet at the same time committed to an instrumentalist rhetoric wherein the value of any activity was understood in terms of its immediate "profit," Renaissance authors could not easily reconcile their desire for a harmonious canon and the permanence it symbolized with their equally potent desire to renew the canon and thereby to demonstrate the special authority of their work, their nation, and their age. In practice, the paradox of permanence and change tended to reinforce the presentism of verbal power since the principle of universalism, with its stipulation that the past or the future could not diverge in any radical way from the present, allowed the orator to concentrate on the specific requirements of the moment. Contingency was thus implicit in every act of self-definition, whether the author was appealing for control or advancement: it was not especially troubling that every new forceful lament or polemic would soon yield to another, new forceful lament or polemic, so long as the sense of conviction could be maintained. From a modern point of view, this element of contingency made for much wastage, since the task of self-definition entailed an ever-renewed rejection rather than reproduction of the literary past. Yet to have acknowledged this contingency would have been unthinkable, denying as it would have the absolute, universalist basis for belief. Hence the appeal of narratives such as neoclassicism, which maintained this absolutism even as it allowed for revision. Authors, however, had to come up with their own self-defining gestures that could reconcile the conflicting functions of order and change, gestures that could explain how it was that the author's lifework was at one with the canon yet equally its productive renewal.

This could be especially problematic for professional authors, who had to deny being motivated by economic self-interest in order to gain legitimacy. Some, like Jonson, could profess laureate ambitions of writing poetry for the common good, but such conventional defences of the literary activity could not indicate how the individual poet's work represented something new and distinctive within the literary system. Unable to justify their practice in terms of economic profit, and deriving only a general sense of cultural authority from the poet's traditional roles, professional authors were obliged to define themselves almost exclusively in relation to the existing literary canon. As a result, their gestures implied a view of art as an activity separable from other socio-political concerns. If print had encouraged a greater sense of autonomy among readers and authors alike, the task of presentist self-determination intensified the process whereby artistic production would be increasingly valued for its ostensible independence from social or economic interests. This process of "autonomization," Bourdieu has explained, "is thus correlative with the constitution of a socially distinguishable category of professional artists or intellectuals who are less inclined to recognize rules other than the specifically intellectual or artistic traditions handed down by their predecessors, which serve as a point of departure or rupture. They are also increasingly in a position to liberate their products from all external constraints, whether the moral censure and aesthetic programmes of a proselytizing church or the academic controls and directives of political power, inclined to regard art as an instrument of propaganda."[45] As the process was inseparable from the rise of professional authorship, it would culminate only later, with the thorough commercialization of the literary system in the eighteenth century. Yet the social diversification which the process implied, and which would mark the undoing of rhetorical culture, was already being signalled in the efforts of the earliest professional authors to distinguish themselves. I will consider three such efforts: Robert Greene's *Vision*, Ben Jonson's 1616 folio *Workes*, and Michael Drayton's "Epistle to Henry Reynolds, of Poets and Poesy."

GREENE'S VISION (1592)

Purportedly "written at the instant of his *death*" yet likely penned two years earlier, Robert Greene's *Vision* is one of a number of posthumously printed pamphlets telling of the author's apparent remorse over a misspent life.[46] The title page's announcement of a deathbed repentance notwithstanding, the narrative describes a healthy if anxious Greene undergoing something of a mid-career crisis. Although his prose romances have made him very popular, especially among women readers, Greene wonders with mock seriousness whether his choice of specializing in this genre has not cost him his chance at getting the everlasting fame he desires. "Povertie is the father of innumerable infirmities," he says, freely admitting that he wrote mainly for money.[47] Greene, one of the self-styled university wits, has felt the stigma against commercial authorship: "Hee that commeth in Print, setteth himselfe up as a common marke for every one to shoote at" (sig. A4r). But it is a charge of licentiousness which has brought on his vision. Having been accused of authoring the scurrilous *Cobler of Canterbury*, Greene is disturbed that his writings have gained him a reputation for immorality, and this prompts him to reconsider his life in letters.

To show that he is mindful of literature's moral obligations, Greene composes a self-admonishing "Ode, of the vanitie of wanton *writings*," in which Ovid is held up as an example of a poet whom Apollo may have crowned with the laurels but whose licentiousness led to his banishment from polite society (B1v). Greene then falls into a dream, where he meets two elderly gentlemen who are identified as Chaucer and Gower, and whom Greene addresses on the subject of his "fond pamphlets": "Grave Laureats, the tipes of Englands excellence for poetry: ... I am driven into a dumpe whether [the pamphlets] shall rebound to my insuing credit, or my future infamie, or whether I have doone well or ill, in setting foorth such amourous trifles" (C2$_{r-v}$). In a debate that follows, a merry Chaucer defends the writing of amorous tales by advocating a plural canon, while moral Gower brings out all of the conventional objections. For Chaucer, authors ought not be restricted to a narrow standard for literary production: "poets wits are free, and their words ought to be without checke" (C3$_r$). Chaucer assures Greene that the poet of imagination, no less than the serious philosopher, is deserving of fame, a claim which he can support by citing his own reception: "If thou doubtest blame for thy wantonnes, let my selfe suffice for an instaunce, whose Canterburie tales are broad enough before, and written homely and pleasantly: yet who hath bin more canonised for his workes, than Sir *Geffrey Chaucer*" (C3$_r$). Like Covell, Greene does not clarify what he means by "canonized," although once again the suggestion is that a poet may achieve earthly immortality in the writings of his disciples.

In reply, Gower dismisses both the content and staying power of Chaucer's works: "men honor his more for the antiquity of the verse, the english & prose, than for any deepe love to the matter: for proofe marke how they weare out of use" (C4$_r$). His language becoming ever more obsolete, Chaucer is no longer acclaimed as the refiner of English, and hence his works have lost much of their utility. Canonicity, argues Gower, is based on a work's instrumental value: "Men that write of Morall precepts, or Philosophicall Aphorismes are more highly esteemed, than such as write Poems of love, and conceits of fancie" (C3$_r$). Accordingly, personal distinction should be less of an incentive to poets than teaching the public how to work towards "an universall profit of their countrey, and how to keepe youth from any touch of idle vanities." Works like Greene's, Gower insists, "greatly prejudice the state of the commonwealth" (C3$_v$). Chaucer and Gower then exchange stories "for the suppressing of jealousie" (D1$_v$), a narrative interlude that allows Greene to use the canonical authority of his precursors to rewrite literary history in his own defence. Chaucer's fabliau, as Gower recognizes, would not have been out of place among the "fantasticall toyes" that so disgraced the *Cobler of Canterbury*, while Gower's story is a moralized romance similar to the type Greene wrote earlier in his career (E1$_r$). Chaucer and Gower are made to represent less the two sides of Greene's conscience than the two extremes of his fiction.[48]

Siding with Gower, Greene concedes that he has never been the darling of moralists and official canon-makers. He admits "the gravest sort, whose mouthes are the trumpets of true report, had spoken hardlie of my labours" (H1ᵥ). But Greene dismisses these critics by introducing another character, King Solomon, who embodies absolute evaluative authority. The fictive Greene has promised Gower that his next work will be the biblical *Mourning Garment* but even this career transformation is not enough for Solomon, who advocates total conversion to devout learning. Declaring himself "wiser than the sons of men," Solomon is graver than any of Greene's usual detractors though equally far more flamboyant than the two English laureates. Solomon is a Puritan "in the habite of a King," a patrician scornful of the liberal arts, who berates Gower for presuming to know the nature of truth as well as "the hidden aphorismes of arte" (H2$_r$–3$_r$). Solomon attempts to persuade Greene of the higher calling of theology yet presents him with incentives that seem altogether Parnassian. If Greene were to follow the path of wisdom, he would "be honoured in the streets" (H2ᵥ). With divine learning come "riches and honour," and were Greene to "drinke of those waters," he is assured by Solomon, "so shalt thou recover thy fame that thou hast lost" (H2ᵥ). The rewards of authorship remain the same for Greene, whether he chooses to write of love or divinity. While Solomon preaches a saintly life, Greene is dazzled by the glamour of canonization. The *Vision* ends with Greene thoroughly converted and promising to instruct his readers in the ways of God: "As you had the blossomes of my wanton fancies, so you shall have the fruites of my better laboures" (H4$_r$).

Greene is precisely the type of popular fabulist who would be banned from a state-sponsored canon like Covell's, or from any canon of moral literature. Yet Greene is not all that much concerned with the health of either the state or his soul. His *Vision* is all about the rewards of professional authorship, as well as the new and sometimes elusive values and pressures that rhetorical canon-making places upon the working writer. Within a modern, secular canon, the author's fame and singular modernity are pre-eminent; they are values without priority, subordinated to neither religious nor kingly authority, and tied only in an ambiguous way to the vicissitudes of the book trade. With the conditions for canonicity no longer clearly defined, it is difficult for an author like Greene to know how to go about becoming a celebrated artist. Though he has achieved considerable popularity, Greene knows that his fictions are not of the kind that would guarantee him a place among the national literary pantheon. And yet, as he points out, his early fictions followed the pleasant vein of England's most canonized poet, Chaucer. Greene is confused about the source of value: his master enjoys the immortality that is forbidden to him. Chaucerian romances have not worked for Greene and he feels the threats of obloquy and oblivion. His initial response, according to the

Vision, is to believe that an acceptance of older traditions, civic humanism or theological study, will assure him a foothold in posterity. His other, more instinctive response is to interpret all prevalent notions of authorship and canonicity so that they agree with his own: just as Solomon tells the fictive Greene exactly what he wishes to hear, so do Chaucer and Gower tell Greene-like tales. Greene has joined their canon because he has recreated the canon on his own terms. At the very moment when, as Solomon, Greene describes the wonders of "divine" fame, he discovers the liberating principle of revisionism.

There is a catch. Revisionism rests on a paradox, Benjamin's paradox, insofar as the transcendental author can define himself only in opposition to the canon his work renews. There can be no transcendence if the canon is left unrevised, and yet without the canon as antithesis, there can be no difference, no modernity, no renewal. In making his precursors seem like more of himself, Greene exacerbates the problem of presentist self-definition, as well as the problem of authenticity that originally brought on the discontent. How can Greene deny having authored the *Cobler of Canterbury* when his own text includes a tale that might have been taken from that very collection? Greene disappears into his own fiction, into the Chaucerian imitations and other popular genres that make up his literary output, into the image he has created for himself and into the texts that bear his name. His repentance, however sincere, becomes nothing more than another "last confession," repeated over and over again in numerous pamphlets, all capitalizing on the value of the Greene name. In desperation, the printer, Thomas Newman, tries to defend the *Vision*'s authenticity: "Manie have published repentaunces under his name, but none more unfeigned then this, being everie word of his owne: his own phrase, his own method" (A3$_r$). To this day, the authenticity of the repentance pamphlets remains unproven. As for Greene, he does achieve something like canonization in the work of his successors. His name and persona continue to appear in print after his death until, at last, in John Dickenson's *Greene in Conceipt* (1598), he is himself cast as a literary ghost telling other people's tales.

THE "WORKES" OF BENJAMIN JONSON (1616)

Both Covell and Greene use "canonised" to suggest something of the new heroic stature of the Renaissance artist, one who may surpass temporal sovereignties in being able, through his writings, to transcend the world of mutable realities. Canonization, in this sense, is the timeless hope of a presentist mentality, given a resonance of

institutional force by the term's ecclesiastical associations. Such resonance is perhaps even stronger in the cognate term "canonical," which
is also being increasingly applied to secular writings during this period,
notably by Donne in his fourth satire, where he looks forward to the
time "some wise man shall, / I hope, esteeme my writs Canonicall" (ll.
243–4). A canonical text achieves its timeless authority less through
the deployment of immortalizing flourishes or other gestures at self-
promotion than through an implicit claim for the force and depth of
its significance. More precisely, a canonical text purports to offer
privileged instruction or value, and it therefore requires of its readers
a special degree of competence, empathy, or skill in interpretation and
judgment. Alvin C. Kibel has proposed a useful distinction between
two types of great books: the cultural document, whose meaning "can
be formulated in other words" – Kibel gives as examples the Reform
Act and Newton's *Opticks* – and the canonical text, whose original
version we seek out because we "insist that its given form is the only
means through which its message can be reliably transmitted." Both
the cultural document and the canonical text possess symbolic value,
an accumulated fame, honour, or recognized authority. But in addition to this symbolic value, the canonical text may also be put to the
service of cultural capital, that is, the measure of recognized expertise
in interpreting and evaluating cultural works and relations. The
canonical text is said to yield a richness of meaning that is nonetheless
accessible only to those of demonstrated competence, an accreditation
which they can accumulate as cultural capital. This is why, in an
objectivist culture, canonical texts are treated as though they were a
continual source of meaning, because this allows for the unlimited
acquisition of cultural capital by social agents who build entire careers
by devoting themselves to the exegesis of even a single canonical
author – I consider Shakespeare's example in more detail in a later
chapter. A canonical text is one so rich in meaning that it is perceived
as impervious to complete reformulation: it is a text, as Kibel suggests,
"whose importance we recognize, although in some radical sense we
are not able to understand it ... Accordingly, its original form is
recognized as the only trustworthy expression of its meaning."[49]
A rhetorical culture like the English Renaissance, as I have been
maintaining, does not value knowledge so much as it does the force
that comes from the skilled and productive use of language; accordingly, its moral economy does not recognize a separable category of
cultural capital in the same way that an objectivist culture does. The
texts that such a culture canonizes are therefore esteemed for the
inexhaustibility of their verbal power, for their endless capacity to
mobilize passions and to persuade judgments. Given this belief in the

force of words, a rhetorical culture may prize the authentic versions of certain of its canonical texts as insistently as an objectivist culture might.[50] The long, complicated history of scriptural reception offers numerous episodes of how a canonical text could variously serve the accumulation of symbolic capital, as it did for the medieval Church with its institutional authority founded on the licensed exegesis of a text purportedly distorted by translation, or the goal of cultural solidarity, as it did for the Reformers who sought out the original text in order to experience fully the boundless force of divine revelation. But whereas the reception of scripture may involve interpreting its message as much as emphasizing its suasive power, the nomination of canonical secular texts in a rhetorical culture carries with it an insistence on textual authenticity less because the text may offer an endless supply of meaning than because it heightens the circulation of symbolic capital. And for this intensification to occur, the text must exert a continual and predictable control over its readers' reactions, which it can accomplish only if all readers confront the text in a version that remains uniform throughout an edition. What I discussed in a previous section – how an emergent print culture prompted some to invoke fictive evaluative communities of "learned readers" – would eventually be taken a step farther, as the fixity that print afforded led to the acclamation of canonical texts whose value lay precisely in their supposed ability to direct readers to a more accordant response.

Ben Jonson's 1616 folio *WORKES* is the first self-consciously canonical edition of an author's works in English literature. Its purpose is to provide an authentic picture of the poet and his *ouevre* at a midpoint in his career. It is meant to substantiate the author's fame, if not necessarily to inflate it. Despite Jonson's pretensions in naming his collection after the Latin *Opera*, the folio – unlike, say, *The Shepheardes Calender* – does not function as a deliberate classic in the way that such classics normally call attention to themselves as historic events. Relatively self-contained, the folio makes no explicit gesture directing attention to possible antecedents, nor has it any elaborate apparatus, intrusive editor, or canonizing declaration heralding the "new poet" as the dawn of a new era in English literature. Even if Jonson wanted to influence the future direction of English poetry, he does not make this claim in his *Workes*. The folio presents the poet in full genuine splendour, locked into no single tradition, recognizing no explicit authority other than his patrons and the well-defined body of his own work. In emphasizing the poet's singularity and authenticity, the folio serves an act of self-advertisement and self-consecration which, unusual for the period, calls attention to its author without signalling how his writings might generate a modern renewal of the canon.

The folio, as has been frequently noted, is designed as an objectification of Jonson's working self, as poet for the stage and for the page, as masque-writer, epigrammatist, panegyrist, satirist, scholar.[51] Others may have performed these roles alongside Jonson but their work is not represented in the folio, nor is there mention of masque designers or Jonson's other collaborators. Commenders aside, the folio gives us only Jonson, though it does not give us all of Jonson: Jonson's commendations of other writer's books are omitted, as are a number of early plays and lesser entertainments. *Every Man in his Humour* has been extensively revised and given a new prologue. *Cynthia's Revels* and *Poetaster* are reprinted in revised versions, though *Bartholomew Fair*, completed in 1614, is excluded. Many of Jonson's revisions are intended to encourage a sense of closure, like the change in the order of the speeches in the final masque, *The Golden Age Restor'd*, a change "designed to give a more significant ending to the Folio" (H&S 7:420n.). In adding a great many stage directions and in annotating his masques, Jonson may be seeking an interpretive closure. Finally and most importantly, the folio contains no apology either for its title, which recalls both *Opera* and large posthumous editions like Speght's *Works of Chaucer*, or for its unprecedented juxtaposition of the "higher" form of panegyric with the less prestigious genres of plays and masques. More than simply raising drama's stature, which is an achievement in itself, Jonson is making the author rather than genre the prime consideration in canon-formation. With his folio, Jonson is putting forward the claim that value resides in the coherence and authenticity of the author's voice, and that this value cannot be measured solely in accordance with conventional perceptions about the different kinds of literature. The folio asserts the worth of Jonson's writings, but in objectifying that worth in the fixity of print, it comes close to embodying a new conception of literary value, one that anticipates later definitions of canonicity.

The folio is nonetheless very much a document of its age. It is perhaps the most extreme example of presentist self-definition in English literary history, since Jonson essentially uses his collection to spatialize temporal relations. This is apparent even from the frontispiece, which shows Jonson surrounded by emblematic representations of the major genres which laureate poets were expected to excel at. One of those genres was pastoral, which Jonson included in his frontispiece despite having not yet gotten around, as he had promised Drummond, to writing any pastoral poetry; Jonson seemed to have designed the frontispiece with a view to his future career, as though his entire poetic progress could be preconceived on a two-dimensional image. Jonson is also relying on the illusion of immutability that comes from the spatial and typographical dimensions of the printed book. He is perhaps the first English author to think of the printed book as a well-defined aesthetic object, a commodity that materializes and preserves on clean and determinate pages of text what was once a fluid, corporate script or a short-lived, contingent event held at a tavern, on a stage, or in a hall at court. In giving the manuscript work an appearance that is standard throughout the run of an edition, the printed book asserts the substantiality of the work, its solid presence in the world of experience, its potential not just for enduring in time but for retaining its order and identity before a great many readers at any given moment.

Jonson shows little concern for the historicity of the traditions he is working in. His self-conscious cosmopolitanism, an *imitatio* based on a wide-ranging intertextuality of ancient and modern texts, treats these influences as Petrarch did, as colleagues to admire or rivals to defy. Jonson's censures of other poets, in the conversations with Drummond and elsewhere, all seem to take place in some timeless setting, an "Apollo Room" just this side of Parnassus: "he cursed Petrarch" (H&S 1:133). Even his classicism, which in its laboured intensity seems less a dictate of the age than Jonson's most effective resource for distinguishing himself from contemporaries, serves to define his singular modernity as much as his purifying anti-modernity: to the Mere English Censurer, "my way in *Epigrammes* seemes new, / When both it is the old way, and the true" (*Ep.* 18:1–2). Priority, influence, and modernity belong to the diachronic relations among authors, whereas Jonson believes in a synchrony, in the presence of his book as a monumentalization of his own authentic identity. In his second epigram, "To His Book," Jonson gives his version of the very same apostrophic gesture English poets from Chaucer and Spenser had used to declare their hopes of entering a canon of their masters. Jonson's version contains echoes of his masters Martial and Horace but no formal request of the book to "go" and walk among the poet's forefathers. Jonson's pantheon, his book, and his self, like many of his lyrics, all seem to stand with calculated, achieved stasis. Jonson treats his book as a natural extension of his person, "nam'd of mee" yet disavowing self-interest as Jonson might: "by thy wiser temper, let men know / Thou are not covetous of least selfe-fame" (*Ep.* 2:8–9). One of Jonson's predominant sets of figures, as is commonly noted, involves the identification of books and persons: "Ben. Ionson his best piece of *poetrie*" (*Ep.* 45:10), "Rare poemes aske rare friends" (*Ep.* 94:6), "Then doe I love thee, and behold thy ends / In making thy friends bookes, and thy bookes friends" (*Ep.* 86:1–4). In a setting that recognizes no change, books speak as timelessly and as actively to "friends" as friends converse among themselves. Even in the brief Ciceronian "*Scriptorum catalogus*" from the *Discoveries* (H&S 8:591–2), Jonson elects a literary canon whose nominees, learned gentlemen and churchmen, could have easily been included (like Savile and Egerton) among the friends and associates assembled in the *Epigrammes*. Canon-formation is social formation, the gathering of disciples and familiars, no mere "riming *Club*" but a "tribe" of sons "sealed" in letters (*U.V.* 30:8; *Und.* 47). As for Chaucer, Gower, Lydgate, and Spenser, they are too remote to be anything like friends of Jonson, who can revive them only through extravagant anachronism in the folio's final masque, *The Golden Age Restor'd*. There, the old poets dutifully appear before Astraea, "To waite upon the age that shall your names new nourish" (H&S 7:425).[52]

In this way, the *Epigrammes*, in particular, are finally less enduring monuments of praise or censure than a dramatic spatialization of the endless conversation of a rhetorical culture, with each subject being placed in a position relative to others, to their moral opposites, and to the central figure of the poet.[53] The latter, of course, seemed forever to engage in persistent position-takings on his own behalf – what Richard Helgerson calls Jonson's "constant, sweaty effort to mark a difference" – in order to distinguish himself from literary contemporaries, to define a legitimate space above the mass market for professional authorship, and to secure his artistic independence from powerful interests: "I a *Poet* here, no *Herald* am," or, addressing the court, "Thy servant, but not slave" (*Ep.* 9:4; H&S 4:33).[54] But it is the totalization of value that is achieved by mapping out social relations in the *Epigrammes* that suggests how the volume functions as a canonical text for its culture, continually distributing its verbal power in order to position its readers. Jonson fills these poems with rhetorical questions that, although meant to praise, seem also to challenge the subject's judgment: "Whom should my *Muse* then flie to, but the best / Of Kings for grace; of *Poets* for my test?" (*Ep.* 4:9–10). Since many of Jonson's questions have to do with determining value, they seem directed as much at the poem's putative subject as at the cultural consensus that is being implicitly asked to respond affirmatively: "Who would not be thy subject, James, t' obay / A Prince, that rules by' example, more than sway?" (*Ep.* 35:1–2). Jonson characteristically leaves his questions unanswered, and this allows for the possibility of closure being forever deferred: "Who shall doubt, Donne, where I a poet bee, / When I dare send my *Epigrammes* to thee?" (*Ep.* 96:1–2). That the question should introduce a spectre of doubt even as it appears to deny it is characteristic of Jonson's manipulativeness, which aims to create a sense not so much of suggestive ambiguity as of a force that can never be quite turned off.

On the surface, Jonson appears to be doing what nearly all of his contemporaries were doing, orienting the reader to a fixed set of responses. The "Reader in Ordinairie/Reader extraordinary" pairing, as I have suggested, merely rehearses a familiar structural opposition that sets learned readers against vulgar dispraisers (H&S 5:432). But Jonson continually elaborates this structure by overstocking the range of audience responses with a proliferation of negative readerly types, from ignorant censurers and the hypocritical "Playwright" to celebrity hunters and plagiarists, ignorant lords, fools, knaves, parrots, beasts, apes, and the rest. If there is a theme to the *Epigrammes*, it is the search for the ideal judge, a search that leads Jonson to acknowledging the intractable diversity of readers: "*In the difference of wits*," Jonson observes, "there are many notes: And it is a little *Maistry* to know them: to discerne, what every nature, every disposition will beare ... There are no fewer forms of minds, then of bodies amongst us. The variety is incredible" (H&S 8:584). This diversity is deplorable because it can disenable sound judgment, for the poet as well as his patrons. Jonson admits that he has "too oft preferr'd / Men past their termes, and prais'd some names too much" (*Und.* 14:19–22). This apparent uncertainty of judgment coupled with the multiplication of undesirable readers make for an unusually complicated reworking of the normal working oppositions that serve to generate belief in a rhetorical culture.

Yet Jonson's doubts about the universal power of rhetoric are merely tactical, and he remains wholly committed to supporting this structure of conviction. His elaboration of its basic codings are designed to intensify his verbal power, to keep his readers in their place by confronting them with a seemingly endless series of position-takings, as if the instrumentality of his rhetoric functioned less to provoke change than to coordinate his subjects according to a cultural grid or network. The ultimate goal of such manipulation is the totalization of value, imagined as a smoothly harmonious community of poets and patrons whose most supreme attribute is that value is in themselves spatialized and "centered"[55]:

> He that is round within himselfe, and streight,
> Need seeke no other strength, no other height; ...
> Be alwayes to thy gather'd selfe the same   (*Ep.* 98:3–4,9)

It becomes a mark of social distinction to embody value in this way and to remain impervious to change, which is routinely imagined as a physical if harmless assault on the still-standing subject: "Fortune upon him breakes her selfe, if ill, / And what would hurt his vertue makes it still" (*Ep.* 98:3–6). The poet, similarly, feels nothing of the fool's "praise or dispraise ... One doth not stroke me, nor the other strike" (*Ep.* 61). Jonson's subjects may acquire symbolic profits from demonstrating not merely disinterest but an ability to keep to their position in the face of adversity and variety:

> But thou, whose noblesse keeps one stature still,
> And one true posture, though besieg'd with ill
> Of what ambition, faction, pride can raise;
> Whose life, even they, that envie it, must praise   (*Ep.* 102:13–17)

It is as though Jonson, prone to thinking of people in terms of books, were objectifying his subjects as canonical texts: authentic, impervious to change, a continual and fixed source of value. In this way, the instrumental value of Jonson's poetry has less to do with directing his readers to any particular course of action than with persuading them to maintain for themselves a position within a cultural complex and to demonstrate their authority by continually *resisting* incitements to change. Jonson's poetry of praise aims to enhance his subjects' authority by persuading them to internalize and adhere to a code against betraying themselves by altering their position. His verse offers a source not of meaning but of verbal power, which allows his readers the opportunity to accumulate symbolic capital by encouraging them continually to reinforce how they define themselves, or at least how Jonson defines them. In effect, Jonson's poetry contributes to the higher goal of legitimizing polite society by repeatedly insisting that it not change.

Jonson's spatialized, presentist conception of value does have one significant consequence, which is that it greatly diminishes the sense, so vital in a rhetorical culture, of value circulating dynamically in society. Exchange is possible in his poetic universe – "giving largely to me, more thou tak'st," Jonson tells Beaumont (*Ep.* 55:5) – and circulation may not matter any if ideally there is to be no differentiating between worthy poets and their worthy patrons, canonical texts and well-centred readers. (In its presentist extremity in positing such an ideal state of complete identity, Jonson's poetry, Stanley Fish has suggested, "does not ask us to do anything or even to learn anything. One can say of it finally what can be said of almost no other verse in the period: it is not designed to be persuasive."[56] In working, though, to ensure that its patrons never change, as if verbal power could defeat time itself, the poetry performs the boldest, most desperate act of persuasion of all.) As he is championing a radical determinacy for books and persons and seeking to objectify himself and his readers in a fixed authentic text, however, Jonson is not far from proposing an objectivist conception of literary excellence, which sees value as being *intrinsic* to the work, to the singular genius of the poet, or to the sensibility of the enlightened reader. Of course, Jonson's standard for literary excellence is one that is fixed and monologic, rather than plural and multiform as in an objectivist culture. Invoking this standard enables Jonson to promote his work using the rhetoric of accuracy, legitimacy, and truth. Jonson does not refer to the good poem but to the "legitimate Poeme," whose rewards both for its subject and its poet must equally be "legitimate fame" (H&S 5:431; *Ep.* 17:3). Evaluative authority Jonson defines as the ability "to vindicate truth from error" (H&S 5:431). "Most commend," he contends, "out of affection, selfe tickling, an easinesse, or imitation: but men judge only out of knowledge. That is the trying faculty" (H&S 5:432). Knowledge here is meant to imply more than the authority of disinterestedness; it denotes almost an objectification of value itself, since Jonson speaks of this "faculty" as if it operated outside the realms of personal choice and desire.

Without a sense of its temporal circulation within systems of exchange, value becomes indistinguishable from meaning. In his opening epigram, Jonson instructs his reader not to judge his book well, but "To reade it well: that is, to understand." And Jonson facilitates this task of understanding, as is routinely noted, by writing verse that is extraordinarily limpid, with similar surface and secondary meanings reinforcing each other to give the impression of the same thing being said several times within the same poem. (It is as though Jonson's poetry, and particularly his poetry of compliment, were attempting to enact the virtue of standing still, and by this effect compensate for their oft-noted lack of specificity about the values they claim to uphold. The poems of praise become each a spatialization of value, removing it from the realms of narrative and change, where any attempt at specifying value must inevitably confront its historicity – narrative being instead reserved for satire, where it serves to enact the futile pursuit of negative values.) Such dense lucidity suggests how divergent Jonson's conception of a canonical text is from modern notions of literary excellence, which insist on the hermeneutic indeterminacy of the text, its inexhaustibility of meaning. Jonson aims instead for an accessibility that ensures that his meaning translates immediately and repeatedly into verbal force. But because that force is designed to control rather than mobilize, there is no clear sense how Jonson's poetry may enable cultural production in his own or later ages, or bring about a renewal of the canon. Poetry for Jonson may have considerable instrumental value in the maintenance and legitimation of polite society, yet as that value is objectified in the textual authenticity of the book, fixed by a transhistorical classicist standard ("the true way"), or concretized in the centred self, it is directed spatially rather than temporally. Jonson can thus define his difference as a poet not in terms of change – modernity, renewal, influence, originality, and so on – but through constant position-takings, from setting himself by the great as their worthiest judge to conjuring up an endless supply of Others to set himself against. And in marking such a relatively autonomous space for himself and his poetic activity, Jonson is auguring the modern field of cultural production, whose definition relies not on a specification of its productive utility but on its sharp differentiation from the fields of socio-economic activity.

Although Jonson received a royal pension and an honorary degree soon after the folio's publication, he cannot be said to have been canonized as a direct result of his *Workes* in the same way that Spenser had been by *The Shepheardes Calendar*. He was instead jeered by the wits for presuming to dignify the drama: "Pray tell me *Ben*, where doth the mystery lurke, / What others call a play you call a worke."[57] The 1616 folio was nevertheless influential because of Jonson's emphasis on the value of the authentic and autonomous authorial voice. Later editions of the works of prominent authors regularly contained prefatory assurances about the genuineness and determinacy of the material, an authenticity that could seemingly account for the author's greatness. Heminge and Condell, in the preface to the First Folio, emphasized "their care, and paine" in assembling Shakespeare's writings which, they claimed, "are now offer'd to your view cur'd, and perfect of their limbes; and all the rest, absolute in their numbers, as he conceived them." An author's powers of conception were perceived absolute, and such powers were no better signified, it seemed, than by a clean and determinate page of text: Shakespeare's "mind and hand went together ... wee have scarse received from him a blot in his papers."[58] Similar sentiments were expressed by Moseley before his 1647 folio of Beaumont and Fletcher's *Works*, where, after insisting on the authenticity of the material, he explained that his authors' supremacy was owing to their mode of composition, for they "never touched pen till all was to stand as firme and immutable as if ingraven in Brasse or Marble."[59] Jonson, of course, ridiculed this growing mythology of authenticity when he criticized the players for admiring everything Shakespeare wrote, but he was after the same clarity and determinacy of voice if not in his foul sheets then certainly in his printed *Workes*.

This idealization of the authorial voice prefigures the cult of originality, yet since there were no cultural or economic reasons for sustaining it, it would soon fade following the Restoration; by then, Shakespeare's works, in particular, would be valued as important cultural documents but ones whose meaning could be reformulated to suit contemporary tastes and understandings. Nonetheless, the ongoing professionalization of letters in the later seventeenth century would have as one its consequences an increasing phenomenalization of textuality, in which the cultural field would be perceived as being distinctive and autonomous by virtue of the special, inherently valuable nature of its products. In the short term, this phenomenalization would be reflected in the tendency among some poets after Jonson to fetishize textuality, as in the vogue for shaped poems, or to believe that the making of an ideal book could represent the realization of an ideal self. This way lies a work like Herrick's *Hesperides*, a text so laboured over that the poet's identity seems completely defined by its formal perfection: "In *Hesperides*, we encounter not only authorship, but a hypercathexis of authorship: for all its squibs of frivolity and its interpolation of seemingly heterogeneous materials, *Hesperides* is unified by the poet's path-breaking insistence on its intimate relationship to himself."[60] So intimate was this relationship, in fact, that the poet permitted no external moral or political constraints to intrude upon the stasis and aesthetic autonomy of his book; even its royalist celebration of rural pastimes and sexual liberty announced the poet's independence from Puritan authorities. Likewise, despite Herrick's injunction that his verses be sung at festive occasions, the book in its perfection seemed designed to resist appropriation by readers: unlike poems disseminated in manuscript, which courtly readers felt free to rework for their own use, the printed text of *Hesperides* was presented to the reader as a self-sufficient Pillar and Pantheon, and as a sentient object which the poet could address directly and repeatedly. In asserting his book's autonomy and monumentality, Herrick was all but declaring that canonical value was something intrinsic to literature rather than instrumentally circulated, something to be cherished as an end in itself rather than deployed as a tool of social intercourse. Good verses were still to be trusted for their traditional immortalizing power, yet such fame was desirable only insofar as the poet's self could be objectified outside history. For Herrick, to live "in my Book's Canonization" was not merely to defy social and political oppression through art, but to transcend life itself.[61]

TO MY MOST DEARELY-LOVED FRIEND HENERY REYNOLDS ESQUIRE, OF POETS AND POESIE (1627)

By the 1620s the English literary system was undergoing an uneasy realignment of its defining structures, with significant conflicts beginning to emerge within the official "learned" canon. Initially, these conflicts were restricted to the formation of rival schools of poetry: the sons of Ben, the Donne circle, Drayton and the Spenserians. Gradually, however, the literary system, which had been rigidly stratified during the Elizabethan period, began to lose some of its "structural integrity."[62] With the growth of the print market and the publication of prestige folio collections, professional authorship was enjoying an increased legitimacy, and on behalf not just of civic-minded laureates like Jonson but of formerly unheralded commercial dramatists like Shakespeare. Emboldened by their new operative authority, professional writers started to challenge the courtiers in their evaluative dominion over contemporary literature, with a view perhaps to forming a new canon after their own image. One target of their challenge was metaphysical poetry, which was chiefly practised among courtly amateurs and which, by its very esoteric style, seemed designed to resist appropriation by the professionals for broad circulation. Drummond, an ally of the professionals, was among the most vocal in dismissing the "Metaphysical Ideas, and Scholasticall Quiddityes," which he claimed were "no more Poesie than a Monster is a Man."[63] Drummond was troubled as much by the obscurity of this faddish verse as by its disregard for convention, which he believed reflected a profound ignorance of the works of "the great Poetes." The metaphysicals preferred rather to keep their own company than to honour a pantheon of their betters and elders. Canon-formation was for them a subject of political satire, as in Donne's mock bibliographical catalogue, "The Courtier's Library." To Drummond's dismay, the metaphysicals seemed to be removing poetry from the center of the national culture and making it the private recreation of determinedly insular coteries.

Whether the coteries were in fact *any more* insular than they had been in the past is unclear.[64] On the one hand, the English court, under Charles I especially, did turn away from older, indigenous traditions that had been observed throughout Elizabeth's reign towards the classicist and baroque paradigms in favour at other European courts. Obliquely reacting to this insularity and to the court's growing absolutism, some oppositional critics upheld the importance of submitting works to a general public for evaluation. For a traditionalist like the amateur Dudley North, the vogue for metaphysical poetry marked a deplorable refusal to address a common understanding. Works of the canon, according to North, had to be generally intelligible, whether or not they were originally intended only for private circulation; modern courtiers, North pleaded, ought to follow the example of their most illustrious precursor, Sidney, whose writings, he claimed, "flourish in applause of all, by a happy and familiar display of their beauties to the meanest."[65] On the other hand, there is evidence to suggest that some gentlemanly amateurs attempted to direct the theatrical tastes of the town, as a number of them tried their hands at play-writing, formerly the exclusive trade of anonymous writers-for-hire. The angry testimony of professional dramatists indicates that this competition from above, accompanied by some imperious courtly opinion-making, was considered a very serious threat to the market for commercial drama. Massinger, lashing out at the courtiers with a class antagonism that would have been unthinkable in a previous generation, accused them of debasing themselves by condescending to write private theatricals:

> Champ on this bitt and then
> Let it bee judg'd whoe are the baser men:
> Wee that descend from our owne height no more
> Then those old Classique Poets did before
> or you o' the wiser few. Indeed you write
> In corners and amonge yo[ur] selves recite
> yo[ur] Compositions ...
> To crie upon an other and soe rest,
> not daringe to indure the publique test.[66]

No doubt fearing reprisal, Massinger did not publish his attack. His statement is nonetheless remarkable. Along with being one of the first to invoke the idea of the "classic," ironically to defend modern commercial authorship, Massinger is here also among the first to accept the idea of the "publique test" and to oppose this test to the courtiers' system of private manuscript circulation. That such a test, with its implicit sense of canon-making by plural consensus, could conceivably yield more legitimacy than courtly privilege suggests how political conflict, along with the democratizing forces of the print market, were beginning to alter prevalent notions of literary value.

The "public test" is a forerunner of the "common reader," though it is equally an expression of nostalgia for the glory days of the Elizabethan era, when the literary system seemed empowered by a harmonious evaluative community – "truly a golden Age," Peacham lamented, "for such a world of refined wits and excellent spirits it produced, whose like are hardly to be hoped for in any succeeding Age."[67] Among the most vocal advocates of a public test was Michael Drayton, who, later in his career, would frequently mourn a lost consensus while bitterly denouncing "these dull yron Times" and "lunatique Age" when "Verses are wholly deduc't to Chambers."[68] Drayton relied heavily on Spenserian complaint for his self-definition, rallying his readers in a valiant struggle against "the unworthiest

Clownes" who dominated both the literary and political systems of the age (1:502). For Drayton, as for his peers, canon-formation was social formation, though Drayton's associates, allied with the opposition gentry, were drawn together by a common ideological antipathy to the age, "When onely Almanack and ballad rimes / Are in request now."[69] That they defined themselves against their age did not make their embattled gesturing any the less presentist in its bearings, aimed as it was to dignify the poets' marginal position and lack of success – Drayton's complaints were loudest in response to the lukewarm reception that greeted his masterwork, the *Poly-Olbion* (1612–22). This marginality and sense of political disappointment did, however, make for a certain loss of faith, since these poets were unsure how their work could contribute to the moral economy of the state. As William Browne asked his friend, "Then why lives *Drayton,* when the *Times* refuse, / Both *Meanes* to live, and *Matter* for a *Muse?*"[70] The question carried with it the assumption that poetry, even Drayton's, could not redeem the times. Drayton's outward reply was scarcely encouraging: "Deare friend, be silent and with patience see, / What this mad times Catastrophe will be" (3:209). Far from being an agent of cultural renewal, poetry could at best survive "in despight of tyranizing times" (1:307), to be rediscovered in some future era as "th'rejected jewels of these slothful times" (3:208).

A poet of laureate ambitions whose accomplishments went insufficiently recognized, Drayton combined the civic-minded ideals of poets of an earlier generation with the still-forming operative legitimations of the increasingly autonomous professional writer. Like most in his culture, he believed that poetry's supreme function was to enable social order and harmony; his cultural pessimism, however genuine, did not prevent him from producing huge works like the *Poly-Olbion,* written to counter the divisions of an iron age with the image of England unified in its people, history, and regions. Yet alongside these traditional values for poetry was a more radical concern for the appropriate status and social function of the print-based author. One of Drayton's chief designs in his writings was to remind his readers of what he believed was the former cultural centrality of poetry and song, a centrality Drayton incarnated in his frequent use of the figure of the bard or druid.[71] The self-romanticization of an alienated poet, Drayton's mythology of "Th'old *British* BARDS, upon their Harpes," which could scarce profit the state as much as the poet, reflected less an authentic longing for the lost authority of the civic poet than the elaborate self-promotion of a professional writer facing the new yet still insecure prominence of professionalism within the literary system (2:344). What Marx said in *The Eighteenth Brumaire of Louis Bonaparte,* about revolutionaries anxiously calling up the names and ideographs of the time-honored dead to secure their new enterprise, is loosely applicable to Drayton's situation as someone quite reluctantly participating in the ongoing ascendancy of the print market, someone who was obliged, in the face of political and career uncertainty, to frame a credible identity by invoking the symbolic authority of a mythic literary genealogy.

Drayton's "sacred" bards and druids are heroic representations whose heroism is not dependent upon kingly authority or iconography but springs instead from their devotion to their art. In the "Ode to Himselfe, and the Harpe," Drayton places himself at the head of a tradition of "right skilfull Harpers" who sing for the sake of music *only* (2:347–9). More strikingly, the bards in *Poly-Olbion* are preternaturally heroic in themselves, possessing a *furor poeticus* that is passed down through each generation of poets "of unmixt blood," down perhaps to Drayton himself:

> They instantlie againe doe other bodies take;
> I could have wisht your spirits redoubled in my breast,
> To give my verse applause, to times eternal rest.   (4:118,2)

Canonical poetry, it was commonly believed, exerted a productive influence on the present, but here the bardic spirit does not circulate dynamically in any larger cultural economy but serves instead the professional poet's desire for personal distinction. For Drayton, such distinction cannot come from the vagaries and degradations of the print market upon which he is obliged to depend, nor is it available from the old literary system's defining hierarchy, under which professional authorship enjoyed little legitimacy. The alternative is to idealize an autonomous realm of art, which has its own unique and self-renewing source of value that infuses the literary canon even as it mystifies how much the canon operates within a broader social economy. Without a sense of its instrumental circulation, cultural production tends to be conceived as a form of compulsion, the innate and spontaneous effusions of the isolated genius or, in Drayton's version, the pure songs of bards

> Addicted from their births so much to Poesie
> That in the Mountaines those who scarce have seene a Booke,
> Most skilfully will make, as though from Art they tooke.   (4:74)

Drayton is not quite prepared to foresake all traditional models of literary production, and, when not celebrating his bards, he will rely on conventional assurances to the reader of the mnemonic utility of his verse. Yet his rhetoric in these addresses sometimes suggests a poet who is searching for an unassailable source of value beyond language, as if verbal power were not enough to ensure solidarity. Of the history in the *Poly-Olbion* Drayton writes, "there is scarcely any of the Nobilitie, or Gentry of this land, but that he is some way or other, by his Blood interressed therein" (4: sig. v*ᵣ). Those who do not demonstrate such innate interest, according to Drayton, are mutations of the race: "outlandish, unnaturall English, (I know not how otherwise to expresse them)" (4:391). Even if this is no more than reactionary emotionalism, it marks possibly the first time that the source of poetic value has been characterized as non-verbally objective, in this case as an organic essence.

Drayton's revisionist mythologizing is less pronounced though no less operative in his verse epistle on the English canon, "To My Most Dearely-Loved Friend Henery Reynolds Esquire, of Poets and Poesie" (1627), one of the last Renaissance catalogues of authors (3:226–31). The poem rehearses some familiar notions of poetry's utility: Chaucer "inrich'd our *English* with his rimes" while Sidney "thoroughly pac'd our language as to show / The plenteous *English* hand in hand might goe / With *Greeke* and *Latine*." The sense of poetry's social function is nonetheless quite muted and rests uneasily alongside Drayton's glorification of productive compulsion, of his fellow poets as "strange kinde of men" inspired by a "fine madness." Unlike the enthusiastic boosterism of the earlier Elizabethan catalogues, Drayton's tone in the epistle is intimate and wistful, with past remembrances so occupying the poet that he begins with not one but two framing reminiscences: first, of his fireside readings with Reynolds of old rhymes stored in "happy memory," and second, of himself as a child asking his master to "Make me a Poet." A similar tone informs the catalogue itself, where Drayton even speaks of still-living authors in the past tense: "proud I was to know, / His poesie," he writes of Drummond, who was to survive him by nineteen years. Drayton's most memorable words of praise are reserved for those poets whose work recalls the spiritual and compulsive origins of literature: Marlowe, he writes, "Had in him those brave translunary things, / That the first Poets had."

Drayton's canon differs most notably from the earlier catalogues in not projecting similitude or harmony. His survey, in addition to offering casual dismissals of writers like Gascoigne and Churchyard who were "not inspired with brave fier," is expressly based on a principle of exclusion, which Drayton announces at the end of his survey: "These be not all / Have writ in numbers." Omitting from his survey the coterie poets, Drayton equates the canon with professional authorship,

and canon-formation with the judgment of the market and the popular voice. Only "workes oft printed, set on every post, / To publique
censure subject" can acquire a legitimate canonicity, in contrast to the
specious aura cultivated in the coteries

> whose poems, be they nere so rare
> In private chambers, that incloistered are,
> And by transcription daintyly must goe;
> As though the world unworthy were to know,
> Their rich composures.

Drayton does not mention that many of the poets he has honoured,
including Chaucer and Wyatt, were served in their lifetime only by
private transcription. Drayton's retrospective look at English literary
history has eliminated all contradiction between the practice of his
forebears and his own. His version of the canon recognizes only a
political division between professionals and courtiers. Drayton even
asserts commonality with "those wits that haunt / Those publique
circuits," the playhouses; says Drayton of the commercial dramatists,
"let them freely chaunt / Their fine Composures, and their praise
pursue." That Drayton fails to identify any of these working dramatists
suggests how his expression of kinship with them is animated less by
affection for the theatre than by a grudging acknowledgment of his
own professional status. The epistle's intimacy, as personal correspondence and fond reminiscence, may also suggest a deep desire on
Drayton's part to recreate something of the aura of the private chamber, not just the "well chosen place" of his evenings with Reynolds but
the select coterie where he, as both a professional and an oppositional
poet, could never quite belong. The "Epistle to Reynolds" reveals no
public poet striving to awaken his community to the productive energies and varieties of its literature. It shows rather a poet willing to
defend his professional status yet who wonders perhaps if his claim
for legitimacy has not cost him a measure of true distinction.

The Muses Elizium (1630) is a continuation of the "Epistle to Reynolds" insofar as it reifies as a "paradice on earth" the ultimate object
of Drayton's desire, a golden world of poetry "farre from vulgar sight"
(3:248). In this poem, Drayton's self-defining nostalgia is itself recast
in presentist terms, as history and oppositional politics are translated
into topography: the pastoral age of Elizabeth lies alongside the
courtly "iron" province of "Felicia," Drayton's "Latin equivalent for the
Greek word that gave the title of Poly-Olbion."[72] Drayton casts himself
as the old satyr who has fled Felicia to find sanctuary in the Elizian
fields, far from the "beastly Brood" (3:324). Abandoning the laureate's

mission to empower his culture, Drayton, who in his final years would be a member of the idyllic Dorset household at Knole, escapes his disappointments by creating a consoling fiction where he might "live in blisse" (3:325). "Pastorals that celebrate the ideal of content," Montrose has suggested, "function to articulate – and thereby, perhaps, to assuage – *dis*content."[73] Where Drayton, in his earlier pastorals, made definite gestures to the world of real affairs, the "ideal of content" in *The Muses Elizium* is reserved for the disaffected poet, while all discontent is attributed to the world and public obligations he has left behind. In this way, *The Muses Elizium* recalls less the pastorals of Spenser and the early Drayton, where there is exalted "the most High, and most Noble Matters of the World," than the aristocratic fictions of Sidney (2:517). "Ease," says Kalander in *Arcadia*, is "the Nurse of Poetrie."[74] With *The Muses Elizium*, Drayton lays claim to this "ease." His poem is a final, great unburdening of *ressentiment*. Drayton, long critical of the insularity of private chambers, projects himself into precisely the kind of arcadian setting associated with the foremost of the coteries.

For a work said to describe the "Poets Paradice," *The Muses Elizium* contains few references to actual poets (3:251). There are the "Orgies" of the Muses in the third Nimphall, but no roll-call of fellow poet-shepherds as there is in Drayton's earlier *Shepheards Sirena*. Drayton has not only withdrawn from contemporary English life, he has forsaken the ideal of a literary tradition, the ideal he had so strongly affirmed in the "Epistle to Reynolds" and in his celebration of native bards. The only poet in *The Muses Elizium* is Drayton the satyr, though in this paradisial context he is a poet without purpose or modernity. In Elizium, the absolute presentist community, there can be no real change, and poetry can serve no function because there is no language to improve, no past to keep alive in verse, no literary tradition to renew. With *The Muses Elizium*, Drayton abandons his professional allies and retreats into pure art, into poetry as compulsion, into production without utility, into an autonomous aesthetic realm where the poet may disavow all interests and responsibilities. As C.S. Lewis has said, the best sections of Drayton's poem "teach nothing, assert nothing, depict almost nothing ... [They are] without weight, ready to leave the earth."[75]

3 The Uses of the Dead

A significant exception to the courtly aversion to print was the funeral elegy, which all poets, career and coterie, would permit to be published in honour of the recently deceased. The solemnity of the occasion, and the seemliness of publicly registering respect for the dead, evidently obviated any embarrassment the poet or his subject might have felt about appearing in print. That the many elegists who mourned Sidney or Prince Henry agreed to do so in print may also suggest an implicit recognition that the printed work was a fit memorial because not only could it be broadly distributed but also it stood a better chance of survival than the private manuscript. A published collection of elegies offered the poet an opportunity to be published in the company of his peers and betters, as would happen with commendatory verses, yet it also allowed the poet to influence with more seriousness than puffery how the subject might be remembered in posterity. Because it held out the possibility of enacting evaluative closure on the subject's writings, the elegy was the pre-eminent poetic genre for rhetorical consecration; this, despite the fact that the nature of elegizing required the poet to confront sentiments that would seem to detract from any thought of literary posterity – sentiments about temporality, mourning shading into self-mourning, the inadequacy of words in expressing loss, and the sense that poetic immortality, the supplementarity of writing beyond the writer's death, may not quite compensate for the fact of human mortality.

In the earliest significant literary elegies, such as Dunbar's "Lament for the Makaris," the making of a canon of dead poets seems only to inspire such sentiments and to confirm death's inexorability. The hope of poetic immortality has no meaning for Dunbar, who sees only the transitoriness and "vane glory" of "Our plesance heir."[1] Yet the effect of the poem, as in most elegies, is paradoxical since death's certainty is matched by the poem's in its refrain. The poem performs an instrumental function even as it asserts the futility of action: so long as poetry exists to articulate a consciousness of mortality, death cannot conquer all. And the fuller Dunbar makes his canon, the more the poem registers ambivalence, for even as there have been so many who have succumbed to physical death, there remain many who have retained an enigmatic identity long after the entombment of the body – "noble Chaucer," "the monk of Bery, and Gower," "Maister Robert Henrisoun," and so on. The movement of the poem is to show how Dunbar, though oppressed by death, is at the head of a tradition that keeps itself alive in and through writing. His self-mourning, like any elegist's, both asserts and defers ultimate closure in announcing a double repetition: death's eternal recurrence, and the ceaseless reproduction of discourse in response to death.

The monumentality of print seemed to magnify many of the paradoxes inherent in writing literary eulogies, as well as this sense of writing within a tradition, as evidenced by the flurry of poetic laments that greeted the successive deaths of Donne, Jonson, and others in the 1630s and 1640s. To some, the materiality of the printed book reinforced the immortality *topos*, as if the object and not just the discourse were capable of perpetuating its own value. Jonson, not surprisingly, invoked this theme in his testimonial before the First Folio: "Thou are a Moniment, without a tombe, / And art alive still, while thy Booke doth live" (*U.V.* 26:22–3).[2] This objectification of the self in print led some elegists to some grotesque identifications of body and text: Henry King assured Jonson that "*thy* Booke shall be *thy Tombe*, / Thou wilt goe downe a *happie Coarse*" (H&S 11:441). As Jonson had foreseen with the publication of his *Workes*, and as confirmed by many of his elegists, the sense of the printed text being an authentic reproduction of the author helped to crystallize the modern notion of author-centred value, fixed by a personal style and moral sensibility in the works and rendering accessible to posterity a unique writerly subjectivity: "Survey *him* in *his* WORKES, and know *him* there" (H&S 11:466). In linking canonical value to an author who could stand outside his context of production, these elegies thus seemed to be contributing to the slow process of cultural autonomization that marked the initial movement away from rhetoricist thinking. As I suggest in this chapter, many of these elegists resisted autonomization and sought rather to harmonize the canon as a means of maintaining their cultural supremacy, particularly following the collapse of their political authority in the period of civil war and Interregnum. These poets would have rather allowed the literary tradition to die than to have suffered their poetry to lose its verbal power in enhancing the effectivity of political discourse. In their desire to dominate canon-making, then, they virtually repudiated, through their gestures, the hope of an enduring indigenous literature.

ELEGIES TO DONNE AND JONSON

Because they were honouring a subject whose poetry had rarely been made public, the coterie poets whose tributes appeared in the first collected edition of Donne's poetry in 1633 were far more sensitive than the sons of Ben to how print could determine an author's posthumous reputation. The edition was evidently the cause of some conflict between Donne's allies and the printer John Marriot, who, in the preface, referred conspicuously to the placement of the elegies at the rear rather than the front of the volume; this unusual arrangement, he claimed, was necessary so that the elegies – some of which had been written well in advance of their possibly unauthorized publication in the volume – would not be read as conventional "Encomiums of the Author" which functioned "in other workes ... to prepare men to digest such stuffe as follows after." Donne's poetry, Marriot declared, "hath the best warrant that can bee, publique authority, and private friends."[3] As I have noted, the notion that public scrutiny of literary works could be as legitimate a test of their value as their private circulation among a cultural elite was a theme commonly expressed during this period by those who opposed the insularity and absolutism of the Stuart court. In speaking up for the authority of the public, Donne's printer may have not only been signalling the increasing independence of the book trade but also obliquely indicating that he had met with courtly resistance in assembling the collection. Certainly, in relegating the elegies to the volume's final pages, the printer hoped to offset the elegists' clear intention of preparing the reader and serving, in King's phrase, as "thy Ashes Guardian," now that his early erotic lyrics were regrettably going to appear alongside the devotional verse of the revered dean of St Paul's (*DCH* 88).

The printer did allow two preliminary commendations, the second of which made clear the courtiers' anxieties: "Yet shew I thee a better way; / Print but his Sermons" (*DCH* 86). The advice going unheeded, damage control is the operative impulse behind most of the elegies.[4] Browne, whose elegy would not be reprinted in later editions of the collection, explicitly denounces "the *Promiscuous* printing of his Poems, the *Looser sort*, with the Religious," and hopes that there might eventually occur appropriate textual excisions that would the *"Fore-skinne* of thy phansie circumcise" (*DCH* 88). Several elegists dismiss the early verse as the productions of heedless youth, or ignore it altogether, emphasizing instead the achievements of the "more matur'd" Donne (*DCH* 92). Others attempt to forestall criticism with verbal antagonism: Walton condemns his "Dull age ... Of black ingratitude" for not adequately mourning Donne's death, while King, addressing Donne, attacks those "Which might prophane thee by their Ignorance" (*DCH* 92, 87). Above all, the elegists deploy a version of the inadequacy *topos* in their repeated claim that no one other than Donne himself can do a proper job of appreciating Donne. Arthur Wilson believes Donne's poems are likely to "lose the glory of their owne cleare bayes, / If they admit of any others praise" (*DCH* 100). Hyde tells Donne "there's not language knowne / Fit for thy mention, but 'twas first thy owne" (*DCH* 89). Even Carew's *tour de force* condensation of Donnian poetics is a version of the *topos*, literalizing as it did the notion that Donne can be praised only in his own mode of expression.[5]

The *topos* has a long history, deriving as it does from protestations of Christian humility and from antique rhetorical formulae of affected humility and incapacity. It is intended to detract from the presumption of the elegists, who make excuses as to why they feel obliged to write their elegies. Donne's elegists volunteer no such excuses, as though for them all elegies were in some sense inadequate, the only suitable response being silence. Richard Corbet says as much in his contribution to the Donne volume. "He that would write an Epitaph for thee," Corbet thinks, "must first beginne to be / Such as thou wert." Corbet maintains that no judgment does Donne justice if it is not identical to Donne's thinking. The elegist has either to imitate Donne faithfully or not to write at all: says Corbet, grimly, "Who then shall write an Epitaph for thee, / He must be dead first" (*DCH* 89–90). The inade-quacy *topos* is supposed to signal the literary tradition's indebtedness to the dead poet, whose influence is said to have been so extensive as to serve as a model for all subsequent production. Yet Corbet's extreme version of the commonplace, along with the notably under-stated articulation of the immortality *topos* in almost all the tributes, suggest that the elegists' overriding concern with protecting Donne's good name has led them to spurn the usual *consolatio* about how discourse may reproduce itself beyond the subject's death.

In extolling how Donne's poetry refined the "Muses garden" and "open'd Us a Mine / Of rich and pregnant phansie," Carew's elegy seems the anomaly in the collection (*DCH* 94). Though literary history associates Carew with the professional Jonson, he was in fact one of the more prominent defenders of Charles I's policy of courtly exclusivity and often expressed fierce animosity toward any notion of "publique authority." It was his attack against what he called the "untun'd Kennell" in the commercial theatres, consuming drama like a piece of "meat," that had provoked Massinger's furious retort.[6] Carew had counselled Jonson, after the failure of *The New Inn* (1629), against seeking "the extorted prayse / Of vulgar breath" (H&S 11:336), while on another occasion he took issue with the idea of the public becoming the arbiters of literary excellence, for that would allow them "an unsafe libertie / To use their Judgments as their tastes, which chuse / Without controule."[7] Yet perhaps because he had not written it with a view to publication, his elegy to Donne is the only one to celebrate openly and without embarrassment the early poet's achievement and to affirm, at the levels of both argument and style, Donne's productive influence on English poetry. And in deploying political metaphors to praise how "to the awe of thy imperious wit / Our stubborne language bends," Carew's elegy self-consciously recalls an earlier mode of commendation that stressed how the subject's eloquence had enhanced the language of political signification and so confirmed poetry's ongoing essentiality within the moral economy of the state. Carew thus appropriates Donne's symbolic value in the service of court ideology, since "describing Donne as a king whose absolute but not arbitrary exercise of power in the 'Monarchy of Wit' corresponds to Carew's flattering vision of Charles I in the political realm."[8]

The metaphors point another way, however, for just as Carew honours Donne for his "fresh invention," he also apotheosizes the poet as a transcendent formalist whose writings will not enable further productivity precisely because they represent an absolute and interable value, "The universall Monarchy of wit." Instead of heralding an emergent Donnian tradition in English poetry, Carew predicts cultural degeneration: Donne's "strict lawes will be / Too hard for Libertines in Poetrie," his refined verse will be displaced by "ballad rime," and ultimately the coming age will see

> The death of all the Arts, whose influence
> Growne feeble, in these panting numbers lies
> Gasping short winded Accents, and so dies   (*DCH* 94–5)

That this simulacrum of Donnian hyperbole is contradicted by Carew's own poem, which successfully executes Donne's poetic "laws," scarcely matters next to the intense rhetorical conviction, the sense both of Donne's inimitability and of cultural exhaustion, that Carew manages to work up in his poem, which proved far more effective at containing responses to Donne than any of the other elegies, as evidenced by Lord Herbert of Cherbury's verse reply to the 1633 edition:

Having delivered now what praises are,
It rests that I should to the world declare
Thy praises, DUNN, whom I so lov'd alive
That with my witty Carew I should strive
To celebrate the dead   (*DCH* 103–4)

It says something about the conflicts in the literary system of this period that the death of poetry has to be proclaimed in order to ensure Donne's consecration and ongoing productive influence. Whereas previous poets like Spenser could both assert their modernity by rejecting an immediate past and look forward to enabling a vital literary culture, the recent literary past is for eulogists like Carew a poetic *ne plus ultra*, whose momentousness is affirmed not simply by differentiating the subject's work from his rivals' but by symbolically renouncing the enabling circulation of value in posterity.

Carew's gesture of canonizing Donne by hailing him as the last poet would be later adopted by Donne's print-based rivals, the Tribe of Ben, for their memorial volume to their poetic father, the *Jonsonus Virbius* (1638), a volume suffused by anxieties of belatedness and by lamentations over an exhausted literary order. Standard accounts suggest that a cult of personality of unprecedented intensity had come to surround Jonson and that the Tribe could not adequately step out from the great poet's shadow.[9] As Randolph puts it in his elegy, the Sons of Ben had been "well content / To glory in the age of your great name" (H&S 11:390); "like Banckrupts in the stocke of Fame," adds Brideoake, "To patch our credit up, we use *thy* Name" (H&S 11:466). Some elegists take aim at Jonson's rivals, notably Shakespeare, or at his detractors – they are, in Henry Coventry's rebuke, nothing less than "*Parricides* in verse" – who had grown more numerous after the failure of *The New Inn* (H&S 11:442); others take to heart the hope of the volume's subtitle in declaring Jonson's poetic legacy "Revived by the Friends of the Muses" (H&S 11:429). But most see little prospect of a vital English tradition. Unable to detach themselves emotionally and creatively from Jonson at his death, these poets mourn not their own temporality but the end of poetry:

Ben is deceas'd, and (by his losse) I feare
A dearth wil follow, good wit wil be dear,
What, is the Muses treasurie exhausted?   (H&S 11:422)

Self-abasement becomes vulgar display as the elegists, surpassing conventional norms for encomiastic exaggeration, indulge in a pornography of failure and negation: Thomas May tells Jonson that "English *Poetry* is dead with Thee" (H&S 11:443); Coventry avers the sons have received "no hereditary beame of *Ben*" (H&S 11:442); without any genuine successor, writes Henry Ramsay, "JOHNSONS *Sceleton* is *Laureate*" (H&S 11:472). To Jasper Mayne, who was also one of Donne's elegists, Jonson's disciples are doomed to marginality in his absence: "So at *thy* fall, / Our *Witt, great* BEN, is too *Apocryphall*" (H&S 11:451). Posterity can be imagined only as backward-looking, postlapsarian: "Every *Age* will looke," writes Godolphin of Jonson's grave, "With *sorrow* heere, with *wonder* on *his* Booke" (H&S 11:450). "Whatsoere the *Subject* be," adds Vernon, "All *Verses* now become *thy* ELEGIE" (H&S 11:449).

In compensation for this productive loss, Jonson's life and writings may yet be valuable for pedagogic consumption. Cartwright promises Jonson that he shall be "read as Classick in *thy life*" (H&S 11:457). Similarly, Richard West predicts Jonson "shalt be read as *Classick* Authors; and / As *Greeke* and *Latine* taught in every Land" (H&S 11:470). These are probably the earliest usages of "classic" to refer to an English author and to proclaim his works worthy of institutional preservation, even if the teaching of those works would appear to serve no constructive purpose. Canon-formation may not be a late occurrence but the normative use of "classic" is. Just as the Latin term, which originally denoted the highest tax bracket, was first used to designate the top rank of authors only in the second century A.D., so its importation into English occurs only in the late 1620s, a time of increasing social divisiveness.[10] The reason for these late debuts is that the idea of the classic implies an awareness of belatedness and the burden of temporality. In these early usages, the term is meant to be taken as a sign of disaffection and despair for present conditions, which are felt to be undergoing a disabling change, a falling off from the absolute value embodied in the classic and in the age in which it was produced. The nomination of classics differs from earlier modes of canonization in that the classic is not said to facilitate ongoing production but may in fact augur its eventual cessation – an idea most fully articulated in T.S. Eliot's essay on the classic, which, he argued, both realizes and exhausts the language and culture of its origin, thereby leaving only "consciously impotent" latecomers in its wake.[11] Thus, Cartwright ends his elegy on a note of agitated self-criticism when he forecasts disaster for English literature:

> When we shall feed on *refuse offals*, when
> We shall from *corne* to *akornes* turne agen;
> Then shall we see that these two *names* are one,
> JOHNSON and *Poetry*, which now are gone.   (H&S 11:459)

The crisis rhetoric intensifies the paradoxes of elegy-writing to such an extreme that canonization seems pointless: English authors begin to be called "classics" at the very moment when English poetry is said to die. So stark are these restatements of the inadequacy *topos* that they threaten to disempower the romance of immortality, the supreme impetus behind all poetic production, including Jonson's.

The sheer number of elegies in the *Jonsonus Virbius*, not to mention the many answer elegies the volume inspired (H&S 11:481–94), at once attests to and belies the elegists' strong feelings of being poetically disenfranchised because of Jonson's death, which has, after all, given them occasion to write en masse. In a way not dissimilar from how Chaucer's disciples openly despaired of literary exhaustion as an oblique means of indicating their allegiance to an ideal of cultural conformism, Cartwright and the others are using the death of poetry as a lapsarian narrative to validate Jonson's consecration and to promote the harmonization of the canon, an ideal equally encoded in most of their other stock themes, such as Jonson's inimitability, which they invoke with numbing invariability: "None but *thyselfe* could *write* a *verse* for *thee*," poetizes Brideoake; of "Worthy *Expressions*," echoes Meade, "none can fully praise *thee* but *thy owne*" (H&S 11:468,471). In Beaumont's emphatic version, the commonplace that Jonson's verbal power could exert a harmonizing influence over English society comes close to resembling a satire on the energetic networkings of rhetorical culture:

> he made our Language pure and good,
> To teach us speake, but what we understood, ...
> His wit and language still remaine the same
> In all mens mouths; Grave Preachers did it use
> As golden Pills, by which they might infuse
> Their Heavenly Physicke; Ministers of State
> Their grave dispatches in his language wrate;
> Ladies made cur'tsies in them, Courtiers, legs,
> Physicians Bills, ...   (H&S 11:438–9)

West forecasts even greater conquests: because of Jonson, the English language is "now all *harmony*," and even "Strangers, who cannot reach *thy sense*, will throng / To heare us speake the *Accents* of *thy Tongue* / As unto *Birds* that sing" (H&S 11:470).

By proclaiming a harmonious canon in the guise of a universally valued patrimony bequeathed by Jonson, and by insisting on the irreproducibility of that inheritance in any other terms but its own, the elegists were engaging not simply in a campaign to enshrine Jonson's authority but in the further autonomization of that aesthetic authority from external moral, political, or economic constraints, an autonomization signalled in West's idealization of a purely formal harmony without "sense" and in the readiness of all the elegists to situate value exclusively in the figure of the author. Such autonomization permitted the elegists, among other things, to misrecognize the complex relations of power that ensured their continued legitimacy as canon-makers. In their view, the mechanisms of reception and reproduction served only to reinforce their structure of conviction:

> The *Court*, the *Universitie*, the heat
> Of *Theaters*, with what can else beget
> Beliefe, and admiration, cleerely prove
> Our POET fi[nes]t in *merit*, as in *love*   (John Ford, in H&S 11:466)

That only a few of the elegists were actually intent on making English poetry conform strictly to Jonson's model did not diminish the force of their project, whose aim was the containment of the literary system, a massive demonstration of tribalistic power over who could participate, and on what terms, in the ongoing production of poetry and the formation of its canon. With its answering elegists scrambling to join the parade once it became clear that, in the words of one, "everie pen shedds inke, to swell a page / in Johnsons Elegies," the *Jonsonus Virbius* succeeded in establishing itself as one of the age's most prestigious vehicles for poetic expression and for claiming distinction in an increasingly unsettled cultural field (H&S 11:485). Looking back a tumultuous decade later, Marvell, in his verses before Lovelace's *Lucasta* (1649), acknowledged that epideictic verses like those to Jonson had functioned for a generation of courtly wits as a vehicle for maintaining their perpetually self-legitimizing conversation: "Who best could prayse, had then the greatest prayse."[12] Many similar volumes, like the set of academic exercises for the obscure Edward King that included *Lycidas*, were undertaken during this period.[13] But with their symbolic violence of pronouncing poetry dead, and of centring value in the author rather than in any broad moral economy, Jonson's elegists made the strongest bid for the exclusivity and productive autonomy of their Cavalier poetics.

PROVING WIT BY POWER

When many of these same elegists gathered a dozen years later to honour one of their own, their expressions of grief had become an outlet for rather different feelings of political belatedness. The record-setting spectacle of fifty-three commendations before Cartwright's *Comedies, Tragi-Comedies, with other Poems* (1651) was plainly a reflexive show of unity among an oppressed group of courtiers recently stripped of their long-held hegemonic power. The real purpose of the Cartwright memorial was signalled by the fact that it appeared some eight years after the dramatist's death but a mere two years after the execution of King Charles in January 1649. Parliament had severely restricted public mourning for Charles. The Cartwright collection was one of several tributes to minor figures, like the earlier elegies to Lord Hastings in *Lachrymae Musarum* (1649), that functioned as thinly disguised laments for the English crown and as opportunities for the Cavaliers to use elegiac conventions for political subversion.[14] In several verses, Cartwright's untimely death is paralleled with the king's, giving ideological point, in Alexander Brome's version, to the familiar *consolatio* of immortality: "So 'tis decreed, spite of Fatality / *Poets, like kings, shall never, nor can dye*" (sig. ***5ᵣ). The further parallel between the date of Cartwright's death and the outbreak of war underscores Richard Iles's contribution, where he announces the death of poetry, as Cartwright had done in the Jonson volume:

So by thy Works Posterity shall know
The merits of thy Age, before the Flow
And Deluges of Blood, which Wars did bring
T'orecome the World, and drown the Muses Spring.   (sig. **7ᵥ)

Still, there is a marked difference in tone between these elegies and the earlier tributes to Jonson, for despite their collective anxiety over the passing of the monarchic order and the consequent degeneration of English cultural life, few speak of literary exhaustion or the impossibility of writing in the absence of paternal authority. On the contrary, several elegists insist on the vitality of the literary tradition, creating for Cartwright a suitably distinguished lineage ("He may be *Johnson's* Grand-Child, *Fletchers* Son," sig. b2ᵥ), which unites former rivals ("In thee *Ben Johnson* still held *Shakespeare's* Quill," sig. b4ᵥ) and begets a Cavalier dynasty in poetry ("from thine Issue a whole *Myriad* springs, / To populate the world: and make us be / *Wits* by a Lineall *Genealogy*," sig. ***5ᵣ).

The Cartwright volume incorporates a number of different political uses of canon-formation. In addition to appropriating the established canon in the service of Royalist propaganda, the elegists were also using the occasion to declare and consolidate their own group allegiances in adverse times. John Leigh's tribute, in particular, functions as a canonizing roll-call of Cavalier wits: Suckling, Carew, Waller, Beaumont and Fletcher, Denham, Newcastle, Davenant, Stapylton, Stanley, Sherburne, Heath, Crashaw, Shirley, "Benlowe's Quarls," Mayne, Cleveland, Berkenhead, Cowley, "Vincent," and "Brown" ("true

Wits though not so publike known," sig. *1$_{r-v}$). Furthermore, the Cartwright volume was one of many similar endeavours by the book-seller Humphrey Moseley aimed at establishing a prestigious author-centred royalist canon, whose cornerstone had been his sumptuous Beaumont and Fletcher folio of 1647, for which he had likewise solicited a conspicuous number of commendatory verses.[15] In monu-mentalizing the works of Caroline dramatists, Moseley was symbolically avenging Parliament's closure of the theatres. As Brome remarked, the Beaumont and Fletcher folio provided the dispersed Cavaliers with the means to gather "in a Troupe t'advance contemned Playes, / And bring exploded *Witt* againe in fashion" (sig. f3$_r$).[16] That Cartwright was an Oxonian divine also gave his commenders the opportunity to retaliate for the successive purges of "the *Court*, and *University*, / (Th'old standing Judges of good *Poetry*)" (sig. [****]3$_r$).[17]

The most interesting Royalist use of canonicity, however, relates to what had seemed in the earlier elegies to Jonson an increasing auton-omization of aesthetics. Annabel Patterson has argued that seventeenth-century authors learned to evade censorship by shrouding their polit-ically sensitive material behind what she calls a "functional ambiguity," a private language that had the ultimate effect of generating the modern view of literature as a peculiarly refined discourse "with rules of its own."[18] There is much evidence to support this argument, as Lois Potter has recently demonstrated, though Patterson's conclusions about the historical development of literature may be somewhat mis-leading. While Royalist writers often emphasized a philosophy of secrecy and even mystery, their system of functional ambiguity oper-ated more like a sophisticated mode of covert allegorization rather than a symbolist poetics of fruitful hermeneutic indeterminacy, of the type that was to be later identified with "literature" in response to the increasing commodification of literary works in the eighteenth century – the contrast here being between a view of meaning that treats it as fixed if highly indirect, and one that sees it as knowable yet multiform and inexhaustible. Such allegorization indicated less a formalization or distillation of verbal art as its radical politicization both inward, in terms of the partisan encoding of rhetorical conventions, and outward, in the application of poetic figuration within a wide variety of verbal and visual discourses. Indeed, in seeking workable vehicles for the transmission of anti-government sentiment, Royalist writers were keen on extending the parameters of polite literature, first to take advan-tage of the disseminatory powers of print, and then to include both colloquialisms and a number of formerly discredited genres, including satire, journalism, romances, and even pornography. Although the courtly aversion to print would temporarily reassert itself following the Restoration, this redefinition of literature's constituent modes and idioms would prove instrumental in the development and ascendancy of Augustan satire, and in the gradual dismantling of both the classicist hierarchy of genres and the rhetorical ideal of eloquence.

Just as much as political oppression led Royalist writers to engage in a highly codified discourse of secrecy and dissimulation, it also led them to embrace opposing principles they had formerly inveighed against, freedom of speech and the idea of determining canonicity by readerly suffrage. Defending the theatre, the commenders in the Cartwright and Beaumont and Fletcher volumes openly celebrated its public nature: to Thomas Philipott, Cartwright embodied a "publique Genius" (sig. ***6$_r$). Other elegists introduced the idea of a trial for authors, an idea most commonly associated with Samuel Johnson, though first (dismissively) proposed by Horace:

> For the try'd Author's Name
> Hath past the test of Fame;
> So known *Classick* Wit,
> That none will question it   (sig. b$_r$)

Uncertain of their audience, the Cavaliers look forward to the verdicts of public authority in posterity. "He shall be read as Canon, / to express what's fit and best," Ralph Bathurst predicts, punning on Cartwright's clerical calling (sig. **2$_v$). The sheer number, as well, of commenders – "we grant here are more than before other Books, and yet we give you not all we have," Moseley assures his reader (sig. a2$_r$) – suggests an implicit dual acknowledgment: first, of the power of published discourse and mass representation, rather than of mere privilege, in the promotion of literary works; and secondly, of the normative authority of public opinion, which the commenders are attempting to influence through their formation of a Caroline canon.

These gestures toward canon-formation by consensus may scarcely approach in seriousness the designs of their republican opponents, notably James Harrington's recommendation in his *Oceana* (1656) that Poets Laureate be elected by popular assembly.[19] Yet the appeals to posterity and public authority nonetheless point to the Royalists' over-riding concern with maintaining their hegemony, if not in a political sphere, then in the perhaps equally crucial sphere of culture. The group exercises, like the Cartwright tributes, may seem to be merely attempts to lift morale and to find some emotional solace in the act of harmonizing the canon along neoclassicist principles.[20] But these compensations were by no means insignificant in a rhetorical culture, whose identity and sense of community depended on a perpetual exchange of verbal persuasions; the symbolic capital which could be gained from exercising dominion over cultural production was closely identified with political authority, whose legitimacy could not be long maintained without the deployment of verbal power. The Royalist wits did not have any genuine political role to fulfil, while the loss of the court and the unsettlement of patronage and audience entailed for their culture its effective disjuncture from all political authority. Even as that culture was experiencing for the first time the severe constraints of political oppression and the consequent exigency of promulgating royalist interests through any available means, aesthetics for the Cavaliers had become, as if by cruel circumstance, autonomized from politics to the extent that literature could no longer assuredly enhance the language of political signification. The Cavaliers' response of politicizing literature enabled them to conduct subversion, to evade censorship, and, above all, to resist the marginalization of their verbal power in the political economy of the state. Yet in the absence of state subvention and courtly authority, particularly after the defeat of 1648, culture became the only field in which the Cavaliers could maintain legitimacy and acquire profits, symbolic if not political or economic. In the words of one contemporary observer, the royalist "cause was devolved from Arms to Pens."[21]

They asserted this legitimacy in part by ridiculing an ostensible republican philistinism. The Cavaliers cast themselves as the curators of high culture, under attack from theatre-hating Puritans and canon-bashing egalitarians seeking to eliminate all distinctions of value. "Were not State-*Levellers* enough!" cried Sherburne before the Cartwright volume, "that yet / We must be plagu'd with Levellers of Wit?" (sig. b*$_r$). The literary tradition was itself appropriated in the struggle: the prologue to the scurrilous *Second Part of Crafty Crumwell* (1648) calls upon "the whole crowd of Poets" from Seneca and Sophocles to Shakespeare, Jonson, Webster, "*Sucklin*, and *Goffe*" to "Blast their black soules, who do despise their laies."[22] More commonly, the Royalists claimed cultural distinction by citing their superior "ease" at poetry, a productivity which, they declared, was indication that they alone knew how to wield the civilizing force of eloquence. The pamphlet prose of the Puritans, they insisted, provoked social divisiveness and conflict, as though their heavy reliance on unmetrical polemics, however effective at mobilizing the populace, signalled their political illegitimacy. Only the "powerful rhythmes" of poetry, wrote Alexander Brome before Lovelace's *Lucasta* in 1649, could redeem

the thick darkness of these *Verseless* times:
These *antingenius* daies, this boystrous age,
Where there dwels nought of *Poetry* but rage ...
Though *Pulpiteers* can't do it, yet 'tis fit
Poets have more *success*, because more *wit*.
Their *Prose* unhing' the State; why may'nt your verse
Polish those souls, that were fil'd rough by theirs?[23]

The frequency with which Royalist wits appeared in elegies and commendatory verses may have likewise served to demonstrate their poetic facility, as if exposure alone could ensure them not only a high profile but ongoing dominance of the cultural field. Some Cavaliers, such as Stanley, Cokayne, and Sheppard, devoted much of their poetic output to epigrams, encomiastic verses, and literary catalogues in which they would memorialise their friends, and their friends' books, with the implicit aim of affirming their political solidarity and cultural authority by the insistent collocation of names. Said a critic of the Cartwright volume, the Cavaliers were out to "prove Wit by Power."[24]

In this effort, they were not altogether successful, which made for some cynicism. No amount of special pleading could install a minor figure like Cartwright in the upper ranks of the canon, while the rage for puffery came to a sudden halt in 1653 when the excessive praise conferred on *Gondibert* by members of the exiled court was ridiculed in a popular collection of mock-commendations written by Denham and other wits based in England.[25] Nonetheless, writing poems remained for the Cavaliers an expression as much of commitment as of hostility: "it is Counsel now to fight the times, / Not in picht Prose, but Verse, and flying rymes."[26] On occasion, this defiance in rhyme caught the attention of Commonwealth authorities. Derek Hirst cites the example of one Royalist activist who was imprisoned on the eve of the southwestern rising of 1655 for publishing a pamphlet collection of tributes to Jonson that was intended to serve as an incitment to rebellion.[27] Such radicalization of literature was designed to counter the autonomization of aesthetics that was threatening to render eloquence politically irrelevant. The Royalists' frequent group appearances in print, along with their tributes to late colleagues, were means of vaunting their productivity and canonical status as evidence of a rightful claim to political supremacy. The fact that they had repeatedly to assert this correspondence between verbal and temporal power, and that their canonizing efforts were largely ineffective politically, suggests, however, that the gradual process of autonomization, accelerated by war yet begun earlier, could not be reversed. The structure of conviction that had supported the totalizing courtly economy, where kings could be received as poets and poets as kings, could not be long maintained in a situation where writing, on either side, had done nothing to prevent revolution and much to foment it – though, for obvious reasons, the Puritans' faith in the Word was greatly reinforced. Although ideals of cultural advancement and hierarchy would be affirmed with renewed emphasis after the return of the monarchy, politics during the Restoration would become secularized, pragmatized, cynical.[28] Poets might continue to pay obeisance to ideals of civic humanism and social harmony, and to draw their legitimacy from their patrons and their relationship to the court, but the ultimate source of value could soon no longer be confidently situated in the verbal power of the state.

"NOR LET US CALL HIM FATHER ANIE MORE"

If the autonomization of aesthetics seemed inevitable, the Cavaliers nonetheless found that they could maintain their social legitimacy through a display of symbolic capital. This lesson would not be lost on their successors among the intellectual elites of the Restoration period, for whom a new cultural absolutism could provide an adequate supplement or even substitute for a failing political absolutism. This cultural absolutism, inspired by the success of its French equivalent, came in the form of a heightened appeal for decorum, regularity, and uniformity. Neoclassicism, still eminently serviceable as a narrative for presentist self-definition and self-promotion, was codified and rigidified into a set of critical formalisms, as though methodizing aesthetic practice could compensate for the dissolution of conviction about the source of value in society. In what is sometimes taken to be a manifesto for Augustan neoclassicism, the preface to Joshua Poole's rhetorical handbook *The English Parnassus* (1657), the ideal of communal solidarity through verbal power has become the patrician goal of refining manners through a correct style: "*We* are then to note, that as the world became more and more civilized, *Harmony*, I mean that of speech and mutual expression one to another, grew more and more into reputation. Hence it is that those languages are considered as the most refined that are most susceptible of *Harmony*, and those most savouring of incivility and *barbarisme*, wherein a man cannot expresse himselfe without harshnesse and discord."[29] One consequence of this formalist discourse was a relative stabilization of the literary system. Although authorial competitiveness and conflicts continued to erupt with undiminished rancour in an ever-growing print culture, poets from Dryden to Pope could define their modernity by reference to notions of formal refinement rather than solely in opposition to their immediate predecessors or rivals. The modern canon was therefore markedly less subject to revision than it had been at the beginning of the seventeenth century: Waller and Denham could enjoy pride of place in the canon for upwards of a century after their deaths, even if their high standing was owing less to what they actually wrote than to the aesthetic paradigms they purportedly represented.

At the same time, the demands of absolutism meant that the canon had almost to be purged of authors who failed to evince an adequate regard for the rules. Shakespeare would be the major topic for debate among Restoration critics, though for the Cavaliers a more problematic case was Chaucer. It has often been noted that Chaucer's reputation fell to its nadir in the mid-seventeenth century. His works had not been republished since Speght's black-letter edition of 1598, though they were evidently still being read, or at least alluded to, by amateur scholars and collectors like Pepys.[30] Edward Phillips, writing in the mid-1670s, reports that Chaucer "through all the neglect of former ag'd Poets still keeps a name, being by some few admir'd for his real worth, to others not unpleasing for his facetious way, which joyn'd with his old *English* intertains them with a kind of Drollery."[31] That Chaucer's language was considered obscure and inadmissable under prevailing standards of eloquence had been true for generations, though as late as 1622 Henry Peacham could still find under Chaucer's "bitter and rough rinde ... a delicate kernell of conceit and sweete invention."[32] The fitful acknowledgment of "his real worth" notwithstanding, the "Father of English poetry" had retained his title in the canon for largely unreflective reasons: the impulse to provide English literary history with a plausible origin, or perhaps a more instinctive desire to maintain the canon's immortalizing authority by making it seem enduring.

The early seventeenth century witnessed several attempts to rehabilitate Chaucer's works for a modern audience. Sometime in the 1610s, Richard Brathwait began to draft his *Comment upon ... The 'Miller's Tale' and the Wife of Bath* (first published in 1665), which offered loose paraphrases of the texts. A modernization of the first three books of *Troilus and Criseyde* was produced around 1630 "for the satisfaction of those Who either cannot, or will not take ye paines to understand The Excellent Authors Farr more Exquisite, and significant Expressions Though now growen obsolete, and out of use."[33] This was followed five years later by the first instalment of Sir Francis Kynaston's Latin translation of the poem (only his parallel-text edition of the first two books was ever published).[34] Kynaston's version indicates that there was interest in sustaining formal recognition of Chaucer's works and even in recuperating his good name on behalf of courtly culture; Kynaston himself believed that the *Troilus* contained many instructive models of courtesy and heroism that ought to be made accessible to youth as well as foreigners. Kynaston's concern with readerly comprehension, manifested in his extensive explanatory annotation, was highly unusual for the period, particularly in being applied to the writings of a medieval vernacular poet. Yet, however forward-looking, his work would be soon forgotten. Kynaston's translation remains a curious footnote to literary history, though odder yet are its English commendations, several of which suggest that Kynaston's efforts are intended to make a Cavalier out of Chaucer: "in White Hall appeare, among those men / For whom thou'lt joy thou art alive agen" (sig. *4$_r$). To Thomas Reade, refurbishing Chaucer into a courtier reaffirms the staying power of verse, which had been obscured by the apparent threat of verbal obsolescence:

CHAUCER, thou wert not dead; nor can we feare
Thy death, that hast out liv'd three hundred yeare.
Thou were but out of fashion; then admit
This courtly habit, which may best befit
Thee and the times.   (sig. **$_r$).

That Kynaston's translation is not without political import is brought home in another testimonial, where the connection is made between Chaucer's welcome at Whitehall and his similar reception in Rome:

surely when the Pope
Shall heare of this and all the sacred Troupe
Of Cardinalls peruse the Worke, and theyle all
In generall Councell mak't Canonicall.   (sig. **$_v$)

Once a Lollard hero in the eyes of Protestant radicals, Chaucer is now Charles's literary emissary to the Vatican.

To the Cavaliers, Chaucer's poetry may have been a significant cultural document but not a canonical text. As another of Kynaston's commenders put it, "the Translation will become / Th' Originall; while that growes dumbe" (sig. *4$_v$). Chaucer's language had little verbal power and, though his writings might still be commendable in substance, they had lost their instrumental effectivity. The act of reclaiming a venerable author like Chaucer for the Caroline court may have had a momentary appeal for the Cavaliers but more significant for them was how, in epitomizing the inevitable decay of language, his name and works could be useful in accentuating rhetorical valuations. The Laudian divine Thomas Jackson could defend the necessity of applying priestly interpretations to scriptural obscurities by citing the example of the vernacular: "our posterity within few years will hardly understand some passages in the Fairy Queen, or in Mother Hubbards, or other tales in Chaucer."[35] Pseudo-Chaucerian idioms could be a convenient device for denoting naivety and rusticity, as in the parodic *A Canterbury Tale Translated* (1641), a satire on Laud and his followers. A "J. Chaucer, junior" contributed one of the Cavalier mockcommendations appended to James Strong's *Joanereidos* (1645), an account of how the women of Lyme Regis repelled a Royalist assault on their town.[36] Still yet, Chaucer could signify for anti-Puritan polemicists a world well lost. Reporting on a series of Christmas riots in Kent, the Royalist *Kingdomes Weekly Intelligencer* for 4 January 1648 described how war had rendered people neglectful of their traditions: "It hath been the custome heretofore to passe away the sloth of these Winter nights with a Canterbury tale or two out of *Chaucer*, but the Gravity of these Times not admitting of such vanities, *Canterbury* hath been at this season so unhappy as to make a tale of herself."[37]

These examples suggest that Chaucer had retained something of a ghostly presence in the popular imagination, if mainly as a symbol of time's ravages. This iconic power may explain why Kynaston's commenders sought to recover Chaucer for the English court and why, after the failure of Kynaston's translation, an effort was made to dislodge Chaucer from the canon. His name was dropped from authorial catalogues, including the formerly comprehensive lists of the canon-matchers: "There is no sort of verse either ancient, or Modern which we are not able to equall by Imitation: we have our English *Virgil, Ovid, Seneca, Lucan, Juvenal, Martial,* and *Catullus*: In the *Earle of Surry, Daniell, Johnson, Spencer, Donne, Shakespeare,* and the glory of the rest *Sandys,* and *Sydney*."[38] Chaucer had become an impediment to proclaiming the modernity of the English canon, which had to be revised in order to preserve its harmony. The most explicit argument for such presentist revision was put forward by the Royalist George Daniel, in a poem entitled "An Essay; Endeavouring to ennoble our English Poesie by evidence of latter quills; and rejecting the former" (1646?).[39] English poetry, Daniel claims, would be better off if Chaucer were no longer uncritically heralded as its patriarch, since his instrumental utility in inspiring contemporary productivity has long since been exhausted:

>   in-authenticke Chaucer's furnishment,
> Adds nothing to our Poesie, in his Store;

Nor let us call him Father anie more ...
Why may not wee better exempt his Name
Then use it? adding nothing to our ffame;
And take the Radix of our Poesie
To honour more in this last Centurie,
The noble Sidney; Spencer lieving Still,
In an abundant fancie; Jonson's Quill
Ever admir'd; these justly wee may call
Fathers; high-placed in Apolloe's Hall.

A blind veneration of native traditions, according to Daniel, has hindered the English from equalling the glory of true antiquity, "the Catalogue of Splendent Rome." Without Chaucer, English poetry will be "noble," "heroicke," a "faire pedigree." The excision of Chaucer from the canon will reinvigorate the literary system, whose working values Daniel, in his related catalogue "A Vindication of Poesie," identifies exclusively with Cavalier poetics. These and not Chaucer, he contends, will "advance / Our English honour."[40]

Declaring Chaucer poetically dead was tantamount to admitting that no English writing could be expected to last. Waller says as much in his poem "Of English Verse," where he claims that Chaucer's example confronts living poets with an intimation of their own mortality, of their words and music fading into obsolescence and oblivion: "*Chaucer* his Sense can only boast, / The glory of his Numbers lost, / Years have defac'd his matchless strain."[41] English poets, Waller suggests, should hope for no more than the solace of "present Love." As in the earlier elegies to Donne and Jonson, the symbolic violence of forecasting poetry's eventual demise was an extreme, embattled gesture at containing the literary system and asserting one's modernity – embattled, because of an anxious recognition that, in a time of social fragmentation, the circulation of cultural value is uncertain and potentially unproductive. Such gestures would soon seem unreasonable and embarrassing in an increasingly objectivist culture, where the making of canons would be considered absurd without a belief in history and a hope in posterity. What Daniel and Waller had done, it would appear, was to resign themselves to the very real yet intolerable contradiction that the making and revising of canons could not but affirm the death of poetry. Hoping to avoid this contradiction, canon-makers in the later seventeenth century begin to insist less on revising the canon as a harmonious similitude and more on treating it as a vital if changing tradition. Notably, there appear fewer Drayton-like catalogues of English authors in Restoration poetry but among the few are several imitations of Ovid's *Amores* 1.15 that are expressly intended to contradict the claims of "detracting Censurers, that the Fame of Poets is Eternal."[42] That Chaucer's name heads the canon in all these rolls suggests that Waller is among the chief targets of these exercises. Yet keeping Chaucer in the canon entails rethinking the nature of literary value. Even more strikingly than the problem of Shakespeare, positioning Chaucer in the canon presented a dilemma for late-seventeenth-century critics, because it involved a difficult compromise between classicist principles and nationalist sentiment, and, more important, because it impelled them to reconsider, if only tentatively, the definition of canonicity that had been for centuries based on the social, political, and cultural idealization of verbal power. Chaucer's language is old, Phillips concedes, but this cannot be just cause for burying his name. To reject Chaucer the father is to reject writing: "if no Poetry should Pleas but what is calculated to every refinement of a Language, of how ill consequence this would be for the future let him consider and make it his own case, who, being now in fair repute & promising to himself a lasting Fame, shall two or three Ages hence, when the Language comes to be double refin'd, understand ... that his Works are become obsolete and thrown aside."[43] Until Dryden would dramatically revaluate the criteria for canonicity in his Preface to the *Fables* (1700), few critics would have anything positive to say about Chaucer though none would deny him his place in the canon.

PART THREE

Defining a Cultural Field

4 Value into Knowledge

The resistance to rhetoric is a feature and perhaps a function of rhetoric itself, and many of the ablest orators have on occasion renounced Parnassus – "for the future," Milton angrily tells the English people in his *First Defence*, "know that words are subordinate to things, not things to words."[1] With the cessation of civil war, in which the utmost tyrannic energies of rhetoric seemed to have been expended, there was sounded the loudest and most persuasive appeal for its resistance, an appeal launched possibly because the apparently victorious Royalist side had profited least from the exercise of verbal power in combating revolution. "And now, when mens minds are somewhat settled," wrote Sprat, rhetoric could be reformed so as "to render our Country a Land of *Experimental Knowledge*." Though rhetoric could not be entirely abolished, Sprat believed, ideally "*eloquence* ought to be banish'd out of all *civil Societies*, as a thing fatal to Peace and good Manners."[2] The ascendancy of a conformist and isomorphic "plain style" during the late seventeenth century, a development commonly identified with the language projects of the Royal Society, may not have entailed as radical a denial of the figural and tropological dimensions of language as it has formerly been supposed, but it did involve an extensive rethinking of verbal power as a source and instrument of value. A new emphasis on probabilistic knowledge, involving the apparent acceptance of contingency, made for a sceptical reassessment of rhetoric's universalizing claims: "Eloquence, the Dress of our Thoughts, like the Dress of our Bodies, differs not only in several Regions, but in several Ages ... And oftentimes in That, as in Attire, what was Lately Fashionable, is Now Ridiculous, and what Now makes a Man look like a Courtier, may within these Few Lustres make him look like an Antick."[3] The statement, from Robert Boyle's 1661 treatise on scriptural style, might not have seemed too remarkable in an earlier age, recalling as it does the formulas of renunciation. Nonetheless, it is representative of an increasingly objectivist mode of thought that would bring about a redefinition of the criteria for canonicity, criteria whose certification would be based less on verbal suasion than proof and its analysis.

It is perhaps likewise a function of modernism that its grand narrative must in every generation be retold in new constructions: Enlightenment; the emergence of Man, Mind, Self, and Nature; the dissociation of sensibility; the rise of empirical science and of the human sciences; the turn to epistemology; the triumphs of method, rationality, probability, and historicism; secularization and the expression of a self-assertive will; the displacement of feudalism and political absolutism by capitalism and bourgeois liberalism; and even the postmodernist rejection of "grand narratives," to name only a few of the most familiar versions. Rhetorical valorizations and oscillations may be embedded in each of these narratives, though they all presuppose a desire to arrive at knowledge of modern experience, a desire whose articulation as a mode of evaluation I have been calling "objectivism." The inadequacy of this term, its brutal simplification of most of the grand narratives I have just listed, is intended to reflect the largely unsystematic way in which canon-formation in the early modern era was altered under pressure from the above historic changes as well as from more material circumstances such as the coming of print. This chapter considers a few of these unsystematic adjustments within Restoration criticism as they relate to notions about the possible sources of literary value, to arguments about what kind of values are to be prized in canonical works, and to claims for the contingent nature of evaluation. Trying to account for the prevalence of change and diversity in human affairs, critics like Dryden, I suggest, began positing a variety of phenomenal foundations for value, foundations which they believed would provide them with at least a partial solution to the relativity of values that their historicist understanding of contingency seemed to present. Yet the solution also required them to reconsider the value and function of literature, in its relation to knowledge, language, and historical change. Dryden, I argue, was the first critic to deal seriously with the paradoxical nature of value, and the first to invoke an historicist interpretation of changing circumstances in defending a plural canon of English literature.

THE GROUNDS OF VALUE

Until the last laureate poet, Pope, would declare its irrelevance in his later satires, most poets who paid court to kings and patrons could abide by the conventional belief that verbal power was vital to the dynamic circulation of value within the moral economy of the state, and that such value could, in principle, be traced to God or at least to the beneficient rule of his temporal sovereign on earth. Dryden, like others, could attribute his age's "refinement of wit" to political restoration and "particularly to the King, whose example gives a law to it" (1:178,181).[4] Under Charles II's influence, wrote Dryden, "our way of living became more free: and the fire of the English wit, which was before stifled under a constrained, melancholy way of breeding, began first to display its force, by mixing the solidity of our nation with the air and gaiety of our neighbours" (1:182). The *Defence of the Epilogue* (1672), in which Dryden makes this claim, may be exceptional among his critical writings in its presentist canonizing, dogmatically contrasting as it does the "vigour and maturity" of the contemporary theatre to the "ill-bred and clownish" wit of the Elizabethan dramatists (1:172,180). Yet Dryden was generally more willing than most poets of the period to equate the source of value with the king, value that for Dryden, on the evidence of his epistle to Charleton, could generate as much the new ideal of scientific knowledge as the advance of eloquence.

The *Defence of the Epilogue* contains, however, a hint of Dryden's characteristically sceptical self-modulation, since he contends that, despite the evident pre-eminence of the language and manners of his times, he can "claim no victory from our wit." Its "advantages," he maintains, can be ascribed merely "to the age" (1:169); or, as he puts it in the epilogue he is defending, "If love and honour now are higher rais'd, / 'Tis not the poet but the age is prais'd" ("Epilogue to the Second Part of *Granada*," 1:167). Dryden seems to believe that the cause of victory, "the age," can be distinguished from its beneficiaries, as though neither his fellow wits nor even the king can take ultimate credit for the victory. Dryden, in his conclusion, allows his generation only a muted triumph: "Without assuming to ourselves the title of better Poets, let us ascribe to the gallantry and civility of our age the advantage which we have above them; and to our knowledge of the customs and manners of it, the happiness we have to please beyond them" (1:183). Dryden is telling his literary peers that they have no right to canonize themselves at the expense of their predecessors, though they may consider themselves fortunate to live in an age of superior refinement from which they can draw in their writing. They can, in other words, define their own modernity and unique value by rejecting an immediate past, but such presentist self-definition cannot serve as a gesture of self-approbation, of self-persuasion leading to conviction. At most, it can lead only to enabling "knowledge" of present customs and manners and of the greater degree of pleasure which contemporary plays can provide an audience.

Barely concealed in Dryden's statement is the paradox of permanence and change, a paradox that confronts Dryden at frequent turns in his criticism. For, it must be asked, which audience will be pleased more with Dryden's plays than Shakespeare's? Dryden may have in mind only a contemporary audience in that he probably does not care how an "unpolished age" like Shakespeare's might respond to, say, *The Conquest of Granada* (1:181). Yet to admit this, as he may realize, would expose his argument to a charge of relativism; his claims for his age's refinement, advantage, and power to "please beyond" would, in such a scenario, function as no more than self-aggrandizing gestures like those he is at pains to preclude. The alternative, absolutist position, that all audiences in all ages would deem Restoration drama superior to its Elizabethan antecedants, might seem initially more desirable if unverifiable, but it would seriously weaken the force of assigning value to "the age" – if the Elizabethans could recognize a superior play when they saw one, why could they not then refine themselves according to the universal standard of value that is implied in the act of being able to acknowledge "superiority"? Dryden's refusal to engage in rhetorical one-upmanship with the Elizabethans has rendered his argument paradoxical: evaluative standards are fixed and eternal but the qualities of an author's work – language, manners, wit, and style – are wholly determined by the circumstances of the age.

The question of value is unabatably paradoxical.[5] Valuations in a rhetorical culture, such as the proclaiming of a neoclassicism that could be at once modern and transhistorical, were unapologetically brimming of paradox, by which the drama of persuasion could be so intensified as to compel audiences into belief. In a sceptical objectivist culture, in contrast, such paradox is felt to be disabling, even as it provokes endless conflicts between absolutist and relativist positions of the kind that cut across critical discourse in the Restoration and beyond.[6] The specific tenets of these positions are in themselves less interesting than the fact that critics on either side hope that the paradox of value can be resolved or at least deferred through knowledge, even though its accumulation would seem only to confirm the problematic nature of valuation. To knowledge, as Dryden suggests, can be ascribed happiness. The assumption is that, though it cannot empower a self-validating structure of conviction, knowledge permits a note of evaluative certainty because it seems to promise even greater returns: an objective, unassailable apprehension of truth, unclouded by desire; a disinterestedness of judgment, the claim of which brings with it a possible reward of symbolic profit and distinction; and an eventual universal agreement about the nature of the most fundamental human values. Expressing such a hope in being able to know value may thus be the most persuasive gesture of all.

The search for certainty in knowledge gave rise in the Restoration to a panoply of foundationalist discourses that figurally reconceptualized value as "grounded" in the phenomenal. These discourses, or paradigms, could be used in support of either relativist and absolutist positions – the moderate Dryden could just as easily write a treatise with the words "Grounds of Criticism" in its title as the more imperious Dennis.[7] In principle, these discourses were intended to provide a point of normative accommodation between two divergent accounts of literary value: a long-standing rhetorical-didactic tradition, which prescribed conventional models for composition as well as emphasizing poetry's instrumental power to please, instruct, and mobilize the passions; and an objectivist reintroduction of the Aristotelian doctrine of imitation, newly reaffirmed in the Davenant-Hobbes debate, which stressed literature's powers of representation in rendering accessible the universal truths of human experience. It is a reflection of the largely untheorized and transitional character of Restoration criticism, particularly in its earlier pronouncements, that its definitions of literary value could often cite both accounts at once. "'Tis true that to imitate well is a poet's work," Dryden could suggest in his *Defence of an Essay of Dramatic Poesy* (1668), but the function of "good verse" was equally "to affect the soul, and excite the passions, and, above all, to move admiration" (1:114). In appealing to foundationalist paradigms such as "the age," critics like Dryden hoped to situate the source of poetic value in something experiential and possibly anterior to language, where such value could then be felt to encompass both rhetorical and mimetic functions. Yet in phenomenalizing this source, these paradigms encouraged the shift from verbal power to knowledge, from valuing persuasion by seduction to valuing persuasion by evidence.

The rules, for example, were usually justified on the grounds that they corresponded to the dictates of Nature, itself certified by the further paradigms of what Rymer in the long title of his *Tragedies of the Last Age* (1678) called "the Practice of the Ancients" and "the Common sense of all Ages." Pope's rendition of the argument in the *Essay on Criticism* (1711) remains the most frequently cited:

> Those RULES of old *discover'd,* not *devis'd,*
> Are *Nature* still, but *Nature Methodiz'd;*
> *Nature,* like *Liberty,* is but restrain'd
> By the same Laws which first *herself* ordain'd.   (ll. 88–91)[8]

Like any set of poetic conventions, neoclassical rules had formerly been regarded as rhetorical options, more or less authoritative depending on how thoroughly poets wished to harmonize the canon. Yet for Restoration critics, whose status as emergent professionals prompted them to seek legitimization in the authority of method, the rules were models for composition that could be treated like knowledge, and knowledge that encoded social determinations of decorum, propriety, character, and so on. At an empiricist extreme, as in Rymer's dismissal of Shakespeare for his "abuse" of history (anachronism in *Julius Caesar*) or psychology (the handkerchief in *Othello*), failure to adhere to the rules made for faulty and unpleasurable representations of experience.[9] Under the rules, many of poetry's pragmatic and utilitarian functions were therefore either devalued or, in the case of pleasure, tied to imitation – a perfect dramatic representation, Rymer believed, "*pleases naturally* in it self."[10] Critics could allow some "profit" with the pleasure though this was increasingly identified with the acquisition of moral knowledge, which, according to Rymer, resulted from "observing" in the best plays "that constant order, that harmony and beauty of Providence."[11]

The rules seemed to provide critics with an absolute objectification of value by which to render judgment disinterested and to fix canonicity: "if people are prepossest," Rymer warned, "we can never have a certainty."[12] That they also provided evaluative certainty with a high degree of specificity within the increasingly prevalent practice of tallying up a work's beauties and faults also accounts for their enduring popularity among critics. Yet in being justified by reference to Nature, the rules could not long be enforced before they began to be challenged by differing perceptions of experience. Working dramatists complained bitterly about how the rules inhibited them from writing anything truly new, which was one way of saying that the rules were inadequate to the changefulness of modern life and "the real state of sublunary nature."[13] The nebulousness of "Nature" meant that it could also be appropriated for valuations of "irregular" authors. "Chaucer followed nature everywhere," wrote Dryden in the Preface to the *Fables* (2:280). And, of course, Shakespeare would be routinely heralded as an archetype of a natural talent that, as Addison suggested, could function for the relativists as "a Stumbling-block to the whole Tribe of these Rigid Criticks" (*Spectator* 592). In Dryden's celebrated version,

Shakespeare "needed not the spectacle of books to read nature; he looked inwards, and found her there" (1:67). The rules were perhaps the last significant expression of a rhetorical will to harmonize the entire canon of English literature according to specific principles of composition. Yet, in being grounded in Nature rather than empowered by a rhetoric of conviction, the rules would ultimately be discarded because they could not be made to embrace the plurality of values that the objectivist pursuit of knowledge about Nature would inevitably reveal – as Foucault notes, "knowledge is not made for understanding; it is made for cutting."[14]

As a secular analogue to God, the evaluative foundations of Nature and its correlate Reason had supreme emotional appeal yet their rhetoricity was difficult to suppress, a fact recognized by Dennis when he attacked Pope for not having spelled out in the *Essay on Criticism* "what he means by Nature, and what it is to write or judge according to Nature."[15] The evidentiary utility of these foundational paradigms was limited since they could be too easily invoked on either side of an evaluative contest, of which there were many during this period: Ancient versus Modern, English versus French, Restoration versus Elizabethan, and so on. These contests were essentially traditional rhetorical agons that had retained their binary structure, wherein self-definition was achieved by verbal apposition, even as the methods of contestation had begun to move beyond simple apposition to an objectivist explication of evidence. The quarrel between the Ancients and Moderns, in particular, had gone from being in its earliest manifestations, as in Meres's canon-matching, an exercise in extended analogy, juxtaposing classical and indigenous authors, to being in its later phase a conflict between rhetorical and objectivist thinking, between orators and scholars, in which either side could barely comprehend the other's assumptions since these were formed according to two starkly opposed processes of thought.[16] In this later phase the quarrel was only tangentially related to canon-formation since the locus of contestation was less the literary system than a broad understanding of cultural value, with each side attempting to humiliate the other according to how each defined that value: Temple and Swift dismissing the scholars for the triviality of their historicist inquiries and their indecorous impudence, Wotton and Bentley embarrassing the classicists for their frivolous, self-deceptive unconcern for truth, as exemplified in Temple's foolish admiration of the spurious *Epistles of Phalaris*. That the quarrel could never be satisfactorily resolved since the contestants could never agree on the terms of debate was the point, perhaps, of Swift's withholding of closure in *The Battle of the Books*. Swift's parody of the quarrel literalized it as a masculinist combat of the type that had long been associated with rhetoric, yet it also ironized the emotional nature of such combats through a bland, journalistic narration ("A Full and True Account of the Battel Fought last Friday"), which worked as a further burlesque of objectivist fact-mindedness.[17]

The quarrel of the Ancients and Moderns, like the other evaluative contests of the period, were implicitly debates over the status and function of evidence in valuation, whether such evidence could be used as proof or as suggestion, as a determination of value or as a mode of punctuation within a rhetorical display. That the contests involved increasingly particularized forms of knowledge to supplement the baldly totalizing paradigms of Nature and Reason suggests, however, that contextualizing value was beginning to be considered an authoritative gesture in critical discourse. Among the more commonly invoked paradigms were language and manners, conceived not in rhetorical terms as productive vehicles for the exchange of value but as experiential conditions by which judgments could be sanctioned. Dryden's claim for the superiority of his own age was primarily founded on the evidence of its wit and manners, evidence that could also authorize comparisons in other directions: a "comprehensive *English Energy*," Roscommon argued, put the English language far above the French.[18] As expressions of desire, the function of such claims scarcely differed from that of earlier rhetorical modes of self-assertion, just as the rhetorical positing of a learned evaluative constitutency often underscored arguments from evidence: "When one compares the best Writers of the last Age with these that excel in this," one modernist typically declared, "the difference is very discernable: even the great Sir *Francis Bacon*, that was the first that writ our Language correctly; as he is still our best Author, yet in some places has Figures so strong, that they could not pass now before a severe Judg."[19] What was different in such moves was that proof was felt to be persuasive in itself and that, implicitly, it could be effectively challenged by other evidence or by its contextualization. Thomas Culpeper, in one of his *Essays* (1671), could easily dismiss the modernist's claim by historicizing it as a perennial "affectation" wherein "every age with us will have the greatest esteem for the Speech they use." Unfortunately for Culpeper, this relativizing gesture could leave him with little more than emotion on which to form his own canon: "I am not so in love with our own times and faces, as that I fancy in our selves a greater excellency, then in our predecessors; who can think that the famous St. [*sic*] *Phillip Sydney*, or the incomparable Lord *Bacon* have been out done in their several kinds, or *Shakespear, Beaumont,* and *Fletcher,* or *Ben Jonson* in theirs, by any of our present writers."[20]

Critics also sought justification in a variety of value determinisms having to do with social or natural conditions. Some of these arguments, like the claim for the normative influence of climate and atmosphere, had been around since antiquity. In the mid-1650s, one self-styled "commender of England" could defend the indigenous canon by overturning what had by then become the commonplace view that "thicknesse of the ayre must breed ... thick witts, but it is not soe ... for what nation can shew more refined witts then those of our Ben, our Shakespeare, our Beaumont, our Fletcher, our Dunn, our Randol, our Crashaw, our Cleveland, our Sidney, our Bacon, &c."[21] Restoration critics took to the idea with a good deal more seriousness, applying it to a host of contradictory valuations. Temple professed himself a believer in judging "from the nature of the People or the Climat."[22] So did the modernist Daniel Baker, who argued that the superiority of English verse could be further established with the evidence of the quality of England's "heavy Soil."[23] And if this were not enough, the "Wit and Valor" of the English, said Rymer, could also have something to do with "our good *Ale*, and English *Beef*."[24]

The rage for party in the latter half of the period similarly encouraged many critics to make the connection between England's poetry and the character of its politics. Gildon, though an advocate of the rules, believed the superiority of English letters was a natural extension of Britain's advantage "in the Honour of *Arms*, or the Wisdom of our Laws."[25] Farquhar, noting the apparent contradiction, declared that the imported laws of the French theatre had no place on the native stage because the English differed from the French "in the complexion and temperament of the natural body as in the constitution of our body politic."[26] The slogans of Tory stability and Whig liberty were often cited as the cause of England's cultural greatness, some loyalists going so far as to attempt a revision of the canon along party lines. Republicans of the 1680s and 1690s strategically republished works by Marvell, Milton, and others to coincide with political crises like the Exclusion Crisis and the Glorious Revolution.[27] Milton's nephew, Edward Phillips, compiled a catalogue of authors, the *Theatrum Poetarum* (1675), that gave short shrift to Cleveland and other Royalist poets. A dozen years later, Phillips's catalogue was rewritten by the Tory William Winstanley, in an effort to restore the reputations of authors like Cleveland who devoted their careers to "Vindicating the Royal Interest, and undeceiving the People."[28] In 1713 Samuel Croxall produced Whig revisions of Spenser, "Design'd as Part of his Fairy Queen but never printed," which provoked an angry response from the *The Examiner*: "to have Treason and Sedition utter'd in the Name and Language of Spenser, is an Iniquity that has few Precedents." Predictably, this Tory critic went on to cite several notably absolutist passages from the *Faerie Queene*.[29] All these examples may indicate a "desperate quest for authentication" among rival factions, although, with Cleveland and perhaps Spenser, it seems as much a case of a political party seeking legitimation in the act of harmonizing the canon as of a minor critic trying to rehabiliate a neglected author with the help of partisan rhetoric.[30]

All these paradigms and determinisms, though seemingly founded in the concrete, could not but seem empty gestures within an increasingly objectivist culture because they did not naturalize the relations of power and value *enough*. On the one hand, the rules could serve to reinforce class determinations of behaviour and speech, yet, in containing spontaneous subjective aspirations too objectively, they soon seemed illegitimate to writers and audiences. On the other hand, linking value to material conditions such as climate could help to underwrite such aspirations, but, in failing to provide an objective order of values, these paradigms could be too easily recontextualized and appropriated on behalf of any cultural or political mythology. In sum, the arbitrariness of all these discourses could not be concealed. The solution in the eighteenth century would be to develop a new series of foundationalist theories that could certify an objective structure of value by being restricted to an autonomous field of cultural production, and yet at the same time be functionally ambiguous enough to sanction the expression of subjective desire vital to the field's renewal. In time, these theories were refined to identify not only a broadly cultural value, but value situated in the author (genius, imagination), in the work (a grace beyond the reach of art, the beautiful and the sublime), and, above all, in the reader (taste, judgment, sensibility). None of these theories provided an answer to the paradox of value – the notorious relativity of taste would be for a long time a favourite topic among satirists.[31] Yet their legitimacy would be difficult to contest. In being based in an ideology of the aesthetic rather than in formal method or material circumstance, they permitted the articulation of desire while seeming to be objectively anterior to language. And in being restricted to a localized conception of the aesthetic experience, they helped critics and readers to misrecognize the material and historical contingencies that determined their judgments.

VALUES IN LITERATURE

The search for evidence, whether in the rules or in experience, had as one of its consequences a heightened impetus among critics to analyse individual works or to provide historical or biographical information that could enable such analysis. Dryden's "examen" of *The*

Silent Woman in the *Essay of Dramatic Poesy*, it is commonly argued, inaugurated a history of critical exegesis that would soon see treatments of various kinds being lavished on canonical English poets: Dennis, Rowe, and Pope on Shakespeare; Patrick Hume, Bentley, and Addison on Milton; John Hughes on Spenser, and so on.[32] Though Dryden's examen, like Rymer's critiques of Shakespeare, was designed as a defence of a particular poetic practice, it was conducted on the assumption that the value of Jonson's play could be objectively perceptible to all as evident fact. In Dryden's telling construction, "*you see in it* many persons of various characters and humours, and all delightful" (1:71, emphasis added). Jonson's resolution, where Epicoene is revealed to be a boy, is contrived so expertly, Dryden argued, that "when it is done, no one of the audience would think the poet could have missed it; and yet it was concealed so much before the last scene that any other way would sooner have entered into your thoughts" (1:74). The language of affectivity, of positing a common audience response, may recall earlier rhetorical fictions of consensus, but what is significant about passages like these is that value is felt to be embedded "in" the text. Instead of circulating value, literature contains it. Value is therefore a form of knowledge which has to be experienced and discerned before it can be appraised by an audience or, for that matter, by other producers. Reception comes first.

For Dryden, craftmanship like Jonson's could make for highly enjoyable spectacle but the source of this pleasure in imitation reached beyond language into experience, enfolding the letter into its referent ("you see in it"). Of Shakespeare, he wrote, "when he describes any thing, you more than see it, you feel it too" (1:67). In such assertions are the first faint incantations of an ideology of the aesthetic, which Eagleton, summarizing de Man's late essays, defines as "a phenomenalist reduction of the linguistic to the sensuously empirical, a confusing of mind and world, sign and thing."[33] Value is naturalized as an experience that fuses perception with cognition, and one that is as much "in" the reader as "in" the text. Indeed, it is also "in" the poet ("he looked inwards, and found her there"); his genius is such that he encompasses the phenomenal in his own transcendent consciousness. In Dryden's influential portrait, Shakespeare "had the largest and most comprehensive soul. All the images of nature were still present to him" (1:67), or, elsewhere, "Shakespeare had an universal mind, which comprehended all characters and passions" (1:260). The aporia of judgment, of determining whether value is assigned by a reader or imparted by the text or its author, is answered by a claim for an endlessly embracing receptivity in authors, readers, or texts that sees value everywhere. In the greatest works, such as Chaucer's, value is bewilderingly profuse and enveloping, sublimely overwhelming the reader in an inexhaustible tide not of rhetoric but of representation and knowledge: "there is such a variety of game springing up before me that I am distracted in my choice, and know not which to follow. 'Tis sufficient to say, according to the proverb, that here is God's plenty" (2:284).

This ideology of the aesthetic would be later developed to provide a plausible justification for the arts, whose function as a repository of fundamental knowledge would be challenged by the claims of a naive empiricism that promised unmediated access to the truth, language being relegated in empiricist discourse to serving as a second-order phenomenon to the first cause of matter – a system of opposition that has, of course, become the central focus of deconstructionist revaluations of "metaphysical" reasoning.[34] Several defenders of the Moderns, like Wotton, believed that nature and knowledge were the purview of science, whereas literary works trafficked in mere opinion and were therefore redundant to an understanding of the truth. The most notorious denigration of the arts, and the one which all subsequent apologists for aesthetics were implicitly attempting to refute, came in the modernist Fontenelle's suggestion that, while eloquence may have formerly been of some use in political debates, poetry had never been "good for anything, under all manner of government; this failing is essential to poetry."[35] Its social utility seemingly negligible compared with science's, poetry could not be readily defended according to any principle of direct instrumentality or referentiality. Rather, it had to be autonomized as a superior form of knowledge, one that attuned truth and meaning to the passions and the imagination, thereby rendering them sensuous and agreeable to a deeper, more intuitive and comprehensive understanding than what the lessons of analytical science could furnish. Mediating between sense and intellect, affect and cognition, the work of art or its equivalent in the reader, the faculty of taste, could serve in theories of moral sympathy as the medium through which there could be apprehended the notion of the good and the fundamental harmony of civil society.[36] Though it could not make anything in particular happen, poetry could be, for Wordsworth, "the breath and finer spirit of all knowledge; it is the impassioned expression which is in the countenance of Science ... The Poet binds together by passion and knowledge the vast empire of human society, as it is spread over the whole earth, and over all time."[37] Severing the values of art from all interests except the transcendent desire for human solidarity, the doctrine of aesthetic autonomy thus became a compensatory move that, in Eagleton's words, "seizes upon the very functionlessness of artistic practice and transforms it to a vision of the highest good."[38]

Phenomenalizing the aesthetic as an experience that folded the word into the world repressed the degree to which meaning was contingent upon language. Dryden's various claims for Jonson's learning and skill in plotting, Shakespeare's sensuous apprehension of nature, or Chaucer's heterogeneous humanity, all treat such knowledge as non-linguistic, independent of any accident of verbal expression. "If Shakespeare were stripped of all the bombast in his passions," Dryden could write, uttering a commonplace view, "we should find the beauties of his thoughts remaining; if his embroideries were burnt down, there would still be silver at the bottom of the melting-pot" (1:259–60). This marks a significant revision of the old rhetorical norms for valuations, under which poets were esteemed principally for their eloquence and refining of the language because the diffusion of symbolic capital had been considered attendant upon verbal power. Dryden's assessment of Shakespeare sharply contradicted the views of his earliest admirers, for whom Shakespeare had been almost exclusively a poet of "sweetness": "The sweete wittie soule of *Ovid* lives in mellifluous & hony-tongued *Shakespeare*," wrote Meres, adding, "the Muses would speak with *Shakespeares* fine filed phrase, if they would speake English."[39] Under the doctrine of imitation, verbal art could, as ever, be highly prized for its power of enhancing signification, just as polished formal craft like Jonson's could be felt to have a measure of substantive import. Yet, as evidenced not only in the polemics of the Moderns but equally in the debate over the related category of wit, eloquence was to a degree released from its cognitive functions, or at least emptied of its ethical and political effects, becoming at an extreme, in the definition that provoked Johnson's censure, Pope's dress of thought: "*True Wit* is *Nature* to Advantage drest, / What oft was *Thought*, but ne'er so well *Exprest*" (*Essay on Criticism*, ll. 287–98). Dryden's version of the argument was even starker in its insistence that, while poetry "must *be* ethical," its ethical nature had nothing to do with language: "the poet dresses truth, and adorns nature, but does not alter them: ... Though the fancy may be great and the words flowing, yet the soul is but half satisfied when there is not truth in the foundation" (1:121).

"Language, wit and conversation," according to Dryden in the *Defence of the Epilogue*, could constitute the advantages of "the age" in the very same way that verbal refinement within a rhetorical culture had always been each generation's source of unique value. If anything, the widespread observance of prescriptions for the drama or the iambic-pentameter line accorded verbal refinement something of the force of law, intensifying in many writers and critics a presentist conviction in the cultural "perfection" of their own age. But, in treating of knowledge as anterior to language, preserved in the eternal verities of human nature, the emphases upon both imitative content and the sensuous aesthetic effect of meaning entailed an appreciable devaluation of verbal art, which was abandoned to the realm of the contingent where, as it happens, it had always been. The implications of this change for literature and for canonicity were enormous. It meant, for instance, that presentist self-definition could co-exist simultaneously with a curious self-abnegation of the kind previously practised under an auctorial order. As ever, it was believed that, the fundamental truths having been already uttered, the living poet's most meaningful function would be to retell those truths anew; but, if language were merely contingent to the age, the poet could not produce anything of lasting value by virtue of verbal skill alone. Dryden, in his epistle to Congreve, could express both satisfaction in the polished art of the "present age of wit," as well as the downcast view that the "second temple was not like the first," for "what we gain'd in skill we lost in strength." Despite their rudeness, or perhaps because of it, the Elizabethans, "the giant race before the Flood," seemed to have a greater grasp of human nature and its passions (2:169–70).[40] Such plaintive gesturing may only be rhetorical, a build-up to Dryden's praise of his younger contemporary, but it does posit a distinction between skill of art and strength of sense, a distinction that, in the long view of history, favours sense above art. The poet may therefore have considered his great works of translation as being no more than productions for the age, and his other writings as being only potentially material for future translators, who might prize their sense as he did Chaucer's: "Another poet, in another age, may take the same liberty with my writings; if at least they live long enough to deserve correction" (2:287).

Lamenting the impermanency of speech was a stock theme among poets eager to harmonize the canon after their own practice, the assumption being that perfection in poetry would stabilize the language in the way that Cicero, Virgil, and other Augustan poets "had by their Writings fix'd the *Roman* Language."[41] In repeating Waller's refrain in the *Essay on Criticism*, Pope was making the same implicit bid for the essentiality of his own project of refinement:

Now Length of *Fame* (our *second* life) is lost,
And bare Threescore is all ev'n That can boast:
Our Sons their Fathers' *failing language* see,
And such as *Chaucer* is, shall *Dryden* be.   (ll. 480–3)

Yet the theme had by this point lost much of its emotional force because it seemed to be contradicted by the knowledge of how some canonical authors had retained a presence in the canon despite the decay of their wit. Pope's lines provoked an ill-tempered rebuke from Dennis: "Now what does young Mr. *Bays* mean by *our second life*, and by *bare Threescore?* If he speaks of himself, and means threescore days, he means too much in Reason: But if he speaks of *Chaucer, Spenser,* and *Shakespear,* and means threescore Years, he means too little in Conscience. 'Tis now a hundred Years since *Shakespear* began to write, more since *Spencer* flourished, and above 300 Years since *Chaucer* died. And yet, the Fame of none of these is extinguish'd."[42] Subscribing as much as Pope to an ideal of verbal perfection, Dennis could not adequately account for these poets' durability, but the point was that these poets had not canonized themselves simply through their eloquence. It is true that, for a few critics, the language of the old poets could itself be appreciated as a valuable form of historical knowledge which presented a challenge to contemporary requirements for poetic expression. The June 1707 number of *The Muses Mercury* contained an essay that reprinted a "proper Spelling" edition of "The Nut-Brown Maid," which the essay contended was not "a *Ballad*; but an Allegorical *Poem*, with more Design in it than many of our late *Odes*." A few years later, Elizabeth Elstob published her *Rudiments of Grammar for the English-Saxon Tongue* (1715), whose purpose, she claimed, was "to shew the *polite* Men of our Age, that the Language of their Forefathers is neither so barren nor barbarous as they affirm, with equal Ignorance and Boldness."[43] Yet such claims obscured the fact that it was the critics' own acts of preservation, and not the language of the old writings, that had brought the works to the attention of contemporary readers. The emergent discipline of philology, though no less informed by nationalist sentiment than the presentist extolling of the contemporary canon, was thus correlated to the growing belief that poetic immortality lay in something other than verbal power.

Being relegated to the temporal, language would subsequently be understood in terms of style, and thereby *revalued* as the particularized mode of discourse through which a writer could define an authorial identity. Whereas rhetoric, Fredric Jameson has argued, had been correlated to "a relatively fixed class standard, as an institution in which the most diverse temperaments [were] able to participate" by speaking in the voice of a common public personality, the concept of stylistics slowly displaced rhetoric as the "essential and constitutive component of the literary work of art" because it accorded with a middle-class culture of individualism.[44] As authorial style became equated with formal attributes of tone, musicality, and versification, it could be applied uniformly to a variety of topics whose treatment had been formerly codified according to rhetorical principles of decorum and scales of address. Perceived as at once contingent and keyed to a powerful and original sensibility, an urbane, polished style like Pope's could serve the creation of a naturalistic voice as *persona* that could take up with an unwavering equanimity "subjects ranging from a pissing contest (in the *Dunciad*) to the theodicy problem (in the *Essay on Man*). The style assumes a form of universality."[45] Verbal refinement could be therefore both a national and a personal project, since the local articulation of a poetic will to distinction coincided with the interests of an upwardly mobile bourgeoisie that was seeking to assert its legitimacy through codes of politeness that could themselves be centred in an aesthetic ideology of individualist sensibility. In time, this emphasis on style encouraged the cult of originality and received legal certification later in the eighteenth century in the heated debates over authorial property. Under copyright legislation as it would eventually be defined, the law could not hinder the commerce in knowledge, but it could protect only the medium or language through which this knowledge was expressed. Accordingly, the formal or stylistic qualities of a work became the focus of legal contention and the determining criteria for authorial uniqueness. The author would be canonized for his or her words, though canonized by others – by editors and commentators – because, without a fixed and uniform standard of expression, words had lost their power to immortalize. At the same time, the ideas in the work would continue to circulate, even to other authors, and this circulation could be considered valuable within a broader moral economy even if these ideas, being not necessarily original with the author, were not considered a work's distinctively aesthetic features. Copyright, in effect, gave legal purport to the depreciation of rhetoric, as the modern author, eager to establish his or her uniqueness, learned to avoid most rhetorical *formulae*, including commonplaces, *topoi*, and traditional figures, while continuing to share with other authors not only ideas but less obviously stylistic conventions of genre, theme, or even allusion.[46]

Because the emphasis on style was initially reflected in presentist codes of refinement, however, the doctrine of originality would not yet be extended to the works of a ruder past. The growing antiquarian interest notwithstanding, the distinction between sense and art accounts for the increasing recontextualization of older English works during this period, from Dryden's modernization of Chaucer to the various critical commentaries and appreciations mentioned above and, as well, to the long-popular "new-modellings" of Shakespeare's plays that were first begun on the Restoration stage.[47] These treatments were all undertaken on the assumption that such works were important as cultural documents, valuable in their meaning but whose message could be largely reformulated in terms not simply more accessible to contemporary understandings but equally more adequate to modern values and desires. The "sense" of those older works, their meaning and its sensuous effect, was felt to be worth preserving but their language had to be in some way elucidated or corrected for the benefit of *both* production and consumption. Such acts of correction were designed to enhance the intelligibility of older works, but they were also expressions of cultural self-definition and of the contemporary literary system's most self-enabling belief in its own special value, its verbal refinement and classicist purification. Reworking the old works were acts of homage as much to the literary past as to its present (and, in the view of many of Shakespeare's revisers, homage far more to the present than the past). In this sense, it is correct to say of Dryden and his generation that they were "the first to establish a canon of English classics."[48] Yet it is a peculiar understanding of the classic that informs these acts of reproduction, one marked not so much by the feeling of belatedness apparent in the term's earliest usages as by the sense of language's inevitable progress. As George Sewell declared in his preface to the seventh volume of Pope's edition of Shakespeare, "what then has been done by the really Learned to the dead Languages, by treading backwards into the Paths of Antiquity and reviving and correcting good old Authors, we in Justice owe to our own great Writers, both in Prose and Poetry. They are in some degree our *Classics*."[49] Here, then, is the objectivist revision of the paradox of canon-making: English writings begin to be called "classics" at the very moment when they begin to seem remote, in need of explication, correction, modernization.

This opening of the canon to writings of appreciable alterity could only occur with a significant pluralizing of the norms for canonicity. In advising critics to "Avoid *Extreams*" between judging the art and assessing the substance, Pope was signalling how evaluation could observe a range of values, any number of which could be discerned in a work (*Essay on Criticism*, l. 384). Harmonization of the canon was becoming less imperative than its ordering according to a hierarchy of values. At the top of this hierarchy were to be placed works, including translations and modernizations, that combined meaning and art in a finished whole – what Pope felt he could achieve by making the sound an echo to the sense. This highest level could still represent for most an ideal of canonic harmony and the animating principle for contemporary production. Yet below this level could also be classed much of the remaining body of established English authors, those like the Elizabethans whose writings lacked an adequate measure of verbal refinement yet still contained matter for "polite learning" – under the prescriptions of the New Rhetoric, poetry could no longer be identified with persuasive speech but had to be reclassified, first under the general category of polite learning, then under the more specific, yet significantly less utilitarian order of the belles-lettres.[50] More difficult to accommodate within this scheme were flashy authors like the metaphysical poets who, as Dryden said of Cowley, seemed to indulge in the "luxury of writing" without benefit of judgment or "solid meat." Bracketed somewhere below the rest, these authors could be included in the canon only if the traditional categories of authorship were radically redefined, as evidenced by Dryden's oddly qualified verdict on Cowley: "though he must always be thought a good poet, he is no longer esteemed a good writer" (2:280). A good poet, it now appeared, wrote with eloquence but a good writer never wrote without sense.

This hierarchy of values would be elaborated and its ranks more precisely defined only later in the eighteenth century, while its rough outlines had much less operative force than the socially determined hierarchy of genres – the greater referentiality of the novel, for one, would not ensure the genre canonical status until much later, when the parameters of aesthetic knowledge could be revaluated. But the reordering of literary standards would nonetheless be decisive for both the composition of the canon and the process of canon-formation. From now on, valuation had to proceed by attending closely to many possible values in a text, as Dryden would do in his comparative appraisals of Elizabethan with contemporary dramatists, or of Chaucer with Ovid and Boccaccio.[51] Discriminations could be made between major and minor writers, while some historicist dispensation could be made for the alterity and "imperfections" of past writings, as though it were appropriate not to judge Chaucer too strictly just because he "lived in the infancy of our poetry" (2:281). Valuation could thus take into account an idea of literary history, in the way that Dryden's resurrection of Chaucer as "the father of English poetry" not only reaffirmed the language's debt to him as its first refiner but equally acknowledged him at the head of a tradition that could still offer the working poet much in the way of inspiration: "Spenser more than once insinuates that the soul of Chaucer was transfused into his body" (2:280, 270). But, above all, the perception that the language, however perfected in the present, had undergone continual transformation meant that the works of the past had lost much of their mnemonic and memorializing power and functions. These works could not survive solely by force of eloquence but had to be preserved in translations, commentaries, and scholarly editions. Canon-formation was now as much about production as reproduction.

At the same time as value was being historicized in this way, so too was it being resituated at a remove from history, contained and fixed in the work despite the superannuation of its linguistic surface. Dryden's most telling praise of Chaucer in this regard was his passing admission that the old poet "is a rough diamond, and must first be polished ere he shines" (2:286). As integral and perdurable as a diamond, Chaucer mirrored nature's splendour; as such, his light had nothing to do with the profit or sweetness of his verse, long since turned to dross. Perceived as at once fixed yet encompassing in its radiance, value was no longer understood to circulate instrumentally among a multiplicity of agents and sources in a dynamic socio-political economy. With increasing frequency in the eighteenth century, critics would refer, rather, to the "intrinsic" merit of canonical works, or to the intrinsic nature of genius or taste, in contradistinction to values that were freely if unprofitably exchanged, such as opinion or prejudice. George Sewell, writing in 1720, remarked that Chaucer's "Fame is taken upon Credit, from the Recommendations of others; and they who speak of him, rather pay a blind Veneration to his Antiquity than his intrinsic Worth."[52] By extension, cultural works that were decried for their morally deleterious effects, such as comedies or novels, were deemed non-canonical precisely because they helped to disseminate undesirable values that in some way impaired or enervated the receptive body. Dennis, expressing a view common among the Augustan satirists, declared that opera is "an effeminate Trifle" that had already, "where-ever it comes, emasculated the Minds of Men, and corrupted their Manners."[53] Intrinsic value had the aura of permanence by being fixed, and of truthfulness by being equated with knowledge. As one defender of the theatre from 1759 would put it, "truth has at length prevailed, and the intrinsic worth of Homer, Shakespeare, Milton, and the Stage will outlast ages of brass."[54] By then, it seemed, modern ages of brass could no longer be polished as brightly as the literary diamonds of the past.

VALUE AND CULTURAL CHANGE

In attributing value to "the age," Dryden was invoking, as he often did, a deterministic theory of historical cycles, a theory that he assigned in the *Essay of Dramatic Poesy* to the modernist Eugenius: "every age has a kind of universal genius which inclines those that live in it to some particular studies" (1:26).[55] This theory, whose degree of determinism Dryden would vary depending on the occasion, was designed to answer the paradox of permanence and change by proposing a hierarchical model of value, whereby the fundamental values in a work rested on the permanent verities of nature and human experience while its lesser qualities could be attributed to that category of phenomena "which religion, customs of countries, idioms of languages, etc., have altered in the superstructures" (1:246). Under this model, adopted in one form or another by various critics, the separations of time and culture, and the implicit relativity of literary values, could be trivialized as superficial accidents of fortune. Yet, as much as it reinforced the traditional equation between value and endurance, the model also had the effect of bringing forward the paradoxical nature of value since it entailed contrasting ever more closely the permanent against the changeable. Whereas in rhetorical valuations canonicity could be adjudged by reference to an evaluative community in the present, that fictive community had now to be extended, as it were, to become the much vaster abstraction of time. The abstraction may have functioned much as the earlier elitist fictions in helping to direct audience responses, with the added suggestion that no contemporary audience could be trusted. Dryden, who often professed himself bound to the tastes of his time, could dismiss the "false beauties" of theatrical spectacle as against the more conclusive edicts of the "test of ages" (1:275). "To please the people ought to be the poet's aim, because plays are made for their delight," Dryden wrote in his *Defence of An Essay of Dramatic Poesy* (1668), "but it does not follow that they are always pleased with good plays, or that the plays which please them are always good" (1:120).

Yet intensifying the universalizing rhetoric in this way had as one of its consequences the idea that poetic value could not be measured solely by a work's effects in its own time, and that this stipulation applied as much to works of the present as of the past. This idea anticipates some modern conceptions of literature which, to cite John Ellis's version, hold that "literary texts are defined as those that are used by the society in such a way that *the text is not taken as specifically relevant to the immediate context of its origin.*"[56] As repositories of truth, canonical texts could be deemed broadly relevant to all societies but not pertaining to any one in particular. The idea, though not fully elaborated until later, had two related consequences. On the one hand, it gave added impetus to the long established practice of lifting canonical works out of their originating context and denying their historicity – much of the commentary on *Paradise Lost* in the eighteenth century was designed to universalize the work for modern readers by devaluing its dense allusiveness as well as its political and theological topicality. On the other hand, it sensitized critics to the possibility that canonical works could not simply be valued for their effects in the present, and that lifting them out of the context of their origin did not necessarily justify appraising them according to prevailing tastes. As much as critics were quick to depreciate the alterity of those texts or their value for ages past, that alterity could also serve as a check against presentist complacency. If contextualizing value was becoming an authoritative gesture in critical discourse, then the knowledge of cultural difference, it was felt, could help critics to arrive at some understanding of what endures and what does not. Yet the inquiry into contingency that such knowledge presupposed had the effect of further abstracting literary value, making it seem far less instrumental and immediate than it had formerly been thought.

Critics could thus undertake to describe the alterity of canonical texts yet at the same time seek to contain the sense of cultural discontinuity by positing an absolute foundation of value. Addison, in his *Discourse on Ancient and Modern Learning* (*c.* 1695), could propose such an undertaking on the assumption that the "present Age seems to have a very true Taste of polite Learning, and perhaps takes the Beauties of an ancient Author, as much as 'tis possible *for it* at so great a Distance of Time. It may therefore be some Entertainment to us to consider what Pleasure the Contemporaries and Countrymen of our old Writers found in their Works, which we at present are not capable of."[57] Frank Kermode has remarked of this passage that it makes the heretofore unimaginable point that "the ideal way to read the classics is to get as close as possible to reading them as contemporaries did."[58] In explicating topical allusions in the ancient texts, Addison was anticipating the mode of historicist accommodation that proposed to overcome the alterity of canonical works by furnishing the reader with as much knowledge as possible of their originating context. Yet, whereas meaning could be to some degree recoverable, Addison believed, the contemporary reader was "not capable of" taking pleasure in that meaning or in the beauties that had already been lost to history. What Addison was saying was that the true value of those texts had to lay elsewhere, in a form accessible even to the present age: "they could see their Author in a Variety of Lights, and receive several different Entertainments from the same Passage. We, on the Contrary, can only please ourselves with the Wit or good Sense of a Writer, as it stands stripp'd of all those accidental Circumstances that at first help'd to set it off: We have him but in a single View, and only discover such essential standing Beauties as no Time or Years can possible deface."[59] Any inquiry into originating contexts could not itself be felt to offer anything more than passing "entertainment" since it could ostensibly deal only with temporal values and not the transcendent value of good sense and polite learning. Yet, in revealing the historical basis for much of the pleasure to be gained from a text, such an inquiry relegated that pleasure among the lesser, temporal values.

Dryden had already made the point more explicitly in one of his most daring rehearsals of his superstructural model of value, his claim in the *Heads of an Answer to Rymer* (*c.* 1677) about how earlier English dramatists could succeed without benefit of rules: "Shakespeare and Fletcher have written to the genius of the age and nation in which they lived; for tho' nature, as [Rymer] objects, is the same in all places, and reason too the same, yet the climate, the age, the dispositions of the people to whom a poet writes, may be so different that what pleased the Greeks would not satisfy an English audience." Stated thus, the paradox of value seemed an untenable contradiction even to Dryden, who did not publish the *Heads*. Nonetheless, Dryden could offer Rymer the concession that "a foundation of truer reason" would show "that the Athenians were a more judicious people; but the poet's business is certainly to please the audience" (1:214). As he would later add, pleasure had to be distinguished from the more lasting rewards of knowledge: "nothing but truth can long continue; and time is the surest judge of truth" (1:278). Pleasure could be an enduring value in a work only so long as every new generation expressed its delight. As Dryden remarked in a preface written not much earlier than the *Heads*, "for generally to have pleased, and through all ages, must bear the force of universal tradition" (1:200). This is among the earliest intimations in English critical discourse that the test of time could involve as much an acknowledgment of the lasting worth of a text as a continual process of reaffirming a text's pleasurable value in changing times. Just as different ages and cultures could in time recognize the fundamental truths embedded in a canonical text, so could they also work toward agreeing over what delighted them in that text. Implicitly, for such agreement to be reached, acts of evaluation had to involve some respectful awareness of how different audiences found enjoyment in literary works.

"The verse of Chaucer," Dryden remarked, "is not harmonious to us; but ... they who lived with him, and some time after him, thought it musical" (2:281). This may not be the first time a historicist argument has been used to broaden the standards of literary practice, but it is the first time such an argument has been used to help retain an acclaimed yet distinctive and inharmonious poet in the English canon. It would never have occurred to previous critics to consider how variously canonical works had been received in the past.[60] Chaucer's original audience had been discredited as rude and ignorant by his Elizabethan admirers, and his greatness dismissed as an historical aberration. That Dryden was willing to show some deference to the views of a distant age might have seemed eccentric to his readers, as might his claim that *The Canterbury Tales* held much historical appeal in presenting "the various manners and humours (as we now call them) of the whole English nation in his age" (2:284). Dryden could make these claims because they dealt with what for him were the contingent values of language and topical referentiality. Chaucer's original audience might have enjoyed hearing his words, but "words are not like landmarks, so sacred as never to be removed; customs are changed, and even statutes are silently repealed, when the reason ceases for which they were enacted" (2:288). Chaucer's enduring value had to do with his meaning: "He is a perpetual fountain of good sense" (2:280). Yet, in praising Chaucer for this transcendent value without making him seem like an anachronism in his own time, the genius among the barbarians, Dryden was asserting continuity with a long-dead audience that evidently took pleasure in Chaucer's meaning as much as his words.

This theme of continuity in change had been implicit in Dryden's long-standing preoccupation with literary paternity and succession. Throughout his writings, Dryden had assembled an impressive stable of literary progenitors whose lineages all presumably concluded with Dryden: in addition to Chaucer, the father of English poetry, Dryden called on, among others, "Father Ben" (1:31), "Scaliger the father" (2:97), Shakespeare, "father of our dramatic poets" (1:70), "Waller, the father of our English numbers," and, remarking on St Evremond's treatment of Virgil, "I could wish that he had not discovered our father's nakedness."[61] Dryden's paternal metaphors served him as a plausible model for literary history, combining as it did the sense of an undying essence co-existing with generational changes in language, manners, and customs. Unlike his superstructural model of value, the idea of a literary genealogy did not necessarily devaluate differences among authors, since it proposed an image of a canon that could be at once plural and internally linked by family resemblances: "Milton was the poetical son of Spenser, and Mr. Waller of Fairfax; for we have our lineal descents and clans as well as other families" (2:270). Literary history and canon-formation could be fused in a myth of inheritance, one that seemed to provide a useful narrative by which to overcome the contradiction between the belief in a uniform human nature and the realities of historical change.

What the narrative could not provide was a satisfactory account of value in diversity, of what made all the various lineal descents canonical. Furnishing such an account required Dryden finally to naturalize and universalize the familial metaphor, and therefore to accept without embarrassment the paradox of permanence and change: "We have our forefathers and great-grand-dames all before us, as they were in Chaucer's days: their general characters are still remaining in mankind ... for mankind is ever the same, and nothing lost out of nature, though every thing is altered" (2:284–5). The contradictions of essential humanity and perpetual alteration all still existed but Dryden removed them from the discourse of canon-making; they were, for him, among the inevitable contradictions of human life. This is the characteristic move of objectivist canon-making, which defers the paradox of value with a dualistic vision of canonicity. In principle, canonical works reveal essential truths about human experience, yet one of the most essential that each work manifests in its turn is the diversity of that experience across time and cultures. Knowledge about that diversity, available from the works and their history, must therefore be accumulated in order that, at some point, some absolute agreement might be reached about those essential truths. The canon in its plurality thus offers, through a multiplicity of perspectives, a hopeful glimpse of what that agreement might seem like.

This dual vision of canonicity is apparent from the increasing tendency in the eighteenth century to classify the divergences among established authors. Addison, in *Spectator* 160, grouped literary geniuses into two classes, the first occupied by "natural" geniuses like Homer and Shakespeare who wrote without the benefit of prescriptive models, the second comprising authors like Milton who "formed themselves by Rules." Yet Addison, risking a relativity of values, refrained from ranking one class above the other: "The Genius in both these Classes of Authors may be equally great, but shews itself after a different Manner." In proposing an interpretation of how geniuses might differ though still achieve equal greatness, Addison hoped to lessen the urgency of deciding between rules or no rules. The differences between Shakespeare and Milton remained, but Addison removed them from the discourse of canon-making; they were for him among the inevitable divergences of human behaviour, psychology, and creativity.

The relativity of Addison's argument could be partially offset by his idea of genius, which, unlike a totalizing concept like Nature, connoted an absolute value yet within a specifically aesthetic sphere. No comparable abstract term, however, existed to accommodate the alterity of older works, since that alterity had as much to do with aesthetics as with history. And no matter how deftly texts could be lifted out of the context of their origin, through allegorizing commentary or through a blank denial of their temporality, a reader coming to the canon for the first time would inevitably be required to overcome any presentist feeling and confront squarely the unsettling otherness of the aged texts. If the canon was to be further expanded and pluralized to include once-marginal authors from the English past, then the question of dealing with cultural alterity had to be seriously addressed. Perhaps the most suggestive discussion of the topic was a brief passage in Hume's essay "On The Standard of Taste" (1757), where he wrote of the difficulty of "reconciling" modern sensibilities to the outmoded and often coarse values in canonical texts. Abiding by the dualistic vision of canonicity, Hume could not believe that the aesthetic values of the past differed in any fundamental way from those of the present, for it was the premise of his essay that a consensual standard of taste, however ample the evidence to the contrary, could be "established by the uniform consent and experience of nations and ages." At the same time, all other human values were to him vulnerable to anachronism, and hence any reader of older works had to struggle to broaden his or her own horizon of expectations in order to appreciate the works fully. Quoting Horace, Hume remarked how the old "poet's *monument more durable than brass*, must fall to the ground like common brick or clay, were men to make no allowance for the continual revolutions of manners and customs, and would admit of nothing but what was suitable to the prevailing fashion." Religious or philosophical "errors" of earlier ages, Hume contended, were the easier to cope with: "There needs but a certain thought or imagination to make us enter into all the opinions, which then prevailed, and relish the sentiments or conclusions derived from them." But, Hume added, the mores and moral values of generations past were a great impediment to the enjoyment of writings from that past: "a very violent effort is requisite to change our judgment of manners, and excite sentiments of approbation or blame, love or hatred, different from those to which the mind from long custom has been familiarized."[62]

It became in the later eighteenth century the hermeneutic task of critics, editors, literary historians, critical biographers, and philologists to enable their readers to undertake this imaginative, violent, *defamiliarizing* effort at making allowances for the inevitable alterity of writings from other ages and cultures. Such an effort would, in theory, bring the reader to an adequate understanding and proper appreciation of the entire, plural canon. Hence Johnson on the need to assess Dryden's work in the context of the Restoration: "To judge rightly of an author we must transport ourselves to his time, and examine what were the wants of his contemporaries, and what were his means of supplying them."[63] Even if it scarcely approached a Herderian emphasis on the discreteness of cultural and historical formations, to maintain a historicist perspective like Johnson's was to allow for the potential relativity of standards. As well, it would no longer be clear whether the reader "transported" modern values to the text, or whether value was intrinsic to the text from the moment of its composition. The hope in the eighteenth century, and into ours, was that this aporia of judgment could be resolved when our shared cognizance of difference would eventually and paradoxically reveal a powerful mental faculty innate to all, or, at least, a fundamental conformism of value: "in consequence of the growing intercourse between all the nations of earth," Joseph Priestley predicted, "and all the *literati* of them, an uniform and perfect standard of taste will at length be established over the whole world."[64] We may have learned to doubt such essentialism, but the belief that literature may help us transcend our own provincialism is still heard to this day: "art, poetry, fiction can sometimes lift us out of ourselves, as when we see or feel experience, or a portion of it, from the perspective of another. Solidarity can be achieved in no other way."[65] It is, of course, a fundamental principle of hermeneutics and of objectivist thinking. Accordingly, though not formulated in any theoretical way until much later, it was an assumption of increasing significance within the critical discourse of the eighteenth century.

5 The Fall of Apollo

Charles Gildon tells of an event, held just prior to the outbreak of civil war, that brought together the Caroline *cognoscenti* to debate the relative merits of Shakespeare and the Ancients in a courtly "trial of Skill": "The place agreed on for the Dispute, was Mr. *Hales*' Chamber at *Eaton*; a great many Books were sent down by the Enemies of this Poet [Shakespeare], and on the appointed day, my Lord *Falkland*, Sir *John Suckling*, and all the Persons of Quality that had Wit and Learning, and interested themselves in the Quarrel, met there, and upon a thorough Disquisition of the point, the Judges chose by agreement out of this Learned and Ingenious Assembly, unanimously gave the Preference to SHAKESPEAR."[1] Within a few years, Falkland and Suckling would both be dead. The court would be dispersed, its members in self-imposed exile and its king executed. The unanimity of the courtiers would be forever shattered. There would be no more trials of skill.

During the Restoration and the eighteenth century there occurred many attempts at recreating this primal scene of English canon-making. Dryden and other Royal Society intellectuals dreamt of establishing a British Academy modelled on the French, where not only the language and its usage might be supervised but where also, in Evelyn's words, "gentlemen and scholars" might "pass censure and bring authors to the touch."[2] Defoe, Addison, Swift, Smollett, and Dick Minim were among the better-known eighteenth-century advocates of a national academy of language and letters. Gildon himself produced a plan for an all-powerful academy that would exercise control over language and written works in all disciplines and would oversee the moral management of playhouses – among other recommendations, he urged that new productions be restricted to plays written by wits aged thirty-eight and over. Gildon made it clear that the purpose of his academy would be to return English letters to their former classical vigour. For Gildon and the others, the appeal of academies sprang from the belief that such institutions might reserve the task of canon-making to those whom Rochester called "the shrewd Judges in the Drawing-Roome."[3]

More than merely enforcing norms of composition, these institutions could, in theory, preserve the select and homogeneous evaluative community of the old courtly order and provide it with a new source of legitimation to supplement a failing political absolutism and a weakened network of patronage. In the absence of such legitimation, the field of restricted cultural production could no longer, it was feared, be properly distinguished from the market of mass production, which was threatening by its continuing expansion to render literary art wholly subordinate to commerce. These fears were, as ever, expressed as elitist jeremiads on the rise of Grub Street and all that it symbolized: the commodification of letters, the impoverishment of literary standards, and the surrendering of culture to the ignorant masses and, for·some, to the increasing numbers of women writers and readers. Yet what these fears actually reflected was the ongoing autonomization of art from the realms of the political and the economic. The threat of commercialization may have been real, but the many contests for cultural distinction that marked the period involved more than just authors like Pope reaping symbolic profits by mocking the mercernary exploits of dunces. They involved redefining what made literary production valuable and legitimate now that it was no longer understood to be central to the moral economy of the state but rather practised as a field of activity unto itself. In this chapter, I examine how the process of redefinition was represented imaginatively in some literary satires of the period and how, in Pope's later work, there began to emerge a new, self-legitimizing conception of literary production. I will then conclude by suggesting, more generally, how this new conception of literary production eventually necessitated the rejection of classicism as the preferred mode of poetic distinction, and the redefinition of the cultural field as deploying its own separable form of cultural capital.

SESSIONS OF THE POETS

If critics have always wished to locate the scene of canon-making in a suitably rarefied institutional setting, poets for their part have long mythologized the canon as a noble refuge, a pantheon or Parnassus safely removed from the routine drudgery of authorship and the burden of temporality. In English literature, the poetic court of canon-making has moved from Chaucer's *House of Fame* to Jonson's throne at the Devil Tavern and Drayton's idyll in Elizium, to end up finally in the Grub Street of Pope's *Dunciad.* Somewhat less familiar are a host of minor genres that also aim to reproduce this scene: commendatory rolls, procession poems, progress pieces, book battles, visits to Parnassus, and searches after wit. "*Albion*'s ancient Sons" have been espied on Parnassus in "dream visions" of the Muses's haunt since at least the sixteenth century.[4] In a visit to the hill in 1564, William Bullein describes Chaucer sitting in "a chaire of gold," Skelton frowning "with a Frostie bitten face," and Lydgate "lurking emong the Lilie."[5] By the mid-eighteenth century, these visions of Parnassus show the conditions for English poetry to have deteriorated under the degradations of the market. An epistle from Parnassus, dated 7 September 1730, tells of the plight of English authors who, excluded from Apollo's Court of the Ancients for their professionalism, are reduced to the status of a Heliconian *petite bourgeoisie.* "*Ben Johnson* sells ale on the side o' the hill, / And *Beaumont* and *Fletcher* go halves in a mill."[6]

More revealing about the changing fortunes of authorship is the minor burlesque genre known as the "session of the poets," where, typically, a medley of major and minor authors compete in a trial of skill for the honour of wearing the English laurels. Introduced by Suckling in "The Wits" (1637) and reaching a height of popularity around the end of the century, the genre had as its ostensible subject the various lobbying efforts and self-prostrating exertions of authors eager to gain the office of Poet Laureate, but what its history actually records is the gradual attenuation of a heroic laureate ideal of civic-minded poetry, an ideal that had served ambitious poets from Spenser to Milton in securing a role for themselves within the literary system. The ideal had been first certified by Petrarch's coronation, an example English poets like Lydgate would follow by bestowing crowns of bay on Chaucer. A Poet Laureateship had enjoyed official or semi-official status in England at least since the fifteenth century: John Kay in Edward IV's reign and Skelton in Henry VIII's each referred to themselves as "Poet Laureate" in recognition of their university training.[7] Dryden was the first Laureate to be given a formal appointment, though both Jonson and Davenant before him held court patents that were generally acknowledged to be the equivalents of Laureateships – the appointment, in this sense, being an official recognition of the heroic ideal, though only fitfully, as in Dryden's tenure, did the post and the ideal actually coincide. As an anonymous elegy to Davenant declared, "There are no Gods, but *Poets Lawreat.*"[8] Ironically, the lustre of the Laureateship began to fade almost immediately after it was formally instituted. Richard Flecknoe, satirizing the elegies for Davenant, reported that the "Officers of Parnassus" had refused the Laureate a "Passport" to Elizium on the grounds that "Bayes was never more cheap than now; and that since Petrarch's time, none had ever been legitimately crown'd."[9] By the eighteenth century, the Laureate had come to symbolize dulness and sycophancy, the supreme dunce around whom the hacks congregate and the world implodes in Pope's revised *Dunciad.* Gray, in turning down the position when it was offered to him, remarked contemptuously that "There are poets little enough to envy even a poet-laureate."[10]

The ostensible reason for the Laureateship's fall into disrepute was that it had become politicized, one more corrupt favour for court flatterers. As Scriblerus says of the laurel in one of his appendices to the *Dunciad,* "it is emblematical of the three virtues of a court poet in particular; it is *creeping, dirty,* and *dangling.*"[11] In actuality, the Laureateship had been politicized from the start. It was instead poetry that had retreated from the chambers of political power, for which poets had always felt a certain ambivalence, because as much as the king and his court had provided legitimacy and patronage for most cultural activities, poets had also long entertained a self-defining conviction in their own independence of judgment and in the supreme power of their eloquence. This independence was what Suckling, of all people, was implicitly reaffirming in his poem, satirizing as he did the upstart wits who were shamelessly vying to replace their late father Ben in the Laureateship. Jonson had epitomized the laureate ideal in presenting himself as a servant but never a slave to the court, yet in his absence the ideal was increasingly compromised as the system of Caroline patronage became ever more consolidated and exclusive. As a highly placed member of the Caroline establishment, Suckling may have also been ridiculing the self-seriousness of this ideal: in addition to pilloring Jonson for his effrontery in publishing his folio, the poem has Suckling himself being called to appear before Apollo only to anger the deity by insouciantly refusing to show up for the competition.

Suckling modelled the action of his poem on an episode from Trajano Boccalini's *Ragguagli di Parnaso* (1613), where Tasso, Apollo's favourite, is awarded the "the Royal Ensigns [that] used to be given to Poets Laureat, of being allowed to keep Parrets in his windows, and Apes as his gate."[12] Yet, unlike the contestants in Suckling's session, Tasso undergoes no rigorous selection process to achieve the post, being a genius who writes without benefit of rules; Suckling may have therefore been also obliquely mocking the very same learned "trial of skill" to which he had earlier participated, where after much ceremony the preference went to another poet who seemed to represent all that was contrary to the classicist pretensions of the polite. In addition, where Boccalini's Parnassus is animated by courtly politics, the theme of Suckling's poem, as of all the "session" poems, is corruption, the unhealthy rapprochement of politics and canon-making, and the physical and spiritual vitiation of the poet. The poem inverts the laudatory parade of poets common to Elizabethan criticism into a survey of dissolution and moral turpitude: the costive Carew, the syphilitic Davenant, and the toadyish Toby Mathew. The poem's ironic close, which sets a pattern for the more than two-dozen later sessions, has Apollo acting out of corrupt self-interest and selling the laurel to an anonymous alderman. Says Apollo, "'twas the best signe / Of good store of wit to have good store of coyn."[13] The suggestion is that, by encouraging poets to surrender their artistic independence, Apollo – the fictive embodiment of the absolutist Charles – has undermined the standard by which he could himself be genuinely praised. To some degree, Suckling likewise stands for the very self-interested blurring of politics and canon-making that he aims to satirize in his poem. The poem evinces some of the cynical self-mockery of the courtier for whom poetry could serve no real social or personal advancement. The first of the "Mob of Gentlemen who wrote with ease," Suckling was a courtly poet who was neither professional nor self-abnegatingly amateurish but who simply enjoyed writing witty verses and plays for his king.[14] Yet, in turning down the chance to become Laureate, in frequently championing an artless Shakespeare, and in being the first English author to uphold the new poetic doctrine of "a certain *je ne scay quoys*," Suckling was also anticipating how the autonomy of poetic art would be later asserted.[15]

An artistic integrity of the kind Jonson professed might have only been a matter of self-presentation, nothing other than the assumed heroic profile of the Renaissance poet – or, more generally, the civic humanist ideal of the self-governing citizen who practised autonomy in the drawing room where he met with his male peers to debate the common good. That it was a poetic profile tenable only for a time in English history seems to be a theme of Marvell's "Tom May's Death," a poem that is closely akin to the session burlesques though marked by a greater ambivalence over the proper political role of the poet. In it, Jonson himself appears as a venerable if slightly comical elder statesman of the Poets' Elizium who renounces a former member of his Tribe, Tom May, for having turned servile scrivener for the Parliamentary side. Marvell's "Jonson" has nothing but scorn for May who, allegedly resentful of being passed over for the Laureateship in 1637, prostituted his art in the service of party. Marvell has his fictive Jonson pull out all of the old Horatian verities of virtue and "spotless knowledge," but there is in Marvell's characterization of a gray-haired Jonson the hint that those ancient verities belong to a former time, when politics and literature were thought to be more readily distinguishable.[16] In the revolutionary period, potential laureates like May or Marvell, who wrote "Tom May's Death" soon after his "Horatian Ode," could not be expected to separate their duty to the state of poetry from the interests of faction. Then again, the poem may be suggesting that, in putting himself and his poetry before politics, Jonson undermined the meaning of the age-old immortality bargain between poet and patron.

In emphasizing the way politics exert an unhealthy influence upon the election of canonical poets, satires like Suckling's or Marvell's reveal the willingness of poets to distance poetry and poetic value from the very political system that had supported almost all major English poets since Chaucer. Initially, sessions like Suckling's restrict their political attacks to the mercenary scribes who either sell their poetic souls to powerful patrons or, in the words of a later session, fish "in the Mud for the Party's Applause."[17] Yet, increasingly, the definition of corruption and sycophancy is widened to include any type of political behaviour. Laureate Dryden's suspect conversion to Catholicism in 1685 provokes a flurry of session-writing, the resulting poems anticipating how in three years' time – following the Glorious Revolution – Dryden would be stripped of his title and pension. A few sessions later, Dryden enjoys a measure of poetic justice when Nahum Tate, the "Bard that had Usurp't the Bays," is himself excoriated for having won the office not by demonstrating poetic talent but by exercising an opportunistic "Cunning of Skill."[18] The retreat from politics, and the attendant displacement of the scene of canon-making from the privy circle of aristocratic power to a wider public sphere, are also signalled in the changing characterization of Apollo and his court.[19] Where Suckling's session is presided over by an autocratic Apollo, a session dated 9 July 1696 proposes a separate class of jurors, one composed of professional critics whose verdicts are binding upon Apollo.[20] The deity's kingly associations also begin to fade as he and the Nine seem to migrate further away from the House of Stuart. Unlike earlier sessions, later examples of the genre untie Apollo from any direct referent and often serve as vehicles for Whig critiques of monarchic power. James II's personal rule comes under abuse in the "Lovers' Session" (1687), when Venus, sitting in for Apollo, throws out a mandamus signed by the king ordering her to award the prize (the best prostitute "in Christendom") to the bearer of the warrant. Says an indignant Venus, "We'll maintain our old way of electing. /

Cunts still have been free, nor can any confine 'em, / Or bring to the beck of their *jus divinum*."[21] The 1688 *Journal from Parnassus* endorses this assertion of literary independence, its Apollo declaring "that the power of Kings, thô it could naturalize Foreigners & legitimate Bastards, never yet extended to the Creation of Poets."[22]

After 1700, sessions become fewer in number, in part because it is difficult to take Anne or any of the Hanoverians seriously as the Apollos for English poetry, and also because the idea of literary evaluation being dominated by autocratic authority becomes increasingly alien to the experience of common readers. The eighteenth-century Apollo is an abstraction. In Sheffield's "The Election of a Poet Laureat in MDCCXIX," Apollo has never even heard of Laurence Eusden, George I's actual choice for the office.[23] Cibber's Laureation in 1730 is accompanied by a host of satires, but few of these are cast as sessions, and many replace Apollo with Queen Dulness.[24] By mid-century, Apollo, like modern royalty, enjoys only a ceremonial role in the governing of Parnassus, which is itself no longer a star chamber but a democracy. In one session from 1754, Apollo is asked to dissolve Parliament "for a general Election in *Parnassus* for proper Members to represent the Republic of Letters."[25] In these later sessions, Apollo comes down from the Mount to join the Minims in the coffee shops. There, he becomes a spokesman for the public, arraigning the critics for their arrogance, as in the session from 1754, where the anonymous contributors to *The Monthly Review* are charged with presuming to "dictate to the Public" its choice of reading. In these late sessions, as the sources of corruption have evolved from privilege to the market forces of Grub-Street capitalism, canon-making has become depoliticized to the extent that authors are satirized not for selling out to party interests but for giving in to the demands of booksellers. Eventually, despite a couple of well-intentioned nineteenth-century revivals, the vogue for sessions dies out as the civic humanist ideal of the laureate poet is eclipsed by a new view of the autonomy of cultural work. Though the Laureateship remains, Apollo and his feudal Parnassus lose their imaginative hold on the minds of readers schooled in the bourgeois codes of taste and individual sensibility, and of poets who had long since left the drawing rooms of state.

The movement from absolutist to democratic politics follows another, less explicit shift from a harmonious to a plural canon. In Suckling's session, several prominent poets like Jonson and Carew are chided for too much self-conscious artistry, as the true Laureate must write with ease, not unlike Suckling. This criterion is later overturned in the Rochesterian "Session of the Poets" (1676), where Wycherley is dismissed as too much the "Gentleman-Writer." The Laureate, the poem suggests, must be a professional, "a Trader in Witt," though not so professional as to write purely for hire; accordingly, the bays are awarded to the actor Tom Betterton, a compromise figure who, in 1676 at least, combined a work ethos with the courtier's contempt for print.[26] By this point, the civic laureate ideal is no longer being taken seriously enough to be considered a credible target of satire, with the result that later sessions are much less specific about the requirements for the Laureateship. Parnassus undergoes a diversification of labour, as its candidates for the bays begin to include not only poets and dramatists but critics, historians, pamphleteers, novelists, journalists, musicians, "Punsters, Quiblers, Songsters, and Translators."[27] One session from 1697, purportedly based on a true event, records the interviewing of several prominent scholars and poets, including Dryden and Congreve, for the position of the first ever Lecturer in Poetry at Oxford – rather unsurprisingly, the poem's ironic close has the position being withdrawn at the last minute for lack of adequate funding.[28] By the time Parnassus is made a republic of letters, authors have begun to compete for office within their respective generic districts: "*Dryden*, and Mr. *Pope* were made the Representatives of *Satyr* ... Lord *Bacon* and Mr. *Locke*, were returned for real and useful Philosophy."[29]

If the laureate ideal had lost much of its authority, and the Laureateship most of its prestige, all the session poets were in agreement about the need to keep Parnassus free of popular authors. In the absence of a heroic ideal by which to legitimize authorship, it had become imperative that, particularly among professional authors who could not boast of genteel affiliations, the poetic activity had to be distinguished more than ever as a restricted field of production. Journalists were first tried by a jury of eminent poets in *The Great Assises Holden in Parnassus* (1645), sometimes attributed to the proudly professional George Wither. In the sessions that circulated among the courtly wits of the Restoration, popular writers were generally ignored, their outright illegitimacy as candidates for the laurels rendering them negligible as satiric fodder. Yet, in the printed sessions that grew more numerous toward the end of the century, lower-class professionals like D'Urfey were routinely given rough treatment, often by their colleagues in the trade. In the second part of the *Visits from the Shades* (1704), Virgil indicts Defoe "for Poetical Treason, in defacing the lawful Image of *Apollo*."[30] In a few sessions, condemning authors to work among the popular hacks is viewed as a suitable penalty for major authors who transgress Parnassian law. One Tory example from 1714 has the "Goddess of Eloquence" sentencing Steele to three years in Grub Street.[31] In other sessions, hopeful candidates improve their chances by assailing their plebeian readers. Gildon is the reputed author of a particularly gruesome *Battle of the Authors* (1720) that includes a scene where several once-popular wits "extend themselves in a wonderful manner by vast slaughters of the common People, in hopes by that means to wash out their former Stains, and Ingratiate themselves with *Apollo.*"[32]

For many of the session wits, the displacement of a heroic ideal for poetry was signalled most clearly by the growing number of women poets. Because of rhetoric's traditional associations with ritual demonstrations of male valour and productivity in the world of practical affairs, the laureate ideal had been espoused by poets from Petrarch to Jonson as an expression of their masculine ambition. In the earliest sessions, Apollo is a princely personification of this ideal, for whom the figure of the woman poet is an affront to the Laureateship because she was usurping the arts of eloquence that were considered essential to the office in fulfilling the duties of public decision making, duties in which she, as a rule, could not participate. In an early "sequel" to Boccalini's journal, the women, being forbidden by Apollo from producing poetry, were obliged to suffer not the banishment decreed on poetasters but the less spectacular fate of being cast, like the Muses, as a silent audience for the competition: "his Majesty commanded that the Ladys shou'd immediately be turn'd out of those honorable Seats which had been prepar'd for the other Sex, for the Reputation of true Poetry."[33] By the 1688 *Journal from Parnassus*, the emergence of professional women writers like Behn had become enough of a threat to Parnassus that they had to be exiled altogether, lest they "soon endeavour a Monopoly of Witt."[34] At most, in the pornographic "Session of the Ladies" (1688), the lecherous women of the town could hold their own competition for the sexual favours of the actor Cardell "Adonis" Goodman. Women writers could be given equal status with hacks in printed sessions only so long as the gendered stereotypes were upheld in the penalties the women were made to incur. In the 1696 session, Mary Pix is brought before the Parnassian court for having "unworthily, fraudulently, and sacrilegiously usurpt, in spight of her Stars, the Province of Poetry," for which she is sentenced by Apollo to "be desperately in Love with several Persons, but not one of them shall regard but despise and laugh at her Passion."[35]

By then, the laureate ideal had become weakened sufficiently for women poets to begin appropriating Apollo in their own defence. Finch, in her "Circuit of Apollo" (1713), has the deity dividing the honours among all women since "they all had a right to the Bay's" and then ceding his evaluative authority to the Muses, "Since no man upon earth, nor Himself in the sky" would dare to rid Parnassus of "three parts in four from amongst woman kind."[36] Apollo has left

England entirely by 1758, in a session by the libertine Charles Hanbury Williams, though not before declaring "that *women* alone for the future shall write."[37] Because they aimed to celebrate a literary constituency that was only beginning to establish itself, these sessions shared with the various catalogues of women writers of the period, notably John Duncombe's *The Feminiad* (1754) and Mary Scott's *The Female Advocate* (1774), the same principle of canonic similitude that had characterized Renaissance inventories of male poets. As in the male catalogues, the harmony of women poets had to be achieved through selective purges of the tradition, in particular of those women writers like Behn and Manley whose reputations for bawdiness and scandal had rendered them unsuitable as literary models under the intensified gender codes of the later eighteenth century. Yet the parading of a unified sisterhood in these sessions and catalogues also reflected the conditions for female authorship during the period, which, in the absence of any socially defined goal of competitive advancement for women writers, encouraged the formation of collaborative circles like the Bluestockings.

The feminization of Parnassus is most evident, however, from the differences between the two greatest Augustan literary satires, *Mac Flecknoe* and the *Dunciad*. Both poems share many of the stock features of sessions: the farcical contest for literary supremacy, the mock ceremoniousness, the concern over bad writing and its possible corruption of the literary system. But the imagining of apocrypha in these works is very different from that of the sessions, where there is always a sense that the author could be a participant in the situation he or she describes. Suckling and the other session wits write local, occasional lampoons about authors with whom they are familiar. Dryden and Pope distance themselves from the events they describe by preserving for themselves a laureate ideal that, unlike what happens in the session burlesques, is not ridiculed by being associated with dunces – aside from one brief reference in the fourth book of the *Dunciad*, the figurehead Apollo is noticeably absent from both satires. Both poets certainly entertained doubts about the relevance of a political ideal of heroism, but these only confirmed for them the necessity of upholding a heroic image of poetic independence. As Robert Folkenflik and others have noted, the tensions throughout Dryden's work over the relation between poet and monarch were heightened following his removal from the Laureateship, and were notably apparent in his late odes, in particular *Alexander's Feast*, where the power of Timotheus's music vanquishes the emperor's passions.[38] Laureate ambivalence becomes outright defiance in Pope's later work, where the traditional heroic image of the Horatian defender of the state's welfare is empowered by the fierce moral autonomy of the Juvenalian scourge of kings and ministers.

The differences between *Mac Flecknoe* and the *Dunciad* have to do with more than their relative treatments of political authority. Though the poem usurps the kingly power of representation in travestying ceremonies of monarchic coronation, *Mac Flecknoe*, written by Dryden during his tenure in the Laureateship, does not subvert the standard by which legitimacy in a poetic sphere is to be measured.[39] Where in the sessions true laureates as well as dunces compete for the same honours, there is no confusing Shadwell's empire for Apollo's: "Great *Fletcher* never treads in Buskins here, / Nor greater *Johnson* dares in Socks appear" (79–80). Flecknoe reigns in the "Realms of *Non-sense*," the antithesis to Parnassus, while Shadwell's coronation is a carnivalesque affair bearing no resemblance to the high ceremony of Petrarchan laureation (6). All the conventional tokens of poetic excellence have been safely eliminated or replaced by absurd equivalents. Shadwell's temples are overspread not with bays but "Poppies" (126), and instead of receiving the Laureate's traditional "tun" of wine, he is himself a "Tun of Man ... but a Kilderkin of wit" (195–6). Everywhere apocryphal, Shadwell's empire confirms by its negativity the authority of the laureate ideal – except, that is, in the one crucial respect that Shadwell's "filial dullness" preserves for his empire as for the laureate ideal a masculine succession (136). Though Flecknoe erects Shadwell's throne near the courts of "Mother-Strumpets," Shadwell is too dull to be a mercenary wit and hence cannot be feminized by being equated with prostitutes (72). On the contrary, Shadwell assumes a semblance of chivalric heroism in being destined to "wage immortal War with Wit" (12). In preserving this masculine order, *Mac Flecknoe* evinces the closed world of the courtly sessions, where satiric deflation is a rhetorical rite, verbal jousting of the kind that had been encouraged among generations of male students.

Unlike Dryden, Pope does not salvage any of the Parnassian apparatus from dulness's onslaught: "the madding Bay, the drunken Vine; / The creeping, dirty, courtly Ivy" (I.303–4), "give from fool to fool the Laurel crown" (IV.98), "The Muse obeys the Pow'r" (IV.628).[40] If the theme of the sessions is corruption, the dominant principle in Pope's "grand Sessions" is the contamination of the harmonious polite canon by its apocrypha in the coming of "The Smithfield Muses to the ear of Kings" (IV.45n.; I.2). Political corruption, in Cibber's partisan Laureation, remains a focal point but the poem's bleakest suggestion is that there exists no operative standard by which to measure this corruption. The poem, smothered in the commentary of the new breed of print-based pedants, records instead the disappearance of learned evaluative communities, of canon-making by coterie and academy. Dulness elects her laureate through universal suffrage: "An endless band / Pours forth, and leaves unpeopled half the land" (II.19–20). Whereas Suckling's Apollo reigned with all the arbitrariness of autocratic rule, Queen Dulness embodies liberal capitalism, whose anarchy has obfuscated all distinctions between selling out to political interests or submitting to the vagaries of consumer taste. As value is wholly determined by the market, participation in any form in this mass culture constitutes, for Pope, prostitution in the extreme, as there is little telling poet from patron, whore from client. This accounts for the substitution of Apollo by Dulness the woman, for Pope's poem is the first significant expression of a gendering peculiar to the modern world, in which, Andreas Huyssen has suggested, "mass culture is somehow associated with woman while real, authentic culture remains the prerogative of men."[41] Applying Huyssen's argument specifically to the *Dunciad*, Catherine Ingrassia has noted how Pope's matriarchal characterization of Dulness, and his virulent attacks on female writers like Haywood, reveal the poet's own anxieties in trying to differentiate himself from the hacks and women with whom he shared some "uncomfortable affinities" in being both a commercial author and someone precluded by his religion and physical ailments from acceding to public office.[42] In depicting the contamination of high culture as the demonic triumph of feminization, the *Dunciad* completes the ironic figuration of negativity and illegitimacy suggested in *Mac Flecknoe*, which had at the last reserved the task of canon-making to the shrewd men in the drawing room. All that remains of the laureate ideal in Pope's poem is its independence and power to judge, barely secured in the lonely refinement of the poet's male voice.

"I LISP'D IN NUMBERS, FOR THE NUMBERS CAME"

Mr. Pope has somewhere named himself the last English Muse ...

Oliver Goldsmith[43]

The feminization of the literary system extended beyond its commercialization or its recognition of increasing numbers of women writers and readers. It involved, as well, the redefinition of poetic values, with greater emphases being placed upon lyrical expressivity, as well as upon feeling, fancy and passion, categories of experience traditionally equated with the feminine.[44] Later in the century, this cultural gendering of aesthetics would provoke intense debate, with Burke being the most notable theorist for a "remasculinization" of the sublime.[45] Yet what this feminization ultimately reflected was "the increasingly marginal position of literature and the arts in a society in which masculinity is identified with action, enterprise, and progress – with the realms of business, industry, science, and the law."[46] In a rhetorical culture, poetry and eloquence had been considered essential to the smooth workings of the feudal state and vital equipment for the warrior, statesman, or courtier who wished to ascend its political hierarchy. With the capitalist privileging of economics, the political value of symbolic representation was greatly diminished. While art and literature would eventually be reconceptualized as a separate sphere of activity that could provide its own special profits, their association with masculinity could not be easily recouped so long as artists and poets, like women generally, were precluded from contributing to the political economy of the state. Yet one category of such compensatory profits was significant enough for a few male poets, like Pope, to see some value in identifying with certain aspects of female authorship. In having been excluded from public decision making, women had the advantage of maintaining an aura of disinterestedness, and of making a claim for the moral autonomy that had always been a mark of distinction for the poet of laureate ambition and even more so now that aesthetics had increasingly to be legitimized through the symbolic disavowal of both economic and political interests.

Pope masculinized this feminine authority most obviously by appropriating the themes of renunciation and retirement that had pervaded women's verse of the Restoration. Writing for a small circle of intimates, poets like Katherine Philips and Anne Killigrew had recreated the closed world of the Renaissance coteries with a far greater degree of exclusivity than had the Restoration courtly wits, who had virtually commercialized their poetry through their extensive networks of scribal publication. Within this circle, the women poets compensated for their inevitable social marginality by disclaiming worldly ambitions and celebrating the ideal of a secluded community of female friends.[47] Finch, in particular, wrote often of the moral and psychological benefits of retirement, assuming in such poems as "A Nocturnal Reverie," "On Myself," and "The Petition for an Absolute Retreat" an attitude almost of social defiance. For Pope, this theme of renunciation had long been certified in the male tradition as the authoritative gesture of the Horatian poet, yet his cultivation of the gesture later in his career was as forceful as Finch's in translating a pose of retirement into the heroic self-dramatization as the isolated, "Unplac'd, unpension'd" poet of opposition – "all the distant Din that World can keep / Rolls o'er my *Grotto*, and but sooths my Sleep" (*Satire* II.i.116, 123–4).[48] And much as the women poets had repudiated this same bustling world in order to avoid being branded as prostitutes in print, Pope used the theme to claim his own commercial disinterest and thereby to resist his own feminization by the market. Indeed, the mock-exasperated plea for privacy that opens the *Epistle to Arbuthnot* ("Shut, shut the door, good *John*!") recalled the theme of public violation that had sometimes been a complaint among women poets whose authorship of their works had been contested.[49]

Yet perhaps the most interesting aspect of Pope's masculinization of female autonomy had to do with his use of the Muses. Walter Ong has suggested that the demise of the Muses is tied to "the entry of post-Gutenberg women in notable numbers into the world of literature."[50] In actuality, the Muses were more commonly invoked by women poets of the period than by the men, who were beginning to call upon other, less conventional personifications. The treatment given the Muses by women poets, as in Finch's "Introduction," was not entirely conventional either, as the poets tended to depict the Muses as fellow women artists, isolated and vulnerable yet perpetually creative. In the male tradition, the Muses had served as one of a number of fictions by which poets could legitimize their writing by mythologizing a moral order that depended on the circulation of verbal power. Parnassus and its denizens had represented the socio-economic conditions for poetic productivity: Apollo as an idealization of the monarch, Helicon as a symbol for the sweet liquor of patronage, and the Muses as embodiments of the traditional incentives of moral instruction, memory, or cultural refinement. The declining fortunes of the Muses during the eighteenth century, their virtual disappearance from English poetic discourse, coincided with the extinction of these traditional models for literary production and of the material conditions which had formerly sustained them. No wonder, then, that their disappearance was well presaged by Apollo's.

For Pope, as for the women poets, the Muses signified a notion of poetic inspiration separate from the material circumstances of production. In the *Epistle to Augustus*, the poet's most extreme statement of laureate ambivalence, Pope rehearses the stock theme of the session poems by surveying the entire tradition of English Laureates, whose relation with the monarch had in some way impaired them all as poets.[51] The Laureateship, the poem implies, had in the past rarely corresponded with a laureate ideal. "Kings in Wit may want discerning spirit," Pope remarks, "The Hero William, and the Martyr Charles, / One knighted Blackmore, and one pension'd Quarles" (385–7), while "Unhappy Dryden" was obliged "To please a lewd, or un-believing Court" (212–13). In those former "Days of Ease," the laureate ideal had been vitiated by the seductive appeal of "the King's Example"

(139, 142). Yet, if "The willing Muses were debauch'd at Court" under the restored Charles (152), the ideal is not even acknowledged by George – "chuse at least some Minister of Grace, / Fit to bestow the Laureat's weighty place" (378–9) – as though, for Pope, corruption were preferable to having no Laureate at all. In this way, Pope's ironic version of the Laureate's conventional apostrophe underscores how the Muses have been essentially exiled from the Hanoverian court: "How shall the Muse, from such a Monarch, steal / An hour, and not defraud the Publick Weal?" (5–6). If anything, the poem suggests that George, by his disdain for verse, has undermined the conditions for poetic production, denying it its traditional refining and immortalizing function. The loss of this last incentive is apparent from the poem's parodying of Laureate procession verses, where England's elder bards presented themselves before the monarch who, it was believed, could sanction their fame.[52] Unfortunately for poetry, however, the Hanoverians have produced only "such forgotten things / As Eusden, Philips, Settle, Writ of Kings" (416–17).

The absence of any clear social purpose for writing poetry is intolerable for Pope, who, even as he laments its impossibility under George, reaffirms the laureate ideal – "a Poet's of some weight, / And (tho' no Soldier) useful to the State" (203–4) – and ironically presents his candidature for the post: "Your Arms, your Actions, your Repose to sing!" (395). In recontextualizing Horace's panegyric to his emperor, Pope further intimates that it is the poet who still wields ultimate control over representation in being able to recreate in verse "such Majesty, such bold relief, / The Forms august of King" (390–1). Yet, in its reworking of the Roman poet's defence of literary modernity, the poem also gives implicit recognition to how market forces have largely supplanted the king's legitimizing authority. The Muses have given way to the dictates of the audience, whose choices for the bays are far more arbitrary: "the People's Voice is odd, / It is, and it is not, the Voice of God" (89–90). Worse yet, in determining canonicity by a readerly consensus of the ages, the public has assumed for itself the poet's fame-making power:

> If Time improve our Wit as well as Wine,
> Say at what age a Poet grows divine?
> Shall we, or shall we not, account him so,
> Who dy'd, perhaps, an hundred years ago?
> End all dispute; and fix the year precise
> When British bards begin t'Immortalize? (49–54)

Pope follows Horace in mimicking the claims of the mindless venerator of the past – "'Who lasts a Century can have no flaw, / I hold that

Wit a Classic, good in law'" (55–6) – yet a more serious consequence than this misguided antiquarianism is the erosion of exclusive standards that had formerly maintained order within the literary system. The growth of the print trade has permitted readers to imagine themselves not only the trustees of the canon but as potential Laureates: "one Poetick Itch / Has seiz'd the Court and City, Poor and Rich: / Sons, Sires, and Grandsires, all will wear the Bays" (169–71). For Pope, commercialization has degraded, marginalized, and feminized the laureate poet without providing an alternative universe of belief wherein the arbitrariness of all the operative tropes for poetic production and canonicity, from immortality to the laureate ideal, could be misrecognized. Many of the basic rewards for writing remained: celebrity, personal advancement, financial profit, and, however reduced in scale, patronage. Indeed, without a controlling structure of conviction, aspiring poets could ever more openly proclaim their pursuit of these rewards. Yet, in the absence of such a determining structure, no poet could attain either distinction or legitimacy.

The *Epistle* does nonetheless contain a very brief indication of what an alternative structure might be founded on. Agreeing with the public's verdict that Cowley's efforts in epic and pindaric are best forgotten, Pope avers, rather innocuously, that "still I love the language of his Heart" (78). The line recalls Pope's eulogizing in the *Epistle to Arbuthnot* of his father who, as a man unfamiliar with the ways of the world, "knew no Schoolman's subtle Art, / No Language, but the Language of the Heart" (397–8). To equate an "Un-learn'd" Pope senior with a poet of subtle art like Cowley might seem odd, but the similar tributes reflect Pope's reluctant engagement with a new conception of poetic value as something not just independent of the realms of the political and economic but unassailable because it is essentially irrational (398). This engagement is most evident in the *Epistle to Arbuthnot*, though it comes at the cost of the poem's unity. In condemning as corruption any poetic practice that serves the government, the patron, or the consuming public, the poem, according to Brean Hammond, seems to suggest that "only the author who is *entirely cut off* from the forces that bring books into existence can be celebrated." Thus, Hammond argues, it is because Pope deprives himself "of any coherent account of writing that contradictions occur on various levels of the poem's articulation."[53] Pope's inability to relate the autobiographical material in the poem to his several repudiations of the conventional incentives for authorship may explain the poem's discontinuities, though its fragmentation, as in many of the later satires, may equally represent Pope's deliberate refusal of one of poetry's most supreme functions, its value in enhancing the state's language of political signification. Yet the poem does, in fact, imply an account of writing, one that does suggest an author entirely cut off from external forces and interests, though one that cannot be made coherent because it is impervious to rational analysis.

This account has to do with one of the most profound consequences of artistic autonomization. The ideology of the aesthetic, as it emerged in the eighteenth century, represented an attempt first to promote art and its appreciation as activities separate from the economic and political, and secondly to relocate the source of artistic and literary value by positing certain innate mental faculties, those of taste, judgment, or moral sense. In grounding value in such faculties, eighteenth-century aesthetic theorists, as I have already suggested, folded the linguistic into the phenomenal; the reality of these faculties might have been undemonstrable, but they were nonetheless said to belong to the realm of the sensuously empirical, a realm of feeling rather than abstraction or convention, of meaning produced by organic natural processes rather than the exchange of the word. Aesthetic value became a matter of felt-experiences within the consumer's deeply embedded moral sense, of meanings perceived by the reader's intuitive judgment, and of the shocks and terrors of the sublime upon the viewer's sensibility. The ultimate source of that value, however, was a providential mystery. The poet could produce a highly rational work, according to Shaftesbury, but the cause of its affective power was beyond rational comprehension: "Though his intention be to please the world, he must nevertheless be, in a manner, above it, and fix his eye upon that consummate grace, that beauty of Nature, and that perfection of numbers which the rest of mankind, feeling only by the effect whilst ignorant of the cause, term the *je ne sçay quoy*, the unintelligible or the I know not what, and suppose to be a kind of charm or enchantment of which the artist himself can give no account."[54] As the source of poetic value was thus unknowable, theorists like Shaftesbury turned their attention from prescribing the right conditions for artistic production to defining the aesthetic experience almost exclusively in terms of the reception of its effects. Their theories, as signalled in their central notion of taste, bespoke an ideology of consumption.

The inevitable consequence of this shift from production to consumption was the suppression of artistic invention within critical discourse.[55] Pope had already sensed the implications of this shift in the *Essay on Criticism*, where he had attempted to bridge the widening gap between production and consumption by writing a poem that, in form and content, argued for the complementary nature of poetry and criticism, and their equal subordination to the law of Nature and its articulation in antique practice. Yet, though it stressed their commensurability, the thrust of the poem, as in much of Pope's early work, was to define its subject by discrimination and contrast, which entailed not merely opposing criticism to poetry but equally exposing just how ambiguous the value of the latter activity had become now that so many of its social functions had been assumed by criticism. That ambiguity was apparent from the poem's opening, which dramatically trivialized the productive effects of verbal power in its suggestion that ill writing was less harmful than poor judgment: "of the two, less dangerous is th' Offence, / To tire our *Patience*, than mis-lead our *Sense*" (4). The terms of Pope's argument in the poem rendered production answerable to reception: judging ill was dangerous because it misled the sense of *readers*, among whom were included the poets, who had to respect the advice of wise critics. This had to be so, since the poem proposed to instruct readers on how to become better, more sensitive consumers of art. Under the aristocratic codes of rhetorical culture, both poets and readers were thought to possess similar innate qualities of good judgment and wit, which were then simply expressed in social and poetic conventions. The bourgeois order heralded in the *Essay on Criticism*, in contrast, brought about both a separation of writing from reading, and an ideology of self-improvement where most of the ideal attributes of the critic (manners, good-breeding, learning, candour, self-restraint, avoidance of partiality, prejudice, and so on) would be a function of learned behaviour. Though ultimate evaluative certainty remained grounded in the natural faculty of "True *Taste*" (12), the reader as critic derived his authority from observing precise rules of socially defined conduct, rules that he could then apply as "*Fundamental Laws*" for literary production (722). In his efforts to refine an "*unciviliz'd*" English culture (716), the critic had thus taken over all of the responsibilities formerly exercised by harmonious evaluative communities of laureates and courtiers. And in claiming the right to bestow the "Poet's *Bays* and Critick's *Ivy*," he could now both determine the canon of literature and form his own pantheon of the "*sounder Few*" among his critical peers (719).

The natural "*Source, and End*, and *Test* of *Art*" that provided the critic with true taste could similarly endow the poet with "true *Genius*" (73, 11), yet the poetic gift was far less accountable, more arbitrary and mysterious than the dictates of the critical faculty. Its power was such that the poet could, at rare moments, violate prevailing rules and "*snatch* a *Grace* beyond the Reach of Art," which, as it "gains / The Heart, and all of its End *at once* attains" (156–7), could be an acceptable transgression of wit's fundamental laws since it returned cultural production to its irrational provenance. Yet, since that source remained irrational, poetic creativity could not be directed, only felt:

In some fair Body thus th' informing Soul
With Spirits feeds, with Vigour fills the whole,
Each motion guides, and ev'ry Nerve sustains;
It self unseen, but in th' *Effects*, remains. (76–9)

Pope may have been here mocking the mythology of the poet's compulsion, as he did later in the poem when he ridiculed the exertions of scribbling wits who run on "in a raging Vein / Ev'n to the Dregs and *Squeezings* of the *Brain*" (606–7). Yet the *Essay on Criticism* provided no alternative to this mythology, no coherent theory of artistic productivity, nor much of a sense of the social function of art. Poetry merely happened to the poet, who had to leave it to the critics to assess its considerable affective force, to harness it if necessary through critical prescriptions, or perhaps to fan "the *Poet's Fire*" (100). Apart from pleasing an audience or providing the instrument upon which critics could demonstrate their taste and expertise, this peculiar inventive discourse seemed to serve no specific purpose other than, potentially, the supreme one of restoring human society to its transcendent, organic, and endlessly renewing source of value in the universal order of nature. As such, all that could be meaningfully said about the practice of poetry pertained to the conditions of its reception, including the poet's own attempts to accommodate this sublime force to the rules of art.

For all of Pope's emphasis upon neoclassical standards for composition, the *Essay on Criticism* marked a major contribution to the increasing tendency among poets and aesthetic theorists alike to consign the causes of artistic production to an origin beyond rational understanding. According to these theories, poetry's unique source of value, of the *je ne sais quoi*, had to be lodged in the poet's *super-sensitivities*, or in some unknown internal energy which the poet-genius seemed to feel more intensely than could the reader. Production was surrendered to pain and compulsion, to the uncontrollable force of imagination, or to repressed psychic energies within the alienated poet. Such notions of poetic genius as compulsion, as I will suggest in the next section, would be increasingly championed later in the period as the poetic activity came more and more to be seen as autonomous. Yet there had been significant antecedents. A few early poets, notably Drayton, proposed transcendent, organic sources of poetic productivity to compensate for their estrangement from the centres of power; most dramatically, Milton, "though fallen on evil days," declared himself divinely guided to write *Paradise Lost* (VII.25). For the Augustan writers, the ongoing commercialization of letters prompted them to toy with myths of compulsion even as they resisted the cultural autonomization which these myths implied. The result was a host of dark fables of painful inspiration: in Augustan writing, as Margaret Anne Doody has noted, "any approach to the central sources of the energies of life or art, or of the creative powers of the poet's mind, takes us toward something monstrous."[56] For Pope, in the *Essay* and subsequent works, the Muses did not so much disappear as become internalized, in the Cave of Spleen or in Eloisa's imprisoned raptures inflamed by thoughts of her lover's mutilated body. That these personifications were often gendered as feminine reflects the identification of women not only with the physiological travails of procreation but with the eruptions of unreason and the perturbations of sensibility – Finch could feel as much poetically enfeebled by the Spleen as empowered by the "dark and terrible" images it inspired in her (78).[57] The satirists, in contrast, could experience only distress at their deepening exile from the drawing rooms of state, and so their poet's masculine fire became transformed into afflictions of the affective body. Dryden, in his later work as a commercial author, frequently complained of his failing memory and of being "a cripple in my limbs."[58] And desire of any kind, Swift alleged, could stem from a mere disorder of the bowels.

By the time Pope writes his *Epistle to Arbuthnot*, his "Muse of Pain" has as much to do with lashing dunces as coping personally and professionally with "this long Disease, my Life" (132).[59] The "Plague" of intruders upon his privacy provoke ailments both real and feigned – "say I'm sick, I'm dead" – just as his renunciation of London literary society is only partially a cure for being "sick of Fops, and Poetry, and Prate" (29,2,229). But writing is itself the most inexplicable of maladies, no longer an animating spirit or informing essence but a chronic nervous disorder, whose cause could be anything from a foul contamination in the writer's well to a pathological infantile ictus:

> Why did I write? what sin to me unknown
> Dipt me in Ink, my Parents', or my own?
> As yet a Child, nor yet a Fool to Fame,
> I lisp'd in Numbers, for the Numbers came.   (125–8)

Unlike what infects the decentred, situational selves of Atticus, Sporus, and the rest, the poetic vocation is a mysterious form of obsessive compulsive behaviour that determines the poet from an early age and thereby provides its own special kind of integrity and unshakeable influence. It may equally afford some initial pleasures but, as Pope had earlier written in the *Essay on Man*, the poet can become among afflicted souls perhaps the most absurdly addicted to his ruling passion:

> See the blind beggar dance, the cripple sing,
> The sot a hero, lunatic a king;
> The starving chemist in his golden views
> Supremely blest, the poet in his muse.   (II.267–70)

In the long term, however, Pope's mad poet, unlike Horace's, feels only the painful burden of his compulsion.[60] His "Bill of Complaint" to his friend and physician Arbuthnot can only repeat a despairing note of incomprehension: "Heav'ns! was I born for nothing but to write? / Has Life no Joys for me?" (272–3).

Yet compulsion has its own authority. The women poets who wrote for no other conventional reason than pleasure recognized that, by their marginality, their *furor poeticus* was distinguished by a certain purity that could justify their claims of disinterestedness and defiance towards public life. Finch, whose poem on the Spleen had been greatly admired by Pope, implied as much in an unpublished preface to her poems:

> For I have writt, and expos'd my uncorrect Rimes, and immediately repented; and yett have writt again, and again suffer'd them to be seen; tho' at the expence of more uneasy reflections, till at last (like them) wearied with uncertainty, and irresolution, I rather chuse to be harden'd in an errour, then to be still att the trouble of endeavering to over come itt: ... tho' itt is still a great satisfaction to me, that I was not so far abandon'd ... to lett any attempts of mine in Poetry, shew themselves whil'st I lived in such a publick place as the Court.[61]

It is this purity that Pope masculinizes in his Horatian self-fashioning. Confessing to Bolingbroke that there is none "half so incoherent as my Mind," Pope makes this self-styled "madness" the source of his poetic uniqueness, the I-know-not-what cause that has made him at once the ultimate outsider and a powerful threat to any common monarch, whose divinity the poet far exceeds by virtue of his remoteness from worldly interests:

> That man divine whom Wisdom calls her own,
> Great without Title, without Fortune bless'd,
> Rich ev'n when plunder'd, honour'd while oppress'd,
> Lov'd without youth, and follow'd without power,
> At home tho' exil'd, free, tho' in the Tower.
> In short, that reas'ning, high, immortal Thing,
> Just less than Jove, and much above a King,

Nay half in Heav'n – except (what's mighty odd)
A fit of Vapours clouds this Demi-god.   (*Epistle* I.i.166, 172, 180–8)

Parts of this could form a portrait of the high-born woman, patrician yet powerless, at home while imprisoned, a person of privilege though oppressed. Yet not only has the male poet come to occupy her eminent station at the social periphery but has equally made a claim on her peculiar purity of feeling: because women are increasingly assumed in the eighteenth century to be not only prone to the "vapours," the traditional diagnosis for female melancholy, but too feeble to dissemble their emotions, they are felt to manifest in both body and sensibility a greater sincerity of response than men, whose firmer constitutions and long habituation in the rational artifices of society, it is believed, help them to arrest any spontaneous outburst of sentiment.[62]

Such fits of sincere feeling and fancy can, however, co-exist with reason and aesthetic discipline in the male poet: "I love to pour out all myself" (*Satire* II.i.51). As a result, he can enjoy all the symbolic rewards of male productivity – honour, prestige, authority, fame – without the corruption and effeminization that is felt, under the new codes of aesthetic autonomization, to attend an author's pursuit of material and political gain. Where other wits write for party, patron, or profit, Pope dramatizes himself as a poet driven by a deep, indeterminate yet determining instinct whose preternatural force renders it morally unassailable – a force that appears, in this way, more unpredictable and transcendent than the reactive indignation of the Juvenalian satirist, who must speak out lest he burst. Replying to the lawyer Fortescue's suggestion that he refrain from satire, Pope can imagine no other outlet for his irrepressible impulse, which would disrupt the poet's sleep as an irruption of the unconscious were it not for the creative catharsis of writing:

Not write? but then I *think*,
And for my Soul I cannot sleep a wink.
I nod in Company, I wake at Night,
Fools rush into my Head, and so I write.   (*Satire* II.i.11–14)

Later in the same poem, Pope, perhaps realizing that with compulsion runs the threat of enslavement, sentimentalizes his moral authority as he had done his father's, by locating it in a masculinized purity of thought and feeling that had formerly been associated with female creativity: "My Head and Heart thus flowing thro' my Quill, / Verseman or Prose-man, term me which you will" (63–4).[63] Such an organic explanation of poetic authority can identify no social function for writing, nor can it be the basis for any conventions by which to structure a work. It only asserts a potential, alternative point of distinction for the "verse-man" and, above all, a new heroic legitimacy for the poetic activity, now seemingly absolute in its autonomy.

Since it can provide the poet with no coherent understanding of poetry's symbolic value in society, maintaining this autonomy comes at a serious cost. By the end of his career, Pope is engaging in bitter, even manic gestures of renunciation, abandoning the English cultural establishment to the dunces, melodramatically presenting himself as the "Last of *Britons*" who draws "the last Pen for Freedom" against an age of vice triumphant in the *Epilogue to the Satires* (II.250, 248), spurning his own evaluative community of political allies in the fragmentary *One Thousand Seven Hundred and Forty*, and declaring to the world "a resolution to publish no more" (*Epilogue* II.255n.). So extravagant and solipsistic is Pope's self-presentation in these late poems that some critics have charged that his rage is all out of proportion to any ostensible provocation. In this vein, Carole Fabricant has written that "the poems appear to lack a convincing objective correlative for the moral outrage and invective expressed, an absence which leaves only the image of a dramatic, bloated, all-consuming, sublime Self that takes over center stage while all else becomes primarily a backdrop which highlights, through contrast, the speaker's virtuous self."[64] From this perspective, Pope's self-definition represents an extreme of rhetorical valorization, where the poet feels compelled to pathologize *everything*, save perhaps for his own "Heav'n-directed hands," in order both to assert his distinctiveness as a poet and to make one final, desperate stand on behalf of poetry's centrality in the moral economy of the state (*Epilogue to the Satires* II.214). For Fabricant and others, Pope's self-defining "combat" is historically significant because it was directed not simply against the traditional civic humanist targets of moral depravity, political corruption, and economic self-interest, but against the new category of modern mass culture; "it was Pope as much as anyone," Hammond suggests, "who established the distinction between 'classic' and 'popular' writers and writing."[65] Yet the binarisms of high and low were nothing new. Pope's cultural combat was something far more spectacular and revolutionary, the culminating struggle in a lengthy historical process whereby professional authorship had sought to liberate itself from social and political authority by proclaiming the sublime autonomy of artistic creativity. Pope's final disavowals, so alienating to most readers, announced the end of writing poetry as a form of social productivity, and signalled the poet's own personal reconciliation to the liberating mythology of the poetic compulsion and its troubling anti-social implications. Though the poet, long since retired to his grotto, could still grandly declare that he could "redeem the land" (*One Thousand Seven Hundred and Forty* 98), he would no longer write in the service of the state, the church, the market, or any other institution or formation. From now on, the poet was to be alone.

THE REJECTION OF CLASSICISM

Within a generation after his death, Pope's pre-eminence in the canon would be challenged by polemicists hoping to rid English poetry of its neoclassical values by proclaiming a new ideal of what Joseph Warton called a "pure poetry" of feeling, as epitomized by Shakespeare's artless tragedies, Spenser's Gothic enchantments, and Milton's boundless sublimities. In a notorious passage in his dedication to Edward Young before his *Essay on the Genius and Writings of Pope* (1756, 1782), Warton made it clear that this revaluation of Pope and other satirists in favour of the poets of the sublime and the pathetic would reaffirm the masculinist hegemony of the canon: "We do not, it should seem, sufficiently attend to the difference there is betwixt a MAN OF WIT, a MAN OF SENSE, and a TRUE POET. Donne and Swift, were undoubtedly men of wit, and men of sense: but what traces have they left of PURE POETRY?"[66] Young seconded Warton's poetic revolution, and his masculinizing rhetoric, with his epochal *Conjectures on Original Composition* (1759), where he heralded poetry's emancipation from classicist imitation. Following antique models, Young wrote, "lays genius under restraint, and denies it that free scope, that full elbow-room, which is requisite for striking its most masterly strokes." If Pope believed he had "pleas'd by manly ways" (*Epistle to Arbuthnot*, 337), Young had simply to reverse the gendering in order to devaluate his former ally's translations of Homer, the single most influential literary event of the century: "by that *effeminate* decoration" of rhyme, Pope emasculated Homer's "various modulations of *masculine* melody" and "put *Achilles* in petticoats." And if Pope's compulsion was an obscure and physically disabling disorder, Young's anti-classicist revolution transformed the poet's pain into a virile force: "For genius may be compared to the natural strength of the body."[67] Such gendering was a common critical gesture of the period, though a change in its conditions of use was here apparent: whereas Pope had asserted his masculine poetic identity so as to distance himself from what was thought to be the feminizing forces of the marketplace, Warton and Young appropriated this masculinity so as to defend themselves from the charge of having feminized literature by promoting a poetry of passion and imagination.[68]

My concern here, however, is less with such gendering than with the possible functions that might have been served by this anti-classicist revolution – a revolution that, arguably, was a logical extension of the cultural autonomization that Pope had already come to embrace in his final writings. In appearance, the rejection of classicism resembled most other such revolutions in being another round in the perennial contest for distinction within the cultural field. These revolutions are usually characterized, Bourdieu has argued, by insurgent avant-gardes within a genre taking on established vanguards by proposing "to question the very foundation of the genre through a return to sources and to the purity of its origins. As a consequence, the history of poetry, the novel or theatre tends to appear as a continuous process of purification through which each of these genres, at the end of a thorough reappraisal of itself, its principles and its presuppositions, finds itself reduced to the most purified quintessence."[69] Bourdieu sees this process of generic purification as resulting from the persistent need to define the cultural field's autonomy as a source of its own special, non-economic capital. The return to a genre's originating essence is a common strategy within what he calls the cultural "game," since it signals a disavowal of economic interest on behalf of refining one's art to its seemingly purest form. And such a disavowal, Bourdieu has repeatedly insisted, is among the most powerful gestures for acquiring symbolic profits within the cultural field.

The poetic revolution that was waged in the critical discourse of the mid-eighteenth century involved, however, more than just a purification of poetic forms or, for that matter, an intensified gendering of literary practices. Classicism's decline as a model for production is especially striking since classicism had long been the preferred discourse for a poet of laureate ambition to claim purity, distinction, and moral autonomy. I have already traced a temporal arc of classicist purification within this narrative, beginning with Petrarch, the first modern poet, who could exalt the classical heritage in order to assert his independence from the inhibitions of a moribund *auctorial* order and to enable his society's progress out of what he termed the "Dark Ages." Social progression became moral and artistic fixity in Jonson's version, a codified formal classicism which he called both "the old way and the true" (*Epigram* 18:2) and which helped him to distinguish his laureate professionalism from the self-interests of the mass market, as well as to secure his artistic independence from powerful influences, Jonson announcing himself to the court as "thy servant, but not slave."[70] Jonson's presentism then became cultural conservatism with Dryden and Pope, whose strategic pursuit of classicist refinement in poetry enabled them at once to disavow economic interest, to assert their moral autonomy, and to present their work as essential in preserving English society from the commercialization and corruption which they felt was threatening to overtake it. After Pope, Johnson supposed, "to attempt any further improvement of versification will be dangerous," but in fact, as I will suggest, no more classicist purification would be undertaken as poetic practice had ultimately withdrawn from the social world.[71]

Classicism had long been a recognized position for a poet eager for distinction to take, and one eminently adaptable to changing circumstances, such as the rise of the vernaculars or of the print trade. It offered the working poet both a legitimizing cultural lineage reaching back to a revered ancient *imperium,* as well as an enabling revisionist narrative of refinement by which to define his modernity. Its decline in the eighteenth century must have coincided with a reorganization of the cultural field so extensive as to alter the relations and position-takings within the field. It is not enough, therefore, to argue that the rejection of classicism reflected an emergent nationalist sentiment that spurned critical doctrines long associated with the French in favour of native genius. Not only was the alternative concept of "pure poetry" itself of French importation, but equally, if Bourdieu's assumption is correct, the goal of an artistic purification not based in classicist principles can only have come about with a further autonomization of the cultural field rather than its yielding to external political interests like nationalism.[72] Nor is it adequate to suggest, as some recent historians have done, that it is only with the establishment of a stable English canon during the period that authors could legitimately relocate the origins of poetic purity from the ancients to a native tradition, in the spirit of "better Ossian than Homer."[73] Pure poetry, according to Lowth, could just as easily be found among the Hebrew Scriptures.[74] Besides, the gesture of proclaiming a pure source among the English had already been proposed authoritatively prior to classicism's ascendancy in the seventeenth century: Drayton, among others, declared himself the herald of a British bardic past, while Spenser could claim to have drawn from Chaucer's well of English undefiled.

Drayton and Spenser, however, were writing within a rhetorical culture whose main currency was symbolic capital – that is, fame, prestige, honour, recognition. Despite being reluctant professionals, Drayton and Spenser were less anxious to define their autonomy from commercial interests than not to compromise their laureate integrity as national poets. They could not be seen to be acting merely out of self-interest, political or economic, since their role as national poets required them to promote the circulation of symbolic capital by using their rhetorical skills to refine the language of political signification; as I suggested in an earlier chapter, these poets were expected to bestow praise and fame on their patrons and the state in the very act of seeking them for themselves. Classicism, with its Horatian or Juvenalian postures of detachment, could thus offer a poet like Jonson or Pope the means not only to assert an antique poetic purity that could seemingly transcend any economic interest, but, more important, to present himself as a public-minded poet of sufficient moral independence to contribute genuinely to the common good in a style proper to his verbal talents. Classicism, in this way, was the cultural analogue to the ideology of civic humanism, with the laureate poet being equivalent to the citizen who practised autonomy in the confined space, the drawing room as it were, where he met with equals; the neoclassical poet-statesman saw his cultural practice as self-governing yet vigorously productive in its deployment of symbolic capital, itself conceived in terms of the masculinist values of honour, prestige, and devotion to the public realm.

As we know from J.G.A. Pocock's work, the values of civic humanism came into conflict in the eighteenth century with a newer ideology of commercial humanism, which reflected the altered historical conditions of capitalist exchange-relations and an emergent liberal republicanism. Commercial humanism emphasized a much broader *polis*, in which the citizen, in exchange for surrendering his autonomy to others who would represent him, became a specialized, private, even decentred individual who refined his moral being through a sympathetic social intercourse among the increasingly complex and *differentiated* human relations and products that commerce could furnish. And among those products and services were the arts, which, it was felt, could help the subject to learn how to modulate the disruptions of passion because they directly engaged the faculties of imaginative sympathy. Within this greatly expanded *polis*, the cultural field would continue to play a role in maintaining the moral order, but it was no longer the *same* role as under a pre-capitalist economy, where it had functioned to help circulate symbolic capital and its attendant ideology of civic humanism. Under commercial humanism, in contrast, the new human relations fostered by commerce and the arts functioned to polish the subject's "manners" rather than to promote an active virtue; these new relations were, therefore, as Pocock has stressed, "social and not political in character."[75] The masculinist values of civic humanism remained appealing to some who were fearful of culture being feminized because of this emphasis on sympathetic social intercourse, just as there were others like Samuel Johnson who continued to abide by the discourse of classicism because they believed in the productive potential of literature to promote virtue directly rather than indirectly through the imagination and sensibility.[76] Yet, whatever the specific values endorsed by writers, the cultural field in general was no longer seen as supporting a set of political relationships and was thus bereft of its former source of legitimacy. In addition, since economic capital had displaced symbolic capital as the main currency of social power, the arts were now in direct competition with all the other commercial goods and services that could facilitate the refinement of manners. In danger of being utterly commodified, the cultural field had to be redefined and more insistently autonomized in order to remain distinctive and legitimate. As a consequence, a new structure of belief began to emerge, wherein the cultural field would be seen as deploying its own separate and special *cultural* capital.[77]

If symbolic capital denotes a measure of accumulated fame, honour, or prestige that can be used within any form of social exchange, cultural capital refers to the level of accredited competence that is required to appreciate the meaning and value of cultural goods and relations. Such cultural products are, according to Bourdieu, to be treated as a sort of code which can be fully deciphered only by those who are recognized to possess the necessary disposition, learning, and skill – this cultural competence thus being credited as a peculiar form of prestige that appears an end in itself, the prestige of aesthetic taste or scholarly expertise, yet in fact represents one category among several of modern social power.[78] The emphasis on learning and skill might seem to align cultural capital with classicism, since the usual polemical charge against the latter was that it was too codified and stressed learning and correctness at the expense of creativity. As Young put it in the *Conjectures*, original genius is characterized by "unprescribed beauties, and unexampled excellence" which were outside the "pale of *learning*'s authorities, and laws."[79] Yet cultural capital does not have to do with prescribed models of production as with the effects of experiencing or learning about art. Whereas classicism had implied an ideology of productive civic participation, commercial humanism did not propose a theory of production, but only one of enrichment through consumption. Production being a feature of the economic field from which the cultural field had to be differentiated, aesthetic theories of the period, as I have suggested, surrendered artistic invention to pain and compulsion. For Pope, prior to his final self-liberation, this surrender could be acknowledged only reluctantly, and then to legitimize strenuous strategic disavowals on two fronts, Pope opposing himself both to Grub Street's commercial contamination of literature and to the traditional target of political corruption. For Young and the other anti-classicists who no longer had to contend with political interests, the poetic compulsion could be celebrated as a sign of how poetry's value and purity transcended all interests. Precisely because the origin of literary invention was irrational and its presence knowable only through its affective power, the value of the aesthetic experience was not to be questioned: "There is something in poetry beyond prose-reason; there are mysteries in it not to be explained, but admired."[80] Others would later attempt to describe the creative process in more detail, but even for Wordsworth the source of invention remained an irrational compulsion, the "spontaneous overflow of powerful feelings."[81]

That creativity could spring from natural gifts had long been entertained in critical discourse, but it is only with the suppression of invention within the moral economy of commercial humanism that the source of poetic purity could be legitimately relocated from a historical practice identified with the ancients to a providential mystery that could only be identified by its effects. On the one hand, this meant that the poets of mid-century, eager to distinguish themselves from their classicist predecessors, could experiment with a broad array of vernacular *and* classical genres, from ballads to Pindaric odes, which they could claim to have served them in purifying English poetry, since this purity had no longer to do with specific poetic practices as with poetry's effects. Yet unlike their predecessors, who had to establish their autonomy from powerful political interests, these modern poets had to devote much of their poetry to asserting the special character and authenticity of their poetic compulsion. After all, eighteenth-century economic man could himself be perceived as a creature of compulsion, "a feminised, even an effeminate being, still wrestling with his own passions and hysterias and with interior and exterior forces let loose by his fantasies and appetites."[82] If their compulsions were not to be mistaken for such degradingly feminine commercial desires, the poets had to rely on the symbolic violence of presenting themselves as *highly* differentiated selves, whether possessed of the elusive poetical character, of a Gothic self-absorption or medieval bardic consciousness, or (in Wordsworth's version) a "more than usual organic sensibility."[83] The poet's uniqueness was not necessarily to be defined in terms of any modernist revision or purification of the existing tradition; despite the nascent cult of originality, these poets' canon-making gestures, notably Gray's "Progress of Poesy," displayed such a respectful awareness of tradition as to seem burdened by the past.[84] Rather, poetic uniqueness was to be measured by its contrast with society and in terms of a power to speak, like Gray's Bard, "with a voice more than human."[85] By extension, the effects that their poetry produced had themselves to be highly differentiated, as partaking of the sublime or the pathetic, in order to heighten the sense that poetry was the supreme discourse of sympathetic engagement: "Poetry, *pure Poetry*," Hurd wrote in a typical vein, "is the proper language of *Passion*."[86] Whereas classicists like Pope had pursued the refinement of poetic conventions as a means to enable symbolic productivity within a moral and political order, their successors saw this project of refinement as profoundly disabling to poetry since the latter's unique affective power, they believed, was inevitably repressed or enervated when subordinated to the requirements of a broadly social discursivity.

On the other hand, with poetry's value keyed to its effects, the experience of poetry could be convertible to cultural capital, since appreciating it now required a recognized measure of refined receptivity – if the Bard spoke with a voice more than human, it would follow that, as the motto before Gray's Odes announced, his poetry was "vocal to the Intelligent alone." In essence, cultural capital rendered amenable to social hierarchization the commercial humanist ideal that intercourse with the arts could help one develop a moral personality marked by a deep imaginative sympathy. Not surprisingly, the period's polemics for pure poetry could easily slide from specifying the nature of genius to insisting on how few readers were possessed of appropriate affectivity and taste. Warton, in the same passage in his essay on Pope where he heralded the idea of pure poetry, claimed that the true poet could be distinguished from the man of sense by virtue of the former's "creative and glowing IMAGINATION, 'acer spiritus ac vis' [the fire and force of inspiration], and that alone, that can stamp a writer with this exalted and very uncommon character, which so few possess, and of which so few can properly judge. For one person, who can adequately relish, and enjoy, a work of imagination, twenty are to be found who can taste and judge of, observations on familiar life, and the manners of the age."[87] By this gesture, Warton was clearly attempting to promote his critical activity, but it is the arbitrariness of his terms that is revealing. First, the true poet was to be differentiated by his "exalted and very uncommon character," but the degree of this differentiation could be measured only indirectly, by analogy with the one reader in twenty who was competent enough to judge of the poetry. Secondly, and more important, the reader who demonstrated such competence, or cultural capital, could claim an apparent moral superiority over the many who relied merely on the ordinary commerce of "familiar life, and the manners of the age" to form their moral being. This cultural hierarchy Warton then went on to reinforce, by analogy, with his ranking of English poets, among the first such efforts in English criticism at systematically hierarchizing the canon. And within this canon, according to Warton, Pope could not be classed in the first rank of poets precisely because his poetry was *too* accessible to ordinary readers, being "fit for universal perusal [and] adapted to all ages and stations." No cultural capital could be gained from demonstrating familiarity with Pope's work, Warton believed, since it "lies more level to the general capacities of men, than the higher flights of more genuine poetry."[88]

Presumably, Warton's competent reader was not simply a refurbished version of the "learned reader" common to rhetorical valuations, since the critic would not have bothered to pen his essay if he had not believed that readers could learn how to acquire the desired competence and to ascend the cultural hierarchy by reading treatises like the essay on Pope. Yet it is on this point that Warton exerted the most implicit of symbolic violence, since he did not actually say whether such readerly competence resulted directly from the experience of poetry, or whether it was rooted in some innate faculty of taste or imagination comparable to the poet's. Eighteenth-century aesthetics theorists often equivocated on this undecidability as to where value resides, in the text or the reader, since the argument from nature could obviously justify a cultural hierarchy while the argument from nurture ensured a social function for the arts in helping to refine the passions. Thus it could be possible for Young to suggest that, while the ultimate source of creativity remained mysterious, the poet could just as much benefit from the poetic experience as the reader: to "men of letters," Young writes in his *Conjectures*, poetic composition "is not only a noble amusement, but a sweet refuge; it improves their parts, and promotes their peace: It opens a back-door out of the bustle of this busy, and idle world, into a delicious garden of moral and intellectual fruits and flowers; the key of which is denied to the rest of mankind." It does not ultimately matter, Young is here implying, whether the cultural capital which is denied to the rest of mankind originates in some providential gift or as a result of an ongoing sentimental education spent conversing among the arts. Nor does it matter, as he puts it, "whether we write ourselves, or in more humble amusement peruse the works of others." What *does* matter is that the poetic experience be consistently opposed to all the other complex and differentiated relations amid "the thronged walks of public life." Young may be arguing against classicist imitation for the gifted poet, but the terms of his argument suggest that the writing and reading of poetry are valuable activities only when conducted in a condition of social withdrawal. The poetic experience, Young insists, is simply more enriching or "improving" than any other human activity, and the more isolated and purer the experience, the better. As he exclaims, "With what a gust do we retire to our disinterested, and immortal friends in our closet ...? How independent of the world is he, who can daily find new acquaintance, that at once entertain, and improve him, in the little world, the minute but fruitful creation, of his own mind?" Within this now-masculinized domestic sphere, such aesthetic disinterestedness nourishes the poet as much as the reader: free from the sordid desires of commercial life, if still materially dependent on the book market, "an inventive genius," says Young, "may safely stay at home ... divinely replenished from within."[89]

The scene of literature, formerly restricted to the drawing rooms of poets and statesmen, had become even more rarefied and autonomous, safely lodged in the reader's mind or the creator's solitary refuge. Only in such a state of seclusion, it seemed, could both the production and reception of poetic value be properly undertaken, for what was said to be most disabling about social life was that its many complex and differentiated relations remained too distracting and "artificial" to allow the artist or reader to develop the requisite disposition that the special experience of poetry demanded. The *"still small voice* of Poetry was not made to be heard in a crowd," wrote Gray, the first notable English poet, if by no means the last, to legitimize an authorial identity by repudiating all claims of a modern social world.[90] The classicists, in this view, had erred not so much because they wrote with ethical or didactic purpose as because, for all their stances of detachment, they had failed to respect poetry's distinctive value in that they had used their writing as a mechanism of social representation and symbolic exchange. Thus, Warton concluded that Pope had forfeited his chance at standing alongside Spenser, Shakespeare, and Milton in the first rank of the English canon, since the satirist had vulgarized his poetic compulsion by having trafficked in scenes of "familiar life." As Warton put it in later editions of the *Essay*, Pope "stuck to describing *modern manners*; but those *manners* because they are *familiar, uniform, artificial,* and *polished,* are, in their very nature, unfit for any lofty effort of the Muse."[91] The idea would subsequently be popularized as the primitivist notion that poetical genius flowered best in "rude and uncultivated" ages: "True Genius," William Duff declared, "removed from the din and tumult of business and care, shoots up to the noblest height." Yet, he added, "Its fate in advanced society, and amidst the croud of mankind, is very different ... Intangled in those vexatious pursuits which interrupt the repose of mankind, its ardor is wasted in the tumultuous career of ambition, and its powers absorbed in the unfathomable gulf of sensual indulgence."[92] Far from returning poetic forms and conventions to their purity of origin, critical gestures such as these were drastically altering the terms of disavowal by which the value of the poetic activity could be defined.

In place of the classicist emphasis on the moral independence of the poet as civic-minded laureate, these gestures were valorizing the autonomization of an entire field of cultural production. The function and distinctiveness of this field had now to be set against the "crowd" in the marketplace, whose multiple sensual delights and subjective relations threatened to render poetry merely one among many possible diversions that could serve the subject in forming his moral being.

The rejection of classicism on behalf of an ideal of pure poetry was thus intimately related to the extended theoretical attempt, from Shaftesbury and Hutcheson to Kant, to define the ideally disinterested yet still valuable nature of the aesthetic experience. Both efforts were part of a larger reorientation of belief about the function of culture in a society increasingly driven by economic exchange. With the ascendancy of commercial humanism, the cultural field, whose autonomy had been for so long defined in opposition to both political and economic interests, was relegated to a depoliticized social sphere where, as its value could only be identified by its effects, it was expected to enable the refinement of manners in much the same way as any other commercial activity or product. In order, then, to preserve the autonomy of the cultural field, and to maintain its utility in legitimizing a social hierarchy, the value of the aesthetic experience had to be converted into cultural capital, which ostensibly furnished the subject with a measure of distinction and moral benefit that were evidently unobtainable through the ordinary commerce among all the other goods and exchange relations of modern life. Pure poetry, in the sense of poetic effects free from all elements except emotion, was the objective correlative to disinterested reading, in the sense of an experience free from all the less refined and refining distractions of the social world. In misrecognizing the arbitrariness of proclaiming such purity and disinterest, the poets and critics at mid-century were contributing to a new structure of belief, which, regardless of the intention of the individual, could not but serve to reinforce a sense of social distinction. As Bourdieu suggests in his critique of aesthetic disinterestedness, "it should not be thought that the relationship of distinction (which may or may not imply the conscious intention of distinguishing oneself from the common people) is only an incidental component in the aesthetic disposition. The pure gaze implies a break with the ordinary attitude towards the world which, as such, is a social break."[93] In rejecting classicism, these poets and critics were not so much staging a retreat from history as they were attempting to isolate and extol the special character of poetry as compensation for the fact that poetry had been denied its former centrality within the political economy of the state.[94] Unlike other poetic revolutions, theirs did not involve a

formal purification of the genre's attributes so much as a social purification of the poetic experience, and this was apparent even when
they attempted to justify pure poetry in formal terms: in Lowth's version, "the poetry of every language has a style and form of expression
peculiar to itself ... the whole form and complexion different from
what we meet with in common life."[95] Only later, when the autonomy
of the cultural field and the legitimacy of its capital were secure, could
the continuous process of purification be once again restricted to
poetic forms, with Wordsworth, the most self-differentiating of poets,
heralding poetry's fully remasculinized return to the "language really
used by men."[96]

PART FOUR

Consumption and Canonic Hierarchy

6 Reading the Canon

Late in his digression on the Ancients and the Moderns (1688), Fontenelle speculated on how, just as the Greeks and Romans had enjoyed an inflated reputation thanks to a recurrent prejudice for the antique, so his literary contemporaries might themselves look forward to being "excessively admired centuries from now, as recompense for the meagre attention we receive in our day. Readers will study our works for beauties that we never imagined putting there, while blatant faults, to which any author would own up, will find the staunchest of defenders."[1] The thought, which Johnson would ridicule in the opening of his Preface to *Shakespeare*, nonetheless correctly prophesied that the works of the Moderns would find a later life as objects of study, their canonicity sanctified in commentaries whose function would be to locate ever-new latent beauties, to make such old works seem timeless in their significance, and to turn faults into virtues by persuading readers to revise their standards. The Ancients, like Scripture, had long been maintained in a position of cultural pre-eminence through such allegorizing commentary, critical consecration, or, beginning in the later seventeenth century, objectivist modes of interpretation founded on rationalist and historicist principles. Yet it is only in the eighteenth century that such forms of attention began to be applied extensively to works of English literature. The works of the English canon had by then been around long enough to warrant not just the prestige of sumptuous editions, as they had been honoured with in the past, but with analyses and arguments that could reveal for the contemporary reader heretofore unappreciated splendours in the text, recover meanings of seemingly universal relevance, or make historicist allowances for the alterity of the aging works. The canon became during this period something to be reproduced.

This change may have been a response to an increased readership at all levels of society, and hence a growing number of readers who were not classically educated and for whom English works, beginning with English translations of the classics, could serve as acceptable substitutes within their acculturation. However, the fact that the English people were encouraged to undertake this process of acculturation, and that the process could be conducted simply by *reading* works of literature, points to much broader ideological and epistemological changes in society, changes that I have been identifying with the ascendancy of an objectivist culture. Not only did commercial humanism, a dominant set of values within objectivist culture, emphasize the refinement of manners through consumption rather than production, but the supreme operative assumption within a modern objectivist culture holds that solidarity can be achieved through the acquisition and systematization of knowledge. Hence reading and literacy were considered increasingly valuable at most or all ranks, if less important to a middle-class woman's formation than a young gentleman's: "Good Taste is for us in Literature, what it is for Women in Dress."[2] A sufficient stock of polite learning was gradually becoming seen as vital to the gentleman's basic moral and social equipment as eloquence had formerly been, and this was signalled in the widening prevalence of the term "literature," used less in its older sense of denoting the quality of being well read as in a more objective sense to identify the materials of polite learning. For Saint-Evremond, in a passage first translated in 1692, there were "no Sciences that particularly belong to Gentlemen, but Morality, Politicks, and the Knowledge of good Literature." Good breeding, Swift mordantly proposed, had to involve becoming acquainted with "an uncommon degree of literature sufficient to qualify a gentleman for reading a play." Young men, wrote John Oldmixon, should follow Arthur Maynwaring's example in forming themselves "*with Polite Literature*, with *Poetry, History* and *Criticism*."[3] (Later, in my concluding remarks, I consider the emergence of "literature" as a central term within critical discourse.)

This deepening of the social significance of the reading activity altered the nature of critical discourse, whose varied functions shifted from aiding the production to regulating the transmission of canonical works, from prescribing how works ought to be composed to supervising how they ought to be read and judged, and from promoting the general symbolic value of writing to ensuring the legitimacy of an autonomous cultural field. Leaving the modes of evaluative practice to my next chapter, I am concerned here with how these new functions required critics to redefine the basis for their authority and, by extension, the norms for canonicity. Something of this new authority is apparent from Shaftesbury's avowal "not only to defend the cause of critics, but to declare open war against those indolent supine authors, performers, readers, auditors, actors or spectators who, making their humour alone the rule of what is beautiful and agreeable … reject the criticising or examining art, by which alone they are able to discover the true beauty and worth of every object."[4] If readers are here differentiated from authors, their activity is not, for both are consumers of the literary work, itself no longer perceived as a mechanism of exchange but as an autonomous "object," whose true beauty and worth only criticism can enable both authors and readers to discern. The critic's authority derives not from adhering to established norms of composition, such as the rules, nor from speaking on behalf of a harmonious evaluative community, but from displaying and teaching special recognized skills of examination, contemplation, and "discovery." Achieving this authority thus involves earning cultural capital, the measure of accredited competence at assessing the meaning and value of cultural goods.

It follows that, for the critic to display a competence superior to the ordinary reader's, these goods must be of a nature that they will contain "true beauty" which requires the critic's special skills and learning to uncover. As a consequence, the critic will tend to focus on those canonical texts whose worth and meaning may not be immediately apparent, and which seem to promise a depth of significance that the critic can then train readers to master. Fontenelle's remark about future readers foraging for unintended beauties in old writings points to the fate of canonicity in a culture where critical and pedagogical institutions are well established: if canonical texts are to be valued not for their persuasive, productive force but for their service in refining the sensibilities and tastes of readers, or in authorizing critics to assist readers in developing certain special forms of attention, it follows that the most continually valued writings are those that are most receptive to contemplation yet equally most resistant to full discovery. Though the relations between a canonical text and its context of origin or use may be quite complicated, the assumption that the canonical text will always have riches in store is central to modern criticism, and modern literary education, for it provides them with an ongoing legitimacy and function and helps to sustain a structure of belief about the exclusivity and special difficulty of acquiring cultural capital.

This assumption only begins to be formulated during the eighteenth century, though the ongoing professionalization of criticism in the period does make for a pressing need to legitimate the critic's role as mediator between reader and text. To authorize their practice, critics begin to rely on a number of gestures for asserting the value of reading canonical English works, including the claim that these works have much to offer readers who seek to refine and display their taste and cultural competence yet are not so accessible that readers may do without the assistance of critics and educators in mastering them. Many of these gestures were introduced in the periodical criticism of the period, and in particular *The Spectator*, where one of Addison's most explicit aims was "to establish among us a Taste of polite Writing" (*S* 58).[5] More than any other cultural phenomenon, *The Spectator* helped to make the reader the focus of critical discourse, to transform the reader from a rhetorical figure used to punctuate assertions of value into a subject whose taste and sensibility could be shaped by discourse; the "great and only End" of *The Spectator*, it is said, "was to institute the very cultural subject to which it was supposedly addressed."[6] This transformation of the reader was effected in part through Mr Spectator's characteristic mode of address, which invited the reader to partake of a cultural conversation seemingly occurring throughout most ranks of English society, and in part through Addison's shrewd popularization and legitimation of the values of commercial humanism, which encouraged the reader to polish his or her manners through a wide-ranging intercourse with modern economic society and its many products. These values Addison most systematically presented in his series on the pleasures of the imagination; but they are equally prevalent in his papers on *Paradise Lost*, which were seminal not simply in raising the stature of Milton's poem but in making it possible for readers to derive cultural capital from the fact of having read works of the English canon.

Addison's influence can be seen not just in the rising number of later critical exegeses devoted to English texts, but also in the changing attitudes towards reading the English canon as expressed in prefaces to literary anthologies, in school textbooks, and in educational treatises of the period, documents that I survey in my second section. Though the universities were beginning to respond to the new divisions of knowledge, with Oxford instituting the first ever chair of poetry in 1708, the formal study of English literature would not be recognized as an university discipline until much later.[7] At lower levels of education, however, there was less resistance to these new divisions, and many eighteenth-century anthologists and schoolmasters began to make the case for including English texts in the education of the young or of the lower orders. The arguments they proposed indicated that English texts were to serve not merely as models for composition but, for many students, as instruments for their moral and aesthetic enrichment. These arguments made it clear that reading was a skill to be learnt, and hence that the English canon had to be introduced to students under circumstances of critical and pedagogical supervision. That said, the period's most spectacular canonization of an English author, Shakespeare's, may have been effected only partly through criticism, since Bardolatry was largely inaugurated on the English stage and symbolically ratified with Garrick's Jubilee of 1769. In my last section, however, I argue that critical discourse gradually displaced the authority of the theatres in terms of controlling the evaluation and interpretation of Shakespeare's texts. This displacement proved successful precisely because the critics, if not the actors, were able to present Shakespeare as an author whose works contained unlimited beauties that could be discovered only through skilled reading. The extended critical effort to define an authentic Shakespearean text thus reflected an altered cultural situation where the cultural capital that could come from reading was becoming recognized as a category of social power.

ADDISON READS MILTON

Perhaps no single campaign of canonization in all of English criticism has been ever been waged so successfully as Addison's consecration of *Paradise Lost* in the eighteen Saturday papers of *The Spectator* that ran from January to May 1712. Milton's reputation among poets and critics had been relatively secure prior to Addison's intervention, but the latter's assault on contemporary taste ensured the poet's work a popularity that Milton himself could never have expected nor possibly desired. Never again would *Paradise Lost* be read merely by a fit audience though few. Addison's essays, reprinted more often than any other work on Milton, became a major influence both in forming opinion on the poem's meaning and in making it respectable for all fashion-conscious readers to acknowledge their esteem for the work of a modern English writer. That Addison may have popularized Milton's epic at the cost of domesticating the poet's radical ideas was recognized at the time, though most critics thought this was on the whole a good thing. Johnson's ironic praise in his "Life of Addison" summed up the general view of the critic's accomplishment: "An instructor like Addison was now wanting, whose remarks being superficial, might be easily understood, and being just might prepare the mind for more attainments. Had he presented *Paradise Lost* to the publick with all the pomp of system and severity of science, the criticism would perhaps have been admired, and the poem still have been neglected; but by the blandishments of gentleness and facility he has made Milton an universal favourite, with whom readers of every class think it necessary to be pleased."[8]

Implicit within Johnson's praise are several assumptions that would not have been possible were it not for Addison's efforts, whose significance for the history of the English literary canon has not been fully understood. Addison helped to redefine the practice of canon-formation in at least three ways, all of which are apparent from Johnson's remark. First, in seeing Addison as a critic who cares more for the poem than for his own system, Johnson is projecting himself onto Addison, transforming his predecessor into a defender of the common reader, one who establishes a work's canonicity by sounding the authority not of neoclassical doctrine but of a readerly consensus. Such a projection may be appropriate to Addison only to a degree, since he in fact declares that he will examine *Paradise Lost* "by the Rules of Epic Poetry" (*S* 267). Yet, in emphasizing a readerly consensus over the prescriptions of "science," Johnson's praise does suggest how much Addison's efforts contributed to the shift within canon-formation from production to consumption, from codifying the rules of poetic practice to specifying the conditions for receiving works of English literature. Secondly, in contrasting the effectiveness of Addison's "blandishments of gentleness and facility" to the dead ends of systematic criticism, Johnson is assuming that modern readers learn to appreciate a work more readily if their instruction is conducted less as a course in method than as a mode of social intercourse, one that prepared "the mind for more attainments." Addison, in this way, altered the role of the critic, transforming it into one of pedagogical supervision as sympathetic engagement, of a type increasingly valorized within the emergent ideology of commercial humanism. Thirdly, in noting acerbically that, thanks to Addison, Milton became an author "with whom readers of every class think it necessary to be pleased," Johnson is indicating that Addison made Milton's work seem valuable not only for the pleasure it may have afforded but equally for the prestige it promised the reader who could claim to have read the poem with pleasure. Because of Addison, readers were inspired to prepare their minds for more attainments because they could now earn social distinction and cultural capital merely by being known to have rightly appreciated Milton and other canonical English authors.

Within a rhetorical culture, as I have suggested, the activity of reading English literature was rarely valued as an end in itself. Reading served the interests of production, in encouraging readers into socially constructive acts or in helping writers to sharpen their skills. The delights of reading could not be distinguished from its utilitarian benefits, and even literary pleasure itself was often expressly valued for its socializing influence. Addison proposes no such utilitarian purpose in his papers on Milton. Occasionally he will gesture rhetorically about how *Paradise Lost* puts to shame what he calls "the vicious Taste which still prevails so much among Writers" (*S* 279). Yet in speaking of the "taste" of contemporary writers and not their practice, Addison deploys the codes of consumption rather than prescription. As for the instrumental functions of reading, Addison must seriously downplay Milton's fierce didactic aims in order to rehabilitate the radical poet into the now-familiar eighteenth-century poet of the sublime.[9] Milton's complex theodicy in *Paradise Lost* is reduced, in Addison's blandly universalizing version, to the unremarkable proposition that "*Obedience to the Will of God makes Men happy, and that Disobedience makes them miserable.*" This moral, Addison asserts, "makes this Work more useful and instructive than any other Poem in any Language" (*S* 369). However large the claim, it is a measure of Addison's desire to deflect controversy that he should restrict his discussion of the poem's moral utility to a single paragraph in the very last paper of his series. Prior to that paragraph, the value of reading *Paradise Lost* is defined solely in terms of pleasure, just as the function of writing about the poem is measured by how well the critic points out the many ways Milton has provided "that sublime Kind of Entertainment, which is suitable to the nature of an Heroick Poem" (*S* 303).

Proposing reading as its own reward is a tricky claim for Addison to make, since seeking pleasure without purpose would seem wasteful, especially to the middle-class readers he is attempting to court.[10] Addison will elsewhere assure his readers that the pleasures of the imagination will, "like a gentle Exercise to the Faculties, awaken them from Sloth and Idleness, without putting them upon any Labour or Difficulty" (*S* 411). That Addison requires eighteen weekly essays just to help readers enjoy Milton's poem may suggest, however, that this pleasure is in fact to be gotten with considerable labour and difficulty, despite the critic's "blandishments of gentleness and facility."[11] Most of those essays are devoted to instructing readers on how Milton's epic ought to be experienced. Of Adam's colloquy in Book VIII, Addison characteristically writes that "The more the Reader examines the justness and Delicacy of its Sentiments, the more he will find himself pleased with it" (*S* 345). Though pleasure may be the end of reading, Addison valorizes the labour of comprehension and reserves his highest praise for how the poem's sublimity makes the reader work: "It is impossible," he says, "for the Imagination of Man to distend it self with greater Ideas, than those which [Milton] has laid together" (*S* 279). To prepare for such attainments of the mind, according to Addison, readers cannot approach the text innocently but ought continually to scrutinize their own interpretive habits. As he puts it, "one who brings with him any implicit Notions and Observations which he has made in his reading of the Poets, will find his own Reflections methodized and explained ... in the Works of a good Critick; whereas one who has not these previous Lights, is very often an utter Stranger to what he reads, and apt to put a wrong Interpretation upon it" (S 291). Though seemingly innocuous, Addison's statement is among the first significant occasions in critical discourse when the act of reading English poetry is said to involve fashioning textual meaning through a process of observation, reflection, and critical methodization. Rarely had the inner dimensions of the reading experience been described before, yet Addison is here telling his audience not simply how to respond to an English poem but how to interpret it. Addison may himself spend much less time elucidating the poem than judging it, but he is clearly attempting to make his critical discourse appear essential to the adequate reception of the canonical text. This may suggest that Addison's manipulation of his readers is little different from what occurs in earlier critical valorizations, and certainly Addison's dehistoricizing of Milton's poem recalls the presentism of rhetorical canon-making. Yet the function of Addison's criticism is not to make producers out of readers, but to reproduce the text in terms of both rendering it accessible to readers and making readers receptive to the text, for no reason *in particular* except the stated aim of doing justice and honour to an English author's work.

Because he claims to be writing "for the Sake of the Poem I am now examining," Addison misrecognizes his own critical authority, locating such authority instead in the text or in the classical precedents he cites for comparison (S 273). Spurning the authoritarian manner of previous commentators, Addison declares that he will not "presume to impose upon others my own particular Judgment on this Author, but only deliver it as my private opinion" (S 262). The congenial populist tone reflects Mr Spectator's self-presentation, which, in transforming cultural discourse into a mode of social engagement, put into practice the values of commercial humanism, with its emphasis on sympathetic social intercourse as enabling the refinement of manners. In expressing these values, Addison's praise of Milton has as its principal theme the commercial humanist ideal that, in appealing directly to the reader's power of imaginative sympathy, the poem, like the arts generally, aided the individual in enriching his or her moral being. Of Milton's portrayal of Adam and Eve, Addison writes, "The Representation he gives of them ... is wonderfully contrived to influence the Reader with Pity and Compassion towards them." They are, he says, "drawn with such Sentiments as do not only interest the Reader in their Afflictions, but raise in him the most melting Passions of Humanity and Commiseration" (*S* 357). The remark recalls Addison's earlier endorsement of popular ballads, which, he wrote, "are able to move the Mind of the most polite Reader with inward Meltings of Humanity and Compassion" (*S* 85). Implicit in these statements is a reply to the view that reading for pleasure is a wasteful activity. For Addison, the pleasure of reading *Paradise Lost* has to do with how the poem deploys imaginative transport to exercise the reader's passions and sympathies. Whatever its didactic aims, the poem does not so much instruct readers on how to be morally sensitive, or persuade them into performing constructive acts,[12] as it offers them a kind of extended imaginative and affective workout: Milton's sentiments, Addison suggests, "convey to the Mind Ideas of the most transporting Passion" (*S* 345); his similes work "very happily to unbend the Mind of the Reader" (*S* 309); his introduction of God "cannot but fill the Mind of the Reader with a secret Pleasure and Complacency" (*S* 315); his imaginative episodes "so frequently produce in the Reader the most pleasing Passion that can rise in the Mind of Man, which is Admiration" (*S* 315).

This type of experience later critics will later identify with the aesthetic, yet what has been unremarked is how Addison has redefined the function of criticism in order to promote this experience.[13] For Addison, the critic's task is neither to submit the work to systematic analysis nor to emphasize its didactic utility, but to supervise the reading process so as to heighten the reader's sympathetic engagement with the text and its sentiments. And since the critic is himself a reader, he ought to demonstrate his own facility at sympathetic engagement. By his demeanour, Mr Spectator appears as much refined by the pleasures of reading Milton as the ordinary reader: "I have taken as much Pleasure in reading the Contents of his Books, as in the best invented Story I have ever met," Addison says (*S* 267). The gesture allows Addison to misrecognize the extent to which he is creating a taste for Milton, since he presents himself as one who partakes as much of the pleasures of the text as any other reader.[14] Though he is effectively teaching readers how to read, Addison prefers to cast himself as their representative, to whom readers may surrender their critical autonomy in much the same way as subjects generally under commercial humanism are expected to consign their political voice to professional delegates. That Addison was effective as both teacher and representative is perhaps what Voltaire meant when he noted that Addison's assessment of Milton "seems either to guide, or to justify the Opinion of his Countrymen."[15]

To legitimize this authority as his readers' professional representative, Addison must teach them more than simply how to respond to the text. In devoting a lengthy set of eighteen essays to show how much is involved in appreciating even a single poem, Addison is transforming the labour of reading into spectacle, into conspicuous consumption, as it were. In previous centuries, the accumulation of polite learning served clear practical ends, as the courtier would use his liberal education in order to refine his speech, to ascend the career ladder, and to legitimize his social authority; the cultural value of learning was not seen as separate from its utility in symbolic exchanges. By stressing the pleasures of reading above its pragmatic uses, Addison is diminishing poetry's value as a mechanism of symbolic exchange and furthering the autonomization of the cultural field from the political economy of the state. Instead, by the example of his massive exposition of *Paradise Lost*, Addison is making the act of having read literature something that could be socially creditable, as if the mere display of learning could function as symbolic currency. Because of Addison, observed Theophilus Cibber in 1753, "it had become unfashionable not to have read" Milton's work.[16] Yet his greater accomplishment is in having valorized the quality of having read, not just Milton but any English text, as a fashionable condition.

What Addison is implicitly doing is converting the display of learning into cultural capital. Reading the poem becomes an opportunity for the reader or critic to demonstrate his skill and acumen and so earn the prestige of being a recognized authority on the poem. Though Addison maintains that *Paradise Lost* is generally intelligible, the poem contains "Multitudes of Beauties," many of which, he claims, "are not so obvious to ordinary Readers" (*S* 321). Thus the function of the "true Critick," Addison suggests, is "to discover the concealed Beauties of a Writer, and communicate to the World such Things as are worth their Observation." Or, as he says in his own behalf, "I hope that I have made several Discoveries which may appear new, even to those who are versed in Critical Learning" (*S* 291). The idea that a work might possess "concealed beauties" was becoming a critical commonplace at the time, though rarely had it been applied to English writings. Addison's contribution is to adapt the commonplace in the service of cultural hierarchization. Whereas once it had been the job of literary modernizers like Dryden to polish the rough diamonds within the English canon, it is now evidently the exclusive province of the critic to uncover these concealed beauties.

More important, it is enough for the critic to alert readers to such beauties merely for "their Observation," since it is through the demonstration of such powers of observation and attention that readers may learn to distinguish themselves from what Addison calls "the Rabble of Mankind" (*S* 291). Addison is here not simply making his own activity appear essential by promoting the acquisition of learning; he is also attempting to posit readerly competence as a social marker. "The most exquisite Words and finest Strokes of an Author," he characteristically suggests, "are those which very often appear the most doubtful and exceptionable, to a Man who wants a Relish for polite Learning" (*S* 291). Whether this claim is true is not so important as the fact that, through such statements, Addison is helping to revise the function of canonical texts. The more such texts are introduced to a wide readership during this period, the more their function is conceived in terms of reception rather than productivity. As such, their utility in legitimizing a social hierarchy has to be redefined. Beginning with Addison, the beauties of canonical texts are increasingly treated as being difficult of access, concealed yet potentially inexhaustible, so that the ability to decipher those textual beauties can serve as a recognized measure of social distinction. Far from being the last word on *Paradise Lost*, Addison's essays are rather among the first in an ongoing industry of readings, the hard labour of which continues to this day to serve the critic and student in acquiring cultural capital. As Addison himself remarks, "It will be sufficient for me if I discover many Beauties ... which others have not attended to, and I should be very glad to see any of our eminent Writers publish their Discoveries on the same Subject." Critical eminence had formerly been attained by adhering to the rules, but now it is to be achieved by repeatedly digging through the same canonical works in search of excellences and meanings "as may have escaped the Observation of others" (*S* 262).[17]

Because Addison is not theorizing what he is doing in the Milton papers, it is easy to overlook just how much he is negotiating a new role for the English canon. First, canonical texts are to be reproduced as being seemingly valuable in themselves, and not simply because they may inspire further productivity or legitimize contemporary practice. Secondly, reading those texts is felt to produce certain effects. Under commercial humanism, any artistic endeavour is expected to help readers modulate their passions by engaging them in acts of sympathetic intercourse. The critic supervises this process by showing readers how to discover hidden beauties in the text upon which they can then exercise their sensibility. Thirdly, since the cultural field has to be autonomized from the field of economic production, its legitimacy in supporting a social hierarchy depends upon its agents being able to identify and extol a competing form of capital that is peculiar to the field. Such cultural capital is, in theory, available to anyone who can display an appropriate degree of competence at negotiating cultural goods and relations, though, for the critic keen on establishing his practice, there is no more recognized way of earning the necessary credentials than to reinforce the canonicity of a text by directing readers to heretofore unobserved beauties within it. Addison's papers on Milton can be seen as contributing to all three of these historical changes. In teaching his audience how to read Milton's poem, Addison was helping to make reception the locus of critical discourse and opening the way for English texts to be canonized through pedagogical transmission. In valuing the experience of the poem as enabling imaginative sympathy, Addison was encouraging a larger reorientation of belief about the arts, a reorientation that would ultimately bring about the formation of an ideology of the aesthetic. And in making it fashionable to have read *Paradise Lost*, Addison was helping as much to popularize the poem as to provide readers with another means by which to demarcate themselves from the populace.

TEACHING TO READ

A few critics prior to Addison had entertained the notion that readers might require a canon dissimilar in presentation from the canon officially sanctioned as the model for production. In the 11 July 1691 number of John Dunton's quiz paper, *The Athenian Mercury*, the Athenians were asked, "Which is the best *Poem* that ever was made and who in your Opinion, deserves the *Title* of the best *Poet* that ever was?" It is likely the first time such an exclusivist question had ever been raised in English criticism, though the Athenians followed convention insofar as their canon was topped by the epic, with the *Aeneid* as its best example, yet quickly devolved into a catalogue of authors to be celebrated in its fullness and harmony, as reflecting a fundamental concord in polite society: "*Grandsire Chaucer*, in spite of the Age, was a Man of as much wit, sence and honesty as any that have writ after him. Father *Ben* was excellent at *Humour*, *Shakespear* deserves the name of *sweetest*, which *Milton* gave him. *Spencer* was a noble Poet, his *Fairy-Queen* an excellent piece of Morality, Policy, History. *Davenant* had a great Genius. Too much can't be said of Mr. *Coley*. Milton's *Paradice lost*, and some other Poems of his will never be equal'd. *Waller* is the most *correct* Poet we have." Two years later, in their number for 24 October 1693, the Athenians were asked a slightly different question: "What Books of Poetry would you Advise one that's young, and extremely delights in it, to read, both divine and other?" In reply, the Athenians offered another catalogue, though one that contained fewer of the standard rhetorical valorizations of their earlier list:

Answ. For Divine, *David's* Psalms, *Sandy's* and *Woodford's* Versions, *Lloyd's* Canticles, *Cowley's* Davideis, Sir *J. Davis's Nosce Teipsum*, *Herbert's* and *Crasshaw's* Poems, *Milton's* Paradices, and (if you have Patience) *Wesley's* Life of Christ. For others, Old Merry *Chaucer*, *Gawen Douglas's* AEneads (if you can get it) the best Version that ever was, or We believe ever will be, of that incomparable Poem; *Spencer's* Fairy Queen, &. *Tasso's* Godfrey of Bulloign, *Shakespear*, *Beaumont* and *Fletcher*, *Ben. Johnson*, *Randal*, *Cleaveland*, Dr. *Donne*, *Gondibert*, WALLER, all DRYDEN, *Tate*, *Oldham*, *Flatman*, *The Plain Dealer* – and when you have done of these, We'll promise to provide you more.

Apart from the openness of this canon, both to authors still living and to "more" works that could yet be provided, its most striking feature was its lack of supporting critical pieties about what values such reading was assumed to impart to the young reader. The Athenians mocked one of their own (Samuel Wesley was one of Dunton's collaborators) and paid unusual tribute to Douglas's Scots translation of the *Aeneid*, a version not widely known in the late seventeenth century.[18] Yet the Athenians did not tell the young reader why he or she ought to read these particular items, since it was already assumed that the reader was seeking only personal delight. Freed from having to specify any instrumentalist functions for literature, the Athenians proposed a canon for reading that was significantly more plural in its composition, much less exclusive and conventional, than the official harmonious canon they had earlier endorsed.

After Addison, this division between canons for production and for consumption grew more pronounced as reading became increasingly a subject of critical discourse and treated as an activity that involved its own distinct set of interests and competencies. Whereas the Athenians assumed that the young reader needed only to be advised on appropriate selections for diversion, critics and educators after Addison began to propose selections that would ostensibly enable students to practise methods of reading with a view to improving their tastes and enlarging their sensibilities. Addison's papers on Milton were likely an inspiration for the many school anthologies of English poetry that would soon appear, anthologies designed to serve the instruction of composition as much as the right appreciation and apprehension of poetry. Within five years of the *Spectator* essays, James Greenwood produced his anthology *The Virgin Muse* (1717), which, he announced, was designed for ready consumption by students, with "the difficult Places" in his verse selections "made easie and intelligible, by the Help of Notes, and a Large Index, explaining every hard Word." This apparatus, Greenwood claimed, made his compilation suitable "for the *Teaching to Read Poetry*."[19] This claim, it is said, "is the first expression in a textbook of the idea that poetry could be taught, and not just presented to pupils ... Only in the study of foreign languages, principally Latin, Greek and Hebrew, is there evidence before now of texts being scrutinised and 'taught' in order to bring out their meaning."[20] As its title indicated, Greenwood's collection was aimed at women or, as he put it, "Youth of either Sex" who wished to study poetry at home – students, that is, who were likely on the margins of polite society. These students had no apparent practical need to know how to write their own poetry; it was evidently enough for them to learn how to comprehend canonical poetry, as if such comprehension was an intrinsically valuable act.

Most textbook anthologies before the later eighteenth century were primarily designed to aid in the instruction of composition and, increasingly, elocution in English; the ideal of verbal power continued to have many adherents, and a distinguished rhetorician like Thomas Sheridan could still confidently declare on the title page of his *British Education* (1756) that "to refine, ascertain, and fix the English Language" through "a Revival of the Art of Speaking" within the schools might help to cure "the Disorders of Great Britain." Few school anthologists actually discussed methodologies for instructing students on how to interpret literature, though many recognized the need for educators to "explain" these texts, including English ones, to their students. Samples from works of English literature were becoming increasingly prevalent within these collections, being set alongside and ultimately displacing the selections from classical texts that had dominated the spelling books and rhetorics of previous centuries. Some educators, particularly from the dissenting academies, advocated the creation of curricula made up chiefly of English texts, which could prove easier for these students to understand and relate to their circumstances.[21] In 1751 Benjamin Franklin sketched his plan for such a school, where "the best English authors may be read and explained; as Tillotson, Milton, Locke, Addison, Pope, Swift, the higher papers in the Spectator and Guardian, the best translations of Homer, Virgil and Horace, of Telemachus, travels of Cyrus, &c." This syllabus, Franklin insisted, would enable youth to "come out of this school fitted for learning any business, calling, or profession."[22] For younger pupils, even certain English texts were thought too demanding in the view of some teachers, who seemed implicitly to recognize how interpretation could be an acquired skill: "In reading," wrote James Barclay in 1743, "I would always put such *English* books in their hands as they were fond of, and understood. Our *Spectators*, *Guardians*, and the like ... are above the apprehension of children."[23] Similarly, women readers, wrote Ann Fisher in her preface to *The Pleasing Instructor* (1756), require special assistance in interpretation because they are often "*misled* in the Sense of what they are about to trace, especially in *circumstancial* Authors, or such as the Generality call *dark* and *obscure* Writers ... They feel an Entanglement, though they *know not* what or where."[24] By 1773 even *Paradise Lost*, according to the grammarian James Buchanan, "has been generally found to be above the capacities of ordinary readers, from the difficulty of the construction." By normalizing Milton's word order in a version designed "For the Use of our most eminent Schools," Buchanan hoped to accomplish what Addison had done for an earlier generation, "to make this first English classic universally read with ease and delight."[25]

The teaching of interpretation had, by the time Buchanan is writing, become much more prominent in literary education than it had been for Greenwood, and it could be seen by some as a valuable form of attention that had to be taught and practised before it could be perfected. One instructor, writing in 1772, claimed that his extracts of English literature were selected to discourage the "bad habits" among pupils "of fancying you understand what you don't, or understanding by halves, or of being inattentive to, or absent from, what is set before you as an object of understanding."[26] Such statements are of notable historical significance, for they suggest how pedagogical practice was being redefined in radical ways during the period. The schoolmasters were apparently coming up with these anthologies and theories of reading in order to meet the demand of a growing populace eager to introduce its youth to English texts, though it could be equally argued that the schoolmasters were helping to generate such a demand in order to legitimize and promote their practice. Whatever the case, these teachers were assuming roles formerly expected of working poets and writers, who had routinely affirmed the staying power of their activity by keeping the works of the past alive through redactions, translations, and modernizations, such as the several accorded Chaucer's writings in the seventeenth century. The responsibility for reproducing the literature of the past, in terms of rendering it accessible to modern audiences and transmitting it to new generations of readers, had passed from contemporary producers to commentators and educators, whose interests differed from the poets' insofar as they were concerned less with perpetuating the immortality *topos*, and all of its attendant ideological functions, than with establishing the indispensability of their profession in developing the moral sensibilities of England's future generations. Ultimately, the institutionalization of literature, which these educators were inaugurating, meant that the academy would gradually assume many or all of the functions traditionally ascribed to literary production, including, among others, canonizing the authors of the past, reproducing their works, standardizing speech, forming readers, transmitting values, and preserving the names of the dead.

Furthermore, these eighteenth-century anthologists and teachers were contributing to a structure of belief about their own self-assumed role as mediators of the reading activity. Reading English texts was now to be perceived as an act requiring pedagogical supervision, as if these texts could present hermeneutic difficulties that could be surmounted by the young reader only with professional assistance. Pedagogical instruction in interpretation during the period scarcely approached the level of routinization associated with twentieth-century modes of "close reading." At most, in a treatise from late in the period, William Milns advised his colleagues

not only to point out and explain in the clearest manner the particular beauties of the chosen passage, but to show how naturally they rise out of what went before, and how admirably they prepare the way for what is to follow them. The attention is not to be confined to the prominent strokes of fancy, wit, or genius: it should also be directed to the less showy, but more important succession of just ideas, solid arguments, and sensible observations, which form, as it were, the tissue of the work, and from which the principal beauties have their source and origin.

This method, Milns insisted, would prevent the students of English literature from getting "wrong impressions of poetical and oratorical excellence" as inhering in "extravagances of style" rather than more rightly in the "less showy, but more important succession" of ideas, arguments, and observations.[27] In effect, the priorities of a rhetorical culture had been reversed, since the elements of style and language had become devalued in favour of those noetic or thematic elements whose appreciation required acts of skilled interpretation. However rudimentary Milns's methodology, interpretation in literary education, as in critical discourse generally, was becoming as important as evaluation, and recognized as a skill in which one could achieve a measure of professional competence. These educators, through their multiplying discourse on the subject of literary education, were helping to create the first interpretive community devoted mainly to English literature, a self-authorizing community that could regulate how this literature was to be reproduced by setting criteria for readerly competence. In time, their efforts would help to redefine the nature of canonicity, as I will suggest in the next section; in the shorter term, they ensured that the term "reading" would slowly lose its primary association with elocution and reciting and become instead equated with the act of interpretation. The Edgeworths, whose many guide-books early in the next century loudly promoted the teaching of English literature "to strengthen the habits of attention and to exercise all the powers of the mind," signalled this change in the titles of their works, going from *Poetry Explained for the Use of Young People* (1802) to *Readings on Poetry* (1816), which offered students explications of "difficult" English poets, including Milton and Gray.[28]

Within their circle of belief, these educators misrecognized the nature of their own participation in the process of regulation. As ever, they routinely insisted on the dangers of permitting students to read novels, the fears of young minds being harmed by their exposure to prose fiction having been reanimated in the later eighteenth century with the emergence of a mass market for books. In addition to all the conventional moralistic arguments, now bolstered with pseudo-scientific accounts of the injurious effects of such reading, some commentators also proposed the newer argument that the problem with novels was that they could be too easily and rapidly consumed: "They fix attention so deeply, and afford so lively a pleasure, that the mind once accustomed to them cannot submit to the painful task of serious study."[29] As in the past, such claims were being put forward in order to assert control over the unguarded reader, but the terms of this control had changed slightly to the extent that novel-reading no longer impaired the reader's productive potential so much as "her" powers of attention and relish for mental exercise – the rapid consumption of novels being commonly gendered as feminine.[30] In essence, educators were asserting their supervisory role over readers by valuing the act of interpretation, an act that was not necessitated in the case of novels "whose merit lies chiefly in [the fact that] the story should be quickly passed through."[31] Like Addison before them, educators were urging their students to surrender their critical autonomy by insisting that the true pleasures of reading could come only in relation to texts of an intellectually demanding nature, whose laborious explication would justify the teaching and supervision of interpretation.[32]

The texts that educators did recommend to their students might not have seemed terribly demanding, the bulk of their anthologies being devoted to selections from *The Spectator* and other periodicals, topical verses by both men and women poets, and standard passages from Pope, Thomson, and Cowper.[33] It is possible that the use of these works as models for composition, often categorized by theme or "sentiment" within the anthologies, accounts for the popularity of essayistic poetry on "various subjects" during the period, in much the same way that school exercises had something to do with the prevalence of elegies and occasional pieces in Renaissance miscellanies. But, with the exception of specialized collections of such genres as ballads, most eighteenth-century anthologies, unlike the earlier miscellanies, were not expressly assembled to reshape the canon by promoting composition in any particular kind of literature, just as their editors, unlike their Renaissance predecessors, seemed reluctant to assert their authority as canon-makers, preferring to present their canons as apodictic. The modesty *topos* was revived as the appropriate gesture of the consumer-friendly anthologist. Elizabeth Cooper, in the preface to her important compilation of pre-stuart verse, *The Muses Library* (1737), left it to her readers to determine why England ought to have its own canon: "Of what real Value polite Literature is to a Nation, is too sublime a Talk for me to meddle with; I therefore chuse to refer my Readers to their Experience." Goldsmith is even more self-effacing before his *Beauties of English Poetry* (1767): "my design was to give a useful, unaffected compilation; one that might tend to advance the reader's taste, and not impress him with exalted ideas of mine ... I claim no merit in the choice, as it was obvious, for in all languages the best productions are most easily found."[34] Though Goldsmith would be criticized by reviewers for his "meek spirit of diffidence and indecision," his manner anticipated how literature would be marketed in the boom for cheap reprints and miscellanies that would follow upon the repeal of perpetual copyright in 1774.[35] In these later miscellanies, English writings are presented to readers as being selected wholly for their private diversion or sentimental edification; as Barbara M. Benedict suggests in her survey of these anthologies, literature is increasingly treated as a "triumph of aesthetic skill, a feast of stylistic beauty, not a vehicle to social action. Rather than conveying political lessons, literature is represented as the enfranchisement of individuals to judge morality and meaning."[36] The school anthologists, for their part, were usually not so forthcoming about what made any particular works worthy of inclusion, beyond making a general claim that, in a typical formulation, the works were "selected with a view to refine the taste, rectify the judgment, and mould the heart to virtue."[37] At the same time, their selections worked to reinforce not only prevailing tastes but intellectual and ideological changes within the cultural field, whose increasing autonomy was recorded in these anthologies: by 1802 Dryden, whose Virgil was long considered an essential pedagogical model of expression in English, was said to be too "political" for young sensibilities.[38]

The most significant consequence of this shift toward interpretation was that literature was turned into an object of study, to be valued less as a mode of symbolic exchange than as a type of moral technology that could enrich students by virtue of the labour required to understand

and appreciate it. Lockean notions of education, which subserved the emergent disciplines of knowledge, made it initially difficult for educators to treat literature as a definable category of learning, and a few were tempted to dismiss literature altogether from the curriculum. In *An Essay upon Study* (1731), schoolmaster John Clarke suggested that poetry "can not, I think, be made subservient to any *important* Purpose of Life."[39] Yet, if writing or reading literary works could not necessarily empower a person to accomplish anything in particular, its study could nonetheless require labour and discipline, of such a nature and intensity that it could prove central to the student's education in preparing his or her mind for more attainments. Poetry ought to be taught, wrote James Buchanan in his 1770 proposal for a grammar school, since its most beautiful passages "tend to mend the heart, at the same time they enlighten the understanding."[40] Such notions pervaded the discourse of aesthetics and moral sympathy during the period but were most notably expressed in relation to the teaching of English literature in Hugh Blair's landmark *Lectures on Rhetoric and Belles Lettres* (1783). Blair had earlier edited the first large-scale uniform edition of *The British Poets* (44 vols., 1773), a collection intended by the Edinburgh booksellers to challenge the London trade's claim of perpetual copyright. Though his lectures had been largely prepared by 1762, Blair had an interest in promoting the mass consumption of English literature, and in defending the cultivation of taste through reading, and he was in an authoritative position to do so as Regius professor of rhetoric and belles-lettres at Edinburgh University. Passages from English poetry had been discussed by previous lecturers at the university, including John Stevenson and Adam Smith, for whom the teaching of English literature could serve the rhetorical and didactic ends of improving style and conduct.[41] Since the university study of literature was still dominated by rhetorical instruction, Blair, too, was expected to emphasize the utility of literary models in composition, but he went considerably further than his predecessors in emphasizing that students could pursue literary study for the sake of either production or consumption: "some, by the profession to which they addict themselves ... may have the view of being employed in composition, or in public speaking. Others, without any prospect of this kind, may wish only to improve their taste with respect to writing and discourse, and to acquire principles which will enable them to judge for themselves in that part of literature called the Belles Lettres."[42] The category of the belles-lettres being the historical antecedent to the modern sense of literature, Blair's definition of the term in his hugely influential lectures, it has been argued, "did more than anything else" to fix the modern range of literature's constituent genres: "orations, historical works, philosophical treatises and dialogues, epistles, fiction, pastoral poems, lyric poems, didactic poems, biblical writings, epic poems, tragedies, and comedies."[43]

Just as significantly, Blair's ideal of belletristic consumption, as he described it in the polemical introduction he wrote for the 1783 volume, popularized the notion of an autonomous aesthetic experience. Whereas rhetoric was taught for clear ethical and instrumental ends, the belles-lettres were works that seemed to have no palpable designs on readers, works they could read in order to engage their moral and imaginative sympathies: "Belles Lettres and criticism chiefly consider [the reader] as a Being endowed with those powers of taste and imagination, which were intended to embellish his mind, and to supply him with rational and useful entertainment. They open a field of investigation peculiar to themselves."[44] Like most theories of taste, Blair's claim here both evinced and denied the aporia of judgment: Blair could not say whether value resided with the "endowed Being" of the reader, or was intrinsic to the bellestristic texts, which could somehow recognize in advance the critical authority of such a reader. Yet in so doing, in positing the reader as endowed Being, the text assumed an authority that preceded the reader's. Reader and text occupied the irreconcilable semantic grounds of subject and object. No matter: the undecidability of where value could be located was negated by the sheer localism of the experience, since both reader and text were made to inhabit "a field of investigation" that was peculiar to itself, inwardly directed, pure and self-governing, a pastoral of value.

Within this localized sphere, the activity of reading literature could seem to be of the highest good, as essential to the subject's moral formation. Literature did not have to be conventionally didactic or instrumentalist in its persuasions, since "the exercise of taste" alone, whatever the subject of the work, "is, in its native tendency, moral and purifying." So long as the activity of reading was conducted with seriousness and discipline, the goal of applying a critical understanding to literature was not to acquire practical learning but to arrive at a much more desirable state of self-knowledge. "The exercise of taste and of sound criticism," Blair declared, "is in truth one of the most improving employments of the understanding. To apply the principles of good sense to composition and discourse; to examine what is beautiful, and why it is so; to employ ourselves in distinguishing accurately between the specious and the solid, between affected and natural ornament, must certainly improve us not a little in the most valuable part of all philosophy, the philosophy of human nature. For such disquisitions are very intimately connected with the knowledge of ourselves." This self-knowledge could then be the moral foundation for all the student's other practical endeavours: "to be entirely devoid of relish for eloquence, poetry, or any of the fine arts, is justly constructed to be an unpromising symptom of youth; and raises suspicions of their being ... destined to drudge in the more vulgar and illiberal pursuits of life."[45] Given the localized, self-referential experience of aesthetic value, to study English literature was ultimately to study oneself, and the more receptive and discerning the student's appreciation of literature, the more he or she was prepared to negotiate the complexities of a world where, under the prevailing codes of commercial humanism, personal enrichment came with ever more refined acts of consumption. Literature functioned as moral technology for the student, not so much by providing direct instruction as by presenting a supreme occasion for the student to hone his or her sensibility and skills of response, and thereby to achieve a condition of self-aware subjectivity without which, it seemed, the student could not be free.

At the very historical moment when the reception and transmission of English literature was beginning to come under pedagogical supervision, literary study was being proclaimed as an avenue to self-formation and autonomy, the measure of which was the student's own eventual ability to show others how to appreciate literature. As Buchanan asked before his *British Grammar* (1762), "When young Gentlemen become well acquainted with the Nature of Ellipsis and Transposition, what immense Advantages must accrue from their construing and resolving every sentence they read in any English Classic whether Prose or Verse? How will this fix Attention, awake Reflexion, and improve the Judgment with respect to a masterly Knowledge of the Subject ...? Nay, in Time, what judicious Critics will they not become?" To teach students how to read works of English literature was to involve them in an emergent economy of belief, where they could be promised "masterly Knowledge" and evaluative independence so long as they perpetuated the critical discourse that had informed their course of literary study. Such a self-sustaining code of professionalism resembled the circle of conviction that had earlier sustained a rhetorical culture, but without the latter's sense of dynamic exchange: ideally within an objectivist culture, the act of consumption was to be autonomous and disinterested, the canonical text was less important in what it imparted than in the quality of response it evoked, and the knowledge this experience provided was productive only in the sense that the reader could direct it inwardly towards self-mastery. At the same time, the cultural capital that the student could earn from such professional training in critical understanding was felt to be highly desirable and widely enabling, perhaps more so than any other kind of skill, precisely because it did not determine the student for any particular interest.

The only significant exception made to this was in the case of the student whom nature had already imbued with the poet's compulsion. George Chapman, in *A Treatise on Education* (1773; 3rd ed. 1784), subscribed eagerly to the new pedagogy in which the "introduction to poetry, and ... perusal of the most celebrated poems in the English language, are thought necessary for giving youth a critical taste." To facilitate this course of instruction, Chapman recommended lecturing directly from well-known works of criticism and pedagogical theory, such as "Trapp's Lectures, Newberry on Poetry, the Preceptor, Rollin's Belles Lettres, and the Elements of Criticism," before sending students off to the school library to read "the best English poets, descriptive, pastoral, and epic, such as, Thomson, Pope, Milton." But, Chapman warned, "as a natural genius for poetry is absolutely requisite for forming a poet, and is not to be acquired by art ... therefore it is not attempted here to impose a study upon youth, which nature has forbid to the generality of mankind." The poetic compulsion, Chapman believed, was to be prized even more than a refined receptivity to art, since it was so far from being driven by any particular interest that it could prove socially *disabling*, rendering the gifted student "very unsuitable to the different circumstances in which men are placed, and the various occupations which they are obliged to follow." The contrast with earlier pedagogical practice could not be more striking. For centuries, students had been required to write in imitation of the ancient poets, and encouraged to essay generic exercises in verse, with the aim of polishing their rhetorical proficiency, without which the young gentleman could not ascend to office, participate in public decision making, or contribute to the common good in a manner suitable to his talents. With the retreat from rhetoric and the concomitant autonomization of the cultural field, the teaching of poetic composition gradually lost much of its immediate practical utility. The value of literary works had therefore to be reconceived so that they might assume a new objective role within the academy; hence, instruction in their comprehension and appreciation was increasingly felt to serve a different kind of good in helping students become ever more sensitive, imaginative, and receptive consumers of the knowledge that was considered essential to achieving mastery of self and the world. Yet, if the fruits of poetic production were to be prized as objects of scrutiny within the student's program of self-realization, poetic productivity had no recognized role to play within modern literary education, which was seen as too routinized and inhibiting, under the growing mythology of original genius, to nourish the young poet. Paradoxically, that young poet, at once highly differentiated and heroically enslaved to a providential compulsion, could not achieve the same measure of self-determination as the young reader who mastered the poet's writings in a regulated course of study. At most, the young poet could have the sympathy of educators like Chapman, who would only reluctantly encourage those "on whom nature has bestowed a poetical spirit, to pursue a path, which is no less hazardous than it is honourable."[46]

INEXHAUSTING SHAKESPEARE

> Criticism, if a science, must be totally intelligible,
> but literature, as the order of words which makes the science
> possible, is, so far as we know, an inexhaustible source
> of new critical discoveries, and would be even if new works
> of literature ceased to be written.
>
> Northrop Frye[47]

Historians of Shakespeare's reception have often expressed dismay at how the many revisions of his plays held the stage for so long during the eighteenth century and beyond. Brian Vickers, voicing a common complaint, says that the "tyranny of the audience" is to blame: "Those who believe in the high and serious calling of literary criticism will be disappointed that many intelligent men and women who cared about Shakespeare and the drama failed to stop the 'new-modelling' of his plays. But the force of theatrical tradition and theatrical conservatism, the homogeneity of taste, were all too strong."[48] Vickers's lament is more an evaluation than an explanation of the phenomenon, and it can scarce account for what seems a more interesting development: how is it that, despite this inexorable force of tradition and aesthetic conformism, there should develop a counter-movement in eighteenth-century editions and critical assessments of Shakespeare towards valuing the real thing, "Shakespeare Verbatim" (to cite the title of Margreta de Grazia's study of Edmund Malone's edition[49]). This counter-movement towards textual authenticity has sometimes been attributed, by de Grazia and others, to the emergent critical doctrines of genius and originality, doctrines born of the heated copyright debates over authorial property. Yet this argument can itself hardly account for the persistent appeal of the theatrical adaptations, which continued to attract audiences into the nineteenth century; besides, the best known polemicist for originality, Edward Young, could declare that even a transcendent genius like Shakespeare committed errors against the "*moral* rule" that ought perhaps be "cleaned" for presentation on stage.[50]

This widening divergence in reproductions of Shakespeare on the stage and on the page is even more significant in light of the fact that, earlier in the century, the editors and the adaptors had been in agreement upon the need to remodel Shakespeare's plays in order to make of him both a modern and a highbrow. A polishing effort like Pope's edition served the same purpose as the theatrical adaptations in making Shakespeare's works conform to prevailing neoclassic standards and polite Augustan tastes. Even the most conservative of Shakespeare's early editors, Lewis Theobald, evidently saw no conflict in "restoring" Shakespeare's text from Pope's emendations while at the same time happily declaring how he had made "some Innovations upon History and *Shakespeare*" in his own theatrical version of *Richard II* (1719).[51] Even though Shakespeare's plays were rarely performed or published "as written," the editors' and adaptors' mutually reinforcing efforts were enormously successful insofar as they ensured Shakespeare's consecration in English culture.[52] Yet, as Michael Dobson has pointed out, a change seemed to occur at mid-century, as adaptations, though still very popular, diminished in critical importance "alongside other means of appropriating and promoting Shakespeare's authority."[53] It is possible to argue that the counter-movement towards authenticity in Shakespeare scholarship can be described as one such strategic position-taking, whereby editors and critics in increasing numbers appropriated Shakespeare's sacrosanct authority in order to promote what Vickers calls "the high and serious calling of literary criticism." In the second half of the eighteenth century, I suggest in this section, there occurred a significant redistribution of cultural capital, marked by an increasing insistence upon the inherent value of reading, that may account for Shakespeare's changing fortunes during the period, first in print and then in the theatre. I emphasize that I am not concerned with either the precise features of the theatrical revisions, their history in performance, or the protracted editorial debates over specific textual matters, much of which has been extensively dealt with by previous scholars. I am only interested in the general arguments for and against these revisions, and so my argument has actually less to do with Shakespeare's reception as with how the nature of literary canonicity was being redefined during the period.

The Licensing Act of 1737 helped to bring about the change towards textual authenticity. Though, as has often been noted, the measure helped in the long term to de-radicalize the theatrical space, the stage was for a brief period so highly politicized following the passage of the Act that any performance could be read for anti-ministerial innuendo. Since many of the adaptors, such as Colley Cibber, were aligned with the government, an opposition group like the Patriots could promote productions of unreworked Shakespeare as if authenticity could signify politically within such a heated atmosphere. Fielding, though suspicious of the Patriots, made the satirical point in *The Historical Register* (1737): "as Shakespeare is already good enough for people of taste, he must be altered to the palates of those who have none."[54] Yet these productions of the genuine Shakespearean text functioned much like adaptations insofar as they appropriated Shakespeare's meaning; inevitably, the adaptations regained the stage once the political fervour had subsided. The only other significant occasion when politics threatened to undermine the legitimacy of the adaptations occurred in response to the Seven Years' War, when critics loudly deplored revisions of Shakespeare that remodelled the Englishman's plays according to the neoclassic rules of the hated French. These ideological complaints were quickly allayed, however, by the managers' presentation of new, highly patriotic adaptations of a kind that would characterize productions of Shakespeare during subsequent periods of political anxiety, such as in the aftermath of the French Revolution.[55] From these examples, it appears that the movement towards an authentic Shakespeare did not seem politically motivated and may in fact have represented a reaction against politics to the degree that, in promoting the value of their critical activity, eighteenth-century editors and commentators were contributing to the autonomization of the cultural from the political field.

Distinguishing the cultural from the economic field was another matter, given the commercial monopoly awarded the patent theatres by the Licensing Act. This monopoly, as has often been noted, had profound consequences for English drama: it discouraged new work and experimentation, encouraged the forming of a conservative repertory dominated by Shakespearean drama, and, most important, solidified the interpretive authority of the managers and acting companies within the patent theatres. These changes were recognized at the time, though most contemporary critics uttered the usual complaints about the managers feeding a taste for pantomime, spectacle, and melodramatic adaptations. And, as usual, the managers defended their productions by citing public demand, even though it was clearly the actors who controlled the taste of the town through their monopoly, and not the town that dictated to the actors.[56] Increasingly, however, a new note is sounded in the managers' self-defences, wherein their authority is asserted over the public's. Revisions of Shakespeare, formerly justified by reference to standards of politeness and correctness, were now upheld on the basis of the public's lack of interpretive skill. Defending Colley Cibber's much-maligned reworking of *King John*, one critic claimed that there is "a *wild Greatness* in some of *Shakespeare*'s Characters, above the Reach of common Readers."[57] Audiences in Garrick's age may have been as discriminating or as unruly as those in earlier eras but, insisted another critic, their authority had to yield to the actor's: "What shou'd prevent a man of Mr *Garrick's* judgment both as a player and a manager from reviving some play in which he finds much merit, tho' many imperfections, with all that merit preserv'd and all those blemishes struck out; instead of forcing upon us pieces which he knows he must despise us for being satisfy'd with."[58]

However innocuous, these statements would not have been possible if there had not then been occurring a slow fragmentation of the collective norms of politeness, norms to which actors, critics, and editors earlier in the century could all subscribe. The rhetoric of refinement remained eminently serviceable, and both editors and adaptors continued to address putatively "polite audiences" and to flatter them by blaming the faults of the old plays on the barbarity of an age when, according to the commonplace, the "Public Taste was in its Infancy."[59] But universalist codes of value were beginning to lose their operative force among contemporary audiences, just as taste was increasingly being situated in individual sensibilities rather than in definitions of the present age. Certainly the old absolutist critical rationales for the adaptations – the doctrine of the three unities and the like – had begun to lose their legitimacy. The adaptors therefore required a new set of gestures both to authorize their cultural practice and to disavow any naked economic self-interest. Garrick, whose influence as an adaptor has been called "pernicious," relied on his charisma and reputation, which he skilfully developed through a shrewd appropriation of Shakespeare's authority.[60] But the authority of charisma, vested as it was not in collective standards but in contingencies of personality, could secure distinction for the actor only if it was defined in opposition to a lesser authority, such as the common reader's. In the version promulgated by the stage publicists of the day, the actor was presented not as a servant of public taste but as a master interpreter who enhanced a playwright's canonicity by educating his audiences on the hidden splendours of the text. Wrote one dramatist from 1753, "I look upon a good Player as the best Commentator; he calls forth latent Beauties from the Poet's Works that a common reader, tho' deeply learned, cou'd never have imagined."[61] From there it was a small step to demarcate the actor's authority absolutely by endowing him with powers of textual decoding superior to any editor's. So Arthur Murphy, writing in the following year: "I cannot forbear mentioning the obligation which the public has to the genius of Mr *Garrick*, who has exhibited with great lustre many of the most shining strokes of *Shakespeare's* amazing art, and may be justly styled … his best commentator. For it is certain, he has done our poet more justice by his manner of playing his principal characters than any editor has yet done by a publication."[62]

Casting the actor as the superior commentator involved appropriating Shakespeare's authority but equally redefining its nature. As critics and adaptors had done earlier in the century, the actor was seeking to promote Shakespeare's symbolic capital – his accumulated prestige, fame, canonical value – and claimed to do so in the name of English culture. Yet as this symbolic capital was by this time relatively well established, the actor as commentator was also engaged in the next stage of canonization, which involved putting Shakespeare's writings in the service of cultural capital. The meaning and value of Shakespeare's plays became increasingly treated as being fully accessible only by those, such as the actor, who were recognized to possess a special level of competence. Whereas Shakespeare's prestige could be appropriated by almost anyone, including adaptors and editors, the cultural capital that came from being a recognized authority on his works was unequally distributed among social classes and agents. It thus became the locus of contestation in a struggle to dominate the cultural sphere. By promoting Garrick at the expense of Shakespeare's editors and common readers, his supporters were rhetorically upping the ante in this struggle for distinction: in praising the actor as best commentator, Murphy was implicitly acknowledging that evaluative authority had now to do with special skills of interpretation, and if this meant that the actor had to become more like an editor and critic, it also meant that not everyone could claim the same level of expertise because Shakespeare's works were now being perceived as more difficult to explicate than had formerly been supposed. Though Shakespeare was by then considered a national treasure, if a somewhat rough one requiring modern polishing, his true genius was becoming difficult of access and the preserve of the privileged few who knew how to grasp his "latent beauties."

Some notable critics and editors were willing to grant Garrick a singular authority over interpreting and canonizing Shakespeare. George Steevens, who revised Johnson's edition three times before producing his own in 1793, presciently recognized that canonicity involved more than just acts of judgment but required a continual process of cultural reproduction which, according to Steevens, owed its success in Shakespeare's case almost entirely to the actor's expertise: "it is Mr. Garrick's singular felicity that his acting has not only been of infinitely greater service to Shakespeare than all the eulogies of his various commentators, but that his corrections have likewise given some of our celebrated poet's chief pieces a certainty of maintaining their ground in the catalogue of exhibiting plays, which, without an assistance of such a nature has probably slept in oblivion, notwith-standing the exalted reputation of their author."[63] Garrick's detractors, meanwhile, increasingly worked to deny Garrick his authority by exposing his commercialism: "the stage," Goldsmith wrote in a typical vein, "instead of serving the people, is made subservient to the inter-ests of an avaricious few."[64] Bashing the sell-out is a familiar gesture within the struggle for the cultural field, whose relative autonomy depends upon a collective disavowal of economic interest. Although cultural undertakings generally cannot function without economic capital, the artist who goes commercial cannot make a name for himself, cannot acquire cultural capital, because he deprives himself of the means to derive symbolic profits from disinterestedness. Gar-rick's detractors were not questioning Shakespeare's symbolic value, only the actor's legitimacy as an interpreter of the playwright's works. If anything, Shakespeare's authority was aggrandized in these attacks since the authentic versions of his texts, unlike the adaptations, were implicitly promoted as being "pure" of commercial interest. Theophi-lus Cibber, on various occasions both an adaptor and a manager, said as much in his 1756 quarrel with Garrick: "These monopolising Vend-ers of Wit, like Fellows that sell Wine in a Jail, consult not the Health or Pleasure of their Customers, but as it adds to their Profit, force a Sale of their Balderdash and then demand the Price of the best Wines … Were *Shakespeare's* Ghost to rise, wou'd he not frown Indignation on this pilfering Pedlar in Poetry who thus shamefully mangles, muti-lates, and emasculates his Plays?"[65]

A similar argument for disinterestedness was apparent from the claims Shakespeare's editors made in support of their own activity, though, as the editors had to misrecognize their own economic inter-est, their version of the argument was necessarily more complicated. In essence, their response to the increasing authority of the actor-man-agers involved not so much directly contesting that authority as redis-tributing the source of cultural capital to the activity of reading Shakespeare. Initially, editors from Pope to Warburton had, like the actor-managers, proclaimed their authority at the expense of the pub-lic's judgment; though ostensibly working to refine Shakespeare's image, early editors evaluated the works on their readers' behalf by signalling "beauties" in Shakespeare's text with asterisks and by placing "faults" at the foot of the page. Yet this practice could only be taken so far, especially following the politicized vogue for authenticity that marked productions of the plays during the final years of Walpole's ministry. More important, the terms of evaluative authority had changed since Pope's day, since the task of reproducing canonical works had passed from the poets to the scholars and critics. Pope,

Warburton declared, had worked "without any particular Study or Profession of [the editor's] Art," and though he had managed "to make his Edition the best Foundation for all further Improvements," these improvements had now to be left "to the Critic by Profession." Such a bold claim of professional jurisdiction over the canon, Warburton intuitively recognized, had to be legitimized before its symbolic violence could begin to be misrecognized. Anxious for such legitimacy, Warburton turned his edition into a furious display of professional expertise, asserting complete dominance over the text by inserting extensive and eccentric emendations, proposing as many esoteric variants as he could devise, and gesturing wildly in his preface about the need to convince readers of the critic's authority. His edition, he wrote, would serve as an exemplar of "*a body of Canons* for literal criticism" that, by its systematic nature, would both "give the *unlearned Reader* a just Idea and consequently a better Opinion of the Art of Criticism" and, more significantly, "deter the *unlearned Writer* from wantonly trifling with an Art he is a Stranger to, at the Expence of his own Reputation and the Integrity of the Text of established Authors."[66] Criticism, Warburton made it clear, was to be no longer a mode of discourse that anyone could excel at merely by observing a set of formal prescriptions like the rules; it was now to be a practice regulated by professional norms of competence, learning, skill, and disposition.[67]

The failure of Warburton's edition had therefore as much to do with his editorial absurdities as with the fact that no critic could assert interpretive authority because no such norms of competence were as yet universally recognized. The numerous attacks that greeted Warburton's edition, notably Thomas Edwards's very popular *Canons of Criticism* (1750), were animated by a desire both to expose his absurdities and to deflate his arrogance in claiming such special competence. In the wake of these attacks, critical practice underwent something of a crisis at mid-century; all of Shakespeare's editors were soon being censured for their textual errors, and there seemed to be no definitive way to establish one's credentials as a commentator in an increasingly noisy critical scene. Shakespeare's text was being opened up, becoming the subject of a conflict of interpretation that was felt disabling because anyone could participate. By the time Johnson was finishing his edition (1765), Vickers remarks, "the English literary world had become enormously conscious of the unsettled nature of Shakespeare's text. Suggesting emendations was almost a national pastime, for which everyone felt himself to be qualified."[68] If everyone could be an authority on Shakespeare, then no one could be. No cultural capital could be gained in the attempt to correct Shakespeare's text, and the editors were fated to be no more successful than the actors in uncovering Shakespeare's hidden beauties. Since "the text of an author is a sacred thing," declared William Dodd in 1752, "it is real honour to elucidate the difficulties in an author's text, to set forth his meaning, and discover the sense of those places which are obscure to vulgar readers"; however, despaired Dodd, Shakespeare's difficulties had proven so intractable that "I think we may venture to pronounce no single man will ever be able to give the world a compleat and correct edition of *Shakespeare*."[69] The solution to the crisis was to make the best of it, as it were, by generating an economy of belief wherein this uncertain state of affairs could be perceived as a condition that was both normal and healthy: first, by welcoming the desires of readers, if not playgoers, in seeking to achieve an understanding of Shakespeare; and second, by celebrating Shakespeare's indeterminacies as providing endless opportunities for editors, critics, and readers to achieve the "real honour" of elucidating, if only ever provisionally, the meaning of his sacred text.

Johnson, whose edition might have seemed authoritative because of his unmatched knowledge of the language, was among the first editors to acknowledge his readers' desire for self-determination. In the proposal for his edition, he suggested that the "only effect" of practices like Warburton's signalling of beauties "is that they preclude the pleasure of judging for ourselves, teach the young and ignorant to decide without principles; defeat curiosity and discernment by leaving them less to discover ... The editor, though he may less delight his own vanity, will probably please his reader more by supposing him equally able with himself to judge of beauties and faults." Accordingly, Johnson promised, his edition would "exhibit all the observable varieties of all the copies that can be found, that, if the reader is not satisfied with the editor's determination, he may have the means of chusing better for himself."[70] Similar statements soon began appearing before most other editions and commentaries. Steevens, prefacing his 1773 edition, believed that an editor passing judgment on portions of a text "will at once excite the disgust and displeasure of such as think their own knowledge or sagacity undervalued."[71] Readerly knowledge was soon being solicited by editors like Steevens, who routinely appealed for aid in explicating textual obscurities. By this gesture, editors could disavow any commercial interest by making their efforts appear collaborative and beneficial to a broad community: the public's assistance, Steevens declared in his proposal, "is not desired with a lucrative view to the Editor, but to engage the attention of the literary world."[72] Warburton's mistake was to believe that the "critic by profession" could assume complete evaluative authority over readers, when in fact by this time the critic and editor could only legitimately present himself as their representative.

Curiously, Steevens was, as I have noted, a sometime advocate of altering Shakespeare for the stage, and he admitted as much in the same passage from his preface when he noted that the reader's independence is irrelevant within the theatre: "There are yet many passages unexplained and unintelligible which may be reformed ... for exhibitions on the stage, in which the pleasure of the audience is chiefly to be considered." Such a statement, and there were many others like it, might have seemed no more than a rhetorical flourish, but it posited a qualitative difference between readers and playgoing audiences in terms of their respective critical faculties: the former were "common" yet possessed of discriminating taste, the latter "polite" yet subservient to fashion and the unthinking pleasures of the theatrical experience. Reading, according to this new argument, was felt to result in a more definitive evaluation of drama than attending a dramatic performance. Hume implied as much when he remarked that Shakespeare's "total ignorance of all theatrical art and conduct, however material a defect, yet as it affects the spectator rather than the reader, we can more readily excuse than that want of taste which often prevails in his productions."[73] One aspect of this argument would receive theoretical articulation in part five of Burke's *Enquiry*, where he maintained that the power of words over the passions was greater than the affect of sensing objects; the argument might, in this formulation, have been a sophisticated expression of the old anti-theatrical prejudice, to the extent that it assumed that theatrical spectacle disabled critical judgment.[74] At the same time, the argument was being reversed by moral philosophers of the period, including Hume and Smith, who notably deployed metaphors of theatricality to describe an ideal state of sympathetic identification. Social relations, according to Smith, were theatrical in character, since human interchange required the individual to act as an impartial spectator who endeavoured "to put himself in the situation of the other" and strove "to render as perfect as possible, that imaginary change of situation upon which his sympathy is founded."[75] Insofar as these theories presupposed a social space where there could emerge a consensus of equals, their reliance on aristocratic metaphors of the theatre reflected a residual civic humanism.[76] Yet, in emphasizing the willed uninvolvement of the spectator, who could imaginatively feel the experience of another, these arguments were also contributing to the emergent discourse of aesthetic disinterestedness, which explains why the theatrical metaphors would soon give way, in the writings of Rousseau and others, to the paradigmatic trope of commercial humanism, the solitary *flâneur*.[77]

For critics of the theatrical adaptations, however, the harmonizing influence of the theatrical situation made for too much sympathetic identification in that it weakened the spectator's capacity to resist uniting with an audience in an uncritical consensual response. In their view, readers who were removed from the distractions of spectacle were in a better position than theatrical spectators to exercise a willed uninvolvement in relation to the literary text, since they had greater opportunity for self-determination. In more extreme versions of the argument, playgoers, blinded by habit and conformity to prevailing tastes, were said to lack the necessary competence to decipher Shakespeare's meaning, which was nonetheless intelligible to the reader of the authentic texts. "The mass of an English audience," announced one scholar in 1769, is "like a herd of cattle"; Shakespeare's "excellence," he claimed, "consists in things which are by no means understood by such people as now frequent our theatres."[78] Free of such herd-mentality, readers could demonstrate a greater disinterestedness and hence claim an interpretive and evaluative authority that was greater not only to the tastes of audiences but to the commercial prudence of actors and managers. Steevens, his patience for alterations having apparently been exhausted, wrote in 1779 that the adaptors had begun to recognize the superior legitimacy of readers' judgments: "These Gentlemen have usually taken care to print a larger Portion of their Originals than is ever suffered to be spoken on Stage. They will risque any Violence to the Poet before a passive Audience, but are commendably afraid of the Tribunal of a discerning Reader."[79]

As we have seen, the rhetorical figure of the discerning or learned reader had long served as a gesture for claiming the distinguishing power of disinterest. Colley Cibber, writing at the beginning of the century, could use the figure to defend his adaptations, leaving, he said, "to the Impartial Reader" to judge how much Shakespeare's plays in their original were "injurious to good Manners."[80] Cibber's appeal to good manners indicates how rarely, in these earlier incarnations, the impartial reader disagreed with reigning standards of politeness and correctness. In contrast, the common reader, whose lack of competence Garrick's defenders had invoked to justify his adaptations, became for the editors a much more sophisticated and critically aware figure, one who demonstrated an independence not only from current fashions but from any collective norm, even the commonality indicated in his name. He was, in Johnson's version, "uncorrupted with literary prejudices."[81] Yet uncorrupted did not mean uninformed; the editors' common reader was by definition a reader, and his legitimacy as canon-maker arose from a sweeping disinterest that was the result of a lengthy education spent reading. Cultural capital was being redistributed from the producers – the artists and adaptors – to the consumers, and the more extensive their reading, and the more isolated from the distractions of the moment, the more authoritative their judgment. This refurbished version of the learned reader was thus especially prominent in canonizing efforts made on behalf of early dramatists other than Shakespeare. George Colman, in his "Vindication" of Massinger, could compare a myopic "Publick Taste" that enjoyed only "one Species of Excellence" to the judgment of the wiser few who were alive to all variety of literary merit: "the eminent Class of Writers," Colman declared, "who flourished at the Beginning of this Century, have almost entirely superseded their illustrious Predecessors. The Works of *Congreve, Vanbrugh, Steele, Addison, Pope, Swift, Gay,* &c. &c. are the chief Study of the Million: I say, of the Million, for as to those few, who are not only familiar with all our own Authors, but are also conversant with the Antients, they are not to be circumscribed by the narrow limits of the Fashion."[82] Though the public had not erred in venerating the modern wits, only a fit audience though few had the skill and acumen to recognize the full depth of the dramatic canon.

All these gestures made for a curious situation. On the one hand, the adaptors and their supporters defended their practice of popularizing Shakespeare by citing the authority of polite taste and the need to educate the public. On the other hand, the critics and editors who prized an authentic Shakespeare did so on behalf of an intellectual elite whose critical authority was vested in a common reader who spoke for no collective or socio- economic interest. Of course, editors like Johnson, Steevens, and the others were ceding final authority less to their readers than to the literary past, just as their annotations and commentaries were, as in earlier editions, all designed to instruct the reader on how best to read and judge documents from another age. But, whereas previous editors, like the adaptors, had asserted their authority over readers by modernizing and evaluating the old texts, later critics and editors did not claim such authority for themselves; instead, they secured it in the alterity of the authentic texts or in idealized readers who could appreciate the value of acquiring knowledge about their cultural heritage. Though spurning self-assertive gestures like Warburton's, these later critics and editors, through their practice, were helping to establish professional norms of competence in terms of the skill and knowledge required to deal with the old texts; as Malone would most emphatically demonstrate in his edition and his subsequent colossal demolition of the Ireland forgeries of 1795, Shakespearean scholarship was quickly evolving into a specialized forensic science whose degree of requisite erudition was beyond the reach of most common readers and amateur emendators. Yet the arbitrariness of these norms of competence was being misrecognized as simply what was to be expected of any editor or critic in performing a professional service on behalf of the text and its readers.

Under these new codes of practice, the modern editor could not appear to stand between the reader and the text. Johnson even recommended to his reader that he first attempt to appreciate Shakespeare's text without consulting the notes, and only "when the pleasures of novelty have ceased, let him attempt exactness, and read the commentators."[83] Unlike his predecessors, the modern editor explicitly rejected adhering to any prevailing moral or artistic criterion for literary production: Malone, in the preface to his edition, expressed wonderment at the rhetorical presentism of Shakespeare's earliest editors, who "seem never to have looked behind them, and to have considered their own era and their own phraseology as the standard of perfection."[84] The modern editor proclaimed to his reader the value of pursuing knowledge for its own sake, unmediated by either current fashions or editorial tampering, and proposed that the painstaking accumulation of such knowledge would eventually provide the reader with the cultural distinction of being able to master the hermeneutic challenges posed by old writings: "all such reading, as was never read," remarked Richard Farmer, reversing Pope's jibe at Theobald, was "the reading necessary for a Comment on *Shakespeare*."[85] Or, as Johnson put it most famously in his Preface, "what has been longest known has been most considered, and what is most considered is best understood."[86]

In a roundabout way, the later editors, though disavowing any such pretension, were setting themselves up as the high priests of Shakespeare's sacred text by claiming the requisite cultural capital not so much for themselves as for the reader who confronted Shakespeare in the original. I can explain this process by once again invoking a distinction Alvin Kibel has proposed between two categories of great books: the cultural document, whose message is open to reformulation, and the canonical text, whose original form is felt to be "the only means through which its message can be reliably transmitted." Shakespeare's adaptors and early editors clearly treated his works as cultural documents, whose symbolic value was acknowledged though whose meaning could be made available in versions more adequate to modern needs and understandings. However, once Shakespeare's dominance within the repertory was secure, in large part owing to the Licensing Act, his meaning became the object of a competition for authority and distinction within the cultural field. Though his message could still be altered, his writings were increasingly treated as canonical works, which Kibel defines as "a body of privileged texts with a reserve of meaning accessible only through special disciplines of interpretation." Yet, while the actors could promote their special skills of performance, their adaptations were clearly intended to make money by rendering Shakespeare's meaning accessible to a broad audience; the actor may have appropriated Shakespeare's aura but at the cost of diminishing the fund of meaning in his plays. A canonical text is one whose meaning is seemingly *inexhaustible*: it is a text, Kibel argues, "whose importance we recognize, although in some radical sense we are not able to understand it ... Accordingly, its original form is recognized as the only trustworthy expression of its meaning, and whatever can be derived from it by way of assertion about the world must be referred to this form for its systematic intelligibility. The very idea of *version* is discredited; that of *original* is put in its place."[87]

The editors, no less than the actors, were seeking commercial and symbolic profits, but instead of appropriating Shakespeare's aura for themselves, as both the actors and earlier editors had done, they enhanced that aura by presenting Shakespeare as an author whose works were so rich in significance that they had to be preserved in their original form lest their meaning be vitiated. Editions of the authentic Shakespeare became requisite for any reader who chose to undertake a life-long exegesis of his writings, and the reader was inspired to do so in order to distinguish himself from the uninformed masses that flocked to see the adaptations. Whereas in the past education functioned as one aspect of class determination, reading for the modern bourgeois consumer was increasingly perceived as an avenue to self-formation, for discovering meanings appropriate to developing a receptive and imaginative subjectivity, and for acquiring symbolic profits from displaying a special aesthetic competence. The reader was thus encouraged to seek out works which ostensibly promised a continual source of signification upon which he could exercise his sensibility (and, increasingly as well, *her* sensibility). Neglected authors were more and more being puffed with statements like the following before an edition of Beaumont and Fletcher's works: "Every good Author pleases more, the more he is examined ... especially when the *Stile* and *Manner* are quite *old-fashioned*."[88] And if the difficulties of even Shakespeare's original text were not enough to convince the reader of the density of his meaning, then, beginning with Johnson's variorum edition, there were notes informing the reader of the wealth of scholarship that had already been devoted to decoding even the briefest of passages.[89] Further confirmation of Shakespeare's resistance to totalization was available from an increasing array of interpretive commentary and, in particular, the burgeoning industry of character criticism, which transformed the plays into heroic portraits of the bountiful enigmas of subjectivity.[90] Unlike earlier critics, who aimed to correct or moralize about Shakespeare, the later critics and scholars did not pretend to exhaust the playwright's significance by reformulating his message, but only to offer a discourse that was vitally enabling of any serious attempt at understanding that message. And whereas editors in the past could assert that their corrections had explained Shakespeare's meaning by fixing his text, later editors would claim to have done no more than to have ascertained an acceptable text upon which exegesis could then proceed: the "first and immediate object" of an editor, Malone insisted, was "to fix what is to be explained."[91]

By the time Malone had completed his edition, Shakespeare's canonicity would be all but absolute, sanctified by a chorus of Bardolatry whose principal theme was the author's preternatural inexhaustibility of meaning. Martin Sherlock, addressing Shakespeare, averred "thy variety is inexhaustible. Always original, always new, thou art the only prodigy which Nature has produced. Homer was the first of men, but thou art more than man."[92] "So much has been written," added another critic from 1792, "concerning our favorite author that if the subject were not inexhaustible, what any one may have to add might very well be dispensed with; but there will ever be cause for the exertion of the most enlightened mind, when the exalted merit of this more than mortal is in question."[93] Such hyperbole may have threatened to render any criticism dispensable, but in fact it helped to make all forms of critical practice invaluable to the reader by promoting the acquisition of cultural capital, by encouraging, that is, the reader to engage in a long and deep immersion in the Shakespearean text, and its attendant commentaries, in order to develop the special form of attention – "the exertion of the most enlightened mind" – required to comprehend and appreciate Shakespeare. As well, by apotheosizing a Shakespeare whose "transcendent" authority seemed impervious to appropriation, these effusive gestures enabled the critical community to misrecognize its economic interests. Inevitably, editors like Steevens, faced with competing publications like Malone's that seemed to provide an ever-more definitive text, were forced to defend their stake in the market by arguing for the indefiniteness of Shakespeare's meaning and for an unceasing conflict of interpretations that could justify the production of still further editions: "The readings which have hitherto disunited the opinions of the learned may continue to disunite them as long as England and Shakespeare have a name ... Our author's text ... on account of readings alternately received and reprobated must remain in an unsettled state, and float in obedience to every gale of contradictory criticism." What were once determinate corrections had since become "readings," as editors had become themselves consumers of the text. Given the insolubility of Shakespeare's cruces, the modern editor might conceivably have difficulty defending his readings as any more authoritative than any other, though an acknowledged veteran like Steevens, in his final edition, could always cash in cultural for economic capital: "I claim the merit of being the first commentator on Shakespeare who strove, with becoming seriousness, to account for the frequent stains that disgrace the earliest folio edition of his plays, which is now become the most expensive single book in our language; for what other English volume without plates, and printed since the year 1600, is known to have sold, more than once, for thirty-five pounds, fourteen shillings?"[94]

Steevens's anxious self-promotion may seem a far cry from Northrop Frye's confident assertion that criticism can be a "science," yet both derive the force of their claims from the belief that literature presents, in Frye's words, "an inexhaustible source of new critical discoveries." To earn cultural capital, the reader must demonstrate competence in deciphering the meaning of cultural goods, yet the more these objects are seen to be indeterminate in their meaning, the more the reader is compelled to surrender his critical autonomy to specialized representatives and pedagogical authorities in order to achieve such competence. As Tony Bennett has noted, the "conception of the literary text as unfathomable – as the site for an endless practice of rereading which can never be wrong yet never be right – is ... an artefact of the relations of correction and supervision inscribed at the centre of modern literary education."[95] If this is the case, many of the central assumptions about canonicity in modern critical discourse may function to perpetuate embedded professional interests within critical and academic institutions: the belief that works of literature can never entirely surrender their meaning, that it is heresy to think this meaning can ever be wholly paraphrased, that the pursuit of the single correct interpretation, however inspiring a hope, is ultimately futile since the canonical text is forever patient of interpretation. At the least, these assumptions enable the cultural field to renew itself continually, since they imply that competence within the field, whether achieved by readers or actors or other agents, can only ever be relative and contingent. But, more significantly, these assumptions reflect a larger cosmology of belief about the value of art and of the aesthetic experience in the modern world. As Bourdieu suggests, the more the cultural field is believed to be independent of political or economic concerns, however commercial the impetus for producing ever-new editions of a canonical work, the more that work is "destined to be *decoded,* hence subject to a *repeated reading necessary to explore, without exhausting it, the intrinsic polysemy* of the work."[96] That the canonical text in its authentic purity offers an inexhaustible supply of meaning is thus a necessary presupposition of an aesthetics of pure and disinterested reading. This cosmology of belief surrounding the English canon, I would argue, had its origins in the critical and pedagogical discourses I have been examining in this chapter.

The modern canonization of Shakespeare and, eventually, of other early English authors went hand in hand with the institutionalization of reading. Scholars, critics, and editors made their activity essential to the cultural field by making the study of literature, to which their contributions were integral, a vital element in the constitution of the subject. In justifying their activity by proposing a text that could somehow reproduce itself fruitfully and in perpetuity, they may seem to us to have been engaging in mystification, both of how much Shakespeare's canonization owed to their efforts and of how much those efforts were motivated by a desire to dominate the cultural field. But their efforts ought rather to be seen as contributing to the field's ongoing autonomization, a change marked by an intensification of cultural capital as a mechanism or currency of social power. As such, their ascendancy was necessarily very gradual and not always perceptible. The theatrical alterations would continue to enjoy considerable popularity because they made Shakespeare relevant to modern concerns and desires, though, by the next century, they had lost their critical legitimacy. Theorists like Coleridge and Lamb were by then urging the reader to avoid the bustle of the theatre and to experience Shakespeare in solitude, safely removed from the world of public affairs.[97] Within a few years, the study of English literature would become an academic discipline with the establishment, in 1828, of the first professorship of English at the University of London; in his inaugural lecture, the first holder of the chair, Thomas Dale, signalled his discipline's indispensability within the endless work of elucidation by heralding what he called the "glorious and inexhaustible subject, the LITERATURE of our country."[98] The acting companies, however commercially successful, could no longer deny that they had surrendered much of their cultural capital to the experts who believed that, at some level, what Shakespeare wrote could never be fully understood. Playgoing had therefore to be more like reading in the way Shakespeare's text had to be approached directly, in its most intellectually demanding form, and with minimal concessions to present values and habits. And so in 1838, in what Vickers calls "a courageous partial revival," Macready inaugurated the repeal of the adaptations by restoring most of the original *King Lear*, though even he lacked the fortitude to play the Fool.[99] The high and serious calling of literary criticism – a calling, one might say, elevated on Shakespeare's fathomless depths – had triumphed over the tyranny of the audience.

7 A Basis for Criticism

The eighteenth century, it is commonly assumed, inaugurated the formation of the English literary canon. It is during this period that the modern terms of value first entered critical discourse: the concept of *aesthetics* was introduced by Alexander Baumgarten in 1735; David Ruhnken, writing in 1768, adapted the term *canon* to refer for the first time to a selection of poets and orators; and the word *literature*, long used to designate erudition among a broad range of polite learning, grew increasingly specialized in its meaning so as to become by the end of the century the most prevalent term given to imaginative writings.[1] The emergence of these conceptual categories went hand in hand with significant changes in critical practice, including what René Wellek identified as "the awakening of the historical sense and modern self-consciousness" that led to the development of literary history as a discipline, culminating during the period with the publication of Thomas Warton's *History of English Poetry* (1774–81).[2] Extending Wellek's argument, Lawrence Lipking has suggested that Warton's work ought to be seen alongside Johnson's *Lives of the Poets* (1779–81) as answering a larger cultural need for an "ordered" canon of English letters: "What the public demanded, and what it eventually received, was a history of English poetry, or a survey of English poets, that would provide a basis for criticism by reviewing the entire range of the art. Warton and Johnson responded to a national desire for an evaluation of what English poets had achieved ... English literary history was shaped by the need for a definition of the superiority of the national character."[3]

That we are part of the historical formation which generated these terms and practices may explain some of the problematic assumptions behind such arguments. Canon-formation, as it is now practised, may have begun in relation to English literature only in the eighteenth century, but, as I have been attempting to show, a notion of canonicity greatly antedated this period and indeed was apparent whenever early writers attempted to publicize their activity. These writers, when promoting an English literary system or evaluating the work of others, may not have framed their canons according to modern conceptual categories, but such categories reflected a division of knowledge that was promulgated only during the eighteenth century. Further, what these writers were doing may not have involved much of a "historical sense," as Wellek defined the idea, but this did not mean that their gestures at presentist self-legitimization were gratuitous. Among the early poetic catalogues of authors that dominated rhetorical canon-making, Wellek could find nothing of scholarly value: "Obviously, no real contribution can be expected from a form that primarily served poetical purposes."[4] Not only does the comment rather unhistorically assume that "poetical purposes" must in all ages be autotelic, but "real contribution" is measured solely in terms of historical information and critical competence. Yet those catalogues did serve clear genuine functions in helping poets to defend their activity and to maintain conviction in the productive value of poetry within the moral economy of English society. Finally, early writers often tried to animate their gestures at self-legitimization by appealing to patriotic feeling, their catalogues of authors were regularly intended by their harmony to suggest the vitality and similitude of the indigenous culture, and certainly early poets declared time and again on their own behalf that they were the ones who could most eloquently proclaim "the superiority of the national character."

The desire for what Lipking calls "a basis for criticism" was real, though it did not necessarily stem from an intensified nationalism. Rather, the appearance of literary histories, interpretive commentaries, and evaluative hierarchies reflected a cultural situation in which the function of canon-formation, of evaluating and reproducing works, had been assumed by an increasingly professionalized critical discourse. This cultural situation, in turn, reflected a vast cognitive shift in society, wherein it could suddenly seem imperative to objectify value through such discourses of "ordering," categorization, and historicization. To order the canon was to imply that it needed ordering, that this order was to be different in kind from the harmony prized in earlier rhetorical valorizations and that it could be achieved by setting norms of competence for the reception and interpretation of canonical texts by systematically ranking what English authors had produced, by contextualizing works with abundant historical facts about their authors and their times, and by supplying huge scholarly narratives about the development of literature in England. These critical practices were developed at least partly to resolve contradictions within the canon, so that it would no longer seem inconsistent to honour both artless geniuses like Shakespeare and peerless craftsmen like Pope. Inconsistencies like these had been apparent in earlier rhetorical valuations, though they were usually ignored in the presentist belief that the canon could be harmonized after contemporary practice. Contradictions only began to be taken seriously as a result of the canon being pluralized in response to changing assumptions about the function of literature. Under these assumptions, the cultural field was at once autonomized from other interests and extolled as providing the consumer with the supreme moral technology for realizing himself in the act of seeing experience from the point of view of others. For this sense of experience to seem as broad and enriching as possible, the canon for consumption was constructed unlike the earlier producers' canon in being *relatively* more inclusive, internally differentiated, and intellectually demanding in its scope, meaning, and alterity. To facilitate and control the consumer's engagement with this plural canon, complex modes of cultural reproduction needed to be developed, and this need was answered by professional critical and academic discourse.

A greater plurality of values thus made for a canon that could seem disordered in the way it consecrated authors as diverse as Shakespeare and Pope, Chaucer and Milton, Spenser and Swift, Dryden and Gray, Cowley and Congreve, even perhaps Richardson and Fielding. With this greater plurality, in other words, came the problem of maintaining evaluative certainty in the face of apparent relativity: how could any act of critical judgment be authoritative if canonicity was no longer determined according to clear prescriptive conventions? Eighteenth-century theories of aesthetics and moral sentiments had defined several potential grounds for judgment, in terms of the special character of the aesthetic experience, the unique mysteriousness of artistic creativity, and the discriminating faculty of taste. Yet, as Hume recognized in his essay on the standard of taste, it was difficult to identify empirically an absolute basis for criticism since everywhere there seemed to exist "great inconsistence and contrariety" in human values.[5] If Hume nonetheless went on to posit a standard of taste because his theory of moral sympathy required such an absolute ground, his argument demonstrates how all considerations of value must eventually arrive at a relativist or absolutist position that requires and confirms the other.[6]

By decrying the confusing multiplicity of human opinion, Hume could thus heighten belief in the necessity of establishing a standard of taste. This rhetorical gambit would occasionally be repeated by literary critics of the period, though in general they were less troubled by the paradoxical nature of value than were the moral and aesthetic philosophers. Critics and literary historians were much more apt to assume that, at some level, there existed an absolute foundation of value, despite what their historicist and hermeneutic inquiries seemed to reveal. The problem was how to articulate this evaluative certainty and yet construct a credible canon made up of a diversity of authors who wrote to different standards, in different ages, and for different purposes. In essence, the problem was one of reconciling the pursuit of knowledge about such differences with the practices of evaluating works and reproducing a plural canon, the ultimate hope being that this knowledge could provide a basis for these critical practices.

THE LOGIC OF DIFFERENTIATION

Canon-making was, as ever, deeply informed by ideological bias, and no canon could be credibly proposed that was so plural as to include much writing by women or popular authors unless, as in the case of the ballads, their work could be appropriated for polite consumption. In addition, many evaluative conventions remained operative in regulating canonicity. Generic hierarchies could still serve to diminish the appearance of inconsistency, particularly in the case of the novelists, who were not usually classed along with the famed poets and dramatists of the past.[7] And authors could always rely on all manner of rhetorical assertion to punctuate monistic revisions of the canon. In opposition to long-standing mythologies about the progress of letters, for example, there could be revived the equally ancient belief that cultural decline was inevitable after too much refinement. Writing in 1759, Goldsmith announced that English poetry had already reached a point of perfection during "the reign of Queen Anne, or some years before," since he believed that this perfection corresponded to the smoothening of the heroic couplet, the supremacy of which, he felt, was being threatened by a modern vogue for the "unharmonious measure" of blank verse.[8] Similar narratives of cultural decline underscored nominations of English works as "classics," nominations which were becoming more frequent now that works of the English moderns had begun to compete with ancient writings as objects of critical reproduction. Elijah Fenton, in a testimonial to Thomas Southerne from 1711, declared his plays "shall stand / Among the chosen classics of our land," yet the thought only sparked Fenton's regret over how foreign operas had since usurped the English stage: "There was an age (its memory will last!) / Before Italian airs debauch'd our taste."[9] By 1765 such an expression of disaffection for contemporary production could be as much of a commonplace for elevating English classics as the old gesture of matching the moderns to the ancients: "Indeed it must be confessed that we have *classic-authors* in our own language also, a proper study of whose elegant works would make us look with contempt on the prettiness so profusely lavished on the compositions of some modern writers. Spenser, Shakespear, Milton and Dryden, Swift, Bolingbroke, Addison and Pope, do not yield in energy of stile, truth of sentiment, or real beauty of diction, to any among the ancients."[10]

For the critic and literary historian who sought to defend a plural canon, rhetorical claims like these may have been forceful in their symbolic violence, but their obvious arbitrariness rendered them unhelpful in arguing for plurality. It was not that they wanted to do away with symbolic violence in canon-making, even if that were possible. If anything, they hoped to retain the forcefulness of absolutist gestures within their evaluative performances while at the same time distributing this forcefulness across a range and scale of values. The difficulty was in developing new gestures of ordering whose normative arbitrariness could be more easily misrecognized than the rhetoricity of simple assertion. The observance of neoclassic rules had suggested one solution, for though the rules eventually proved too restrictive in not permitting the cultural field to renew itself, their initial legitimacy was owing to both their specificity and the absoluteness of method with which they could be applied to the appraisal of literary works. Thus, in the earliest hierarchical rankings of authors in English critical discourse, evaluative certainty could be simply an effect of apparent methodological precision. Preparing to undertake a proposed dictionary of British poets sometime in the 1720s or 1730s, Joseph Spence was possibly the first to suggest a systematic comparative scale to guide readers through the canon:

To distinguish ye Characters of the Poets one might use the known marks for ye different magnitudes of the Stars.
1   a great Genius, & fine writer.
2   a great Genius.
3   a fine writer.
4   a good poet in gen[era]l.
5   a tolerable Poet for ye times he lived in.
6   a middling Poet.
7   a bad Poet.
†   one never to be read.[11]

Roger de Piles's *jeu d'esprit*, "La Balance des Peintres" (1708), inspired at least two English imitations in which canonical authors were graded in various categories such as "Versification," "Genius," "Taste," and "Incidental Expression." In the first, from Dodsley's *Museum* (1745) and likely penned by Akenside, a number of canonical English and European authors were judged under eight criteria on a scale from one to twenty, with "eighteen the highest that any Poet has attained." Despite scoring a zero in "Critical Ordonnance," Shakespeare was ranked highest, alongside Homer, with a "final estimate" of eighteen. In the second of these charts, from *The Literary Magazine* (1758), twenty-nine English authors, from Chaucer to the Augustans, were ranked under four "qualifications" on a similar scale of one to twenty, "of which 19 may be attained in any one qualification, but the 20th was never yet attain'd to." Pope scored highest with 71, followed by Milton, Dryden, and Addison. At the next level stood the improbable trio of Shakespeare, Cowley, and Swift, each awarded a total of 66. Among authors singled out as too marginal for measurement were Rochester, Wycherley, and Shadwell ("he is below all criticism").[12]

In ludicrousness and simplicity, these scales and tallyings recall early exercises like Meres's canon-matching, but they also suggest how much critical evaluation had been transformed since Meres's day. The canon was now understood to be ideally selective and hierarchical rather than full and harmonious, while the accomplishments it recognized were to be valued according to divergent measures and criteria rather than sharply valorized by apposition to an apocryphal other. The canon was to be organized not by genre – the criteria were "applied equally to every Species of poetry," Akenside insisted – but by either the formal attributes of art, such as versification, or the creative disposition and historical circumstances of the author: fine writing, according to Spence, did not necessarily correspond with great genius, while a poet might be passable only in relation to the "times he lived in." As in Meres's canon, an absolute value was assumed as the basis for judgment, but it was now believed to exist only potentially, being "never yet attain'd to." As a consequence, the modern canon remained open and provisional, for though the poets' relative rankings were seen as stable in relation to this absolute standard, the "Degree of absolute Perfection" could not, in principle, be known since it was "beyond even the Taste of Knowledge of the best Critics at present." In fact, according to Akenside, a score of twenty was only a metaphysical hypothesis, since "the nineteenth Degree is the highest of which the human Mind has any comprehension." Perfection was something to be continually striven for, if never yet achieved, and was to be predicated in terms not of current poetic practice but of the limits of human knowledge, taste, and comprehension. This contingency of judgment, Akenside confessed, related equally to his own powers of discrimination, since he could rank the poets only "according to the best Information which my private Taste could afford me." Accordingly, he told readers, "I shall be extremely glad if any of your ingenious Correspondents will correct me where I am wrong." Meres's canon, which appeared in a rhetorical handbook for authors, offered Elizabethans an absolutist image of harmony that could empower them with the belief that their society could be as productive as the ancient empires. The later scales and balances of poets, written for the benefit of consumers by literary historians and reviewers, proposed a canon that was revisable, internally gradated and categorized by "qualification," and composed with a view to refining the "Taste of Knowledge" among readers and critics in the hope that an understanding of human perfection might be achieved at some distant future time.

Above all, these later canon-makers believed that judgment could be made objective by codifying the norms of canonicity within a discourse of scientific taxonomy and quantification. The rankings of poets, Spence indicated, could be identified by the same "known marks" used to identify the "different magnitudes of the Stars." The feeling that criticism could aspire to the character of a science was prevalent during this period, as it usually is in an objectivist culture whenever a professionalized critical discourse is felt to be in need of legitimation. Of the pleasures of poetic beauty, Johnson declared in the *Rambler*, "Criticism reduces those regions of literature under the dominion of science, which have hitherto known only the anarchy of ignorance, the caprices of fancy, and the tyranny of prescription."[13] Criticism, it was believed, could observe its own set of precise and repeatable rules of practice, and these would differ from earlier neoclassical doctrines in not serving as prescriptions on poetic production but as mechanisms for systematizing the reception of literature. Accordingly, critics insisted that these rules were to be derived from "observation," with the basis for judgment, as Hume remarked, being "the same with that of all the practical sciences, experience." Despite the empirical difficulties in determining, in Hume's words, "what has been universally found to please in all countries and in all ages," canonicity was to be a quantifiable measure of the transhistorical patterns of literary consumption, and classifiable by the observable attributes and effects of art.[14] It did not seem to matter that estimations of value were necessarily comparative and contingent, or that slippages in measure were bound to occur as a result of interpretation. The discourse of scientism was desirable because it provided criticism with an air of certainty at a time when it was seeking to establish a plural canon that was ostensibly not determined by the values of contemporary production. Canon-making in the past had been the province of poets, but now their self-service and present-mindedness made their gestures seem illegitimate to critics: "nothing is more dangerous in literary matters," wrote the contributor to *The Literary Magazine*, "than to follow the testimony given by one living author to another." Whether the critics' own gestures at scientific objectivity were any the less informed by the values of the day, or by self-service in legitimizing their profession, is not as significant as the fact that these gestures were felt to carry an evaluative authority greater and more disinterested than the rhetorical campaigns poets had formerly waged on their own behalf. Persuasion by proof and method now seemed more effective than persuasion by verbal seduction.

The scientism also accorded with the commercial humanist emphasis upon difference, since the search for knowledge brought with it continual specification and "cutting," as Akenside happily acknowledged when he noted that his category of taste could "admit of several Subdivisions; for some Poets are excellent for the Grandeur of their Taste, others for its Beauty, and others for a kind of Neatness." The ideology of individualism that informed the cults of originality and personal style could find expression in the claim that English authors could be severally differentiated in both kind and degree of skill, disposition, learning, taste, and moral sensitivity. So differentiated, the author presented a unity of both discourse and subjectivity, since his writings seemed to form a canon as harmonious as any proposed in early critical discourse yet one signifying a coherence of self rather than of English society: "an author's peculiar character," wrote a contributor to *The British Magazine* for June 1760, "is stampt upon his works, and may be discovered under the disguise of different forms in all his compositions."[15] At the same time, the fact of the author's individuality, it was felt, rendered comparative estimations and hierarchical evaluations all the more authoritative for being precise: "Nothing can be more conducive to form the taste than to draw a parrallel between the genius's of such as have distinguished themselves in any branch of literature, and, by weighing their merits in the ballance of criticism, enable ourselves to ascertain with exactitude at which side the scale of excellence preponderates." How the author's "peculiar character" related to the merits of the writings was left undefined but the implication was that comparing authors would yield an exact sense of each author's particularity; this interpretive sense, in turn, could make for evaluative certainty, as if specificity of analysis brought with it its own axiological force. For this essayist, the logic of specification and differentiation inevitably determined the terms of praise, since

Shakespeare could seem to him at once authorially unique and sub-limely multiform, "so various and fertile that 'tis hardly possible to point out what he excels most in, or shew the predominant beauty of his works." This logic, where not only authorial uniqueness was prized but evaluative certainty was correlated to how definitively an author's uniqueness could be demonstrated, pervaded the critical discourse of the period, becoming for the Romantics the maxim Wordsworth attrib-uted to Coleridge: "every great and original writer, in proportion as he is great or original, must himself create the taste by which he is to be relished."[16]

As much as this logic accorded with the differentiating forces of the marketplace and the individualism of an emergent commercial humanism, its prevalence was more directly related to the changing cosmology of a cultural field that was evolving towards an ever-greater autonomy. Now that people from most ranks and occupations could learn to read and write literature without being directly answerable to a dominant class, both the terms of entry into the field and the "rules of the game" within it had to be redefined.[17] First and foremost, a threshold had to be proposed to distinguish cultural work from other forms of human endeavour, and in particular to keep it opposed to the cash nexus: for the cultural field to be a meaningful entity, one had to be able to identify certain activities as being uniquely cultural. The discourse of aesthetics had already begun to generate terms for signalling the cultural, terms like taste, judgment, and imagination. Yet, because their definitions had to remain sufficiently ambiguous to allow for the field's renewal, these terms, unlike neoclassical laws for poetry, did not propose fixed requirements for entry into the field or come with precise evaluative criteria for cultural work. Accordingly, critics keen on systematizing the canon were obliged to find some way of translating such terms into workable normative boundaries as to what constituted literature or what made a work canonical. These critics thus abided by the logic of differentiation in the belief that such boundaries could be ever more finely specified.

In actuality, what propelled this logic had less to do with defining literature than with achieving dominance within the cultural field. As the absolute value of cultural activity could be stated only as a hypo-thetical possibility, so the exercise of judgment could only ever be contingent, an open-ended process of comparison. In addition, the more the autonomy of the field was asserted, the more cultural works were to be evaluated solely in comparison with other works within the field, as if their value was, as Bourdieu suggests, to be "derived only from the structure, hence the history, of the field, increasingly barring the 'short circuit,' meaning the possibility of passing directly from what is produced in the social world to what is produced in the field." As a consequence, success within the field became increasingly measured by how well one could demonstrate "a *differential* perception, distinctive, drawing into the perceiving of each singular work the space of compossible works, and hence attentive and sensitive to the *deviations* in relation to other works, contemporary but also past."[18] Simply put, the more refined and informed the act of discrimination, the more authority it seemed to possess. The logic of differentiation had now become the rules of the game, the terms for participation if not entry within the field. Placing works relationally to one another might not necessarily reveal what made them worthy of attention, just as selectively distributing value across the history and totality of the cultural field could not compensate for the uncertainty over the source of that value. All the same, the art of fine discrimination now served the interests of all who strove for position within the field, much as acts of rhetorical apposition had done for earlier generations.

THE WARTONS ON THE CANON

This confusion over differentiation, as providing as a basis for criticism when in fact it could serve only to map out the cultural field, can be seen in the period's most elaborate ranking of English poets, in Joseph Warton's *Essay on the Genius and Writings of Pope* (1756, 1782). Warton divided the canonical English poets into "four different classes and degrees." At the top were "our only three sublime and pathetic poets; SPENSER, SHAKESPEARE, MILTON; and then, at proper intervals, OTWAY and LEE." In the second rank were those authors who "possessed the true poetical genius, in a more moderate degree, but who had noble talents for moral and ethical poetry. At the head of these are DRYDEN, DONNE, DENHAM, COWLEY, CONGREVE." Below them were the "men of wit, of elegant taste, and some fancy in describing familiar life. Here may be numbered, PRIOR, WALLER, PARNELL, SWIFT, FENTON." And in the lowest class were the "mere versifiers, however smooth and mellifluous some of them may be thought ... Such as PITT, SANDYS, FAIRFAX, BROOME, BUCKINGHAM, LANDS-DOWN." By this scheme, Warton could then adjudge Pope, after an extensive examination of his works (and subsequent revision of the rankings), to be deserving of pre-eminence in the second class, "*next* to *Milton*, and *just* above *Dryden*," as his poetry was primarily "of the *didactic, moral,* and *satyric* kind; and consequently, not of the most *poetic* species *of poetry*." Pope's imagination, Warton concluded, "was not his predominant talent."[19]

Warton has been ridiculed for the monotonous predictability of this conclusion, and it is commonly assumed that Johnson was referring to the *Essay*, a work he otherwise admired, when he took on the polemicists for pure poetry at the end of his "Life of Pope": "To circumscribe poetry by a definition will only shew the narrowness of the definer, though a definition which shall exclude Pope will not easily be made."[20] From the point of view of the history of canon-making, however, Warton's scheme is of considerable interest precisely because Warton felt he had to rely on a compendium of then-prevalent gestures in order to avoid seeming too restrictive while remaining authoritative in his evaluations. In a sense, he did not need his canonical rankings to make his case against Pope, since he could have simply criticized Pope's writings for their lack of imagination and sublimity and found them wanting as "pure poetry." The result might have seemed limited in its monistic account of poetic value, though not necessarily tautological or any more dogmatic than similar Romanticist revaluations of Pope, and his canon would have had the force and harmony of earlier rhetorical valorizations. Yet he claimed to revere Pope and did not wish to form a canon that would have excluded him entirely. In fact, Warton was aiming to recognize as many authors as possible under his scheme: in addition to the poets named in his opening lists, he filled his argument with comparative assessments of numerous ancient, medieval, and modern authors, as if he were trying to position all Western authors within an ordered canon. By this logic of differentiation, Warton believed that evaluative certainty could come only by precisely defining Pope's place within this canon, and if his conclusions were wildly overdetermined, this was not as significant as his attempt to form a definitive yet plural canon, one that earned its authority by specifying a diversity of criteria while managing not to appear inconsistent.

Warton's scheme essentially conflated five divergent norms or conditions of canonicity, which were aligned in a rather complicated manner with his four "different species" of authors. At the outer limits of his canon was the boundary of craft, as signalled in the technical criterion that English poets had at a minimum to be versifiers, and in the qualitative distinction that their verse had to be smooth and mellifluous in order to be remembered within any canon. Within this boundary, Warton then identified a traditional hierarchy of genres, a sense usually connoted by the term "species," though one limited to two levels: the highest occupied by epic and heroic verse, with other kinds ("*didactic, moral,* and *satyric*") falling below this level. He subsequently qualified the evaluative force of this two-tiered hierarchy by introducing the deterministic notion, increasingly popular at the time, of how excellence in epic and heroic poetry was out of the reach of authors bred in more refined eras. "In no polished nation, after criticism has been much studied, and the rules of writing established, has any very extraordinary work ever appeared," Warton claimed. This primitivism reversed an earlier classicist belief in progressive refinement, and just as Dryden once blamed Shakespeare's failings on the barbarity of a past age, so Warton was perhaps palliating Pope's limitations as a unfortunate accident of his modernity. The idea allowed him to reinforce the central formal division within his hierarchy as historically inevitable, while at the same time weakening its normative authority insofar as it implied that dispensations were to be made for the circumstances determining a poet's accomplishments: "We can never completely relish, or adequately understand any author ... except we constantly keep in our eye his climate, his country, and his age." This gesture, fast becoming a commonplace at the time, may not have had as much of a relativizing force for Warton as his statement appeared to suggest, but his resorting to historicism was indicative of his anxious need to seem both flexible and assured in criticizing a cherished and only recently dead poet like Pope.[21]

Yet, whereas Dryden's periodizing was for him an adequate basis for criticism, Warton had to add another set of conditions to explain how, in a heroic age like Shakespeare's, there could also thrive lesser poets like Donne, Sandys, and Fairfax. To position these poets, Warton proposed the criterion of authorial disposition or faculty, of which he recognized three essential categories, the mere versifiers, the men of wit and taste, and the true geniuses. This last disposition could, in theory, be found as much among the Shakespeares as the Popes, but owing to historical circumstance, these last possessed it only "in a more moderate degree." With this criterion, Warton could revise his traditional order of genres by introducing his prime operative standard of imagination, according to which Shakespeare could be classed among the epic poets and Pope just below, since "*good sense* and *judgment* were his characteristical excellencies, rather than *fancy* and *invention*." For Warton, this standard could represent an absolute value, independent of time or place, since it was possible for "the vigorous and creative imagination of MILTON" to be "superior to the prejudices of his times."[22] Yet, if the poet's imagination could transcend any historical determinism, this might have meant that Pope, unlike other lesser geniuses, could have written poetry of the first rank had he not been so distracted by his prosaic age. After all, Warton knew that Pope's defenders could always point to the fantastical apparatus in *The Rape of the Lock* as proof of the poet's inventive powers. Anticipating such claims, he added a fifth point of differentiation, namely that poets could be ultimately classed, in one of three categories, by the social content of their work: the nere versifiers, who exhibited little adequate sense of their world; the ethical poets like Pope and the men of wit like Swift, who trafficked with ease in the scenes of "familiar life"; and, above all, the poets of heroic imagination, who dealt in supreme fictions that were to be appreciated not for their familiarity but for their sublime and pathetic effects. Warton's ideal of pure poetry had to be fundamentally opposed to modern society, with its adverse influence on the creativity of lesser geniuses, yet he recognized that his criterion of imagination might not be enough to signal the anti-social nature of this ideal. *The Rape of the Lock* may have been inventive, but it dealt with contemporary life and mores. This last criterion was therefore the decisive one for Warton in relegating Pope to a lower class, for the satirist's ultimate failing was not a demonstrable lack of imagination but his regrettable choice in having "stuck to describing *modern manners*, [and] those *manners*, because they are *familiar, uniform, artificial*, and *polished*, are, in their very nature, unfit for any lofty effort of the Muse."[23]

Read closely, Warton's canon-making is a marvel of differentiation that appears to rehearse most of the defining values of canonicity, aside from utilitarian interests, that were then operative: (1) considerations of the formal and technical attributes of poetry as a verbal art, (2) considerations of genre and mode of discourse, (3) considerations of historical context and of divergences in cultural beliefs, (4) considerations of the qualitative and aesthetic attributes of poetry as a fictive or figurative art, and (5) moral and ideological considerations. In one version or another, these criteria had been around since antiquity and remain operative to this day, but what was remarkable about the *Essay* was that, despite invoking all of these criteria in a furious display of critical gestures, its classifications could still seem at once narrowly conceived and irrelevant. "*Where*, then," Warton asked after completing his lengthy review of Pope's writings, "according to the question proposed at the *beginning of this Essay*, shall we with justice be authorized to place our admired POPE?"[24] The problem for Warton was that, no matter how finely discriminating his appraisals of Pope's poetry, none of his initial assumptions of value could be justified by differentiating Pope as a poet, that is, by describing the qualities of his work, the features of his authorial character, or the specific nature of his accomplishments relative to other poets' work. It was not simply that Warton's advocacy of pure poetry determined the exclusionary nature of his highest class: monistic conceptions of canonicity have long been proposed as authoritative, just as it is still possible to hear some critics today confidently declaring that Shakespeare or Milton are the strongest poets in the language or the most ideologically freighted. Rather, no matter how many poets Warton could manage to categorize within his plural and internally differentiated canon, those categories could only seem increasingly arbitrary the more he appeared to objectify them as the basis for his criticism. Once a critic starts going down the road of plurality and differentiation, his task of justifying any assumption of value, maybe even plurality itself, becomes all the more logically difficult – if perhaps less imperative than in the case of an absolutist canon. Modern critics may misrecognize their assumptions by complicating their acts of judgment, by appearing not to judge a work by fixed and specifiable criteria but submitting it instead to a seemingly particularized and open-ended critical treatment, or by presenting their assumptions as provisional in leading to a potential absolute value without dictating rigid codes of evaluations.[25] For an eighteenth-century critic like Warton, however, no canon could have seemed authoritative without a declaration of absolute principles, moral and cultural interests, or determinable criteria. Warton could always try to suggest such valuative certainty by varying the size and number of his canonical classes, but such differentiation remained a comparative and unfixed exercise, just as the competence he claimed to demonstrate as a judge of the canon could itself only be measured as a relative degree, as cultural capital that could be prized precisely because only one in twenty readers could possess it.[26] In the end, what Warton had failed to do was to identify a unique and enabling source of value for his canon because the need to determine such a source could not easily accord with his desire to order a plural canon.

A similar conflict was apparent within the emergent practice of literary history, beginning with the pioneering efforts of the cataloguers Leland and Bale, who had hoped that their immense histories of British letters could serve to promote a tradition at once extensive and monolithic. Yet Leland and Bale were in the highly unusual position of having to try to promote the importance of old writings at the moment of their impending destruction, and their resulting categories were thus deeply conflicted exercises in attempting to wed antiquarian research with absolutist claims. Subsequent scholars, if they took notice of literary works at all, were much less concerned to derive from their researches any narrative of its development. It was left to the poets, in their encomiums to their age and colleagues, to suggest how such a narrative might aid canon-making, particularly if the "lineal descents and clans" of English poetic progress could be seen to culminate in a contemporary literary culture. With the lessening of such presentist thinking, eighteenth-century poets proposed ideas on how a more scholarly narrative might be organized, though the emphases in these early sketches remained on the productive influence of the author. Pope proposed a historical "classification of the poets" that ordered English poets according to schools, many of which were identified by a dominant poet and his followers, such as the "School of Chaucer" that, according to Pope, spawned Lydgate, Hoccleve, Skelton, and "Walter de Mapes." The implication was that the history of English poetry would confirm a canon made up of major figures and lesser acolytes; as Pope elsewhere remarked to Spence, "'Tis easy to mark out the general course of our poetry. Chaucer, Spenser, Milton, and Dryden are the great landmarks for it."[27] Spence's own brief manuscript history of English poetry, penned in French, diverged from Pope's plan in setting poets within historical periods, including Spence's own "Age Augustaine," though it was constructed upon the rhetoricist principle that the poet's canonicity was attendant upon verbal refinements: Dryden, wrote Spence, "releva beaucoup nôtre poësie, et nôtre langage."[28] Revising Pope's plan, Gray recommended to Thomas Warton that his history continue the model of grouping poets by school; however, his own outline gave prominence to earlier, non-classicist poets of "Provençal invention" like Chaucer and Spenser over the later "School of France, introduced after the Restoration."[29] In all these plans, literary history was made to serve particular revisions of the canon, where certain texts, styles, or genres were upheld by positing an author or mode of discourse as the harmonizing paradigm for an historical period, such as the "Age of Pope," to the exclusion of different authors or genres from the same period.

Warton, notoriously, rejected all these plans for his *History* in favour of a loosely chronological, self-consciously unsystematic approach that stressed both canonic plurality and the far-ranging particularization of knowledge. The "mechanical" arrangements proposed by Pope and Gray, he believed, would "destroy that free exertion of research with which such a history ought to be executed, and [were] not easily reconcileable with that complication, variety, and extent of materials, which it ought to comprehend."[30] Warton's critics have long deplored the consequences of his decision to eschew all principles of organization, and they have often pointed out how the unfinished *History* seems divided between Warton's stated aim of recording the progress of learning and the refinement of manners and his apparent mourning for a time when English poets felt more keenly the vivifying "fictions that are more valuable than reality."[31] This "contrast between romance and learning," Lipking has noted, is the fundamental dialectic of the unfinished *History*, apparent both from Warton's theme of the struggle between reality and fiction and from the historian's conflicting desire at once to record the facts "faithfully" and to make those facts fit an oblique lapsarian narrative of imagination lost.[32] In accordance with this dialectic, the *History* contrasted its own submerged canon of fine fablers against an expanding apocrypha of misguided poets who "became ambitious being thought scholars." Gower sacrificed his "native powers of invention ... to the pride of profound erudition," while "Petrarch would have been better poet had he been a worse scholar." Chaucer's poetic "feelings were too strong to be suppressed by books." Hawes's *Passetyme of Pleasure* "is almost the only effort of imagination and invention which had yet appeared in our poetry since Chaucer." Wyatt's "genius was of the moral and didactic species: and his poems abound more in good sense, satire, and observations on life, than in pathos or imagination."[33] Even Spenser and Shakespeare could flourish as epic and heroic poets only for a time in English poetic history because their era, nominally "the most POETICAL age of these annals," represented the last precarious balance, "a sort of civilized superstition," before the eclipse of the imagination inevitably set in.[34]

This impulse to oppose imagination to learning made for a complex structure of values within the *History*, since Warton's own groundbreaking scholarship seemed to represent just the kind of intellectual effort that moved society further away from the true sources of poetry. The utility in providing a history of English poetry, Warton insisted, was much like that of any other rationalist enquiry in providing a surer understanding of the world. By the logic of differentiation, the more precisely and thoroughly the history of the cultural field could be mapped out, the more the historian "teaches us to set a just estimation on our acquisitions." That estimation could be both comparative in its methodology and absolute in its conclusions: "We look back on the savage condition of our ancestors with the triumph of superiority ... arising in great measure from a tacit comparison of the infinite disproportion between the feeble efforts of remote ages, and our present improvements in knowledge."[35] In being itself an unsurpassed display of information, the *History* amply demonstrated this disproportion, as if the knowledge of past learning confirmed the relative superiority of modern erudition. Yet Warton was hesitant to recognize a progressive teleology in areas other than learning. Though his history emphasized how the refinement of manners was attendant upon the advancement of knowledge, it would have been unusual for someone of Warton's age not to believe in the universality of moral standards: "It is in vain to apologise for the coarseness, obscenity, and scurrility of Skelton, by saying that his poetry is tinctured with the manners of his age. Skelton would have been a writer without decorum at any period."[36] More difficult to establish was the transhistorical prevalence of norms of creativity, since Warton's own narrative of imagination's decline suggested far otherwise. At the same time, Warton had to believe in the essentiality of these norms so that not only his own judgments of poets might seem objective, but equally the imagination might have as strong a claim as a source of value in modern life as learning and morality.

In his earlier *Observations on the Fairy Queen* (1754), Warton had relied on a familiar relativizing gesture to encourage readers to overcome their presentist feelings: "It is absurd to think of judging either Ariosto or Spenser by precepts which they did not attend to. We who live in the days of writing by rule, are apt to try every composition by those laws which we have been taught to think the sole criterion of excellence. Critical taste is universally diffused, and we require the same order and design which every modern performance is expected to have, in poems where they never were regarded or intended. Spenser, and the same may be said of Ariosto, did not live in an age of planning."[37] By historicizing classicism as a recent development, Warton hoped he could weaken its absolutist claims – one of the possible functions of literary history being to help defeat arguments for the non-contingent nature of canonicity by showing how the canon has never been unchanging in its composition. Whereas Spenser's detractors had assumed that his epic's lack of conventional order had resulted from the poet's ignorance of the universal truths set out in classical practice, Warton simply asserted the opposite claim that learning was a temporal condition that obscured the fundamental source of poetic value in natural genius: "Born in such an age, Spenser wrote rapidly from his own feelings, which at the same time were naturally noble."[38]

Yet Warton could not go far with this argument before making any endeavour in modern learning, including his own literary history, seem arbitrary because of its historicity and in apparent conflict with its primitivist attitudes. Though the *History* made clear that the progress of learning had unfortunately obstructed the expression of genius, that progress could not be presented as a reversible historical aberration. Warton instead had to rely on a somewhat different set of historizing gestures, one whose main assumption of value was implicit in the above claim though more pronounced in a later passage from the *Observations*: "In reading the works of a poet who lived in a remote age, it is necessary that we should look back upon the customs and manners which prevailed in that age. We should endeavour to place ourselves in the writer's situation and circumstances. Hence we shall become better enabled to discover, how this turn of thinking, and manner of composing, were influenced by familiar appearances and established objects, which are utterly different from those with which we are at present surrounded."[39] Here canon-formation would be served by literary history, in its most widely recognized function of rendering older works accessible and relevant to modern readers by contextualizing their meaning and significance. Encouraging readers to engross themselves in learning about the past, Warton was hoping to pluralize the canon by promoting the absolute value of acquiring knowledge. In the earlier gesture, Warton had asserted that it was unfair of readers to judge older works by contemporary models of production. In this subsequent gesture, he went further in positing a distinction between modern expectations about production and the appropriate conditions for consumption. Reading the literature of the past, he was suggesting, had to be conducted not simply without preconceived notions about how works ought to be written, but in the spirit of wanting to become "better enabled" and more disinterested readers. Accordingly, the absolute basis for criticism was less the poet's natural genius than the ability of the reader to learn so deeply about the past as to transport himself sublimely into the writer's "situation and circumstances." In effect, Warton was celebrating works of the imagination by celebrating the exercise of imagination that was required to read them.[40]

The very form of his *History* encouraged this exercise. The mass of information he provided on all manner of social, religious, political, philosophical, and technical matters was intended to envelop the reader in the past, to enable the reader as much to appreciate the works of the past as to experience that past vicariously: "the manners, monuments, customs, practices, and opinions of antiquity ... are objects which forcibly strike a feeling imagination."[41] The ages of chivalry and superstition which Warton described in detail were the very stuff of romance whose passing he was lamenting. If modern learning had dimmed the power of creative invention, it nonetheless provided an opportunity for the reader to indulge an escapist self-immersion in the past. Vicesimus Knox felt that the appeal of anti-quarian histories like Warton's was deceptive because they diverted readers from appreciating the true source of poetic value: "By an effort of the imagination, we place ourselves in the age of the author, and call up a thousand collateral ideas which give beauties to his work not naturally inherent."[42] And yet, in a significant way, Warton was con-tributing to the autonomization of the literary experience that was implicit in Knox's contrast between "collateral ideas" and "inherent" beauties. Although Warton was greatly concerned with showing how literary activities in the past had interacted with all aspects of early English life, not only were works of the imagination to be opposed to modern learning and manners, but the study of those works and their history did not seem to have any particular moral influence on modern readers. Even if readers could place themselves imaginatively in a distant past, they remained free of the superstitions, credulities, and "barbarities" of the past that "are the parents of imagination."[43] Secretly delighting in the old romances despite their better judgment, it seemed, modern readers were restrained by their reason from either writing such trifles or taking their values and meanings to heart.

For Warton, the old texts could be either purely of fictive interest or purely of documentary interest in providing records of a distant era; any other possible values they may have once expressed as poetry or rhetoric were to be dismissed as belonging to a temporal realm. As he remarked in the postscript to his *Observations*, the works of the English past "preserve many curious historical facts, and throw considerable light on the nature of the feudal system. They are the pictures of anti-ent usages and customs; and represent the manners, genius, and char-acter of our ancestors. Above all, such are their Terrible Graces of magic and enchantments, so magnificently marvelous are their fictions and fablings, that they contribute, in a wonderful degree, to rouse and invigorate all the powers of imagination: to store the fancy with those sublime and alarming images, which true poetry best delights to dis-play."[44] In fact, the romantic fictions of the past did not seem to have any direct instrumental effect on their original audiences, at least none comparable to the changes wrought by learning. Satiric and didactic works may have wielded some persuasiveness in helping, say, to expose abuses of religion, but such a direct engagement with social reality rendered these works less poetic and imaginative. In contrast, the romantic fictions of the past appeared only to reflect the beliefs and manners of their age; further, they did not have a defined role to play in the moral economy of a particular era, providing only "entertain-ment" for readers of all eras.[45] Warton even dismissed as unfounded the humanists' distrust of romances translated from the Italian, adding tersely, "I have nothing to do with the moral effects of these versions. I mean only to shew their influence on our literature, more particularly on our poetry."[46] Writers and audiences in the past may have believed that literature served utilitarian ends in helping to circulate moral or ideological values, but from the point of view of the historian, these functions were unappreciable, irrelevant to a history of literature, and of no consequence to the modern reader.

Here, then, was the basis for criticism which would allow the literary historian to form a plural yet authoritative canon. Both Wartons eagerly wished for a transcendent poetic standard of imagination that would banish the classicists and moralists to a lesser rank, but Thomas's application of this standard seemed less arbitrary than his brother's because it was sewn into an evidently disinterested reconstruction of English poetic history that seemed, on the surface at least, to acknowledge all variety of early poetic activity without positing any prescriptive classifications of poets. The *History* may have presented a series of running judgments distinguishing the real poets from the versifying scholars, but a more profound assumption within the *History* was that the study of the literature of the past involved an exercise of the imagination which could be conducted free of moral or pragmatic considerations. Joseph's version of the canon had recognized an outer boundary of verbal craft, but this boundary was the traditional defining criterion of rhetorical "making," the long-observed enclosure of the producers' canon, which presupposed an instrumentalist notion of value that neither Warton could abide. Thomas's version, conversely, was a canon for consumers, the outer limit of which was defined less by the technical requirement of verse than by the criterion of literature as an imaginative experience. In reading the many divergent works of the past, or their semblance in the Ossian and Rowley forgeries, consumers could benefit morally in having their affectivity and sensibility refined while remaining untouched by any moral beliefs promulgated in these works because these were at a comfortable historical remove from them intellectually. Likewise, the study of English literary history could benefit readers in extending their knowledge and sharpening their powers of discrimination, but such mapping of the field was merely collateral to the inherently imaginative experience of reading past literature. Both Wartons believed the source of value lay in imagination, yet the *History of English Poetry* made imagination not only the central criterion of poetic production but equally the condition of consumption. The historian could therefore present a canon that was more plural and inclusive, and much less symbolically violent than the critic's, because the source of value in imagination could be made to involve many different works in the act of reading. At the same time, in localizing this special experience of imaginative reading as separate from other interests, this source of value could be made to seem uniquely enabling. Appearing as a neutral and scholarly digest of historical material, Warton's history may not have proposed any particular revision of the canon, though, like any objectivist literary history, it helped to perpetuate the reproduction of the canon by promoting the study of literature. Yet, in situating the study and experience of literature within an autotelic and disinterested realm of the imagination, the *History*, which would be treated as a standard work well into the next century, was one of the most important documents in a cultural movement that was decisively altering the nature of canon-formation.

JOHNSON AND THE PARADOX OF VALUE

Johnson, by his own account, resisted this movement. Distrustful both of the imagination and of the attempts to champion it, he held on to the most central beliefs of rhetorical thinking about the canon: that literary value was predicated on the essential uniformity of human nature, that this value did not inhere in literary works but rather in the moral and psychological truths these works helped to communi-   *Intro* cate, that one of the writer's supreme functions was to refine the language so as to enable the promulgation of these truths, and that the canon represented a harmonious consensus of human opinion. His *Dictionary*, with its abundant illustrative quotations, was massive confirmation of the rhetorical premise that the "chief glory of every people arises from its authours" because of their efforts in establishing the verbal power of the vernacular.[47] His edition of Shakespeare was presented as public recognition of an author who, by having "gained and kept the favour of his countrymen," could heroically "assume the dignity of an ancient, and claim the privilege of established fame and prescriptive veneration," as if Shakespeare's canonization were a symbolic gesture much like a ritual of laureation.[48] Above all, his *Lives of the English Poets*, the most sustained and celebrated critique of English literature to appear prior to the nineteenth century, presented a canon that seemed founded on the traditional rhetorical principles that a work's moral character could be intimately related to its author's, and that the pre-eminent value of all writings, biographies included, was to provide persuasive models of conduct "to enable the readers better to enjoy life, or better to endure it."[49]

I end with Johnson because his criticism was to be the last significant expression of a residual rhetoricist understanding of literary value, at a point when rhetorical culture had ceded its hold on Western thought to the rigours of an ascendant objective rationalism. From the vantage of such rationalism, at odds with rhetorical assumptions, Johnson's rhetoricity seems primarily a function of the astatic and robust performativity of his style. With its endless bifurcations and qualifications that seem as much to undercut as reinforce the generalizing conviction of his argument, it is a style designed to win assent by seeming to leave room open for all provisionalities and contingencies while still appearing to be moving towards a definitive summation.[50] In its Latinate thickness and couplet rhythms, the style appears to announce its

ın artificiality, a conventional oratorical strategy for making the
speaker seem credible and ingenuous.[51] But Johnson goes much further than previous rhetors in complicating this strategy, in risking
outright contradiction in order, he believes, to arrive at truth. *Adventurer* 95 provides an impressive, almost self-parodic example of how
Johnson's mode of essentialist assertion can end up curving back on
itself almost to the point of self-cancellation, in order to make the
original presupposition seem all the more considered.[52] Ostensibly a
defence of authors against the charge of plagiarism, the essay provides
Johnson with an opportunity, one he relishes, for him to affirm once
again the fundamental sameness of human nature. Authors have often
treated of the same topics, he begins, because the same topics have
forever occupied humanity: "Writers of all ages have had the same
sentiments, because they have in all ages had the same objects of
speculation; the interests and passions, the virtues and vices of mankind, have been diversified in different times, only by unessential and
casual varieties." At most, Johnson avers, books differ only for particular and contingent reasons: "some will be clear where others are
obscure, some will please by their stile and others by their method,
some by their embellishments and others by their simplicity, some by
closeness and others by diffusion."

Save for Johnson's manner of piling on examples, his central opposition between human essentiality and the accidents of history was one
that had been assumed in English critical discourse for centuries. But
it is precisely Johnson's characteristic multiplying and differentiating
of examples that is so rhetorically unusual. What is more, he multiplies
his examples in support of both sides of his defining opposition, often
moving back and forth between sides within the same argument, as
he does in this essay. Works of morality, he observes, are bound to be
similar because "right and wrong are immutable," yet there will always
be reasons for writing them, since there is "in composition, as in other
things, a perpetual vicissitude of fashion." In fact, there are numerous
ways for the moralist to be an original writer: "he may familiarise his
system by dialogues after the manner of the ancients, or subtilize it
into a series of syllogistic arguments; he may enforce his doctrine by
seriousness and solemnity, or enliven it by sprightliness and gayety; he
may deliver his sentiments in naked precepts, or illustrate them by
historical examples; he may detain the studious by the artful concat-
enation of a continued discourse, or relieve the busy by short strictures
and unconnected essays." Within a paragraph, Johnson is already
countering this list of possibilities with a parallel list of certainties
about the universality of the passions: "their influence is uniform, and
their effects nearly the same in every human breast: a man loves and

hates, desires and avoids, exactly like his neighbour; resentment and ambition, avarice and indolence, discover themselves by the same symptoms, in minds distant a thousand years from one another." Yet such certainties, he adds, may be manifested in a host of divergent human actions throughout history, and hence writers "are to observe the alterations which time is always making in the modes of life, that they may gratify every generation with a picture of themselves."

There then follow two more internally differentiated lists of examples, the longest in the essay, that bring together both the argument for human essentiality and its antithesis ("Thus love is uniform, but courtship is perpetually varying ... "). By the end, Johnson has asserted as well as demonstrated by his mode of illustration that writers may choose from "an inexhaustible variety" of examples, a conclusion that would seem to deny his original absolutist proposition, were it not for the implication that the perennial fact of change and plurality confirms that humanity must at some level remain the same: "The mutability of mankind will always furnish writers with new images." Whatever his conclusion, Johnson's performance has apparently been rhetorical all along, a wholly serious exercise whose aim has been to confirm both a sense of human diversity and its ultimate insignificance. As Robert DeMaria, Jr has said of Johnson's characteristic mode of evaluative practice, "to diversify and multiply binary oppositions to the extent that Johnson so often does is to suggest that formal dualities are, after all, fictitious – merely ways of speaking about the mixed nature of human experience in which nothing is really the opposite of anything else."[53]

In this essay, as in much of his critical writing, Johnson was rehearsing the central paradox of value – between absolute and relative, transcendent and temporal, permanent and changing – the paradox I have equated with Benjamin's dictum on originality and tradition, and the paradox that Dryden baldly, almost helplessly conceded in his Preface to the *Fables*: "mankind is ever the same, and nothing lost out of nature, though everything is altered." It could be argued, indeed, that Johnson's greatness as a critic lies in his being the first since Dryden to confront this paradox in all its aporetic irresolvability and to acknowledge it in the act of judgment. Both Dryden and Johnson resolutely believed in human essentiality as the absolute basis of judgment, but where Johnson differed from Dryden was in how much more readily he enumerated its opposites in the pluralities and contingencies of value. And because he multiplied his terms and arguments for both generality and particularity, his order of values seemed far less arbitrary or narrow than the orthodox neoclassicism Dryden tried to work from. At times, Johnson's estimations of authors could even appear objectivist in their empirical precision, in the range of his criteria, in his diminished concern for the productive functions of literature, and in his emphases on the diversity of authors' accomplishments, on the changing conditions for writing, and on the "wild vicissitudes of taste."[54] Johnson may have "loathed" historicism but he also repeatedly insisted that cultural change ought always to be considered when judging a writer's work.[55] He could praise Dryden for having "first taught us to determine upon principles the merit of composition," but he resisted stipulating iterable criteria or systematic definitions for poetry, preferring to respond to particular works with a changing arsenal of evaluative formulas.[56] He believed in the harmonizing authority of an essential human consensus, but this evaluative community he adduced from a host of divergent measures, from the test of time, to a work's popularity, to the common reader who spurned the edicts of polite authority. He could refer to the "ranks of literature" and to how some poets could be placed in hierarchical classes, but he steadfastly rejected any attempt to publicize his criticism, and in particular the *Lives*, as providing a definitive ordering of the English canon since he knew that not only the permanence that such an effort promised might prove illusory, but the fallible judgment of one writer could hardly be the only determinant in the formation of a national canon of letters.[57] Johnson's authoritativeness in his evaluative practice had therefore as much to do with how, as he said of Dryden's, "the author proves his right of judgement by his power of performance," as with his complicated sense of plurality and permanence in human affairs, which rendered his style and approach finely suited to the distributive art of judgment.[58]

Johnson's criticism ought therefore to be understood as resting primarily on rhetoricist assumptions, even as his arguments often deployed the language and gestures of objectivist thought. His work can be seen as perhaps concluding a long-standing oratorical and civic humanist tradition in English writing that, since Dryden and his skeptical awareness of paradox, had gradually come to acknowledge if not entirely accept the authority of the new discourses of knowledge by incorporating some features of their style or scientific method. The author most deeply suspicious of these new discourses, Swift, had himself used the plain style of a naive empiricist discourse ironically against itself, as a satiric weapon, at a time when this style was no longer being treated as a rhetorical option but as an accepted vehicle of truth. Johnson's aim was similarly tactical, since his evaluations possessed great suasive force because of his reliance on the discourse of differentiation, and all the more force because such differentiation was believed at the time to assure an objective certainty. His criticism may have accordingly seemed far different in appearance from earlier modes of rhetorical valuations, yet differentiation remained for Johnson a mode of rhetoric and not its own self-justifying logic: being analytically precise was for him an authoritative gesture in assessing a plural canon, yet the gesture could never appear to him an end in itself but useful only in leading to an understanding of human essentiality. No one knew how to play the rules of the differentiating game better than Johnson, but the absolute value of human endeavour remained for him always within sight. And because he believed that this value was potentially discernible within all activities, Johnson refused to think of cultural work as constituting a separate and self-enclosed field.

In this way, perhaps the earlier English rhetor with whom Johnson can be most instructively compared is his namesake Ben. If the earlier Jonson intensified his evaluative authority by complicating his rhetorical appositions within a presentist network of spatialized value-relations, the later Johnson achieved a similar result by complicating his oppositions along an open-ended range of temporal possibilities. Both authors believed in the dynamic power of rhetoric to affirm a common humanity. Yet, whereas Ben Jonson felt such commonality to be conceivably obtaining in the timeless moment of poetic utterance, Dr Johnson saw the achievement or revelation of commonality as an ongoing process, as if he had grasped how it was that the instrumental nature of rhetoric made for ceaseless change. "What was it like to be Johnson," Lipking has speculated, "was to relish the notion of a stable, unchanging self. It was also to keep on the move."[59] An almost identical argument has been advanced for the earlier Jonson and his ideal of a "centered self," though this is not surprising because value was often affirmed in a rhetorical culture by opposing stasis to movement.[60] The difference between the two rhetors was that the later Johnson, always on the move, was far more cognizant of change and human diversity, and consequently more willing to see how the effort to establish a perfect commonality had to be continually renewed even if it could never be concluded in this life.

Accordingly, there is a binary quality about Johnson's criticism, a quality that is rhetorical in its certainty of belief yet not exclusive in the earlier Jonson's manner. What has been celebrated as Johnson's flexibility as a critic, his refusal to systematize his principles and his willingness to risk contradiction, is rather a characteristic of his criticism to move back and forth dramatically between absolute and contingent positions, between generalizing and differentiating claims, and between ideas of permanence and empirical accounts of change and diversity. For a rhetor like Johnson, there is no question of explaining the precise relations between these positions, since there exists no separate cultural field whose totality and internal structure needs to be marked out. As a result, his criticism presses the paradox of value to an extreme of rhetorical oscillation, and this has significant consequences for his understanding of literary value and the basis for criticism. As I will suggest, Johnson's critical practice may bear some discursive resemblances to an objectivist mode of valuation, but it may equally involve certain ideas about the act of judgment that are strikingly similar to those being heralded in his age by the very cultural movement he was bent upon resisting.

The norms of canonicity seemed to float severally throughout Johnson's criticism without being unmoored to a fundamental order of value. His prime criterion was the one most closely tied to this foundation, the value of literary art in providing "just representations of general nature," just as the greatest poets were for him the poets of nature, Homer and Shakespeare.[61] To limit the core of his canon to so few authors is indicative of Johnson's willingness to find value throughout the diversity of the canon, and to avoid harmonizing the canon around a central value even if that value was precisely the one of presenting such harmony in images of human commonality. It is, in fact, unclear which English author might come closest to Shakespeare under this criterion: Dryden, who "had a mind very comprehensive by nature," seemed to have the greatest claim yet "every other writer since Milton must give place to Pope," and the excellence of neither of these poets consisted in a deep commitment to general nature.[62] At the same time, the core of Johnson's canon did not necessarily correspond to the highest rank in a hierarchy since, in principle, all authors shared in a common humanity, in their lives if not always their works, and so this core could not be for Johnson a sharply exclusive category. This is the most significant difference between Johnson and critics like the Wartons who invoked the criterion of literature as a fictive art. It is not simply that Johnson equated this criterion with an Aristotelian sense of representation while the others thought of it in sublimer terms, as betokening the power of imagination to enable flights beyond reality into the figurations of fancy and desire. It is that the latter more fundamentally saw the imagination as uniquely providing the means to view experience from the point of view of others, whereas Johnson saw this as conceding too much to otherness and human division. For Johnson, the function of art was to provide the means to see oneself as much in others as others in oneself, and to experience how it is, as he said of Dryden, to be "another and the same."[63]

Johnson, like Dryden, drew his postulates mainly from a Horatian tradition, and the universal truths of common humanity could be morally effective in leading to goodness only if they were made clear and appealing: "The end of writing is to instruct; the end of poetry is to instruct by pleasing."[64] Interestingly, this central tenet of the rhetorical tradition gave Johnson a good deal of difficulty when applying it to the judgment of particular works. Throughout his career, he could abide by the idea of writing's moral instrumentality in the abstract, and he could invoke the idea when dealing generally with genres like biography or the novel or running down non-literary writers like Jenyns. Yet devotional poetry, in reducing the truths of divinity, could never be truly beneficial for Johnson, while the overwhelming sublimity and didactic intensity of *Paradise Lost* made reading it "a duty rather than a pleasure."[65] Addison's life and works evinced nothing "but purity and excellence," yet *Cato* left Johnson cold.[66] Most troublingly, the greatest poet in the language appeared "to write without any moral purpose," even as his plays pleased above all others by being so revealing of general nature. As this moral purposiveness involved how an author directed readers to respecting this generality, it had to be a transcendent norm, derived from "laws of higher authority than those of criticism." Yet, even as it was "always a writer's duty to make the world better," this criterion could not have exclusive force within the canon if, as in Shakespeare's case, his works could instructively reveal human nature without pointing a moral.[67] That Johnson could recognize a distinction between a work's moral content and its ethical purposiveness suggests that he was willing to concede something to the growing contemporary disfavour towards the didactic tradition. Adhering to utilitarian notions of writing's function in society, he could not support the newer ideas on the moral affectiveness of literature in helping to refine the tastes, receptivity, and sensitivity of readers. However, he seemed not to hold any strong rhetorical conviction in the suasive power of art, at least none comparable to the structure of belief that early English writers had helped to maintain on their own behalf.

If Johnson rarely used the same formula twice to denote his central principle of human generality, he was equally loath to cry up the principle with the codes he had inherited from the rhetorical tradition. His ideal evaluative community was a fully inclusive consensus generated amid diversity, and never an elite society to be defined in the usual rhetorical manner by opposing it to a fictive dissensus of unlearned readers. Many of the gestures he relied on therefore possessed a certain objectivist facticity in appearing to propose quantifications of this consensus. Sales figures, he implied on one occasion, could be taken as evidence of lasting value: *The Pilgrim's Progress*, he told Boswell, "has had the best evidence of its merit, the general and continued approbation of mankind. Few books, I believe, have had a more extensive sale."[68] Popularity as an index of value could not be readily dismissed by a commercial author like Johnson: "he who pleases many must have some species of merit."[69] Yet, since there were always temporary fashions, popularity could be deceptive if it was not measured over generations, in "length of duration and continuance of esteem." Johnson is usually credited with having reintroduced the test of time into critical discourse, though in his Preface to *Shakespeare* he properly treated the idea as having general acceptance: "He has long outlived his century, the term commonly fixed as the test of literary merit."[70] Johnson may have been skeptical of such a test, since he knew that the figure of a hundred years had been mocked by Horace and his imitator Pope as reflecting an unthinking prejudice for the antique. For the earlier satirists, a quantifiable standard was too arbitrary a gesture to be credible, even within a rhetorical argument. In contrast, the currency of objectivist thinking in Johnson's age meant that this arbitrariness could be more readily misrecognized. For Johnson, then, the gesture had acquired at least some degree of rhetorical force.

Johnson relied on the gesture to assure readers that a human commonality of values was not perpetually indiscernible but could become apparent at some point. Shakespeare could claim "prescriptive veneration" after outliving his century because one had to believe in the possibility of consensus; in principle at least, the lengthy process whereby "works tentative and experimental [were] estimated by their proportion to the general and collective ability of man, as it is discovered in a long succession of endeavours," had to arrive at some plausible conclusion.[71] Yet invoking the test of time remained for Johnson merely a device for suggesting if not establishing this consensus. Accordingly, he could elsewhere propose other figures, such as the fourteen years it took *The Rape of the Lock* to become "settled" in the canon.[72] The protracted legal wrangling with Tonson over the Shakespeare copyright seems to have prompted Johnson to vary his ideal number, since he went from advocating a sixty-year term of copyright protection in 1763 to a hundred-year term in the year of his Preface to *Shakespeare* and then back down to a fifty-year term nine years later when perpetual copyright would finally be abolished.[73] Johnson was likewise ready to point out exceptions to the test: of Cowley's *Davideis*, he remarked, there "are not many examples of so great a work produced by an author generally read and generally praised that has crept through a century with so little regard."[74] Ultimately, the artificiality of the gesture meant that, at an extreme, it could be turned on its head: if consensus was impervious to temporal change, no test would be required to measure the canonicity of those "few transcendent and invincible names, which no revolutions of opinion or length of time is able to suppress."[75]

Johnson's best known symbol of consensus, the common reader, was more directly rooted in a rhetorical tradition, even if it reversed the class polarities of the learned reader familiar from earlier critical gesturings. The common reader was a presentist conception, since the consensus it signified needed no time to emerge but could be heard passing judgment on a relatively recent work like Gray's *Elegy*. As a rhetorical figure, moreover, the common reader could only be negatively identified. The term often designated for Johnson the reading public in contrast to polite or learned authorities, as when he used it to identify the non-specialist who had little use for the abstruse terms for versification or the generalist who little frequented the "recesses of learning" from which the metaphysical poets drew their conceits.[76] Yet, in his most famous formulation, he actually defined it in opposition to the kind of personified abstractions that walked through much of Gray's poetry: "By the common sense of readers uncorrupted with literary prejudices, after all the refinements of subtilty and the dogmatism of learning, must be finally decided all claim to poetical honours." This version of the common reader functioned much like the learned reader in personifying a stance of impartiality, but the disinterestedness that Johnson idealized here and elsewhere was described not in terms of a social distance from a world driven by political or commercial interest. Rather, impartiality was for him a condition of dissociation, with the common reader preternaturally untouched by temporal prejudices and caring not at all for rationalist and erudite sophistications. In this late incarnation, the common reader could appear even more disinterested than the critic, who could happily point out that Gray's *Elegy* had provided him with an unusual opportunity to find commonality with this readerly innocent ("I rejoice to concur with ... "). Johnson could reduce the common reader even further, allowing him only a reactive and not notably self-aware affinity for Gray's poem: "The *Church-yard* abounds with images which find a mirrour in every mind, and with sentiments to which every bosom returns an echo."[77] The common reader was among Johnson's most authoritative gestures in his later criticism yet was barely a rhetorical figure at all, at least not one denoting consensus in diversity, but seemed rather a starkly isolated creature of "naked sensibility."[78] In this respect, the common reader was indistinguishable from the finely receptive figure who, in the aesthetic discourse of the period, was increasingly being seen to occupy the autonomous space of the aesthetic experience and, in Blair's version, to share with literary texts a privileged moment "peculiar to themselves."[79]

What happened to the common reader in this late transformation reflected perhaps a certain irresolution in Johnson's criticism, one that became more recondite the more his critical evaluations were based on criteria other than his fundamental source of value in human commonality. Always the source of risk in rhetoricist thinking, this irresolution had to do with the rhetorical oscillation in his arguments and how arbitrarily he could relate his several criteria of judgment to the basis for criticism in general nature. The irresolution may appear so only from a modern perspective; for Johnson, it seems, differentiations of authors may, at some level, have all been rhetorical acts that, by their multiplication and diversification, functioned to show how human divisions were ultimately unimportant. But on the surface at least, Johnson's evaluative practice resembled objectivist discourse in its empiricism and modes of specification, and this was particularly apparent the more he moved out in his canon from its central criterion of human commonality in order to consider the temporal conditions of canonicity.

Of such considerations, Johnson was especially sensitive to arguments for making historicist allowances in valuation, since these more directly involved the dialectic of the impermanent and the essential. An author's originality, he knew, could be assessed only in context, and if Dryden's *Essay on Dramatic Poesy* did not afford the modern reader "much increase of knowledge or much novelty of instruction," this was only because its tenets had become so absorbed in modern critical thought as to seem truisms; hence Johnson's provision in his "Life of Dryden" that "to judge rightly of an author we must transport ourselves to his time, and examine what were the wants of his contemporaries, and what were his means of supplying them."[80] Yet, if even a single work of criticism had so changed perceptions of literature that its importance was only apparent in careful retrospect, this might indicate that, just as present attitudes owed much to Dryden's thinking, his work marked a significant discontinuity with whatever went on before. Dryden might be said to have rediscovered universal truths first set down by the ancients, but this would have greatly diminished any claim for his originality and would have raised the question of how important was his rediscovery if a great poet like Shakespeare could have done without these truths. Because Johnson refused to indicate how Dryden's originality could be correlated to human commonality and continuity, his historicizing gesture could seem either purely formal or openly relativistic.

The gesture had probably less relativizing force for Johnson than it did for either Warton, though it had enough for him to assuage his strong religious and rational antipathy towards the witches in *Macbeth*: "In order to make a true estimate of the abilities and merit of a writer, it is always necessary to examine the genius of his age, and the opinions of his contemporaries." The gesture could equally be applied the other way, in relation to Shakespeare's reception in the present: Shakespeare's work, Johnson observed, "has scenes of undoubted and perpetual excellence, but perhaps not one play, which, if it were now exhibited as the work of a contemporary writer, would be heard to the conclusion."[81] How much significance the gesture had for Johnson remains unclear, however, since he seemed rather more reluctant than Dryden to demarcate clearly the lasting from the transient in literature. Dryden's list of contingent values in his superstructural model ("religion, customs of countries, idioms of languages, etc.") would have readily been endorsed by Johnson, who would have added to the list many more categories of beliefs, manners, fashions, and "temporary prejudices."[82] The only categories, it seemed, that Johnson would not allow the dispensations of history were the two transcendent categories of general nature and its productive complement in morality, the absolute values that were "independant on time or place."[83] Yet, as in *Adventurer* 95, Johnson could go to elaborate lengths to complicate these categories with examples of how the enduring truths of human nature could be realized in all manner of temporal activities and experiences. The consequence for his criticism was that these absolute values appeared so abstract, no matter how variously he identified them, that only very implicitly could they be related to most of his more specific historical claims for literature.

Like Dryden, Johnson could affirm a conventional classicist belief in refinement – since Dryden's time, he typically remarked, "it is apparent that English poetry has had no tendency to relapse to its former savageness" – yet the claim could seem considerably more arbitrary than Dryden's because it did not appear to be legitimized with reference to either human commonality or moral justice.[84] The problem was not so much the performative aspect of the gesture, however ungrounded it may now appear, as how by this gesture Johnson could instruct readers on human nature and morality or direct them to the sources of value in these essential categories. A century before Johnson, Dryden was already having qualms about announcing his age's superiority over the last because he did not want the gesture to be merely one of self-congratulation. Initially in his career, Dryden could believe, like most previous poets, that society could be harmonized by the power of language, and that the permanent source of this power lay with God, king, or the state. Yet, with the rise of objectivist thinking, Dryden wanted what he believed was a more concrete source of value, and this he located in his notion of the age, the contingent advantages of which, he claimed, had benefited his peers by enabling them to surpass the work of their predecessors. The knowledge of being advantageously if not absolutely blessed could thus be a basis for criticism, even if it could not serve to maintain a rhetorical circle of conviction. In positing such a foundation, however, Dryden was supporting another structure of belief, one centring on the idea that the more such knowledge could be accumulated about the phenomenal experiences of nature or the age, the closer one could get to the source of absolute value. Yet, just as ultimate harmony was continually deferred in rhetoricist thinking by language's oscillations and oppositions, so the riskiness in this objectivist thinking was that its searches after knowledge would lead only to ever more differentiation and specification, and that its arrival at ultimate truth would as a result be forever deferred.

For Johnson, human division could still, in principle, be overcome through verbal power, even though his spiritual guilt over this division was deep enough that he could not presume to think that lasting harmony could be achieved in this world. He could be considerably more forthright than Dryden about fashions and prejudices, about the contingencies of the age or the varieties of human experience, because these could serve as rhetorical categories whose significance would diminish the more they were multiplied. Yet, as I have said, the terms of his actual evaluative practice had much in common with objectivist discourse. Not only was his central value of human commonality objectified in the phenomenal foundation of nature, but he could speak much like Dryden about how temporal conditions could greatly determine the character of a work and its author: "Every man's performances, to be rightly estimated, must be compared with the state of the age in which he lived." He could likewise defend Pope for his "civilizing" alterations to the *Iliad* because he "wrote for his own age and his own nation."[85] Just how much importance these gestures accorded to human change, however, Johnson purposefully left undefined. The gestures may have been largely rhetorical in the sense that the "state of the age" was in the last instance irrelevant beside the essential value of human commonality. Yet, for Johnson the empiricist, knowledge of the "state of the age" provided the critic with a degree of evaluative precision, even if the relativizing pursuit of such knowledge appeared to take him further away from the fundamental values informing the canon. In accordance with the logic of differentiation, Johnson's critical practice recognized a highly diversified canon, where the worth of each author could be distinguished with a great deal of specificity because Johnson was willing to consider a wide range of criteria and contingencies, including the value-determinants of "the age." As he wrote in his review of Warton's essay on Pope, "Barely to say, that one performance is not so good as another, is to criticise with little exactness."[86] Yet breaking down his canon into such plurality and exactness seemed inevitably to lead the critic away from his absolute source of value in commonality. The more Johnson distributed value across his internally differentiated canon, the less this canon appeared directly empowered by this enabling source.

How Johnson's central source of value flowed to the outer limits of his canon was especially unclear since those boundaries rather vaguely corresponded to a wide variety of criteria having to do with a work's formal attributes, its subject, argument, and the like, criteria that Johnson often found easier to identify by negatives. The criterion most frequently invoked was the productive qualification of craft, as Johnson routinely relegated poets to the margins for the staleness of their figures, the harshness of their diction, the dissonance of their rhymes, or the dullness of their verse. But craft was no guarantee of merit since, as Pope had done in the *Essay on Man*, the "seductive powers of eloquence" could be wasted on "penury of knowledge and vulgarity of sentiment" and could finally "oppress judgement by over-powering pleasure." Technical skill and innovation could not likewise compensate for the more serious faults of "ideas physically impure," of irreverence or irrelevance, of perverseness of thought or studied cleverness, or of pretension in affecting too much novelty or archaism.[87] Though Dryden could be praised for refining English verse, the norms of style and craft seemed among the most contingent of values for Johnson, since they were often distorted by passing vogues or the idiosyncrasies of the author. Johnson cherished certain broadly defined stylistic qualities of clarity and ease, yet it did not appear that craft could serve, as it once had, as a dominant criterion of value around which to harmonize either the canon or public discourse generally.

In fact, as his comment on Pope's oppressive rhetoric suggested, Johnson could seriously downplay any sense of the productive utility of eloquence and verbal power. The chances of fame were so slender in Johnson's view that poets could have little reasonable hope of immortalizing either themselves or their subjects. Though authors could be the chief glories of a people because of their contributions to the language, Johnson could also make clear in the "Preface" to his

Dictionary that linguistic change was inevitable, whatever the contributions. Poetic refinement, for generations a central classicist preoccupation, seemed to him to have already reached, with Pope, a point after which "any further improvement of versification will be dangerous." Most significantly, Johnson's evaluations frequently relied on the language of affectivity, as in the example of the common reader's response to Gray's *Elegy*, yet an affectivity that seemed to involve little direct and positive instrumentality. Rare was it for Johnson to speak in Longinian terms, as he did of Congreve's *The Mourning Bride*, about how its reader could enjoy "for a moment the powers of a poet" (the phrase is ambiguous, since the reader could either feel empowered like a poet or be affected by a particular poet's power, namely Congreve's).[88] Even more striking was the negative example of his dismissing Swift's didactic prose because "it instructs, but does not persuade." Johnson evidently meant that the moral learning Swift offered was not expressed forcefully enough to draw the reader's attention.[89] Yet to posit such a distinction in this way was to conceive of instruction as inert information, and of persuasion as an ability to appeal to readers but not to direct their behaviour or to stir them into action. Johnson may or may not have shared his age's growing disinclination towards didactic poetry, but he evidently saw instruction in writing as providing a form of moral knowledge that could purposively present models of conduct to readers and could fix their attention if articulated with polish or energy, but it could not necessarily convince or compel them to do anything in particular.

Similarly, in *Rambler* 136, Johnson could maintain that "to encourage merit with praise is the great business of literature," yet in another number qualify this by indicating that such encouragement of merit could not be considered an instrumental act within a dynamic moral economy: "to praise us for actions, or dispositions, which deserve praise, is not to confer a benefit, but to pay a tribute."[90] True, Johnson often remarked on the moral depravity of distributing unmerited praise, as he felt Dryden had done too frequently, but the negative effects were largely centred on the poet's judgment or the quality of his work.[91] In general, Johnson could find it easier to criticize a work for failing to do good than to praise another for its power of moral suasion or mnemonic consecration: "I do not see that *The Bard* promotes any truth, moral or political." At most, he recommended, authors ought to "keep themselves harmless" and to "exert the little influence which they have for honest purposes."[92] Literature had moral value for Johnson, and ideally a moral intentionality as well, but such value did not operate within a productive economy of "profit." Literary works could communicate the fundamental truths of common human experience, and could do so in a pleasurable way, yet they did not circulate those truths.

As a consequence, few of the conventional defining features of artistic discourse, from formal craft to theme and subject matter, could be definitively related to the fundamental source of value in general nature. These features could be useful in "attracting and detaining the attention. That book is good in vain which the reader throws away."[93] Yet this implied that a book could be "good" without these features, even if the reader threw it away for lacking such attributes, or it might not be good even if it possessed several. The suggestion here was not simply another version of the old rhetorical fear that eloquence might render immoral subjects appealing. Rather, Johnson's greatly diminished sense of poetic productivity rendered ambiguous the canonical status of works whose popularity and esteem were owing primarily to the pleasurable qualities of their technique, subject, narrative, and even invention. *The Rape of the Lock* was so canonized as to be "no longer at the mercy of criticism," but its poet could not be said to have "made the world much better than he found it." Similarly, Johnson's gestures at ranking works according to artistic excellence – *Paradise Lost*, "considered with respect to design, may claim the first place, and with respect to performance the second" – could seem both unequivocal and perfunctory, as if they were merely rhetorical and not actually positing a fixed canonic hierarchy. Indeed, the pleasures of art were for Johnson much less substantial, more arbitrary, and perhaps even of a lesser kind than the pleasures of truth, since "Nothing can please many, and please long, but just representations of general nature."[94] In principle, all canonical works demonstrated something of general nature, and did so in different ways, but Johnson refused to provide much sense of how this value could be distributed across his canon, from its core to its margins. He found it easier to judge a work's pleasurable attributes than to indicate how it could fulfil a larger moral purpose in directing readers to a sense of their commonality. His canon, particularly as it is presented in the *Lives*, may have rested on a strong empiricist notion of truth and been precisely internally differentiated in terms of each authors' accomplishments as practitioners of literary art. Yet the relative lengths of the *Lives* told the reader more about the order of this canon than did Johnson's various criteria.

In much the same way, Johnson's discounting of poetry's productive value allowed him to entertain certain notions of creativity that might not have otherwise been easily reconciled with a belief in human universality. In particular, he could subscribe to some small degree in the growing mythology of poetic genius, "that power which constitutes a poet; that quality without which judgement is cold and knowledge is inert; that energy which collects, combines, amplifies, and animates." Genius was not necessarily a compulsive force for Johnson, yet it did seem to mark the poet out as a being somewhat separate from the rest of humanity, one blessed with "native force" and "original powers." In Imlac's impassioned account, the poet wrote "as a being superior to time and place." For Johnson, Dryden had not compromised his art to the demands of the literary trade, he had prostituted his poetic gift: "Such degradation of the dignity of genius, such abuse of superlative abilities, cannot be contemplated but with grief and indignation."[95] Johnson may have been here projecting onto Dryden some of his own mythology about the hardships of the professional writer, just as he may have been judging Dryden by the civic humanist codes of laureate independence. Yet, if Johnson could converse at length about the labours of authorship, he showed little interest in theories of poetic creativity, in part because of his distrust of contemporary claims being made on behalf of the power of imagination. At most, he would define the "true Genius" in much the traditional sense as "a mind of large general powers, accidentally determined to some particular direction."[96] Johnson did not wish to distinguish the poet from general humanity, and he had little respect for poets like Gray who elevated themselves by spurning common life. He likely relied on terms like genius only out of rhetorical convenience, since he had little patience for the growing mythology of the poet's compulsion. All the same, both poetic invention and the instrumental productivity of poetry were subjects deeply suppressed in his critical practice, and it was because of this suppression that he could differentiate the unique features of a poet's character and work without ever having to account for the cause of this uniqueness or its consequences for general nature. In this and in many other respects, his canon rested on a deep irresolution as to the precise relation between its absolute and its relative values, between commonality and plurality.

As much as Johnson's canon was a producers' canon that proposed only an attenuated conception of literary productivity, it was also a consumers' canon that recognized a rather reduced sense of the possibilities for reading literature. The edition of Shakespeare and the *Lives*, as well as the criticism from the periodical essays, were intended to aid the reproduction of English literature on behalf of readers, and while Johnson made clear his general standards for poetry, his criticism was not designed to promote particular prescriptive models for writing. His *Dictionary*, he hoped, would help to stabilize such things as spelling and accentuation, but he did not concern himself in his criticism with the function of reading in helping to assist composition, elocution, or the exercise of interpretation. Like any other writing, he believed, literary works were supposed to present readers with universal truths or provide models better to enjoy or endure life, and, unlike other works, they did so in a way that could please. A literary work might be browsed or contemplated for any number of reasons, "but the most general and prevalent reason of study, is the impossibility of finding another amusement equally cheap or constant, equally independent on the hour or the weather." As an instrument of pleasure, poetry was a "luxury," not a necessity.[97] Reading literature did not necessarily shape the sensibility, facilitate the refinement of manners, or require special faculties of taste – as Hawkins reported, Johnson disdained the advocates of the "Shaftesburian school" who pretended to "tastes and perceptions which are not common to all men."[98] Certainly Johnson refused any suggestion that esteemed English works ought to be considered required reading, either for moral or patriotic reasons, for the acculturation of the subject, or for the pursuit of symbolic honours in being recognized as specially competent in the assessment of literature. The portrait of the professional Minim who could ascend to critical eminence through a mechanical display of such competencies was the obverse of Johnson's idealized common reader, in that both figures embodied his contempt for any attempt to transform reading and criticism into modes of acquiring cultural capital, into vehicles of fashion and prestige, and into means for distinguishing oneself from others.

In sceptical moments, as in his final contribution to *The Adventurer*, Johnson acknowledged that the task of evaluating and canonizing works of literature could fall to a select few who, though not necessarily blessed with deeper critical penetration than a common reader's, were better prepared or better placed to influence the reading public: "whoever has remarked the fate of books, must have found it governed by other causes, than general consent arising from general conviction. If a new performance happens not to fall into the hands of some, who have courage to tell, and authority to propagate their opinion, it often remains long in obscurity, and perhaps perishes unknown and unexamined. A few, a very few, commonly constitute the taste of the time."[99] Acknowledging himself to be among those few, Johnson may have grasped the historical irony that, champion of the common reader that he was, he wrote his *Lives* as prefaces to an edition that was deliberately designed to divert attention from the one reprint series, Bell's, which the common reader could afford. Johnson's was the prestige edition, the "elegant and accurate edition of all the English Poets of reputation," which the London booksellers believed might help them preserve at least a symbolic hold on the canon following the defeat of perpetual copyright.[100] But Johnson refused to capitalize on his authority and recommended only five authors for the edition, the bulk of poets having been chosen by the booksellers as those they most wished to claim as their privilege. He refused the role of final authority over the canon because of his deep commitment to the consensual "voice of the people."[101] As he wrote indignantly on his receipt for the 1783 edition of the *Lives*, "It is great impudence to put *Johnson's Poets* on the back of books which Johnson neither recommended nor revised. He recommended only Blackmore on the Creation and Watts. How then are they Johnson's? This is indecent."[102] Negotiating the demands of the marketplace with the interests of common humanity, Johnson cast himself as the arbiter of canonicity as much as the representative of readers, the highly discriminating critic of English letters as much as the spokesman for universal humanity.

Johnson may have offered readers his detailed impressions and assessments of English literature but he believed that all readers had finally to exercise their own judgment. If readers were to arrive at an understanding of general nature despite the prevalence of diversity in the world, Johnson felt, it was through repeated acts of judgment that they could learn to discount this diversity and all the distractions of the moment. Perpetually aware of the many influences that could distort judgment, Johnson frequently surrounded his valuations with observations on the various interests and prejudices that the reader had to set aside in the search for truth. Declaring sympathy for some forms of emotional favoritism such as patriotism, Johnson claimed to regret having to list the faults in *Paradise Lost*, "for what Englishman can take delight in transcribing passages, which, if they lessen the reputation of Milton, diminish in some degree the honour of our country?" At other times, he could declare his own predilections for truth in advertising, as when he felt that Cowley's love poetry was not so estimable once it was known that the poet denied having been himself in love. He also recognized that certain disproportions were unfortunately bound to be reflected in the canon: of Ambrose Philips's poems, he noted that "if they had been written by Addison they would have had admirers: little things are not valued but when they are done by those who can do greater." And then there were always the exigencies of deadline and idiosyncracy that disinclined the critic from hazarding "either praise or censure" of works he could not bother to reread.[103]

Yet, ideally, the literary critic exercised his judgment much like the common reader, in a condition of self-restraint and subtraction. However much Johnson followed a political agenda in his criticism, his typical gesture was to abjure politics as a criterion in evaluation, particularly of authors like Akenside whose views he opposed: "With the philosophical or religious tenets of the author I have nothing to do; my business is with his poetry."[104] Political influence in valuation was the type of distortion Johnson claimed to be most sensitive to, and there were occasions when he wrote as though canon-formation could be depoliticized or at least conducted in a cultural sphere relatively separate from politics. Whereas Renaissance postulators happily promoted English literature by ranking its canonical authors according to social degree, such a practice seemed greatly illegitimate to Johnson and his age, for whom cultural activities like canon-making had to be defined by a disavowal of political interest, like the one that prefaced the "Life of Halifax": "in this collection poetical merit is the claim to attention; and the account which is here to be expected may properly be proportioned not to [Halifax's] influence in the state, but to his rank among the writers of verse." To separate value from interest in this way was to imply that value did not circulate in a dynamic social economy nor was it something that could be assigned to a work. It was to assume that value was neither productive of desire nor something constructed in language but rather situated in a realm emptied of the differences and divisions that gave rise to desire – the ultimate risk in an objectivist culture being that value might be trivialized and emptied out the more the attempt was made to specify it. For the critic as for the common reader, valuation corresponded to an act of personal divestment that could be fully achieved only in the finality of time: "favour and flattery are now at an end; criticism is no longer softened by his bounties or awed by his splendour."[105]

Divestment of commercial interest was more complicated. Johnson's professionalism may have made him scornful of authors' repudiations of economic interest yet his own self-defining disavowals were implicit in routine complaints against the "Age of Authors," in censures against Dryden for pandering to his audience and his patrons, or in expressions of regret over Shakespeare's willingness to sacrifice "virtue to convenience."[106] For a critic who spent much time judging works by how much pleasure they afforded him, Johnson held deeply conflicted attitudes towards pleasing for a trade, for as much as he was personally reminded of how authors "must please to live," he could not condone the servility of those like Dryden who wrote only to please. Pleasing the people, he believed, was not the same as respecting the consensual voice of common humanity if the poet saw no distinction between aesthetic pleasure and his own material satisfactions. As he made clear when comparing Dryden to Pope, Johnson felt that the earlier poet's judgment was compromised because he refused to repudiate his self-interest in furnishing pleasure: "He wrote, and professed to write, merely for the people; and when he pleased others, he contented himself." The critic could himself profess to have been moved to write the *Lives* "by the honest desire of giving useful pleasure," but he could not allow this desire to seem selfish in origin and intent.[107]

Gestures of disavowal like this, even from a commercial author, may have been utterly conventional, but Johnson refined them to an unusual degree, and with the aim not of protecting the definitional integrity of the artistic field but of trying apparently to rid himself of self-interest. Thus, the rhetorical commonplace that an author motivated by material designs could purchase only a local popularity for his works became for Johnson a central theme of his criticism. It is as if he were attempting to persuade himself and his age that it was possible to write for a living and yet not do so purposely, for to do so as an only motive was to set oneself apart from common humanity. In this belief, Johnson was firmly within the rhetorical tradition, which centrally assumed that human division resulted from a regrettable assertion of the individual will. The truly enduring work, Johnson believed, was not composed to do anything in particular for its author or its audience, nor could the writer "expect it to be received with eagerness, or to spread with rapidity, *because desire can have no particular stimulation.*"[108] To be desirous without particular stimulation would seem to be a logically impossible state to achieve, given that the desire to achieve it had itself to be a particular stimulation. Yet for Johnson, always on the move, it was a state of being, the real state of sublunary nature, and only by a particular stimulation of the will could one diverge from it.

The act of judgment for Johnson, then, was ideally the articulation of a natural state of general desire in which the critic and common reader managed to arrest the self-differentiating desires of the will. Humility demanded that this state could never be assumed to be sustainable in this life, just as discrimination was necessary because "faults and defects every works of man must have." But the act of discrimination, of fault-finding and comparing authors and assessing their relative merits, was a "subordinate and instrumental" art that, ideally, occurred only *after* works had been read in the assumption that they could convey universal truths in representations of general humanity. Reading had to be conducted in good faith, and for Johnson this meant that readers had to deny themselves as many particular interests as possible in order to approach a work in a condition of general desire. In such a state, readers coming to a canonical text like Shakespeare's would find a "mirrour of life" in which their identity would be indistinguishable from its textual reflection because at such a moment text and readers would in effect *be* universal truth, occupying the same moment of commensurability as texts and "learned readers" of old were supposed to.[109] This shared experience of commonality would be an absolute value because, however momentary, it marked the fulfilment of a natural state of general desire, whose objective was precisely to overcome human division. At such moments, criticism would be both superfluous and an impertinence of the assertive will: had Gray written more poems like the *Elegy* that could find a mirror in every mind, "it had been vain to blame, and useless to praise him." Likewise, there had always to remain "an appeal open from criticism to nature" because it would have been presumptuous to insist that this general desire could be perpetually satisfied by prescribing models of composition.[110] Rejecting "the cant of those who judge by principles rather than perception," as if judgment without principles were possible, Johnson believed that the critic ought to draw on experience to formulate norms of discrimination yet still recognize that the initial pleasurable perception of truth resulted from a pure and undifferentiating desire.[111]

If, according to Johnson, the fate of books was seldom decided by "general consent arising from general conviction," consensus was most likely to occur in relation to the works of the past, which, though partaking of "the condition of human things" to grow in some aspects obsolete "by accident and time," were in their alterity less likely to distract the reader from the pure act of judgment because they did not tend to inspire a local and interested response.[112] The edicts of time not only rendered criticism redundant but gradually distanced the work from both the particular interests of its author and the history of partisan valuations it may have originally elicited. Johnson sometimes spoke in objectivist terms of a work's "intrinsick value," as when he observed that, since Garth's *Dispensary* "has been no longer supported by accidental and extrinsick popularity, it has been scarcely able to support itself."[113] More generally, Johnson argued in functionalist terms concerning the temporal values that could win an author a fleeting celebrity. Either works written according to the demands of fashion would "catch hold on present curiosity, and gratify some accidental desire, or produce some temporary conveniency," or the author too studious of fame laid "hold on recent occurrences, and eminent names, and delighted their readers with allusions and remarks, in which all were interested, and to which all therefore were attentive."[114] In other words, the impermanent work did something in particular, whether its author intended it or not, and thus the work made a difference in the negative sense of diverting readers from their commonality.[115] Reputation might be conferred by "the fondness of friendship, or servility of flattery," yet this equally presupposed an instrumental economy.[116] In time, however, these instrumental functions would become lessened until at last there would remain nothing about the work that could stimulate readers to differentiate themselves or their age from common humanity. At such a point, the work would be of no particular interest, except as a document of its own failure.

The enduring work, in contrast, would in time lose its temporal values as an instrument of change yet remain open to readers in its fundamental value as a non-productive mirror of universal identity. In this way, the test of time, as Johnson described its workings in the Preface to *Shakespeare*, involved as much a set of received comparative estimations of the playwright's works as a gradual fading away of once-dominant and distracting fashions and interests:

He has long outlived his century, the term commonly fixed as the test of literary merit. Whatever advantages he might once derive from personal allusions, local customs, or temporary opinions, have for many years been lost; and every topic of merriment or motive of sorrow which the modes of artificial life afforded him now only obscure the scenes which they once illuminated. The effects of favour and competition are at an end; the tradition of his friendships and his enmities has perished; his works support no opinion with arguments, nor supply any faction with invectives; they can neither indulge vanity nor gratify malignity, but are read without any other reason than the desire of pleasure, and are therefore praised only as pleasure is obtained; yet, thus unassisted by interest or passion, they have past through variations of taste and changes of manners, and, as they have devolved from one generation to another, have received new honours at every transmission.

Most of these interests were, in Shakespeare's age, inseparable from the values a learned reader might have been expected to consider in making a judgment. Though Johnson cautiously added that judgment "never becomes infallible," the implications of his argument were clear: true judgment, disinterested and dispassionate, was most likely to occur in relation to the works of the past, whose long pedigree of productive utility time itself had helped to repress. Going back to the classics, readers could transcend what Johnson called "the modes of artificial life," both of Shakespeare's time and of their own, and could read and judge authentically. "Time and place will always enforce regard," Johnson elsewhere conceded, knowing that valuation could never entirely escape the tastes and pressures of the moment, yet the remark implied that the act of judgment had ideally to be achieved in a state independent of time and place, an utterly objective realm where the reader, like Imlac's poet, would be a foundational being, one wholly commensurable with the absolute values of general nature and moral justice.[117] Short of achieving this state, readers in this life were to arrive at authentic judgment not by treating the work as an object to be consumed, in the sense of assimilating it as part of their own subjectivity, but by suspending any feeling they might have of reading the work with a view to deriving any particular benefit or profit for themselves except the transcendent pleasure of truth. The test of literary merit was as much a test of readers as of books, because for readers to be able to recognize with pleasure a just representation of human commonality, they each had to read not as an individual but as the species, just as their initial act of judgment had to be a paradoxical one of non-differentiation.

The differentiating game remained a deeply serious activity for Johnson. Yet, far from defining the boundaries of cultural work or enabling one to achieve a position of distinction within a cultural hierarchy, it led instead in an opposite direction, towards ascertaining all the temporal values that could divert one from an understanding of common humanity. Accordingly, it is not quite right to say that the irresolutions in Johnson's criticism played themselves out like a self-consuming artifact, in the sense that they functioned merely as a rhetorical stratagem to compel readers into accepting a truth that was inexpressible in discourse. The irresolutions were rather a real and unavoidable consequence of believing, as Johnson did, that common humanity was resistant to definition. Though, as Johnson insisted throughout his writings, common humanity could be recognized empirically by its manifestation in perennial forms of conduct, it could not, in principle, be broken down into its constituent features or described in its full enabling presence. It could only be asserted in abstract terms or suggested by describing what it was not, namely those temporal values that could themselves be differentiated, analysed in a work, or related to the specific circumstances of the work's production or its author's life.

Arriving at common humanity therefore necessitated a process of subtraction, in which readers could pleasurably experience this absolute value only by identifying and ideally setting to one side all the many lesser values, including the pleasurable ones of style or novelty, whose standards were subject to change. It was not that these temporal values were to be eliminated altogether, even if that were possible, but only that they were not to be mistaken for general nature. Much like an earlier Jonson who was wont to define his positives by negatives, Johnson risked irresolution in attempting to affirm a source of value that could not be specified because it existed outside the realms of change and difference. If the newer discourse of aesthetics had begun to generate foundational terms so vague that they were impervious to essentialist definition, Johnson refused to differentiate his essential value, or to articulate its precise relation to social and historical diversity, in order that it be understood to underlie all human activity. This is why his canon-making, whether seen from the perspective of producers or consumers, seemed so diminished in its account of literature's specific value or utility. If literature was to be truly valuable and in accord with common humanity, then there could be nothing special or unique about it. And this is why, poised between production and consumption, the fully disinterested exercise of judgment was for Johnson as necessary a basis for criticism as the absolute value of general nature, because at some fundamental level they were the same.

A foundation of value beyond time or place, a reader of unformed sensibility, a canonical text that evinced purposiveness without serving any specific purpose, a wholly disinterested act of judgment that could make for a sense of human solidarity within the reader, and a plural and internally differentiated canon whose pleasures were best felt by a reader who had discarded the immediate prejudices of the age and self: all these modern conceptions of value were being introduced in the aesthetic discourse of Johnson's time, and their similarity to some of Johnson's critical ideas might indicate how removed even Johnson was from a rhetorical culture. Yet it would be a mistake to assume that this similarity went much deeper than a surface resemblance. Seeking an objective source of value, aesthetic theorists and critics located it in the intrinsic value of the work, the reader's faculty of taste, or the author's providential genius; needing to legitimize a function for literature, they proposed that it was the finer breath of knowledge that could help form the tastes and sensibilities of readers; hoping to distinguish literature from all the other commercial goods and activities that could fulfil the same function, they celebrated it as an art without purposiveness yet whose very inutility made reading it an experience of the highest moral good; endeavouring to define this experience, they envisioned it as an autotelic refuge from interest, where the reader could define his or her moral autonomy in the very act of imaginatively perceiving experience from the point of view of another; and attempting to relate this experience to English literature, they ordered a canon that, by its diversity, seemed to encourage the vital exercise of the reader's imagination. Johnson's criticism evinced much of the same empiricist discourse of differentiation that characterized objectivist valuations, yet for him this discourse could render judgment more precise only with respect to values other than general nature. In starting from the assumption of human universality, Johnson's beliefs were the obverse of objectivist: essential value was not something that could be isolated in the text, its reader, or its author because it designated this universality; his common reader was unformed yet in a natural state of general desire; his canonical text did not do anything in particular for anybody but rather helped to satisfy this universal desire; the act of judgment may have been ideally disinterested but not autonomous, because in judging readers had to deny their own desire for self-determination in order to be another and the same; and, as a function of acknowledging the fact of human division, the writings of the canonical English authors had to be precisely distinguished and evaluated, yet only after the attempt had been made to recognize in them as in oneself any signs of universality. Johnson's structure of conviction was among the least authoritarian yet in its way as elemental as *auctoritas* itself. For Johnson, no book or rhetorical performance, no act of writing or reading, could ever truly produce the supreme value of human commonality, and this was so not simply because no work of humankind could achieve perfection, but because this value was not something to be "produced" at all but rather something that, perpetually and with effort, had to be discerned in all human endeavour.

How Poesy Became Literature

The idea of literature, it has often been noted, is of relatively recent emergence. In Foucault's version of the claim, the idea was born of a radical realignment of the disciplines of knowledge, a realignment that, by the nineteenth century, had left a space for the "pure act of writing" to curve back upon itself and to reconstitute itself as an independent "form of language that we now call 'literature.'"[1] That the modern sense of "literature" has not been part of Western thought for long should not be taken to mean that before the nineteenth century the word itself had not been in usage nor that there was no collective term for identifying the peculiar "form of language" that we would now equate with the literary. Yet a change did occur, and this change I would identify with the protracted cultural shift that I have outlined in this narrative, the shift in canon-formation from production to consumption. Poetry, or "poesy," as I have already suggested, had long been used as the prevalent term to designate the category of verbal and fictive art because, at its root, it pertained to "making" and to the values of rhetorical productivity. Aristotle understood this when he adopted the term in the *Poetics*. Eager to defend this art from Plato's strictures against its dangerous moral and psychological affectivity, Aristotle wanted a term that might identify not so much the art's verbal power as what he believed was its essential quality as a mode of fictive representation. With reluctance, he accepted the common designation of "poetry," a term that could refer to any rhythmic utterance: "people do attach the making [that is the root of the word *poiētēs*] to the name of a metre and speak of elegiac-makers and hexameter-makers; they think, no doubt, that 'makers' is applied to poets not because they make *mimēseis* but as a general term meaning 'verse-makers.'" Not every fool, Aristotle added, who wrote a medical treatise in verse ought to be called a poet, but that was unfortunately what was happening.[2] Though "poetry" would do for now, Aristotle seemed to be saying, more refined distinctions were needed if critical discourse was to be a meaningful activity.

Despite Aristotle's protests, the conventional distinctions remained in place throughout much of the history of European criticism. "Maker" was the prevalent term in Dunbar's time, "poet" in Shakespeare's. A medical treatise written in verse could still conceivably be praised as the work of a poet into the eighteenth century, and even into ours: an extract from John Armstrong's *Art of Preserving Health* (1744) has made it into Roger Lonsdale's first Oxford collection of eighteenth-century verse. Yet, owing perhaps to Aristotle's influence, and certainly Horace's, poetry before the nineteenth century was less a technical designation for verse than a normative category of fictive or rhetorical art. In Sidney's famous formulation, "there have bene many most excellent Poets that never versefied, and now swarme many versefiers that neede never aunswere to the name of Poets."[3] Within this category there could belong poems, plays, fictional works, and discursive prose of a peculiarly refined nature. Sidney included within his definition More's *Utopia*, the romance *Amadis de Gaule*, and the ballad *Chevy-Chase*. Some, like Bacon, emphasized the fictionality of poetry while others, like John Dennis a century later, privileged its linguistic peculiarities: "the great Art of Poetry consists in saying almost every thing that is said figuratively."[4] The efflorescence of the novel in the eighteenth century might have conceivably necessitated a realignment of the category but, then, Fielding could quite easily describe his works as comic epics in prose. The entry of the novel did not seem to enlarge the traditional category of "poesy," though the term itself was fast becoming obsolescent by Fielding's time because the art of metrical speaking and fine fabling was no longer prized for its verbal power. By then, the social function of poetry had changed fundamentally as a rhetorical culture had been largely displaced by an objectivist understanding of experience.

The new term, "literature," had in actuality been around for some time. *Litteratura* for the Romans denoted either the ability to form letters or, more usually, the quality of being widely read. In an age when books were comparatively scarce, being widely read meant being well read. This sense survived in vernacular derivations of the term: "literature" initially designated erudition among a broad range of polite learning, while its cognates, "literate" and, later, "literary," referred to the condition of what has lately been termed "cultural literacy." Bacon had this sense in mind when, in his dedication before *The Advancement of Learning* (1605), he praised his king for being "so learned in all literature and erudition, divine and humane."[5] Literature was the polite *paideia*, with its own hierarchical syllabus. In John Clarke's curriculum from 1731, "The Value therefore of the several Parts of Literature is to be measured by their Tendency"; at the top, for their promotion of virtue, Clarke placed "*Divinity* and *Morality*." Next came mathematics and natural philosophy, for their contributions to scientific and technological advancement. Other parts of learning, Clarke went on, "that indirectly serve either of the two 'fore-mentioned Purposes, as *Languages*, take the third. And in the last and lowest Rank come those, that scarce, I think, serve any other Purpose in Life, than that of immediate Pleasure, or Amusement: Such are *Poetry, Plays* and *Novels*; which are not indeed so properly Parts of Learning, as Ways of exercising the Invention, that require some Knowledge of Letters, in order to a Man's acquitting himself handsomely therein."[6] Clarke's hierarchy suggests how, in the eighteenth century, poetry was increasingly opposed to both learning and "languages" as pragmatic notions of utility were gradually being displaced by the newer disciplines of knowledge. Literature was still, in Clarke's time, a term capacious enough to subsume both verbal art and these new disciplines, but cultural activity was now occupying its own separate sphere.

Literature was not just books. It was the name given to all reading that could be considered valuable, and the name for the valence of reading. The term was nonetheless a relatively loose one. Johnson, for one, used it in a variety of contexts. At times, he seemed to equate it generally with reading. In the "Life of Milton," he wrote that the "call for books was not in Milton's age what it is in the present. To read was not then a general amusement; neither traders, nor often gentlemen thought themselves disgraced by ignorance. The women had not then aspired to literature, nor was every house supplied with a closet of knowledge." "General literature," he added, "now pervades the nation through all its ranks."[7] At other times, Johnson had something more specific in mind. Boswell reported that what Johnson read at college, "he told me, was not works of mere amusement, 'not voyages and travels, but all literature, Sir, all ancient writers, all manly.'"[8] Literature was functional and exclusive reading – polite and phallogocentric reading if Johnson's remark is taken seriously. But Johnson, who recognized the potential rigidities of canon-formation, preferred a broadly literate society to a selectively learned one:

We must read what the world reads at the moment. It has been maintained that this superfoetation, this teeming of the press in modern times, is prejudicial to good literature, because it obliges us to read so much of what is of inferiour value, in order to be in fashion; so that better works are neglected for want of time, because a man will have more gratification of his vanity in conversation, from having read modern books, than from having read works of antiquity. But it must be considered, that we have now more knowledge generally diffused; all our ladies read now, which is a great extension.

"Modern writers," Johnson concluded, "are the moons of literature; they shine with reflected light, with light borrowed from the ancients."[9] Johnson believed the extension of literacy and knowledge to women was a good thing, and indeed, as I have already suggested, the increasing prevalence of "literature" in the eighteenth century reflected the fact that the qualities denoted by the term had come to seem as being as central to the young person's equipment as eloquence had formerly been. What is noteworthy about Johnson's statement, however, is his use of the phrase "good literature," which indicates that, in an age when books had become much more readily available and the activity of reading far more encouraged among the general public, the normative dimensions of the original category had to be reinforced. Ideally, the idea of literature was now to be set against the present, the "superfoetation" and fashion of the moment, and the pale fire of the moderns. In reading the works of the past, men and women could transcend their own vanities and prejudices and escape the immediate pressures of common life, where so many demands could be placed on one's time and attention.

The examples that René Wellek has cited as the earliest English usages of "literature" as a term for a specific body of writings, and not just any learning, all had to do with older writings. "Shakespeare and Milton," wrote George Colman the elder in 1761, "seem to stand alone, like first-rate authors, amid the general wreck of old English literature." And Johnson, in a letter of 1774, expressed the hope that "what is undeservedly forgotten of our antiquated literature might be revived."[10] There was much reviving of old literature going on in the later eighteenth century: Colman's essay appeared before an important edition of Massinger's plays, and Johnson within five years went on to produce his *Lives* as prefaces for a major anthology of post-Interregnum verse. Percy published his *Reliques of Ancient English Poetry* in 1765, Warton came out with his *History of English Poetry* between 1774 and 1781, Tyrwhitt produced the first modern edition of Chaucer's *Canterbury Tales* in 1775–78, just about everybody had a say in editing Shakespeare's works, and even working poets were fooling the public with the forged medievalisms of Ossian and Rowley. This revival of old authors, furthermore, was not being done in the name of either composition or moral utility: Massinger could never conceivably be defended as a model of eloquence or a fount of useful wisdom. Rather, these editions and histories were sold to be read, as Johnson put it in his Preface to *Shakespeare*, "without any other reason than the desire of pleasure."[11] This new emphasis on simple appreciation and pleasure resulted in a considerable broadening and pluralizing of the English canon, which, since its inception, had been keyed to the demands of production, to each generation's standards for poetic expression and rhetorical instrumentality. The canon became, in Johnson's age, something for readers to make. We can even mark the date of this change.

On 22 February 1774 literature in its modern sense began. On that day, the House of Lords elected to defeat the notion of perpetual copyright so long claimed by the London bookselling monopoly over works of the English canon. The Lords had been persuaded by the novel idea that the canon ought to be fully accessible in multiple editions to general readers, for their benefit and pleasure. The moment was highly symbolic, for it marked the official recognition of the needs and desires of a consuming public. From that moment, the canon of English literature, now conceived of as comprising only *old* works, was valued as public domain, cultural goods for everyone to enjoy and esteem: as one contemporary account put it, "the Works of *Shakespeare*, of *Addison*, *Pope*, *Swift*, *Gay*, and many other excellent Authors of the present Century, are, by this Reversal, declared to be the Property of any Person."[12] Never before in English history had it been possible to think that the canon might belong to the people, to readers. From that moment, the canon became a set of commodities to be consumed. It became literature rather than poetry.

Early English writings, in other words, first became widely available in cheap editions at the moment when they were no longer being thought of as useful models of verbal power but rather things people might find pleasurable or, better yet, might find essential in helping them to sharpen their taste and refine their sensibility. The canon of the dead was felt more suitable for this purpose than contemporary works because it was free of the incrustations of modern prejudice. Readers could more directly experience and value the works of the past than those that had not yet survived the test of time. Literature was thus a more adequate term for these writings than poetry, or the interim term belles-lettres, because it designated a category removed from the values of productivity and instrumentality. It was a term that had to do exclusively with reading, reading isolated from received opinion, considerations of utility, and the pressures of reality. As Isaac

D'Israeli declared in 1795, "whatever some authors may imagine, the concerns of mere literature, are not very material in the system of human life." In the literature of the past, D'Israeli claimed, readers could rise above the ordinary commerce of life and even find refuge from the horrors of the French Revolution: "Literary investigation is allied neither to politics nor religion; it is a science consecrated to the few; abstracted from all the factions on earth; and independent of popular discontents, and popular delusions."[13] And if reading canonical works was to be ideally done in a state of splendid withdrawal, it followed that the activity would have nugatory effects on the world outside. Vicesimus Knox said as much in an essay on reading early English poetry: "Mistakes in matters of mere taste and literature, are harmless in their consequences to society. They have no direct tendency to hurt any interest, or corrupt any morals."[14] Knox's trivialization of literature would have been unheard of in ages past. Not that Knox undervalued poetry. On the contrary, it was for him a discourse purer than the rest, one that suffered tremendously when contaminated by other interests. As he suggested in a later essay, politics were harmful to literature:

Poetry, philology, elegant and polite letters, in all their ramifications, display their alluring charms in vain to him, whose head and heart still vibrate with the harsh and discordant sounds of a political dispute at the tavern. Those books, whose tendency is only to promote elegant pleasures or advance science, which flatter no party, and gratify no malignant passion, are suffered to fall into oblivion; while a pamphlet, which espouses the cause of any political men or measures, however inconsiderable its literary merit, is extolled as one of the first productions of modern literature.

"From a taste for trash, and a disrelish of the wholesome food of the mind," Knox added, "the community, together with literature, is at last deeply injured."[15] Knox was not quite equating literature with imaginative productions, but the normative import of his categories was clear: literature, no longer synonymous with reading or learning, was a canon of works of evident "literary merit" that could not be judged according to the terms of other, mundane discourses. Reading this canon may have been a harmless and ineffectual activity as long as it was done in an appropriate state of disinterestedness. The reader of literature was at once emancipated from worldly concerns and powerless to alter that world.

At the moment, then, when canonical texts were becoming easily available to a broad reading public, the experience of literature was increasingly defined, by Knox and others, as an isolated and autonomous activity. Defining this autonomy entailed a series of progressively refined demarcations, initially from politics and religion and commerce, and then, later, from science and facticity, ideas and abstractions.[16] David Bromwich is no doubt right in saying that the idea of aesthetic autonomy was a myth "of which the more skeptical romantics were free from the start."[17] But there is the sense in the later eighteenth century of aestheticizing the act of reading and of isolating the ideal state of mind for experiencing the canon. In his essay "Of the Choice of Reading" (1797), William Godwin went so far as to argue that "the impression we derive from a book, depends much less upon its real contents, than upon the temper of mind and preparation with which we read it."[18] "Literature" came to imply such detached, well-tempered reading. Archibald Alison, writing in 1790, suggested that literary art was best approached by a mind "vacant and unemployed," and whose "imagination is free and unembarrassed" by "the labour of criticism."[19] *Pace* Foucault, the act of *reading* literature was made to seem so pure and unique that there could occur no aporia of judgment since there was no telling intellect from sensibility, merit from affect. It was almost as though the subject was himself aestheticized: he was left so alone with the text that you could not tell the reader from the reading.

Of course, Knox, Colman and the others were all helping to instruct readers on how best to read and judge literature. Their editions made older works ready for consumption by correcting, annotating, and contextualizing them. Their critical commentaries brought together the authority of received opinions and present tastes and so pointed readers to the role they were to play within the test of time. Perhaps most important, in valorizing and institutionalizing a prestigious form of competence at reading literature, they were impressing upon readers a need and desire to undertake the lengthy and difficult process of achieving an adequate understanding and proper appreciation of the entire plural canon. The critical discourse of the eighteenth century was therefore helping to regulate the reception and formation of the canon in a manner far more elaborate and complex than it had been determined in the past. The autonomization of the reading experience might in this way be seen as a reaction to the opening up of the canon to a broad readership, as an attempt to retain polite control over culture by denying general readers both a specific social function for reading as well as the cultural capital required to appreciate the canon. Yet, as I have argued, this autonomization ought rather to be understood as being part of a much larger reorganization of human activities that followed upon the cognitive shift from rhetorical and objectivist thinking, and indirectly, upon a multiplicity of extensive material changes. What these critics and aesthetic theorists were attempting to do was to define a plausible and special function for literary works now that these works were no longer considered of any particular use in a modern commercial society. The pure experience of reading was for them valuable precisely because it could not be made to serve any specific purpose; instead, it performed a general, even supreme good in encouraging readers to refine their sensibilities, to improve their tastes, and to form their moral being. By reading literature, and particularly the diverse literary works of the past, one could leave behind one's selfish desires and local prejudices and transport oneself imaginatively into the life of another.

So autonomized from local interests, the act of reading literature was itself differentiated as an intensely local experience that could somehow bring about in readers a defamiliarizing, perhaps decentring transcendence out of their own common identities. Where poetry had offered the gentleman at once the eloquence necessary to participate in wordly affairs and the verbal power vital to maintaining a presentist belief in the moral economy of the state, literature took the reader out of a public world and into a personally enriching yet radically private encounter with difference. In time, this experience would be identified with particular modes of writing, those that, because of their alterity or affectivity or fictiveness, most seemed to enable such an experience. Yet to define literature in this way as a body of imaginative writings may be somewhat misleading, since it locates the imaginative act in the work and not the reader, the object and not the subject. Literature designates those canonical if secular writings whose reproduction and transmission necessitates, and perhaps encourages, an act of imaginative sympathy, a creative reading that leads to dialogic understanding and solidarity. It may be misleading, as well, in the way it ignores how critical and academic institutions mediate this transmission and so regulate these acts of understanding, interpretation, and evaluation. Measuring the extent of this mediation, whether as it exists at present or in the past, remains no simple matter, however. Literary canons, whether they posit at their center standard authors or alternative values, are the products of complex identity politics that only with reduction can be equated merely with hegemonic authority.

Poetry is composed and spoken, literature read and studied. The inevitable consequence of the shift from production to consumption was the loss of any coherent notion of invention within the cultural field. The Romantic theory of the poet-genius who creates "the taste by which he is to be enjoyed" was spiritual compensation for the degradations of commodification, and poor compensation at that: not only was Wordsworth's claim something that Jonson or Pope might have thought was implied in their role as cultural refiners, but even to speak of "taste" was to abide by the terms of consumption. Likewise, Wordsworth's sympathetic reader who evinced a "co-operating *power*" with the poet's emotions was little more than spiritual kin to the learned reader of old. Perhaps this may account for why Wordsworth's final court of appeal was a suprahistorical audience far removed from present-day readers: "Towards the Public, the Writer hopes that he feels as much deference as it is entitled to: but to the People, philo-sophically characterised, and to the embodied spirit of their knowl-edge, so far as it exists and moves, at the present, faithfully supported by its two wings, the past and the future, his devout respect, his reverence, is due."[20] Only an immortal audience could be utterly free of local interests or presentist complacency, and utterly receptive to all literature, regardless of its age or culture of origin. In this, we can recognize the next stage in the movement Foucault traced in Western culture, a movement that saw the attribute of heroism pass, in an emergent world of representations, from the hero to the poet-maker whose task it had been to represent him.[21] In an emergent world of reproduction and consumption, those epic dimensions of heroism and immortality passed finally from the poet-maker to the reader.

Notes

I have modernized *i/j* and *u/v* throughout. I have retained original capitalization and punctuation, except in passages quoted from modern editions where these have been emended.

INTRODUCTION

1 Julie A. Smith traces the history of this symbolism in "The Poet Laureate as University Master: John Skelton's Woodcut Portrait," in *Renaissance Rereadings*, ed. Maryanne Cline Horowitz *et al.* (Urbana: University of Illinois Press 1988), 159–83.

2 The frontispiece appears before the reprint volume, *The Universal Visiter and Memorialist. For the Year 1756* (London 1756).

3 The periodical could also include one of Johnson's satires on the proliferation of authors that, he claimed, left so few readers that "every man must be content to read his book to himself" [1 (April 1756): 162]. The remark, however, suggests how much consumption had by Johnson's age become the measure of production.

4 "Reproduced" here refers to the activities of both physical preservation (printing, libraries, etc.) and cultural transmission (the institutions of criticism, pedagogy, etc.) This is the sense in which John Guillory uses the term in his entry for "Canon" in *Critical Terms for Literary Study*, ed. Frank Lentricchia and Thomas McLaughlin (Chicago: University of Chicago Press 1990), 233–49. Guillory rightly notes that canon-formation, at least in its modern conception, involves both the evaluation and the preservation of literary works: acts of judgment, he

suggests, "are necessary rather than sufficient to constitute a process of canon-formation. An individual's judgment that a work is great does nothing in itself to preserve that work, unless that judgment is made in a certain institutional context, a setting in which it is possible to insure the *reproduction* of the work, its continual reintroduction to generations of readers" (237). See also Guillory's important critique of the current canon debate, *Cultural Capital: The Problem of Literary Canon Formation* (Chicago: University of Chicago Press 1993).

5 Northrop Frye, *Anatomy of Criticism* (Princeton, N.J.: Princeton University Press 1957), 344–5.

6 Hans Ulrich Gumbrecht contrasts feudal to bourgeois concepts of literature in "'Phoenix from the Ashes' or: From Canon to Classic," *New Literary History* 20 (1988): 141–63. See also Jean-Marie Goulemot, "Histoire littéraire et mémoire nationale," *History and Anthropology* 2 (1986): 225–35. Though both Gumbrecht and Goulemot deal specifically with the making of the French literary canon during the eighteenth century, I am indebted to both for their suggestions about how modern canon-formation displaced an earlier rhetorical tradition in criticism. Gumbrecht's argument, in particular, closely parallels mine in identifying a change in the way literary value is defined: "The value of literature," Gumbrecht writes in relation to the eighteenth century, "is now being measured less by the functions it performs for society than by its effects on *individual readers*" (151). I develop this idea in my later chapters.

7 "At the beginning of the seventeenth century," according to Foucault, "thought ceases to move in the element of resemblance. Similitude is no longer the form of knowledge but rather the occasion of error ... Resemblance, which had for long been the fundamental category of knowledge – both the form and content of what we know – became dissociated in an analysis based on terms of identity and difference; moreover, whether indirectly by the intermediary of measurement, or directly and, as it were, on the same footing, comparison became a function of order; and lastly, comparison ceased to fulfil the function of revealing how the world is ordered, since it was now accomplished according to the order laid down by thought, progressing naturally from the simple to the complex. As a result, the entire *episteme* of Western culture found its fundamental arrangements modified" (*The Order of Things* [New York: Random House 1970], 51–4).

8 C.S. Lewis once noted how early English culture appeared so alien to modern sensibilities because of its deep immersion in rhetoric: "Rhetoric is the greatest barrier between us and our ancestors ... Nearly all our older poetry was written and read by men to whom the distinction between poetry and rhetoric, in its modern form, would have been

meaningless" (*English Literature in the Sixteenth Century, Excluding Drama* [Oxford: Clarendon Press 1954], 61). Since then, much work has been done on the shift from a rhetorical to an modern empirical culture, in particular Walter J. Ong's numerous studies on the subject, including *Rhetoric, Romance, and Technology* (Ithaca, N.Y.: Cornell University Press 1971), and *Interfaces of the Word* (Ithaca: Cornell University Press 1977). The consequences of this shift for the history of literary theory and practice have been the subject of many studies and surveys, too numerous to mention. These generally agree that a gradual movement is discernible in English critical discourse, a movement from rhetorical-didactic to imitative-objective theories, as developed from classical precedents in the Platonic-Aristotelian-Horatian debate over the function of poetry. Though my concern in this survey is not so much with literary theory as with the practice of evaluation, such practice is obviously informed by what John D. Boyd, in a representative formulation, calls "two fundamentally different views of poetry itself, one of which sees it as an autonomously meaningful structure, and the other, more rhetorically conceived, which views it as an instrument for molding opinion or moving an audience to action" (*The Function of Mimesis and Its Decline* [New York: Fordham University Press 1980], xii). M.H. Abrams's summary of these theories in the introductory chapter to *The Mirror and The Lamp* (Oxford: Oxford University Press 1953) has long been standard, but see also Abrams's revision of the chapter, as well as his important essay on "Art-as-Such: The Sociology of Modern Aesthetics," in *Doing Things with Texts* (New York: Norton 1989), 3–30 and 135–58.

The idea of an "epistemological shift" has of course been a central thesis in much pragmatist and deconstructionist exhumations of rhetoric, notably Richard Rorty's seminal *Philosophy and The Mirror of Nature* (Princeton, N.J.: Princeton University Press 1979), and the work of the contributors to *The Rhetoric of the Human Sciences*, ed. John S. Nelson, Allan Megill, and Donald N. McCloskey (Madison: University of Wisconsin Press 1987). My own schematic comparison of rhetoricist and objectivist thinking loosely corresponds to Stanley Fish's summary account of the quarrel between rhetorical and "foundational" thought, in his essay on "Rhetoric" in *Doing What Comes Naturally* (Durham, N.C.: Duke University Press 1989), 471–502. In writing a history of early canon-formation, I suppose that my own affinities, unlike Fish's, lean towards objectivism, though even to speak of a schematic "quarrel," however essentialist its content, is to propose a divisive rhetorical structure for my argument. My term "objectivism" may be unfortunate, yet, as I explain at the beginning of my fourth chapter, the term is meant to denote a host of beliefs and discursive formations associated with modernity – empiricism, rationalism, realism, foundationalism, etc. – while equally suggesting something of the unsystematic manner in which these discourses were first invoked in relation to canon-making.

9 "Solidarity" is Richard Rorty's term for the sense of community that may be generated through pragmatic or rhetorical accounts of experience. To this, he opposes the desire for "objectivity," which seeks to ground the understanding of experience by reference to an ultimate Truth in a nonhuman reality (see, in particular, "Solidarity or Objectivity?" in *Objectivity, Relativism, and Truth* [Cambridge: Cambridge University Press 1991], 21–34). Rorty might therefore object to my equating solidarity to a conception of "ultimate" value. Yet, however pragmatic its procedures, rhetorical thinking, especially in its pre-modern articulations, generally functions on the universalist principle that verbal power is to be deployed in the service of achieving an ultimate goal of human solidarity.

10 The idea that discourses of knowledge may themselves be a form of performative rhetoric is of course a central premise of received deconstruction. In a succinct formulation of the claim, Paul de Man criticizes Stanley Fish's model of affective stylistics for relegating "persuasion, which is indeed inseparable from rhetoric, to a purely affective and intentional realm and makes no allowance for modes of persuasion which are no less rhetorical and no less at work in literary texts but which are of the order of persuasion by *proof* rather than persuasion by seduction" (*The Resistance to Theory* [Minneapolis: University of Minnesota Press 1986], 18, emphasis in original).

11 The phrase is Frank Kermode's, from the title of one of his several meditations (*Forms of Attention* [Chicago: University of Chicago Press 1985]) on how, in modern culture, works of art come to be treated as canonical and deserving of "the most energetic efforts of criticism and interpretation" (xiii).

12 Richard McKeon, "Canonic Books and Prohibited Books: Orthodoxy and Heresy in Religion and Culture," *Critical Inquiry* 2 (1975): 794.

13 "Embarrassment" is E.D. Hirsch, Jr's term, from his account of the shift from "instrumentalist" to "intrinsic" theories of literary value, in "Two Traditions of Literary Evaluation," *Literary Theory and Criticism*, ed. Joseph P. Strelka (Bern: Peter Lang 1984), 287. Hirsch's account anticipates mine in several of its emphases, though our readings of this shift differ considerably. In particular, Hirsch suggests that "the ancient instrumental theory was predicated on the uniformity of human nature" (287), whereas intrinsic theories are responses to historicism and its embarrassing recognition that tastes and sensibilities are "relative to time, place, person, and culture" (296). It seems to

me, rather, that universality (or "solidarity," to use Rorty's term) is the fundamental hope and purpose of both rhetorical and objectivist cultures, the basic difference between them being merely one of how to achieve such universality. Whereas the former asserts a common humanity even as its verbal power relies on coercive distinction-making, so the latter strives for total self-knowledge for all even as it is embarrassed by what its researches into life's contingencies reveal.

14 Ben Jonson, *Timber; or, Discoveries*, in *Works*, ed. C.H. Herford, Percy Simpson, and Evelyn Simpson, 11 vols. (Oxford: Clarendon Press 1925–52), 8:636.

15 Cicero, *Of Oratory*, 1.8.33, trans. E.W. Sutton and H. Rackham, in *The Rhetorical Tradition: Readings from Classical Times to the Present*, ed. Patricia Bizzell and Bruce Herzberg (Boston: St Martin's Press 1990), 204. In Puttenham's version, "Poesie was th'originall cause and occasion of [men's] first assemblies," and since poets "were from the beginning the best perswaders," they acted as "the first lawmakers to the people, and the first polititiens, devising all expedient meanes for th'establishment of Common wealth, to hold and containe the people in order and duety by force and vertue of good and wholesome lawes, made for the preservation of the publique peace and tranquilitie" (*The Arte of English Poesie* [London 1589], 3–6).

16 William Oldys, pref. to *The British Muse*, ed. Thomas Hayward (London 1738), vii.

17 The phrase is Richard A. Lanham's, in *The Motives of Eloquence: Literary Rhetoric in the Renaissance* (New Haven, Conn.: Yale University Press 1976), 1. Stanley Fish adopts the phrase in *Doing What Comes Naturally*, 482–5.

18 Longinus, "On Sublimity," trans. D.A. Russell, in *Ancient Literary Criticism*, ed. D.A. Russell and M. Winterbottom (Oxford: Clarendon Press 1972), 467.

19 In ancient critical practice, Hans Robert Jauss has argued, "there was little investigation into reception. The canon of works and authors was extended to their posthumous fame, passing over in silence their impact on recipients, the very bearers of tradition." Jauss cites the notable exception of Aristotle's *Poetics* (to which might be added Book Ten of Plato's *Republic*) but concludes that "classical aesthetics saw any inquiry into the effects of art as outside the purview of art" ("The Theory of Reception: A Retrospective of its Unrecognized History," *Literary Theory Today*, ed. Peter Collier and Helga Geyer-Ryan [Ithaca, N.Y.: Cornell University Press 1990], 60).

20 Daniel Defoe, *A Vindication of the Press: or, An Essay on the Usefulness of Writing, on Criticism, and the Qualification of Authors* (London 1718), 12. Defoe's authorship of this pamphlet has been much contested. See the

evidence collected by Maximillian E. Novak, "*A Vindication of the Press and the Defoe Canon*," *Studies in English Literature* 27 (1987): 399–411; and Laura A. Curtis, "The Attribution of *A Vindication of the Press* to Daniel Defoe," *Studies in Eighteenth-Century Culture* 18, ed. John Y. Yolton and Leslie Ellen Brown (East Lansing, Mich.: Colleagues Press 1988), 433–44.

21 Bourdieu sees culture (in its restricted sense) as a site of struggle where a dominant class uses the symbolic capital of cultural artifacts or agents in order to maintain its power over a dominated class. This "cultural game," as Bourdieu calls it, is marked by struggles for "legitimacy" (acceptance and authorization by those above within a social hierarchy), and for "distinction" (demarcation from those below). To acquire legitimacy, the social agent must demonstrate a degree of cultural capital, which may be a certain critical disposition or body of knowledge, "an internalized code or a cognitive acquisition which equips the social agent with empathy towards, appreciation for or competence in deciphering cultural relations and cultural artefacts ... The possession of this code, or cultural capital, is accumulated through a long process of acquisition or inculcation which includes the pedagogical action of the family or group members (family education), educated members of the social formation (diffuse education) and social institutions (institutionalized education)" (from the editor's introduction to Pierre Bourdieu, *The Field of Cultural Production*, ed. Randal Johnson [New York: Columbia University Press 1993], 7). Bourdieu analyses the particular features of this struggle in his massive empirical study of the French cultural system, *Distinction*, trans. Richard Nice (London: Routledge and Kegan Paul 1984).

In his most recent work, *The Rules of Art*, Bourdieu has applied the theoretical models that he first set out in his early programmatic essays (collected in *The Field of Cultural Production*) to a full-scale sociology of the literary field as it existed in mid-nineteenth-century France. In doing so, he revises some of his original categories. Notably, he places greater emphasis upon the accumulation of symbolic capital within the field, since he is more concerned with authors' "position-takings" than with the cultural capital that readers may seek to acquire. Nevertheless, in charting the consequences of the field's "autonomization" from economic interests, his findings are directly relevant to this study, even though he is examining the history of the field's "rupture with the bourgeois" (that is, within an economy already defined by consumption and the cash nexus), whereas I am dealing with an earlier stage of this history, the rupture with the feudal (that is, within an economy where consumption is beginning to displace production as its defining principle). Though Bourdieu warns that evidence for such autonomization prior to the nineteenth century "remains ambiguous, even contradictory," he concedes that its history could be traced back to the beginnings of writing itself: "Although it has to be admitted that the slow process which made possible the *emergence* of different fields of cultural production and the full social recognition of corresponding social figures (the painter, the writer, the scholar, etc.) reached its culmination only at the end of the nineteenth century, there is no doubt that one could push back its first manifestations as far as one likes, even to the moment when cultural producers first appeared, fighting (almost by definition) to have their independence and particular dignity be acknowledged" (*The Rules of Art: Genesis and Structure of the Literary Field*, trans. Susan Emanuel [Stanford, Calif.: Stanford University Press 1996], 366n.1, 387n.62. Emphasis in original). It is this early history that I have attempted to undertake in this study.

Critics have noted several problems with Bourdieu's sociology of aesthetics: his almost exclusive focus on French culture, which is arguably more rigidly stratified than cultural systems in other societies; his tendency to equate value with interest or to reduce it to status-distinction; his inadequate conception of class, which he views in terms of a fixed linear hierarchy; his overly functionalist account of social relations, which objectifies the cultural field to such a degree as perhaps to eliminate any possibility of risk or aleatory occurrences; and his reluctance to situate his own critical practice in relation to the fields he is examining. John Frow outlines some of these problems, while still accepting many of Bourdieu's principles, in *Cultural Studies and Cultural Value* (Oxford: Clarendon Press 1995), 5–7, 27–47. For a critique of how Bourdieu's formalist mapping of social relations virtually aestheticizes the cultural field, see Jonathan Loesberg, "Bourdieu and the Sociology of Aesthetics," *ELH* 60 (1993): 1033–56. Though not all of these problems impinge upon this study, I have taken them into account and modified Bourdieu's approach and assumptions accordingly – notably, in relation to the element of risk within a cultural economy. Then there is the problem of Bourdieu's appallingly opaque prose. As Richard Jenkins has remarked, Bourdieu's writing is "unnecessarily long-winded, obscure, complex and intimidatory. He does not have to write in this fashion to say what he wants to say" (*Pierre Bourdieu* [London: Routledge 1992], 9–10). Some of Bourdieu's cumbersome neologisms have unavoidably found their way into this study, though I agree with Jenkins in believing that, for all of its flaws, Bourdieu's work remains "enormously good to think with" (11).

22 Raymond Williams, *Keywords*, 2nd ed. (London: Fontana 1983), 87.

23 Frye, *Anatomy of Criticism*, 341.

24 The phrase, "aporia of judgment," is Howard Caygill's, from his remarkable study of how eighteenth-century aesthetic theorists dealt with this "undecidability," *Art of Judgement* (Oxford: Basil Blackwell 1989), 1.

25 Of course, objectivist arguments against the immanent value of literary works are frequently heard, and usually emphasize how value is determined either by sensitive readers or within social and institutional practices. Value is nonetheless perceived as situated within the realm of consumption, to which production is subordinate. In Terry Eagleton's account, "literary value is a phenomenon which is *produced* in that ideological appropriation of the text, that 'consumptional production' of the work, which is the act of reading ... The histories of 'value' are a sub-sector of the histories of literary-ideological receptive practices" (*Criticism and Ideology* [London: Verso 1978], 166–7).

26 A recent controversial attempt to describe the economy of literary evaluation is Barbara Herrnstein Smith's *Contingencies of Value* (Cambridge, Mass.: Harvard University Press 1988). Though sharply agonistic, Smith's ostensibly relativistic account seems to derive its force less from her critique of axiology (the belief in an absolute foundation of value) than from the promise she holds out of furnishing an exhaustive exposition of evaluative contingencies, an exposition that, she hopes, will demonstrate the need for "the continuous development and refinement of more richly articulated, broadly responsive, and subtly differentiated nonobjectivist accounts of, among other things, 'truth,' 'belief,' 'choice,' 'justification,' and 'community'" (172). In subscribing to such a goal, Smith rather unself-consciously reveals her attachments to objectivist assumptions ("objectivist" in the sense that I am using the term), in the way she posits as a value the refinement not of verbal power but of accounts of "difference." Commenting on the passage just quoted, Steven Connor quite rightly observes that the "more Smith insists on the necessity not to impose universalist accounts falsely or prematurely, the more commitment she displays to the ideal of an expanded, more richly diversified sense of community. This value appears to be absolute rather than relative, since it is the expression of the principle of the desirability of general improvement" (*Theory and Cultural Value* [Oxford: Blackwell 1992], 29). In contrast, Bourdieu's work, which Smith has adapted for her own purposes, has been criticized for its "sociological relativism" (Frow, *Cultural Studies and Cultural Value*, 6).

27 Terry Eagleton, "The Subject of Literature," *Cultural Critique* 2 (1985/ 86): 98. Ellipsis and emphasis in original.

28 Eagleton's own account of this history, *The Ideology of the Aesthetic* (Oxford: Basil Blackwell 1990), extends the critique that de Man had launched in his late essays, now collected as *Aesthetic Ideology*, ed. Andrzej Warminski (Minneapolis: University of Minnesota Press 1996).

29 Among the numerous reception histories now available, the relevant volumes in the Critical Heritage series, and such compilations as

Caroline F.E. Spurgeon's *Five Hundred Years of Chaucer Criticism and Allusion (1357–1900)* (3 vols. [Cambridge: Cambridge University Press 1925)], have provided important source material for this study. References for case histories, such as those devoted to Spenser, are noted in the text. Histories of taste and literary appreciation were largely a preoccupation of early-twentieth-century compilers, though John Buxton's *Elizabethan Taste* (Brighton, U.K.: Harvester Press 1963) is a relatively recent example. Histories of criticism and aesthetic theory are too numerous to mention; I briefly discuss the work most directly related to this study, René Wellek's *The Rise of English Literary History* (Chapel Hill: University of North Carolina Press 1941), in my final chapter. I discuss Lipking's *Ordering of the Arts* (Princeton, N.J.: Princeton University Press 1970) and Weinbrot's *Britannia's Issue* (Cambridge: Cambridge University Press 1993) below and at several points in the text and notes.

30 One notable work that deals with the emergence of "literature" in relation to political, scientific, and philosophical discourses is Timothy J. Reiss's *The Meaning of Literature* (Ithaca, N.Y.: Cornell University Press 1992). Though Reiss covers much of the same period I examine, his argument differs considerably from mine both in treating ideas about literature within a wider European intellectual context, and in proposing a large historical hypothesis about how these ideas were developed in response to a perceived collapse of consensual norms that had dominated Western thought until the later sixteenth century.

31 An important recent study on one such phenomenon, and that covers much of the same period as I do, is Barbara M. Benedict's *Making the Modern Reader: Cultural Mediation in Early Modern Literary Anthologies* (Princeton, N.J.: Princeton University Press 1996). Though Benedict's work appeared too late for me to address her findings fully within my argument, many of her conclusions, particularly about the relation of canon-making to a consumer culture and the emergent middle-class ideal of reading for improvement, anticipate mine. Much of her analysis, however, consists of a detailed consideration of how editorial practices during the period both presupposed and encouraged changes in how the reader was conceived, whereas I am more concerned with how changing definitions of "the reader," among others, reflected larger historical developments, including the emergence of an autonomous cultural field.

Another work that came to my attention too late for me to consider its evidence fully is Kevin Pask's *The Emergence of the English Author: Scripting the Life of the Poet in Early Modern England* (Cambridge: Cambridge University Press 1996). Pask offers an illuminating Foucauldian analysis of how early life-narratives of English poets attached increasing significance to the "author-function," a development that, he claims, should be read as "a sign of the authority accorded to vernacular literature" (2). Though I believe that Pask, like his mentor John Guillory, places too much emphasis upon how "the school" may have influenced English canon-making in its early stages, his account complements mine in several respects, notably in its focus upon how the cultural value of the canon was enhanced by literary biography, a genre that I have dealt with only in relation to the specific examples of Johnson's *Lives* and the catalogues of Leland and Bale.

32 Wendell V. Harris, "Canonicity" *PMLA* 106 (1991): 115–19.

33 Weinbrot, *Britannia's Issue*, 114. In Weinbrot's defence, he is concerned primarily with the formation of a "British" literary identity as it emerged following Britain's cultural expansion into both a united kingdom and an imperial trading power. However, his argument strikes me as echoing the kind of ideological, unhistorical myth-making that has characterized cultural self-advertisements since the Middle Ages. In this vein, Weinbrot argues that, over the course of the eighteenth century, "more readers saw the canon as friendlier, less divisive, and its sane variety consistent with the heterogeneous British character. To require a single valued canon, after all, violates British 'freedom,' cherished idiosyncracy, and theory of ample room in Parnassus for nonclassical emulative talents" (*Britannia's Issue*, 135–6; see also his "Enlightenment Canon Wars: Anglo-French Views of Literary Greatness," *ELH* 60 [1993]: 79–100). As I note in my second chapter, nativist arguments against classical values had been voiced well prior to neoclassicism's ascendancy in the seventeenth century. The apparent pluralizing of the canon that seemed to occur during the eighteenth century, I am arguing, may have been promoted through such myth-making, yet it actually reflected a profound historical change in how literature was valued. This same change, I suggest in my final chapter, accounts for the increasing desire that Lipking has identified among eighteenth-century critics to "order" the canon by means of hierarchical rankings, scholarly editions, and literary histories.

34 J.G.A. Pocock has provided the fullest explication of these terms, notably in *The Machiavellian Moment: Florentine Political Thought and the Atlantic Republican Tradition* (Princeton, N.J.: Princeton University Press 1975), and *Virtue, Commerce, and History* (Cambridge: Cambridge University Press 1985). I consider civic humanism in relation to Petrarch and the Renaissance coteries in my first chapter, and commercial humanism in relation to the rejection of classicism in my fifth chapter.

35 With the huge popular success of works like Allan Bloom's *The Closing of the American Mind* (New York: Simon and Schuster 1987) and Harold Bloom's *The Western Canon* (New York: Harcourt Brace 1994),

the canon debates have become a boon industry in academic publishing. Useful compilations of position papers on the topic include *Canons*, ed. Robert von Hallberg (Chicago: University of Chicago Press 1984), *The Hospitable Canon: Essays on Literary Play, Scholarly Choice, and Popular Pressures*, ed. Virgil Nemoianu and Robert Royal (Philadelphia: Benjamins 1991), and *Falling into Theory: Conflicting Views on Reading Literature*, ed. David H. Richter (Boston: Bedford Books 1994). The theory of canonicity and canon-formation, however, has only recently begun to receive extended treatments. I have already noted important works by Guillory, Bourdieu, Kermode, Frow, Herrnstein Smith, Connor, and Harris. To these may be added Charles Altieri's *Canons and Consequences: Reflections on the Ethical Force of Imaginative Ideals* (Evanston, Ill.: Northwestern University Press 1990), and Michael Bérubé's *Marginal Forces / Cultural Centers: Tolson, Pynchon, and the Politics of the Canon* (Ithaca, N.Y.: Cornell University Press 1992).

CHAPTER ONE

1 Richard McKeon, "Canonic Books and Prohibited Books: Orthodoxy and Heresy in Religion and Culture," *Critical Inquiry* 2 (1975): 792.

2 See Jack Goody, "What's in a List?" in *The Domestication of the Savage Mind* (Cambridge: Cambridge University Press 1977), 74–111.

3 Ernst Robert Curtius, *European Literature and the Latin Middle Ages*, trans. Willard R. Trask (New York: Harper and Row 1963), 256, 396. Frank Kermode examines how canons present fictional "packages" in *History and Value* (Oxford: Clarendon Press 1988), 109–27.

4 Bourdieu defines gesturing in this way as "a truth whose sole meaning and function are to deny a truth known and recognized by all, a lie which would deceive no one, were not everyone determined to deceive *himself*," in *Outline of a Theory of Practice*, trans. Richard Nice (Cambridge: Cambridge University Press 1977), 133. Elsewhere, Bourdieu analogizes misrecognition to a willing suspension of disbelief, rather like how an audience responds to a magic show, save that the codes of misrecognition are operative throughout the "whole logic" of a discipline or field of activity (*The Rules of Art: Genesis and Structure of the Literary Field*, trans. Susan Emanuel [Stanford, Calif.: Stanford University Press 1996], 169).

5 Michel Foucault, *Language, Counter-Memory, Practice*, ed. Donald F. Bouchard, trans. D.F. Bouchard and Sherry Simon (Ithaca, N.Y.: Cornell University Press 1977), 73.

6 On aesthetic self-legitimation within modern literary systems, see Pierre Bourdieu, *The Field of Cultural Production*, ed. Randal Johnson (New York: Columbia University Press 1993), 115–20.

7 "Widsith," in J. Duncan Spaeth's partial translation, in *Old English Poetry: Translations into Alliterative Verse* (New York: Gordian Press 1967), 76–7.

8 On *Widsith* as a begging poem, see Norman E. Eliason, "Two OE Scop Poems," *PMLA* 81 (1966): 185–92. On *Widsith* and Christianity, see Robert P. Creed, "Widsith's Journey through Germanic Tradition," *Anglo-Saxon Poetry: Essays in Appreciation*, ed. Lewis E. Nicholson and Dolores Warwick Free (Notre Dame, Ind.: University of Notre Dame Press 1975), 386.

9 Walter Benjamin, "The Work of Art in the Age of Mechanical Reproduction," in *Illuminations*, ed. Hannah Arendt, trans. Harry Zohn (New York: Harcourt 1968; New York: Shocken 1969), 223.

10 "Deor," *Anglo-Saxon Poetic Records III: The Exeter Book*, ed. George Philip Krapp and Elliott van Kirk Dobbie (New York: Columbia University Press 1936), 179.

11 For early Christian commentators, God was not merely the author of all created things but the only possible source of inspiration for human writings. See A.J. Minnis, *Medieval Theory of Authorship* (London: Scolar Press 1984), 36–9.

12 The idea is implicit in another of Benjamin's dicta: "In every era the attempt must be made anew to wrest tradition away from a conformism that is about to overpower it" (*Illuminations*, 255).

13 Bede, *Ecclesiastical History of the English People*, ed. Bertram Colgrave and R.A.B. Mynors (Oxford: Clarendon Press 1969), 415.

14 Seth Lerer analyses Bede's story of Caedmon, Aelfric's use of literary authorities, and Alfred's learning projects as examples of canon-making in *Literacy and Power in Anglo-Saxon Literature* (Lincoln: University of Nebraska Press 1991), 1–3, 34–5, 56–9.

15 Alcuin, in his selective catalogue of the library at York (*c.* 780), placed Aldhelm and Bede immediately following his list of patristic *auctores* and invoked pagan symbolism to describe how Aelberht trained students "to blow on the Castalian pipe, / And run with lyric step over the peaks of Parnassus" (*Versus de Patribus Regibus et Sanctis Euboriencis Ecclesiae*, ed. Peter Godman [Oxford: Clarendon Press 1982], 125, 113). For centuries such rhetoric had been uttered with little seriousness by most poets. The more conventional gesture was to abjure the mythology and to declare, rhetorically, a belief in moral truth over creative eloquence: Aldhelm, prefacing his *Aenigmata* (*c.* 700), echoed Persius in denying that he ever slept on Parnassus (*Poetic Works*, ed. Michael Lapidge and James L. Rosier [Cambridge: Cambridge University Press 1985], 70). Still, the image of an Englishman on Parnassus suggests that even indigenous *auctors* could be treated as moderns to be judged by the standard of the ancients. William of Malmsbury, in

his ecclesiastical history of England (*c.* 1125), praised Aldhelm's sermons for how well their "English solemnity" were enlivened by "Greek acumen" and "Roman elegance" (*De Gestis Pontificum Anglorum,* 5 vols., ed. N.E.S.A. Hamilton [London 1870], 4:336). On the scholarly reading of Old English texts at Worcester, see Christine Franzen, *The Tremulous Hand of Worcester* (Oxford: Oxford University Press 1993).

16 The shift that McKeon identified in the history of Christian doctrine, which I cited in my introduction (see p. 7), had by this time become institutionalized, with the symbolic value of scriptural and patristic writings, now perceived as works requiring special skills of interpretation, having been almost fully converted to the Church's equivalent of intellectual capital.

17 As Minnis points out (*Medieval Theory of Authorship,* 9–39, 73–117), this was the dominant view of authorship during most of the Middle Ages, though the *auctor* system was probably more rigid in principle than in practice: "The term *auctor,*" Minnis writes, "may be profitably regarded as an accolade bestowed upon a popular writer by those later scholars and writers who used extracts from his works as sententious statements or *auctoritates,* gave lectures on his works in the form of textual commentaries, or employed them as literary models" (10).

18 As the medieval curriculum was structured around specialist disciplines (the trivium and quadrivium) that emphasized the truth content of works rather than their formal attributes, poetry played a very limited role in the instruction of grammar. Only later, with the establishment of a humanist curriculum, with its canon of classical texts and *copia* of literary techniques, would poetry regain the pedagogical prestige it had enjoyed under classical rhetoric. See John Guillory, *Cultural Capital: The Problem of Literary Canon Formation* (Chicago: University of Chicago Press 1993), 70–2. It has been suggested, however, that the copying of the Anglo-Saxon poetic *codices* may have been undertaken to promote instruction in English. Patrick Wormald entertains this possibility in "Anglo-Saxon Society and its Literature," in *The Cambridge Companion to Old English Literature,* ed. Malcolm Godden and Michael Lapidge (Cambridge: Cambridge University Press 1991), 18.

19 Giraldus Cambrensis, *Historical Works,* trans. Thomas Wright (London 1863), 4–5.

20 Walter Map, *De Nugis Curialium,* ed. and trans. M.R. James, C.N.L. Brooke, and R.A.B. Mynors (Oxford: Clarendon Press 1983), 405, 313. On the erroneous attribution of Map's work, see Minnis, *Medieval Theory of Authorship,* 10–11.

21 The pathologizing of the Other is a theme common to early varieties of Renaissance New Historicism, notably Stephen Greenblatt in his *Renaissance Self-Fashioning* (Chicago: University of Chicago Press, 1980),

where he records examples of pathologizing at its fiercest: "Self-fashioning is achieved in relation to something perceived as alien, strange, or hostile. This threatening Other – heretic, savage, witch, adulteress, traitor, Antichrist – must be discovered or invented in order to be attacked and destroyed" (9). Barbara Herrnstein Smith has argued that "the privileging of the self through the pathologizing of the Other remains the key move and defining objective of axiology," in *Contingencies of Value* (Cambridge, Mass.: Harvard University Press 1988), 38.

22 Map, *De Nugis Curialium*, 405.

23 Donald E. Pease, "Author," in *Critical Terms for Literary Study*, ed. Frank Lentricchia and Thomas McLaughlin (Chicago: University of Chicago Press 1990), 107.

24 Alastair Fowler describes varieties of generic modulation, and revisions to the generic hierarchy, in *Kinds of Literature: An Introduction to the Theory of Genres and Modes* (Cambridge, Mass.: Harvard University Press 1982), esp. chaps. 11 and 12.

25 Michel de Certeau has emphasized how popular culture obscures the distinction between production and consumption because its "making" at once defies textuality and emphasizes "tactics" of appropriation whereby the lower orders make use of official culture for their own ends and interests. Official culture cannot, in this sense, fully contain popular culture because the latter represents an alternative form of production: "A rationalized, expansionist, centralized, spectacular and clamorous production is confronted by an entirely different kind of production, called 'consumption,' and characterized by its ruses, its fragmentation (the result of the circumstances), its poaching, its clandestine nature, its tireless but quiet activity, in short by its quasi-invisibility, since it shows itself not in its own products (where would it place them?) but in an art of using those imposed on it" (*The Practice of Everyday Life*, trans. Steven Rendall [Berkeley: University of California Press 1984], 31). Certeau's remarks on the topic are evocative, but their familiar polarization of high and low render popular culture merely parasitic upon official culture, and they ignore the equally complex processes of consumption that ensure the reproduction of official culture.

26 Geoffrey Chaucer, "Sir Thopas", ll. 897–900, in *The Riverside Chaucer*, ed. Larry D. Benson, 3rd ed. (Boston: Houghton Mifflin 1987), 216. Subsequent references are to book and line number.

27 See Paul Strohm, "Chaucer's Audience," *Literature and History* 5 (1977): 26–41.

28 Anne Middleton examines the social and literary ideals of this new group in "Chaucer's 'New Men' and the Good of Literature in the

Canterbury Tales," in *Literature and Society*, ed. Edward Said (Baltimore, Md.: Johns Hopkins University Press 1980), 15–56. Middleton cautions that the phrase "new men" is usually reserved "for those lower gentry and civil and legal professionals who attained office and privilege in significant numbers under the Tudors," but, she adds, their cultural ideals were broadly similar to those of Chaucer's audience and pilgrims (15). It is perhaps equally anachronistic to refer to these ideals as civic humanism, an ideology that, in the fourteenth century, was only beginning to be formulated in Italy. Yet these ideals were broadly humanistic insofar as they emphasized the moral virtue of the individual and not the perpetuation of universal order.

29 Alvin Kernan, *The Imaginary Library* (Princeton, N.J.: Princeton University Press 1982), 37.

30 "Laureate" is Richard Helgerson's term, in *Self-Crowned Laureates: Spenser, Jonson, Milton and the Literary System* (Berkeley: University of California Press 1983). Helgerson identifies three separate categories of authorship in the literary system of the Renaissance: amateurs like Sidney and Donne, laureates like Spenser and Milton, and theatrical professionals like Shakespeare. Laureates and amateurs, unlike the professionals, were schooled in a tradition of civic humanism, which taught them the importance of using their poetic abilities in the service of a public life. Laureates and amateurs "differed, however, in how they hoped to accomplish that service – the amateurs as churchmen and statesmen, the laureates as poets. For the amateur, poetry was ... a way of displaying abilities that could, once they had come to the attention of a powerful patron, be better employed in some other manner. For the laureate, poetry was itself a means of making a contribution to the order and improvement of the state" (29). Laureates also differed from amateurs in actively publicizing their activity and in seeking out canonization.

31 To be precise, the ideology of civic humanism represents a dominant set of socio-political values within rhetorical culture but does not encompass all possible forms of symbolic capital within this culture. The auctorial order presented its own set of institutionalized values, yet still operated according to the modes of rhetorical thinking.

32 J.G.A. Pocock's *The Machiavellian Moment: Florentine Political Thought and the Atlantic Republican Tradition* (Princeton, N.J.: Princeton University Press 1975) provides the fullest history of civic humanism in its later articulations.

33 Quoted in Minnis, *Medieval Theory of Authorship*, 212.

34 Because rhetoric was taught to young males being trained in public decision making, it became associated with masculine puberty rites; its elaborate codes and formalities were compared to jousting and other

forms of male chivalry, and its study was linked to the development of masculine courage. See Walter J. Ong, *Rhetoric, Romance, and Technology* (Ithaca, N.Y.: Cornell University Press 1971), 14–15.

35 See Theodor E. Mommsen's classic essay, "Petrarch's Conception of the 'Dark Ages,'" *Speculum* 17 (1942): 226–42.

36 On how "purification" often underscores claims for modernity and cultural distinction, see Bourdieu, *The Field of Cultural Production*, 187–91.

37 Hans Robert Jauss, *Aesthetic Experience and Literary Hermeneutics*, trans. Michael Shaw (Minneapolis: University of Minnesota Press 1982), 260.

38 This is the version of Benjamin's paradox that Paul de Man sees as disabling any assertion of modernity, in "Literary History and Literary Modernity," *Blindness and Insight*, 2nd ed. (Minneapolis: University of Minnesota Press 1983), 142–65.

39 Richard de Bury, *Philobiblon*, trans. Archer Taylor (Berkeley: University of California Press 1948), 61.

40 John Gower, *Works*, ed. C.G. Macaulay, 4 vols. (Oxford: Oxford University Press 1899–1902), 2:2.

41 Gower, *Works*, 2:1.

42 David Piper describes the tomb in *The Image of the Poet: British Poets and their Portraits* (Oxford: Clarendon Press 1982), 11.

43 Gower, *Works*, 2:2–4.

44 On Gower's editorial practices, see Derek Pearsall, "The Gower Tradition," in *Gower's "Confessio Amantis,"* ed. A.J. Minnis (Cambridge, U.K.: D.S. Brewer 1983), 182–4.

45 The verses are reprinted in C.G. Macaulay's edition of Gower's *English Works*, 2 vols. (London: EETS 1901), 2:479.

46 Translation quoted from Russell A. Peck's edition of Gower's *Confessio Amantis* (Toronto: University of Toronto Press 1980), 494n.1.

47 A.J. Minnis contrasts the good-humouredness of Gower's poem to the poet's conventional claims of *auctoritas* in the commentary. See *"De Vulgari Auctoritate*: Chaucer, Gower and the Men of Great Authority," in *Chaucer and Gower: Difference, Mutuality, Exchange*, ed. R.F. Yeager (Victoria, B.C.: English Literary Studies 1991), 51–63.

48 See Minnis, *Medieval Theory of Authorship*, 177–90.

49 See Chaucer's prologue to his *Treatise of the Astrolabe* (*Works*, 661).

50 On Chaucer's use of these terms, see Glending Olson, "Making and Poetry in the Age of Chaucer," *Comparative Literature* 31 (1979): 272–90.

51 A.C. Spearing writes that Chaucer's use of apostrophes and invocations expresses "a revealing and amusing tension (and it was always an important part of Chaucer's skill to make his difficulties into a matter for amusement); for he is fascinated by this new conception of the vernacular poet as prophet, yet he cannot quite adopt the role as

wholeheartedly as Dante does" (*Medieval to Renaissance in English Poetry* [Cambridge: Cambridge University Press 1985], 24).

52 For versions of this argument, see Middleton, "Chaucer's 'New Men,'" 17–18, and Alice S. Miskimin, *The Renaissance Chaucer* (New Haven, Conn.: Yale University Press 1975), 122.

53 George Kane, *Chaucer* (Oxford: Oxford University Press 1984), 36.

54 Proposing candidates for whom Chaucer really intended as his "man of great auctoritee" is one of the great pastimes of Chaucer criticism, though I am inclined to agree with A.J. Minnis that the the figure's precise referent is less significant than the man's lack of identity. Minnis thinks Chaucer had in mind a fictive *auctor* with no known book, such as his Lollius from *Troilus* ("*De Vulgari Auctoritate*," 45). I would suggest rather that Chaucer is acknowledging the venerable yet fading aura of *auctoritas* just prior to its historical disappearance. Jacqueline T. Miller offers a reading of the poem's ending similar to mine: the "*House of Fame* breaks off, perhaps concludes, before this ambiguous figure of authority speaks or acts, but the poem as it stands has worked to show that no authority can maintain its status or offer an unassailable system upon which an author may safely rest when called upon to justify the legitimacy of his art ... The narrator's silence at the end acknowledges the limitations of his own voice but also recognizes and predicts the inevitable failure of the 'man of gret auctorite' to maintain his status, and it recalls the evidence of similar failures that have occurred throughout the poem. No truly authoritative voice has been discovered; no authorial stance can be validated; and the poetic voice and enterprise end" (*Poetic License: Authority and Authorship in Medieval and Renaissance Contexts* [New York: Oxford University Press 1986], 69–71).

55 Thomas Hoccleve, *The Regement of Princes* (1412), quoted in *Five Hundred Years of Chaucer Criticism and Allusion (1357–1900)*, ed. Caroline F.E. Spurgeon, 3 vols. (Cambridge: Cambridge University Press 1925), 1:21.

56 "The Life of Our Lady," ll. 1628–35, as reprinted in Spurgeon ed., *Chaucer Criticism*, 1:19.

57 *The Court of Sapience*, in Spurgeon ed., *Chaucer Criticism*, 1:16, where it is attributed to Lydgate.

58 Lois A. Ebin provides an exhaustive survey of these terms in *Illuminator, Makar, Vates: Visions of Poetry in the Fifteenth Century* (Lincoln: University of Nebraska Press 1988).

59 *Book of Curtesye* (ll. 400–1, 405–6), ed. F.J. Furnivall (London: EETS 1868), 41.

60 David Lawton, "Dullness and the Fifteenth Century," *ELH* 54 (1987): 791, 787.

61 John Walton, trans. of Boethius's *De Consolatione Philosophiae*, in Spurgeon ed., *Chaucer Criticism*, 1:20.

62 Seth Lerer, who provides a full account of Chaucer's canonization in the fifteenth century, argues that these poets' efforts involved "the projection rather than enactment of laureate performance – a self-fashioning not of professional or amateur, but of the patronized and the subservient" (*Chaucer and His Readers: Imagining the Author in Late-Medieval England* [Princeton, N.J.: Princeton University Press 1993], 5).

63 Lawton, "Dullness and the Fifteenth Century," 793.

64 John H. Fisher, "A Language Policy for Lancastrian England," *PMLA* 107 (1992): 1170.

65 John Shirley, headnote (*c.* 1450) to Chaucer's "The Knight's Tale," in Spurgeon ed., *Chaucer Criticism*, 1:54.

66 William Dunbar, *Poems*, ed. James Kinsley (Oxford: Clarendon Press 1979), 37.

67 Lydgate, *Life of Our Lady*, in Spurgeon ed., *Chaucer Criticism*, 1:20; *Fall of Princes*, ll. 153–4, quoted in Richard Firth Green, *Poets and Prince-pleasers: Literature and the English Court in the Late Middle Ages* (Toronto: University of Toronto Press 1980), 148.

68 Osbern Bokenham, *Legend of St. Margaret* (*c.* 1450), ed. Mary S. Serjeantson (London: EETS 1938), 12.

69 John Skelton, "Philip Sparrow" (*c.* 1507), ll. 784–5, 800–7, in *Complete English Poems*, ed. John Scattergood (Penguin 1983), 91.

70 Skelton, *Garlande of Laurell*, ll. 442–6, in *Complete English Poems*, 324.

71 On Skelton's poem as a personal and political catharsis, see Alistair Fox, *Politics and Literature in the Reigns of Henry VII and Henry VIII* (Oxford: Blackwell 1989), 191–200.

72 Skelton used the self-appelation (*vates ille / De quo loquntur mille*) in the epigraph to *Why Come Ye Nat to Courte?* (1522), in *Complete English Poems*, 311.

73 Skelton, *Garlande of Laurell*, ll. 404–6, in *Complete English Poems*, 323. Andrew Hadfield equates Skelton's revisionism with Derrida's notion of the supplement, as the new self-crowned laureate "is both to work as an adjunct to [the tradition] and to overgo it" (*Literature, Politics and National Identity* [Cambridge: Cambridge University Press 1994], 29).

74 Thomas Berthelet, preface to his 1532 edition of Gower's *Confessio Amantis*, in Spurgeon ed., *Chaucer Criticism*, 1:78.

75 Sir Brian Tuke, preface to William Thynne's 1532 edition of Chaucer's *Works*, in Spurgeon ed., *Chaucer Criticism*, 1:80.

76 Stephen Hawes, *The Passetyme of Pleasure*, ed. William Edward Mead (London: EETS 1928), 54–5.

77 Alcuin's epistles on the raid have been edited by Colin Chase, in *Two Alcuin Letter-Books* (Toronto: Centre for Medieval Studies 1975), 50–6.

78 John Bale, ed., *The laboryouse Journey & serche of Johan Leylande, for Englandes Antiquitees ... with declaracyons enlarged* (London 1549; rpt. Amsterdam: Theatrum Orbis Terrarum 1975), sig. A7ᵥ. This work, hereafter cited as *laboryouse Journey,* contains Leland's "New Year's Gift" of 1546/7 to Henry VIII, to which Bale has added extensive commentary.

79 John Leland, letter to Thomas Cromwell, dated 16 July 1536, quoted in part in Anthony à Wood, *Athenae Oxonienses,* ed. Philip Bliss, 3 vols. (London 1813), 1: col. 198. Wood notes that he saw the original letter "among the papers of state," but it has since been lost.

80 Though these catalogues offer generally reliable information, especially about post-Conquest writings, their utility for modern scholars has been eclipsed by the antiquaries' notebooks, which contain valuable library references and some tantalizing quoted extracts unobscured by commentary. One of Bale's notebooks has been edited by Reginald Lane Poole and Mary Bateson under the title *Index Britanniae Scriptorum,* in *Anecdota Oxoniensia* 9 (Oxford: Clarendon Press 1902).

81 In addition to the sources noted above, see Bale's letter to Matthew Parker, dated 30 July 1560, edited by H.R. Luard in *Cambridge Antiquarian Communications* 3 (1864–76): 157–73. It is impossible to get even an approximate figure on how many books were destroyed or dispersed, but it is clear that the losses were very heavy. C.E. Wright surveys some of these losses in "The Dispersal of the Monastic Libraries and the Beginnings of Anglo-Saxon Studies. Matthew Parker and his Circle: A Preliminary Study," *Transactions of the Cambridge Bibliographical Society* 1 (1951): 208–37; and "The Dispersal of the Libraries in the Sixteenth Century," in *The English Library before 1700,* ed. Francis Wormald and C.E. Wright (London: Athlone Press 1958), 148–75.

82 Antonia McLean has noted "there is no proof that the state was directly responsible for the loss or destruction of books on a large scale. The monastic libraries were dispersed through government indifference rather than by deliberate intention." *Humanism and the Rise of Science in Tudor England* (New York: Neale Watson Academic Publications 1972), 90. Clearly, however, the policy of Dissolution helped to undermine the entire system of book preservation that had existed throughout the medieval period.

83 Wood, *Athenae Oxonienses,* 1: col. 198.

84 Extending a tradition of medieval cataloguers dating back to St Jerome, Leland and Bale drew upon previous attempts in England at producing bibliographical records of library contents. In the fourteenth century, a monk at Bury St Edmunds compiled a catalogue which surveyed the lives and works of 674 authors, "for the use and convenience of students and preachers." See R.H. Rouse, "Bostonus

Burienses and the Author of the *Catalogus Scriptorum Ecclesiae*," *Speculum* 41 (1966): 471–99. Bale's catalogue includes an entry describing the "Herculean labours" of one Alan of Lynn, a fifteenth-century Carmelite prior who is reputed to have indexed all available copies in England of important medieval works (*Illustrium Maioris Britanniae Scriptorum ... Summarium* ["Ipswich," i.e. Wesel, 1548], 185). And Bale, before his conversion, wrote a sizable "bio-bibliographical" study of the literature of his fellow Carmelites, the as yet unpublished *Anglorum Heliades* (1536). On this work, see Leslie P. Fairfield, *John Bale, Mythmaker for the English Reformation* (West Lafayette, Ind.: Purdue University Press 1976), 50–3.

85 In his New Year's Gift (*laboryouse Journey*, sig. C7ᵥ), Leland indicated that he had given his catalogue the Petrarchan title "*De Viris Illustribus*," though it would be later retitled as *Commentarii de Scriptoribus Britannicis* (2 vols., 1709) by the Oxford printer Anthony Hall.

86 Bale, ed., *laboryouse Journey*, sig. A2ᵥ.

87 Bale, *Summarium*, 6–8. These imaginative accounts of England's origins were a rejoinder to similar propaganda made on behalf of other nations, such as a number of French claims that had declared the erudition of Gallic bards superior even to Roman learning. For more on this contest of bards, see Herbert Weisinger, "Who began the Revival of Learning?" *Papers of the Michigan Academy of Science, Arts and Letters* 30 (1944): 625–38. One episode related to this contest was the so-called Debate of the Heralds, where spokesmen from England and France boasted of their respective nation's glories, canons of learned men and women included. A contemporary of Bale's, John Coke, fired one of the last shots in this debate, in *The Debate between the Heralds of England and France*, rptd. with *Le Débat des Hérauts D'Armes de France et D'Angleterre*, ed. Léopold Pannier and M. Paul Meyer (Paris 1877).

88 Bale, ed., *laboryouse Journey*, sig. B2ᵣ.

89 Leland, "New Year's Gift," in Bale, ed., *laboryouse Journey*, sig. D5ᵥ.

90 Bale, ed., *laboryouse Journey*, sig. H5ᵥ.

91 Leland, "New Year's Gift," in Bale, ed., *laboryouse Journey*, sig. C5ᵥ.

92 Bale, manuscript note in his epitome of Leland's *De Viris Illustribus*, quoted in Fairfield, *John Bale*, 116.

93 Once the reformers had achieved political power, observes F. Smith Fussner, it became incumbent upon Protestant apologists like Bale "to justify the origins of authority by appealing to history, largely because Protestant churches were not *institutionally* legitimized by tradition or history in the sense that the Roman Catholic Church was," in *Tudor History and the Historians* (New York: Basic Books 1970), 293n.92. Emphasis in original.

94 J.G.A. Pocock, *Politics, Language and Time: Essays on Political Thought and History* (New York: Atheneum 1971; rpt. Chicago: University of Chicago Press 1989), 179–80.

95 Bale, *The vocacyon of Johan Bale to the bishoprick of Ossorie in Irelande* ("Rome," i.e. Wesel, 1553), sig. B3$_r$.

96 Bale, *vocacyon*, sig. B7$_r$.

97 Leland, "New Year's Gift," in Bale, ed., *laboryouse Journey*, sig. B8$_r$.

98 Leland's interest in antiquities may have predated the Dissolution, having developed out of his early acquaintance with continental humanist scholars. This view is supported in general terms by Joseph M. Levine, who states flatly that the "antiquarian impulse was born of the revival of antiquity," in *Humanism and History: Origins of Modern English Historiography* (Ithaca, N.Y.: Cornell University Press 1987), 73. Antonia Gransden offers the counter-argument that "ultimately the alterations which took place in historical writing were less the result of ideas derived from the study of the classics, than of political and religious exigencies." See *Historical Writing in England*, 2 vols. (London: Routledge and Kegan Paul 1974–82), 2:469.

99 Leland, "New Year's Gift," in Bale, ed., *laboryouse Journey*, sig. C2$_r$-C3$_r$.

100 Leland, "New Year's Gift," in Bale, ed., *laboryouse Journey*, sig. D7$_v$.

101 Bale, ed., *laboryouse Journey*, sig. B4$_r$.

102 Leland, *Commentarii*, 421–2.

103 See, for example, John Leland's elegy on Wyatt, *Naeniae in mortem Thomae Viati equitis incomparibilis* (London 1542), esp. sig. A4$_v$.

104 Leland, *Commentarii*, 428. Quoted from translation given in John H. Fisher, *John Gower: Moral Philosopher and Friend of Chaucer* (New York: New York University Press 1964), 14.

105 Bale, ed., *laboryouse Journey*, sig. G3$_r$.

106 Bale, *Scriptorum Illustrium maioris Brytanniae ... Catalogus*, 2 vols. (Basel, 1557–59), 1:526. Quoted from translation given in Spurgeon, *Chaucer Criticism*, 3:26.

107 Bale, *Summarium*, fol. 154$_v$.

108 Bale, ed., *laboryouse Journey*, sig. H6$_r$.

109 Bale, *Summarium*, fol. 154$_v$.

110 Bale, ed., *laboryouse Journey*, sig. H5$_v$.

111 Bale, ed., *laboryouse Journey*, sig. "Cv$_{r-v}$" (i.e., C3$_{r-v}$).

112 John Foxe, *Acts and Monuments*, ed. George Townsend, 8 vols. (London, 1843–49), 3:720.

113 Bale, ed., *laboryouse Journey*, sig. F6$_r$. Protestant controversialists greatly exaggerated the Catholic aversion to printing. As Eamon Duffy has shown, "tens of thousands of Latin primers," in addition to numerous liturgical books and devotional tracts, were produced by English

presses prior to the 1530s. See *The Stripping of the Altars: Traditional Religion in England, c.1400–c.1580* (New Haven, Conn.: Yale University Press 1992), 77–87.

114 Bale, ed., *laboryouse Journey*, sig. F8$_v$.

115 Benedict Anderson, *Imagined Communities*, 2nd ed. (London: Verso 1991), 46.

116 Even then, the old manuscripts possessed little value for scholars trained in the New Learning. The universities may not have discouraged the destruction. As Bale suggested, the schools were "not all clere in this detestable fact" (*laboryouse Journey*, sig. B$_v$). In a letter dated 12 September 1535, Cromwell's most ruthless henchman, Richard Layton, proudly reported that he had seen the works of Duns Scotus "banished" from Oxford, the "leaves of Dun" left to blow in the wind or used as "blawnsherres" (scare-sheets) to frighten away the deer (in G.H. Cook, ed., *Letters to Cromwell and others on the Suppression of the Monasteries* [London: John Baker 1965], 46).

117 On the dispersal of Bale's library, see Honor McCusker, "Books and Manuscripts Formerly in the Possession of John Bale," *The Library*, 4th ser., 16 (1936): 144–65.

118 On Leland's activities on behalf of the Royal Library, see J.R. Liddell, "'Leland's' Lists of Manuscripts in Lincolnshire Monasteries," *English Historical Review* 54 (1939): 88–95.

119 Bale, ed., *laboryouse Journey*, sig. D3$_v$.

120 Bale admitted that some of the violence was caused by "men godly mynded" who laid waste indiscriminately to all they could get their hands on in the abbeys. His "declaracyons" appended to Leland's "New Year's Gift" were thus meant in part as a plea to the English not to emulate the harmful "fury or frantycke madnesse of the Anabaptistes" and other fanatical groups (*laboryouse Journey*, sigs. E8$_v$–G2$_v$).

121 "A Short View of the State of Knowledge, Literature, and Taste, in this Country, from the Accession of King Edward I to ... Henry IV," *New Annual Register for the year 1784* (London 1785), xii.

122 None of Paston's books have survived. Paston's list is reprinted in *Chaucer: The Critical Heritage*, ed. Derek Brewer, 2 vols. (London: Routledge and Kegan Paul 1978), 1:70–1.

123 Richard Tottel, pref. to *Songes and Sonettes, written by the ryght honourable Lorde Henry Haward late Earle of Surrey, and other* (1557), rptd. as *Tottel's Miscellany*, ed. Hyder E. Rollins, 2nd ed., 2 vols. (Cambridge, Mass.: Harvard University Press 1965), 1:2.

124 "Until recent times," Walter J. Ong has remarked, "the rhetorical tradition, which, with the allied dialectical or logical tradition, dominated most written as well as oral expression, helped in the fictionalizing of the audience of learned works in a generic but quite real way. Rhetoric

fixed knowledge in agonistic structures ... From Augustine through Thomas Aquinas and Christian Wolff, writers of treatises generally proceeded in adversary fashion, their readers being cast as participants in rhetorical contests or in dialectical scholastic disputations" (*Interfaces of the Word* [Ithaca, N.Y.: Cornell University Press 1977], 76).

125 Arthur F. Marotti suggests that, by exhorting his readers "to learn to be more skilfull," Tottel "implicitly accepts a model of intellectual and moral self-improvement that is basic to print culture and to developing notions of social progress" (*Manuscript, Print, and the English Renaissance Lyric* [Ithaca, N.Y.: Cornell University Press 1995], 215). Yet exhortations like these had been common in rhetorical addresses to audiences since antiquity. Tottel in fact confronts his readers with conflicting signals: he assures them of the poetry's courtly origins and yet implies that they have a right to possess this material, he scolds the unlearned for their rudeness yet equally condemns the poetry's courtly owners as "ungentle," and he promotes his volume in terms of readerly "profit" and yet defends it by calling upon the aid of learned readers who, presumably, do not require further self-improvement. As Mary Thomas Crane suggests, Tottel's gestures evince "the mixed attitude of humanist logic and rhetoric, promising to make available to the public a form of discourse that is both common and uncommon, public and private, enabling and controlling" (*Framing Authority: Sayings, Self, and Society in Sixteenth-Century England* [Princeton, N.J.: Princeton University Press 1993], 168).

126 Robert Weimann has identified this cultural objectification of values as the primary function of canon-formation: "As a cultural institution, a literary canon may be defined as a publicly circulating, usable body of writing which, by definition, is held to be as much representative of certain national or social interests and traditions as it is unrepresentative and exclusive of others. In fact, the very representativity of this privileged body of writing appears as a sine qua non for its function as a tradition or heritage, for receiving and projecting patterns of social, cultural, and national identity" ("Shakespeare (De)Canonized: Conflicting Uses of 'Authority' and 'Representation,'" *New Literary History* 20 [1988]: 68). I derive the phrase "evaluative community" from both Benedict Anderson's notion of "imagined communities" and Stanley Fish's theory of "interpretive communities."

127 Gary Waller, *English Poetry of the Sixteenth Century* (London: Longman 1986), 44.

128 See J.W. Saunders's classic essay, "The Stigma of Print: A Note on the Social Bases of Tudor Poetry," *Essays in Criticism* 1 (1951): 139–64. Stephen W. May questions whether this stigma was consistently observed in practice, in "Tudor Aristocrats and the 'Stigma of Print,'"

Renaissance Papers (1980), 11–18. Whatever the practice, the stigma was clearly a common self-defining gesture among courtly authors. Wendy Wall considers how the gesture often involved gendered metaphors of intimacy and transgression, in "Disclosures in Print: The 'Violent Enlargement' of the Renaissance Voyeuristic Text," *Studies in English Literature* 29 (1989): 35–59, and more generally in *The Imprint of Gender: Authorship and Publication in the English Renaissance* (Ithaca, N.Y.: Cornell University Press 1993).

129 As Gary Waller suggests, Tottel's anthology "became part of the courtly consciousness. It became an essential guide to the kinds and modes of poetry that would deck out the aspiring courtier's taste" (*English Poetry of the Sixteenth Century*, 21).

130 Walter Benjamin suggests that the aura of work, its unique value, "has its basis in ritual, the location of its original use value," in *Illuminations*, ed. Hannah Arendt, 224.

131 For more on the desirability of scribal idiosyncracy in manuscript publication, see David R. Carlson, *English Humanist Books: Writers and Patrons, Manuscript and Print, 1475–1525* (Toronto: University of Toronto Press 1993), 118–21. Carlson cites the example of the printer Colard Mansion, who bankrupted his business by trying to imitate scribal irregularities through a multiplicity of fonts. On the commercialization of manuscript dissemination, see Harold Love, *Scribal Publication in Seventeenth-Century England* (Oxford: Clarendon Press 1993), 35–89.

132 Robert Darnton, *The Kiss of Lamourette: Reflections in Cultural History* (New York: Norton 1990), 157. The processes of reading were, however, discussed insofar as they related to the widely cultivated arts of memory.

133 Robert L. Montgomery surveys some of these reader-oriented instrumentalist arguments in *The Reader's Eye: Studies in Didactic Literary Theory from Dante to Tasso* (Berkeley: University of California Press 1979).

134 Thomas Blundeville, *The true order and method of writing and reading hystories* (London 1574), sigs. H2$_v$-H3$_r$.

135 George Puttenham, *The Arte of English Poesie* (London 1589), 132.

136 An important exception were the Catholic authorities and reformist polemicists who believed that the greater textual uniformity and dissemination afforded by print offered the means to create a harmonious religious community centred around a corpus of canonical reading matter. On Reformation attempts to create a corporate culture based on a printed canon of "Great Books," see John N. Wall, Jr, "The Reformation in England and the Typographical Revolution: 'By this printing ... the

doctrine of the Gospel soundeth to all nations,'" in *Print and Culture in The Renaissance,* ed. Gerald P. Tyson and Sylvia S. Wagonheim (Newark: University of Delaware Press 1986), 208–21. On Catholic publishing practices, see Eamon Duffy, *The Stripping of the Altars,* 77–87.

137 Marotti examines several of these "answer" poems in terms of the "social textuality" of manuscript dissemination (*Manuscript, Print, and the English Renaissance Lyric,* 159–71).

138 As Walter Benjamin suggests (*Illuminations,* 224), mechanical reproduction does not necessarily lead to "democracy," but it does make the question of determining artistic excellence a matter of politics rather than ritual.

139 Elizabeth L. Eisenstein, *The Printing Press as an Agent of Change,* 2 vols. (Cambridge: Cambridge University Press 1979), 1:229.

140 Richard Smith, "The Printer in commendation of Gascoigne and his workes," pref. to George Gascoigne, *The Posies,* 2nd ed. (1575) sig. ¶¶¶¶iij$_v$.

141 Puttenham, *Arte of English Poesie,* 6.

142 Stefano Guazzo, *The Civile Conversation,* trans. George Pettie (1574), quoted in Frank Whigham, "Interpretation at Court: Courtesy and the Performer-Audience Dialectic," *New Literary History* 14 (1983): 630.

143 Sir Philip Sidney, *The Defence of Poesie,* Ponsonby ed. (London 1595), sig. H2$_v$. Daniel Javitch has suggested that the growth of English poetry in the later sixteenth century was stimulated by both the Tudor court's preference for the vernacular and, more significantly, by the stylistic pressures which the court exerted, pressures that favoured the informality and playfulness of poetic discourse over the rigours of classical oratory. Poetry was thus considered the ideal vehicle for the social conversation of the Tudor courtiers. See Javitch, *Poetry and Courtliness in Renaissance England* (Princeton, N.J.: Princeton University Press 1978), 15.

144 J.G.A. Pocock, *Virtue, Commerce, and History* (Cambridge: Cambridge University Press 1985), 42.

145 John Donne, *The Sermons,* ed. Evelyn M. Simpson and George R. Potter, 10 vols. (Berkeley: University of California Press 1962), 7:410.

146 William Covell, *Polimanteia* (Cambridge 1595), sig. Q4$_r$. I discuss this work in more detail in my next chapter.

147 Edward Hake, *Newes Out of Powles Churchyarde,* 2nd ed. (London 1579), sig. A3$_r$.

148 Francis Davison, pref. to *A Poetical Rhapsody* (1602), ed. Hyder E. Rollins, 2 vols. (Cambridge, Mass.: Harvard University Press 1931), 1:5.

149 John Lily, pref. to Thomas Watson, *Hecatompathia, or Passionate Centurie of Love* (London 1582), n.p.

150 Bourdieu, "The Market of Symbolic Goods," in *The Field of Cultural Production*, 112–41.

151 William Webbe, *A Discourse of English Poetrie* (London 1586), sig. A4$_r$.

152 Bourdieu, "The Production of Belief," in *The Field of Cultural Production*, 74. Distancing his sociology from Marxist economism, Bourdieu has recently argued that economic capital may be subordinate to symbolic capital even in capitalist economies, since acts of exchange may not be possible without symbolic gestures of disavowing economic interests: "In an economy which is defined by the refusal to recognize the 'objective' truth of 'economic' practices, that is, the law of 'naked self-interest' and egoistic calculation, even 'economic' capital cannot act unless it succeeds in being recognized through a conversion that can render unrecognizable the true principle of its efficacy. Symbolic capital is this denied capital, recognized as legitimate, that is, misrecognized as capital," in *The Logic of Practice*, trans. Richard Nice (Stanford, Calif.: Stanford University Press 1990), 118.

153 Bourdieu, *The Field of Economic Production*, 75. Bourdieu stresses that such a disavowal of economic concerns is "neither a simple ideological mask nor a complete repudiation of economic interest," but necessary within any cultural practice whose authority and legitimacy derive from that practice's apparent autonomy from the realms of the economic and political. Disavowal and disinterest are thus practical *negations* employed by social agents within a practice who "can only work by pretending not to be doing what they are doing" (74–6).

154 See Arthur F. Marotti's controversial argument in "'Love is not love': Elizabethan Sonnet Sequences and the Social Order," *ELH* 49 (1982): 396–428.

155 According to *OED*, "legitimation" was used in the mid-seventeenth century to designate the canonical authority of a literary work: "The fact that it is the work of its reputed author; authenticity, genuineness."

156 John Lyly, pref. to *Euphues* (1578), in *Complete Works*, ed. R. Warwick Bond, 3 vols. (Oxford: Clarendon Press 1902), 1:182.

157 Stanley Fish describes how Jonson used rhetorical structures to posit an almost hermetic coterie of like-minded readers, in "Authors-Readers: Jonson's Community of the Same," *Representations* 7 (1984): 26–58. One must always be careful with Jonson, who manages to assert his independence even when he is relying upon the most conventional of patrician fictions: in spurning the "reader-in-ordinary," Jonson insults the taverngoer but he is also punning on *lecteur ordinaire du roi*, the title held by an official in the French court who was charged with reading books to the king. William Nelson provides evidence of a similar, informal position in the English court, in "From 'Listen, Lordings' to 'Dear Reader,'" *University of Toronto Quarterly* 46 (1976/77): 113–15.

158 Foucault, *Language, Counter-Memory, Practice*, 124.

159 Gascoigne, *The Posies*, sig. ¶iiij$_v$-¶¶$_r$.

160 This closed system of value operates all the more tightly the more the field of cultural production is perceived as autonomous, separate from economic or political concerns. In such a field, symbolic value, according to Bourdieu, becomes nothing more than "the degree of recognition accorded by those who recognize no other criterion of legitimacy than recognition by those whom they recognize," in *The Field of Cultural Production*, 38.

161 Webbe, *Discourse of English Poetrie*, sig. H4$_v$.

162 Sir John Harington, *A Preface, or rather a Briefe Apologie of Poetrie*, pref. to translation of Ludovico Ariosto, *Orlando Furioso* (London 1591), sig. ¶2$_v$.

163 Alexander Brome, *Song and other Poems* (London 1664), A7$_v$.

164 Of course, such gentler versions of the fiction merely mask didactic designs, as J. Paul Hunter suggests in his authoritative study of reading in the eighteenth century, *Before Novels: The Cultural Contexts of Eighteenth-Century Fiction* (New York: Norton 1990), 236–9.

165 William Vaughan, *The Golden-grove* (London 1600), sig. Y6$_v$-Y7$_r$.

166 See Jonas Barish, *The Antitheatrical Prejudice* (Berkeley: University of California Press 1981), 117.

167 Sidney, *Defence of Poesie*, sigs. H2$_v$, H4$_r$.

168 Sidney, *Defence of Poesie*, sig. F3$_r$.

169 Sir Nicholas Bacon, from the State Papers for 1567, cited in D.M. Londes, "The Theory and Practice of Censorship in the Sixteenth-Century England," *Transactions of the Royal Historical Society*, 5th ser., vol. 24 (1974), 142.

170 William Prynne, *Histriomastix, the Players Scourge* (London 1633), sig. **6$_v$.

171 "I.G.," *A Refutation of the Apology for Actors* (London 1615), 56.

172 Edward Dering, *A brief & necessary instruction, verye needeful to bee knowen of all housholders* (London 1572) sigs. Aij$_r$-Aiij$_r$.

173 William Lambarde, quoted in Marjorie Plant, *The English Book Trade: An Economic History of the Making and Sale of Books*, 3rd ed. (London: Allen and Unwin 1974), 48.

174 Puttenham, *Arte of English Poesie*, 49.

175 Sir Edward Dering, pref. to Richard Robson, "The Kent Petition Against Episcopacy (Root and Branch Petition)" (1640), in *Proceedings, principally in The County of Kent*, ed. Lambert B. Larking, *Camden Society Publications* 80 (1861): 32.

176 Walter J. Ong, *Rhetoric, Romance, and Technology*, 14.

177 Stephen Gosson, *Plays Confuted in Five Actions* (1582), in *Markets of Bawdrie: The Dramatic Criticism of Stephen Gosson*, ed. Arthur F. Kinney, (Salzburg: University of Salzburg 1974), 162.

178 Roger Ascham, *The Scholemaster* (London 1570), sig. I3$_v$.

179 Foucault notes how the rise of humanism made for a change in the perception of madness: "Whatever obscure cosmic manifestation there was in madness as seen by Bosch is wiped out in Erasmus; madness no longer lies in wait for mankind at the four corners of the earth; it insinuates itself within man, or rather it is a subtle rapport that man maintains with himself .... There is no madness but that which is in every man, since it is man who constitutes madness in the attachment he hears for himself and by the illusions he entertains," in *Madness and Civilization*, trans. Richard Howard (London: Tavistock 1967), 26. Foucault does not, however, make a connection between this shift in the definition of madness with the changes to discourses in general that were brought about by the coming of print culture.

180 Mathias Prideaux, *An Easy and Compendious Introduction for Reading All Sorts of Histories*, 2nd ed. (Oxford 1650), 348.

181 Gosson, in *Markets of Bawdrie*, 186.

182 Juan Luis Vives, *A very frutefull and pleasant boke called the Instruction of a Christen Woman*, trans. Richard Hyrd (London *c.* 1540), sigs. E3$_v$,F2$_r$. Vives's work was widely disseminated throughout Renaissance Europe; Hyrd's translation alone went to nine editions through 1592. See Valerie Wayne, "Some Sad Sentence: Vives' *Instruction of a Christian Woman*," in *Silent But for the Word: Tudor Women as Patrons, Translators, and Writers of Religious Works*, ed. Margaret Patterson Hannay (Kent, Ohio: Kent State University Press 1985), 15. On the humanists' motives in condemning tales of chivalry, see Robert P. Adams, "Bold Bawdry and Open Manslaughter: The English New Humanist Attack on Medieval Romance," *Huntington Library Quarterly* 23 (1959/60): 33–48.

183 Not surprisingly, women writers of the period were far more likely than men to affect humility in their prefaces to readers, whom they routinely addressed as "courteous" or "gentle readers." See the examples collected in *The Paradise of Women: Writings by Englishwomen of the Renaissance*, ed. Betty Travitsky (Westport, Conn.: Greenwood Press 1981).

184 As Montgomery observes, "*Praxis* is a more important end than *gnosis*" in a rhetorical culture (*The Reader's Eye*, 117).

185 "L.N.," "To the Reader, if Indifferent," pref. to *England's Helicon* (1600), ed. Hyder E. Rollins, 2 vols. (Cambridge, Mass.: Harvard University Press 1935), 1:6.

CHAPTER TWO

1 William Covell, *Polimanteia* (Cambridge 1595), sigs. Q2$_r$-R3$_v$. The tract has been attributed to Covell on the basis of its place of publication and the dedication, which is signed "W.C." On Covell, see E.A.J.

Honigmann, *John Weever* (Manchester, U.K.: Manchester University Press 1987), 17–18.

2 Canonization was not necessarily a term of commendation. Nashe used it to condemn Harvey: "From this time forth for ever, ever, ever, evermore maist thou be canonized as the *Nunparreille* of impious epistlers," in *Works*, ed. R.B. McKerrow, 5 vols., corr. rpt. (Oxford: Basil Blackwell 1966), 1:317.

3 Francis Thynne, Epigram 38: "Spencers Fayrie Queene," in *Emblems and Epigrames* (London 1601), ed. F.J. Furnivall (London: EETS 1876), 71.

4 Stephen Greenblatt develops this standard neohistoricist theme in his entry for "Culture" in *Critical Terms for Literary Study*, ed. Frank Lentricchia and Thomas McLaughlin (Chicago: University of Chicago Press 1990), 225–32.

5 Though the immortality topos received its strongest articulation in the poetry of this period, particularly in the poetry of professional authors of laureate ambition, the theme was often eschewed by courtly amateurs who, in affecting a rhetorical humility, dismissed the staying power of their literary entertainments and youthful "fancies." John Lyly, addressing "the Gentlemen Readers" before *Euphues* (London 1578), claims that he is "content this winter to have my doings read for a toye, that in sommer they may be ready for trash ... [A] neww worke should not endure but three monethes," in *Complete Works*, ed. R. Warwick Bond, 3 vols. (Oxford: Clarendon Press 1902), 1:182.

6 Thomas Churchyard, *A praise of poetrie* (London 1595), sig. G3$_r$.

7 Richard A. Lanham, *The Motives of Eloquence: Literary Rhetoric in the Renaissance* (New Haven, Conn.: Yale University Press 1976), 4.

8 Earl Miner, "Assaying the Golden World of English Renaissance Poetics," *Centrum* 4 (1976): 7; Arthur B. Ferguson, *Clio Unbound: Perception of the Social and Cultural Past in Renaissance England* (Durham, N.C.: Duke University Press 1979), 385.

9 Gabriel Harvey, "Letter-Book" (ms., *c.* 1580), in *Elizabethan Critical Essays*, ed. G. Gregory Smith, 2 vols. (London: Oxford University Press 1904), 1:123–4.

10 Sir Philip Sidney, *The Defence of Poesie*, Ponsonby ed. (London 1595), sig. H2$_r$.

11 Thomas Nashe, "Preface to Robert Greene's *Menaphon*" (1589), in *Works*, 3:323.

12 Gabriel Harvey, marginalia from his copy of Chaucer's *Works* (1598), in Virginia F. Stern, *Gabriel Harvey: His Life, Marginalia and Library* (Oxford: Clarendon Press 1979), 126.

13 Francis Meres, "A Comparative Discourse of our English Poets with the Greeke, Latine, and Italian Poets," in *Palladis Tamia, Wits Treasury* (London 1598), 286.

14 Barnabe Googe, pref. to his translation of Marcellus Palingenius, *The Zodiake of Life* (London 1565), sig. (‡)3ᵥ; William Webbe, *A Discourse of English Poetrie* (London 1586), sigs. Lᵥ-L2ᵣ.

15 Barnabe Barnes, *Foure Bookes of Offices* (London 1606), sig. H2ᵣ.

16 Nashe, *The Anatomie of Absurditie* (1589), in *Works*, 1:23–4.

17 John Lane, dedic. to M.S. *Guy of Warwick* (*c.* 1615), quoted in *Bishop Percy's Folio Manuscript*, ed. John W. Hales and F.J. Furnivall, 3 vols. (London 1868), 2:523–5.

18 George Puttenham, *The Arte of English Poesie* (London 1589), 33–4.

19 Puttenham, *Arte of English Poesie*, 86, 34.

20 Samuel Daniel, *A Defence of Ryme*, appended to *A Panegyrike Congratulatorie* (London 1603), sig. G3ᵥ.

21 On the quantitative movement and Daniel's invention of a Gothic tradition of rhyme, see Richard Helgerson, *Forms of Nationhood: The Elizabethan Writing of England* (Chicago: University of Chicago Press 1992), 25–40.

22 Richard Carew, "The Excellency of the English Tongue," in William Camden, *Remains Concerning Britain*, ed. R.D. Dunn (Toronto: University of Toronto Press 1984), 43–4.

23 John Jones, pref. to *The arte & science of preserving bodie & soule in healthe* (London 1579), 2.

24 An important exception was Spenser, whose work made Chaucerisms popular for a time, to the disdain of neoclassicists like Jonson. Elizabethan critics seemed, for the most part, ambivalent about Spenser's experiments, which would be praised in less uncertain terms only much later. Richard Graham, Viscount Preston, writing after the Restoration, declared that Spenser's "design was noble; to shew us that our language was expressive enough of our own sentiments; and to upbraid those who have indenizon'd such numbers of foreign words" (*Angliae Speculum Morale; The Moral State of England* [London 1670], 68).

25 Barnaby Rich, *Allarme to England* (London 1578), sig. *3ᵥ.

26 Gabriel Harvey, *Pierces Supererogation* (London 1593), sig. C1ᵣ; Charles Fitz-Geffrey, *Sir Francis Drake, his honorable life commendation* (London 1596), sig. B5ᵣ; Thomas Edwards, *Narcissus* (London 1595), sig. H4ᵥ; Roger Portington, commendatory to Robert Greene's *Mamillia* (London 1583).

27 John Webster, *Complete Works*, ed. F.L. Lucas, 4 vols. (London: Chatto and Windus 1927), 3:319.

28 William Drummond of Hawthornden, *Poetical Works*, ed. L.E. Kastner, 2 vols. (Manchester, U.K.: Manchester University Press 1913), 2:123. The inclusion of George Buchanan in this pantheon is striking. Buchanan was the author of a controversial history of Scotland, first

published in 1582, that upheld the right of the Protestant nobility to depose Mary Stuart in favour of her son James. After Charles's execution, according to David Norbrook, Buchanan's work "was frequently cited by defenders of the regicide" ("*Macbeth* and the Politics of Historiography," in *Politics of Discourse: The Literature and History of Seventeenth-Century England*, ed. Kevin Sharpe and Steven N. Zwicker [Berkeley: University of California Press 1987], 93). Drummond himself wrote a *History of Scotland* (1655) that was intended as a Royalist riposte to Buchanan.

29 Ben Jonson, *Works*, ed. C.H. Herford, Percy Simpson, and Evelyn Simpson, 11 vols. (Oxford: Clarendon Press 1925–52), 7:313. Subsequent references are to this edition, hereafter cited as H&S. Parenthetical documentation for Jonson's poems, from volume 8, will identify the collection and line number: *Epigrammes* (*Ep.*), *The Underwood* (*Und.*), ungathered verse (*U.V.*). Notes for the *Discoveries* and the "Conversations with Drummond" will refer only to volume and page number.

30 Jonathan Goldberg discusses James's cultivating of the image of the "poet-king," in *James I and the Politics of Literature* (Baltimore, Md.: Johns Hopkins University Press 1983), 17–28.

31 Edward Topsell, *The Historie of Foure-Footed Beastes* (London 1607), sig. A3$_v$.

32 Anthony Stafford, *The Guide of Honour* (London 1634), sig. A8$_r$.

33 Richard Barnfield, *Poems: In divers humors* (London 1598), sig. A3$_r$.

34 Gascoigne drew himself kneeling before Elizabeth in the illuminated presentation copy of the "Hermit's Tale" (1576), Brit. Mus. Royal MS. 18.A.XLVIII, f.1, reproduced in Roy C. Strong, *Portraits of Queen Elizabeth* (Oxford: Clarendon Press 1963), 101. In the same year, Gascoigne is portrayed singly in the frontispiece to his *Steele Glas.*

35 Harold Ogden White records that it was only "shortly before 1600" that "plagiarism" first appeared in English discourse, in *Plagiarism and Imitation during the English Renaissance* (New York: Octagon Books 1965; orig. pub. 1935), 120. Stephen Orgel has argued that the accusation of plagiarism was typically launched against an author who stole from a single source, but that drawing from a multitude of classical and modern sources, as Jonson did in his *Discoveries*, was considered by many an aesthetic ideal ("The Renaissance Artist as Plagiarist," *ELH* 48 [1981]: 476–95).

36 R.R., pref. to Joshua Sylvester's translation of Guillaume de Salluste du Bartas, *Devine Weekes and Workes* (London 1605), sig. A9$_v$.

37 Thomas Lodge, *Wits Miserie and the Worlds Madnesse* (London 1596), sig. I$_r$.

38 Harvey, *Foure Letters, and certaine sonnets* (London 1592), sig. A4$_r$; *Pierces Supererogation*, sig. Z4$_v$-Aa1$_p$.

39 Thomas Edwards, *Narcissus* (London 1595), sig. H3ᵥ.

40 E.K., pref. to Edmund Spenser, *The Shepheardes Calender,* in *Works,* Variorum ed., ed. Edwin Greenlaw *et al.,* 10 vols. (Baltimore, Md.: Johns Hopkins University Press 1932–58), 7:9.

41 E.K., in Spenser, *Works,* 7:111.

42 E.K., in Spenser, *Works,* 7:10.

43 Louis Adrian Montrose, "The Elizabethan Subject and the Spenserian Text," in *Literary Theory/Renaissance Texts,* ed. Patricia Parker and David Quint (Baltimore, Md.: Johns Hopkins University Press 1986), 320. Other studies that emphasize the historic "moment" of *The Shepheardes Calender* include Montrose's "'The perfecte paterne of a Poete': The Poetics of Courtship in *The Shepheardes Calender,*" *Texas Studies in Literature and Language* 21 (1979): 34–67; David L. Miller, "Authorship, Anonymity, and *The Shepheardes Calender,*" *Modern Language Quarterly* 40 (1979): 219–36, and "Spenser's Vocation, Spenser's Career," *ELH* 50 (1983): 197–231; Michael McCanles, "*The Shepheardes Calender* as Document and Monument," *Studies in English Literature* 22 (1982): 5–19; and Richard Helgerson, *Self-Crowned Laureates* (Berkeley: University of California Press 1983), 55–82.

44 Richard Zouche, *The Dove: or Passages of Cosmography* (London 1613), sig. E6ᵥ. The only other significant occasion when the idea of reproducing English writings was raised during this period was in connection with the editing of older works, particularly Chaucer's. Editors from Caxton to Speght expressed concern over obtaining adequate copytexts of the poet's works, a concern that suggests some conception of authenticity. Francis Thynne, noting the "imperfections" in Speght's edition, criticized the bookseller for not paying enough attention to how a work from the past "must needes gather corruptione, passinge throughe so manye handes, as the water dothe, the further yt runnethe from the pure founteyne" (*Animadversions* [m.s., *c.* 1598], ed. F.J. Furnivall [Chaucer Society, 1876], 6). Of note, as well, is Francis Beaumont's letter to Speght (1597) telling of how Chaucer's works were diligently read by "those auncient learned men of our time in Cambridge," who eagerly commended "them to others of the younger sorte" (rptd. in *Chaucer: The Critical Heritage,* ed. D.S. Brewer, 2 vols. [London: Routledge and Kegan Paul 1978], 1:139).

45 Pierre Bourdieu, *The Field of Cultural Production,* ed. Randal Johnson (New York: Columbia University Press 1993), 112–13.

46 Though not specifically attributed to Greene, the pamphlet was published under the title *Greenes Vision.* On the date and authorship of the tract, see the evidence gathered by D. Nicholas Ranson in "The Date of Greene's *Vision* Revisited," *Notes and Queries,* n.s., 22 (1975): 534–5.

47 Nashe reported that Greene, whom he called the "Homer of women," "made no account of winning credite by his workes ... his only care a spel in his purse to conjure up a good cuppe of wine with at all times" (*Strange Newes*, in *Works*, 1:287).

48 On how Greene's tales compare with those of his medieval predecessors, see Neil Gilroy-Scott, "John Gower's Reputation: Literary Allusions from the Early Fifteenth Century to the Time of *Pericles*," *Yearbook of English Studies* 1 (1971): 43; and Richard Helgerson, *The Elizabethan Prodigals* (Berkeley: University of California Press 1976), 96–100.

49 Alvin C. Kibel, "The Canonical Text," *Dædalus* 112 (1983): 239–41.

50 By authenticity is not meant originality. Authenticity is an ahistoricist notion, whereas originality, as David Quint has explained, implies an idea of change: "As a concept of value, originality is the byproduct of a historicist criticism which considers the work of art within its historical context without necessarily assigning value to the context itself. The comparison of the work to other similarly evaluated works measures what is distinctive and inimitable in it alone" (*Origin and Originality in Renaissance Literature: Versions of the Source* [New Haven, Conn.: Yale University Press 1983], 5). Quint notes that Renaissance historicism impelled authors to look for "versions of the source," but he concedes that a fully developed notion of originality did not enter critical discourse until much later.

51 Among the many important studies dealing with the *Workes* and with Jonson's relation to the emergent print culture are: Richard C. Newton, "Jonson and the (Re-)Invention of the Book," in *Classic and Cavalier: Essays on Jonson and the Sons of Ben*, ed. Claude J. Summers and Ted-Larry Pebworth (Pittsburgh: University of Pittsburgh Press 1983), 31–55, and "Making Books from Leaves: Poets Become Editors," *Print and Culture in the Renaissance*, ed. Gerald P. Tyson and Sylvia S. Wagonheim (Newark: University of Delaware Press 1986), 246–64; Timothy Murray, "From Foul Sheets to Legitimate Model: Antitheater, Text, Ben Jonson," *New Literary History* 14 (1983): 641–64; Joseph Loewenstein, "The Script in the Marketplace," *Representations* 12 (1985): 101–14; Richard Dutton, *Ben Jonson: To the First Folio* (Cambridge: Cambridge University Press 1983); the essays collected in *Ben Jonson's 1616 Folio*, ed. Jennifer Brady and W.H. Herendeen (Newark: University of Delaware Press 1991); and Arthur F. Marotti, *Manuscript, Print, and the English Renaissance Lyric* (Ithaca, N.Y.: Cornell University Press 1995), 238–45. I have drawn on the work of all these authors though a few of our conclusions differ. I maintain that it is not quite precise to argue, as some of these authors do, that Jonson is using the *Workes* primarily to assert interpretive or proprietary control over his writings. Jonson's folio is a statement of value more than it is a claim of ownership.

52 Given his antipathy to the historicism that narrative implied, Jonson could not think of epic poetry as anything other than a version of canon-making. As he told Drummond, "he had ane intention to perfect ane Epick Poeme intitiled Heroologia of the Worthies of his Country, rowsed by fame, and was to dedicate it to his Country" (H&S 1:132).

53 On Jonson's ordering of his "transcendent society" in the *Epigrammes*, see Edward Partridge, "Jonson's *Epigrammes*: The Named and the Nameless," *Studies in the Literary Imagination* 6 (1973): 153–98, and Achsah Guibbory, "The Poet as Myth Maker: Ben Jonson's Poetry of Praise," *Clio* 5 (1976): 315–29.

54 Helgerson, *Self-Crowned Laureates*, 183. Peter Stallybrass and Allon White see Jonson as "trying to stabilize and dignify an emergent place for authorship at a distance both from the aristocracy and the plebeians" (*The Politics and Poetics of Transgression* [Ithaca, N.Y.: Cornell University Press 1986], 74).

55 Thomas M. Greene explored this theme in a seminal essay, "Ben Jonson and the Centered Self," *Studies in English Literature* 10 (1970): 325–48.

56 Stanley Fish, "Authors-Readers: Jonson's Community of the Same," *Representations* 7 (1984): 56.

57 *Wits Recreations*, no. 269, rpt. in H&S 9:13.

58 John Heminge and Henrie Condell, pref. to Shakespeare's *Comedies, Histories, & Tragedies* (1623), in *The Complete Works: Original-Spelling Edition*, ed. Stanley Wells and Gary Taylor (Oxford: Clarendon Press 1986), lix.

59 Humphrey Moseley, pref. to *Francis Beaumont and John Fletcher: Comedies and Tragedies*, ed. James Shirley (London 1647), sig. A4$_{r-v}$.

60 Leah S. Marcus, "Robert Herrick," *The Cambridge Companion to English Poetry: Donne to Marvell*, ed. Thomas N. Corns (Cambridge: Cambridge University Press 1993), 174.

61 Robert Herrick, "To His Kinswoman, Mrs. Penelope Wheeler," l. 2, in *Poetical Works*, ed. L.C. Martin (Oxford: Clarendon Press 1956), 188.

62 As Helgerson explains, the Elizabethan hierarchy of courtly amateur/ laureate/anonymous professional provided authors with a set of enabling definitions and a "clarity of outline from a structure of sharply opposed forces. Humanist expectations played against amateur prodigality; amateur prodigality, against laureate seriousness; laureate seriousness, against professional anonymity. But by the time the Caroline poets began to make themselves known, the tension had gone out of this system of oppositions and had not yet redistributed itself to create a new pattern of authorial roles. The old building still stood, but nothing was holding it up" (*Self-Crowned Laureates*, 186).

63 William Drummond of Hawthornden, "A Letter on the True Nature of Poetry, Addressed to Dr. Arthur Johnston," *Poems and Prose*, ed. Robert H. MacDonald (Edinburgh: Scottish Academic Press 1976), 192.

64 In an influential essay, Peter Thomas has contrasted "the growing isolation, exclusiveness and repression of the court" in the 1630s with the "patriotic high seriousness and protestant nationalism" of earlier literature ("Two Cultures? Court and Country under Charles I," in *The Origins of the English Civil War*, ed. Conrad Russell [London: Macmillan 1973], 184–90).

65 Dudley North, "Concerning petty Poetry," ed. L.A. Beaurline, in "Dudley North's Criticism of Metaphysical Poetry," *Huntington Library Quarterly* 25 (1962): 305–7.

66 Philip Massinger, "A Charme for a Libeller," ed. Peter Beal, in "Massinger at Bay: Unpublished Verses in a War of the Theatres," *Yearbook of English Studies* 10 (1979): 199.

67 Henry Peacham, *The Compleat Gentleman* (London 1622), sig. O2$_r$.

68 Michael Drayton, *Works*, ed. J. William Hebel, rev. Kathleen Tillotson and Bernard Newdigate, 5 vols. (Oxford: Shakespeare Head Press 1931–61), 1:506, 4: sig. v*$_r$. Subsequent references are to volume and page number.

69 Henry Peacham, *Thalias Banquet* (London, 1620), sig. B3$_r$. On how Drayton's hostility to the court is signalled in his poetry, see Jane Tylus, "Jacobean Poetry and Lyric Disappointment," in *Soliciting Interpretation: Literary Theory and Seventeenth-Century English Poetry*, ed. Elizabeth D. Harvey and Katharine Eisaman Maus (Chicago: University of Chicago Press 1990), 174–98.

70 William Browne, pref. to Drayton's *Poly-Olbion*, *Works*, 4:393.

71 See Geoffrey G. Hiller, "'Sacred Bards' and 'Wise Druids': Drayton and his Archetype of the Poet," *ELH* 51 (1984): 5.

72 Richard F. Hardin, *Michael Drayton and the Passing of Elizabethan England* (Lawrence: University Press of Kansas 1973), 129.

73 Louis Adrian Montrose, "'Eliza, Queene of shepheardes,' and the Pastoral of Power," *English Literary Renaissance* 10 (1980): 155.

74 Sir Philip Sidney, *The Countesse of Pembrokes Arcadia* (London 1598), sig. B2$_r$.

75 C.S. Lewis, *English Literature in the Sixteenth Century, Excluding Drama* (Oxford: Clarendon Press 1954), 535.

CHAPTER THREE

1 William Dunbar, *Poems*, ed. James Kinsley (Oxford: Clarendon Press 1979), 178–81.

2 References are to Ben Jonson, *Works*, ed. C.H. Herford, Percy Simpson, and Evelyn Simpson, 11 vols. (Oxford: Clarendon Press 1925–52), hereafter cited as H&S. Jonson's poems appear in vol. 8, and are cited by number and line. Elegies to Jonson are cited by volume and page number only.

3 M.F., pref. to Donne's *Poems* (1633), in *John Donne: The Critical Heritage*, ed. A.J. Smith (London: Routledge and Kegan Paul 1975), 85. Hereafter cited as *DCH*.

4 Michael P. Parker remarks of King's elegy that it "suggests an attempt to shield Donne's memory from other, unauthorized elegists and to avert the discussion of the Dean's unedifying early career that such elegies would surely entail" ("Diamond's Dust: Carew, King, and the Legacy of Donne," *The Eagle and the Dove: Reassessing John Donne*, ed. Claude J. Summers and Ted-Larry Pebworth [Columbia: University of Missouri Press 1986], 191).

5 Joshua Scodel interprets Carew's poem as a self-conscious attempt to demonstrate what "the loss of original poetic force" entails. Noting that Carew adopts a Horatian stance in praising Donne for not imitating the Greek models Anacreon and Pindar, Scodel suggests that Carew "does 'worse' than imitate such Greek originals, since he himself imitates neither Anacreon nor Pindar but the Latin imitator of both Greek poets, Horace. In the elegy Carew is twice removed from the original invention he seeks to capture. The elegy thus wittily reveals that imitation of Donne can only lead to a highly successful enactment of poetic defeat" (*The English Poetic Epitaph: Commemoration and Conflict from Jonson to Wordsworth* [Ithaca, N.Y.: Cornell University Press 1991], 131).

6 Thomas Carew, pref. to William Davenant, *The Just Italian* (1630), cited in Peter Beal, "Massinger at Bay: Unpublished Verses in a War of the Theatres," *Yearbook of English Studies* 10 (1979): 190.

7 Carew, pref. to Davenant's *The Witts* (1636), cited in Diana Benet, "Carew's Monarchy of Wit," in *"The Muses Common-Weale": Poetry and Politics in the Seventeenth Century*, ed. Claude J. Summers and Ted-Larry Pebworth (Columbia: University of Missouri Press 1988), 88–9. Benet persuasively links Carew's distrust of readers to the absolutism of the Stuart court.

8 Scodel, *English Poetic Epitaph*, 138.

9 On belatedness among Jonson's eulogists, see Jennifer Brady, "'Beware the Poet': Authority and Judgment in Jonson's *Epigrammes*," *Studies in English Literature* 23 (1983): 95–112.

10 The *OED*'s earliest entry for "classic," as an adjective denoting the literature of ancient Greece and Rome, dates from 1628. On the normative usage of "classic" in antiquity, see Ernst Robert Curtius, *European*

Literature and the Latin Middle Ages, trans. Willard R. Trask (New York: Harper and Row, 1963), 249.

11 T.S. Eliot, *What is a Classic?* (London: Faber 1945), 15. That classics are the absent presences against which latecomers define themselves is evident from a revealing statement by Charles-Augustin Sainte-Beuve near the end of his essay "What is a Classic?" (1850): "Let us be satisfied with feeling them [the classics], with interpreting them, with admiring them, and for ourselves, latecomers that we are, let us try at least to be ourselves" (in *Critical Theory Since Plato*, ed. Hazard Adams [New York: Harcourt Brace Jovanovich 1971], 562).

12 Andrew Marvell, *Poems and Letters*, ed. H.M. Margoliouth, 3rd ed., rev. by Pierre Legouis and E.E. Duncan-Jones (Oxford: Clarendon Press 1971), 3.

13 On the popularity of funeral elegies as school exercises, see Alberta S. Turner, "Milton and the Convention of the Academic Miscellanies," *Yearbook of English Studies* 5 (1975): 86–93. The 1630s and 1640s saw not only a rise in elegy-writing. See the figures compiled by Franklin B. Williams, Jr on the dramatic increase in preliminary testimonials, in "Commendatory Verses: The Rise of the Art of Puffing," *Studies in Bibliography* 19 (1966): 1–14.

14 On the "oblique mourning" for the King in the *Lachrymae Musarum*, see Michael Gearin-Tosh, "Marvell's 'Upon the Death of the Lord Hastings,'" *Essays and Studies* 34 (1981): 108. In his entry on Cartwright, Aubrey says "'Tis not to be forgott that King Charles 1st dropt a teare at the newes of his death," in *Brief Lives*, ed. Oliver Lawson Dick (Penguin 1962), 152.

15 Moseley's canon included works by Davenant, Suckling, Carew, Waller, Cowley, and many others, though he also printed Milton's first collection of verse. "By the time of the Restoration," Arthur F. Marotti has suggested, "thanks partly to Moseley, the single-author edition of lyric poetry was a familiar phenomenon in the world of publication" (*Manuscript, Print, and the English Renaissance Lyric* [Ithaca, N.Y.: Cornell University Press 1995], 262).

16 Interestingly, the only recorded criticism of the Cartwright volume came from commenders of plays put out by rival publishers. "J.B." alludes to the Cartwright volume in verses before Richard Brome's *A Jovial Crew* (1652): "There comes / A Shole, with Regiments of *Encomiums* / On all occasions, whose *Astronomie* / Can calculate a Praise to *Fifty three*" (sig. A3$_v$). Moseley was unrepentant: "if you think He hath too many *Commenders*, it is a sign you knew him not: we grant here are more than before other Books, and yet we give you not all we have" (sig. a2$_r$). "J.B." may be John Berkenhead, a close friend of Cartwright.

17 On Moseley's royalist subversion, see Lois Potter, *Secret Rites and Secret Writing: Royalist Literature 1641–1660* (Cambridge: Cambridge University Press 1989), 19–22; and John Curtis Reed, "Humphrey Moseley, Publisher," *Oxford Bibliographical Society Proceedings and Papers* 2 (1930): 57–142.

18 Annabel Patterson, *Censorship and Interpretation: The Conditions of Writing and Reading in Early Modern England* (Madison: University of Wisconsin Press 1984), 4–18; Potter, *Secret Rites*, xiii–xiv, 38–71. See also the related argument by Michael McKeon, "Politics of Discourse and the Rise of the Aesthetic in Seventeenth-Century England," in *Politics of Discourse*, ed. Kevin Sharpe and Steven N. Zwicker (Berkeley: University of California Press 1987), 35–51.

19 James Harrington, *Political Works*, ed. J.G.A. Pocock (Cambridge: Cambridge University Press 1977), 354.

20 P.W. Thomas has discussed the relation between Cavalier "morale-boosting" gestures like the Cartwright volume and the crystallization of a classicism that "images the centralizing and institutionalizing tendencies of the aristocratic elite, tendencies only fortified by the upheaval of 1646." See *Sir John Berkenhead 1617–1679: A Royalist Career in Politics and Polemics* (Oxford: Clarendon Press 1969), 133–40, 176–9.

21 John Davies, pref. to J. Hall, trans., *Hierocles upon the Golden Verses of Pythagoras* (London 1656), sig. b3$_v$.

22 "Marcurius Pragmaticus," *The Second Part of Crafty Crumwell* (London 1648), sig. A2$_r$. Thomas Goffe (1591–1629) was a divine, minor tragedian, and notorious "woman-hater" (*DNB*). On other attempts to claim a national tradition in the royalist cause, see Derek Hirst, "The Politics of Literature in the English Republic," *The Seventeenth Century* 5 (1990): 142–3. *The Great Assises Holden in Parnassus* (1645), a satire on royalist newsbooks possibly written by Wither, tries to obviate criticism of Roundhead philistinism by selectively recuperating the established canon. The effort, however, requires considerable revision of literary history, such as having "Cary" repudiate his "vain *Rapture*" (sig. E$_r$).

23 Alexander Brome, *Songs and Other Poems*, 2nd ed. (London 1664), 260–1.

24 J.B., in Brome, *Jovial Crew*, sig. A3$_v$.

25 The precipitous decline of Cartwright's reputation, and of commendatory verses generally, underlies a running joke in Thomas Shadwell's *Bury-Fair* (1689), where the character "Oldwit" is only too happy to advertise his musty credentials: "I ... was *Jack Fletcher*'s Friend, *Ben Johnson*'s Son, and afterward an Intimate Crony of *Jack Cleaveland*, and *Tom Randal* ... writ before *Fletcher*'s *Works* and *Cartwright*'s" (II.i).

26 Pref. to Christopher Wase, *Electra of Sophocles* (1649), cited in Hirst, "Politics of Literature," 140.

27 Hirst, "Politics of Literature," 133.

28 Christopher Hill, *A Nation of Change and Novelty: Radical Politics, Religion and Literature in Seventeenth-Century England* (London: Routledge 1990), 220.

29 J.D., pref. to Josua [*sic*] Poole, *The English Parnassus* (London 1657), sig. a2$_r$.

30 "Probably there were more admirers and readers of Chaucer in the seventeenth century than has been allowed; but they were not literary men," reports D.S. Brewer, in "Images of Chaucer 1386–1900," in *Chaucer and Chaucerians*, ed. D.S. Brewer (London: Nelson 1966), 256.

31 Edward Phillips, pref. to *Theatrum Poetarum* (London 1675), sig. $^{xx}2_v$.

32 Henry Peacham, *The Compleat Gentleman* (London 1622), 94.

33 Jonathan Sidnam, *A Paraphrase upon the three first Bookes of Chaucers Troilus and Cressida, Translated into our Moderne English* (MS., *c.* 1630), cited in *Five Hundred Years of Chaucer Criticism and Allusion (1357–1900)*, ed. Caroline F.E. Spurgeon, 3 vols. (Cambridge: Cambridge University Press 1925), 1:203.

34 Sir Francis Kynaston, *Amorum Troili et Creseidae Libri duo priores Anglico-Latini* (London 1635). On Kynaston's completed translation, see Richard Beadle, "The Virtuoso's *Troilus*," in *Chaucer Traditions*, ed. Ruth Morse and Barry Windeatt (Cambridge: Cambridge University Press 1990), 213–33.

35 Thomas Jackson, "Of Christ's Session &c," *Works*, 12 vols. (Oxford: Oxford University Press 1844) 11:287.

36 Satirizing the convention in testimonials of setting the work beside celebrated titles, several of the mock-commendations mix misogyny and patrician contempt in comparing Strong's poem to a canon of popular narratives: "Arms, and the man I sing, whose lines rehearse / The Western wenches doughty deeds, in verse; / More high, then (earst) the acts of *Guy* of *Warwicke*, / *Southamptons Beavoys*, or the *Knight* of *Barwicke*" (sig. A2$_v$).

37 Cited in Joseph Frank, *The Beginnings of the English Newspaper 1620–1660* (Cambridge, Mass.: Harvard University Press 1961), 335.

38 *Vindex Anglicus; or, the Perfections of the English Language Defended, and asserted* (Oxford 1644), 3.

39 George Daniel of Beswick, *Poems*, ed. Alexander B. Grosart, 4 vols. (Boston, Lincolnshire 1878), 1:79–84.

40 Daniel, *Poems*, 1:32.

41 Edmund Waller, "Of English Verse," *Poems, &c, Written upon several Occasions, and to several Persons*, 5th ed. (London 1686), 237.

42 "To detracting Censurers, that the Fame of Poets is Eternal," *Miscellany Poems and Translations by Oxford Hands* (Oxford 1685), 154–8. Other examples of this sub-genre include John Evelyn *fils*, "The Immortality

of Poesie," *Poems by several Hands, and on several occasions*, ed. Nahum Tate (London 1685), 90–3, and "In imitation of the 15th Elegy of Ovid Lib. I Amor. By a Gentleman of Oxford," *The Grove* (London 1721), 104–8.

43 Phillips, *Theatrum Poetarum*, sig. $^{XX}2_v$.

CHAPTER FOUR

1 John Milton, *The First Defence of the People of England*, in the Samuel Lee Wolff translation, *Works*, ed. Frank Allen Patterson *et. al*, 18 vols. (New York: Columbia University Press 1931–38), 7:353.

2 Thomas Sprat, *The History of the Royal-Society of London* (London, 1667), 42, 111, 114. On the political nature of the Royal Society's language projects, see Brian Vickers, "The Royal Society and English Prose Style: A Reassessment," in *Rhetoric and the Pursuit of Truth* (Los Angeles: William Andrews Clark Library 1985), 1–76.

3 Robert Boyle, *Some Considerations Touching the Style of the H. Scriptures*, 2nd ed. (London 1663), 164. Richard W.F. Kroll has questioned the assumption that Restoration discourse abided by a naive empiricism that treated language as a transparent medium of knowledge. On the contrary, he suggests, authors of the period were wholly aware of the artificiality and performativity of language, yet went beyond earlier rhetorical thinking in emphasizing the contingency and phenomenal properties of language and submitting it to analysis much like any other particular of experience: "Neoclassical scepticism about eloquence does not constitute an outright rejection of rhetoric, because that very scepticism commands a more rigorous commitment to the partial, inferential, and analogical terms that define human knowledge" (*The Material Word: Literate Culture in the Restoration and Early Eighteenth Century* [Baltimore, Md.: Johns Hopkins University Press 1991], 186).

4 References are to John Dryden, *Of Dramatick Poesy and Other Critical Essays*, ed. George Watson, 2 vols. (London: Dent/Everyman's Library 1962).

5 Acceptance of this "unabatable paradox" is the recommendation of Steven Connor's shrewd assessment of contemporary accounts of value, *Theory and Cultural Value* (Oxford: Blackwell 1992), 2.

6 Emerson Marks summarizes the positions in *Relativist and Absolutist: The Early Neo-Classical Debate in England* (New Brunswick, N.J.: Rutgers University Press 1955). Recent useful discussions of the neoclassical debates include Lawrence Manley, *Convention, 1500–1700* (Cambridge, Mass.: Harvard University Press 1980), chap. 5; Douglas Lane Patey, *Probability and Literary Form: Philosophic Theory and Literary Practice in the Augustan Age* (Cambridge: Cambridge University Press 1984); John L.

Mahoney, *The Whole Internal Universe: Imitation and the New Defense of Poetry in British Criticism, 1660–1830* (New York: Fordham University Press 1985); James Engell, *Forming the Critical Mind: Dryden to Coleridge* (Cambridge, Mass.: Harvard University Press 1989); and Kroll, *The Material Word,* chap. 8.

7 John Dryden, *The Grounds of Criticism in Tragedy* (1679); John Dennis, *The Grounds of Criticism in Poetry* (1704).

8 Line references are to Alexander Pope, *Poems,* Twickenham ed., ed. John Butt *et al.,* 11 vols. (London: Methuen 1939–69).

9 Thomas Rymer, *Critical Works,* ed. Curt A. Zimansky (New Haven, Conn.: Yale University Press 1956), 164. On the consistency of Rymer's empiricism, see Kroll, *The Material Word,* 298–302. A similar empiricist codification of fact as value is at work in the harangues of the moralists. Collier, writing on *The Relapse,* advised that the "*Poet* must be careful to hold his *Persons* tight to their *Calling* and pretentions ... To manage otherwise, is to desert *Nature,* and makes the *Play* appear monstrous and Chimerical. So that instead of an *Image of Life,* 'tis rather an Image of Impossibility" (*A Short View of the Immorality, and Profaneness of the English Stage* [London 1698], 219).

10 Rymer, *Critical Works,* 19.

11 Rymer, *Critical Works,* 75.

12 Rymer, *Critical Works,* 18.

13 Samuel Johnson, "Preface to *Shakespeare,*" in *Works,* ed. A.T. Hazen *et al.* (New Haven, Conn.: Yale University Press 1958–in progress), 7:66.

14 Michel Foucault, *Language, Counter-Memory, Practice,* ed. Donald F. Bouchard (Ithaca, N.Y.: Cornell University Press 1977), 154.

15 John Dennis, *Critical Works,* ed. Edward Niles Hooker, 2 vols. (Baltimore, Md.: Johns Hopkins University Press 1939–43), 1:403.

16 My argument here is loosely similar to Joseph M. Levine's in his splendid *The Battle of the Books: History and Literature in the Augustan Age* (Ithaca, N.Y.: Cornell University Press 1991), where he proposes that the quarrel was chiefly about the rival claims of history and literature.

17 Jonathan Swift, *Prose Works,* ed. Herbert Davis, 14 vols. (Oxford, U.K.: Shakespeare Head Press 1939–68), 1:141.

18 Wentworth Dillon, Earl of Roscommon, *An Essay on Translated Verse* (London 1684), 4.

19 Gilbert Burnet, pref. to his translation of Sir Thomas More, *Utopia* (London 1684), sig. A4$_v$-A5$_r$.

20 Sir Thomas Culpeper, *Essayes or Moral Discourses,* 2nd ed. (London 1671), 108–11.

21 Henry Belasye, *An English Traveler's First Curiosity* (MS., 1657), cited in *Donne: The Critical Heritage,* ed. A.J. Smith (London: Routledge and Kegan Paul 1975), 133.

22 Sir William Temple, "Of Poetry," in *Miscellanea. In Two Parts*, 5th ed., 2 vols. (London 1697), 2:357.

23 Daniel Baker, *Poems upon Several Occasions* (London 1697), 1.

24 Rymer, *Critical Works*, 9. René Wellek surveys some eighteenth-century arguments for environmental determinism in *The Rise of English Literary History* (Chapel Hill: University of North Carolina Press 1941), 54–60.

25 Charles Gildon, *Miscellaneous Letters and Essays* (London 1694), sig. A3ᵣ.

26 George Farquhar, "A Discourse upon Comedy," *Complete Works*, ed. Charles Stonehill, 2 vols. (Bloomsbury, U.K.: Nonesuch Press 1930), 2:337.

27 On the publishing activities of the republican "Calves-Head Club," see A.B. Worden, ed., *Edmund Ludlow's A Voyce From the Watch Tower*, Camden Society Publications, 4th ser., 21 (1978): 17–21.

28 William Winstanley, *The Lives of the Most Famous English Poets* (London 1687), 220.

29 Samuel Croxall, *An Original Canto of Spenser Design'd as Part of his Fairy Queen but never printed* (London 1713), and *Another Original Canto of Spenser* (London 1714); *The Examiner* 5.6 (14–18 December 1713): 2.

30 Kevin Sharpe and Steven N. Zwicker, "Politics of Discourse: Introduction," in *Politics of Discourse* (Berkeley, Calif.: University of California Press 1987), 13.

31 "Of all the various subjects that have yet exercised the geniuses of modern writers," wrote a contributor to *The World*, "that of Taste has appeared to be the most difficult to treat; because almost all of them have lost themselves in endeavouring to trace its source" (No. 67, 11 April 1754). For other examples, see the list compiled by R.W. Babcock, "The Idea of Taste in the Eighteenth Century," *PMLA* 50 (1935): 922–6.

32 Dryden, according to Robert D. Hume, is "the key figure in a transition from composition-based to appreciation-oriented criticism" (*Dryden's Criticism* [Ithaca, N.Y.: Cornell University Press 1970], 24–5).

33 Terry Eagleton, *The Ideology of the Aesthetic* (Oxford: Basil Blackwell 1990), 10.

34 In the strong version of the deconstructionist argument, there can be no positing of first causes or grounds of the "real" which cannot be ultimately be shown to be dependent upon a textuality that is posited as secondary or derivative. In Derrida's summary, "what is produced in the current trembling is a reevaluation of the relationship between the general text and what was believed to be, in the form of reality (history, politics, economics, sexuality, etc.) the simple, referable exterior of language or writing, the belief that this exterior could operate from the simple position of cause or accident" (*Positions* [Chicago: University

of Chicago Press 1981], 91). As Kroll suggests (*The Material Word*, 1–6), it is a simplification to equate Restoration culture with a naive empiricism, yet the defenders of the Moderns were prone to opposing poetic figuration to scientific discourse.

35 Bernard le Bouvier de Fontenelle, *Digression sur les Anciens et les Modernes* (1688), appended to later editions of his *Entretiens sur la Plurality des Mondes* (orig. 1686), ed. Robert Shackelton (Oxford: Clarendon Press 1955), 168 (translation mine). Douglas Lane Patey discusses the importance of the quarrel of the Ancients and Moderns in relation to changing definitions of poetry's utility in "'Aesthetics' and the Rise of Lyric in the Eighteenth Century," *Studies in English Literature* 33 (1993): 587–608.

36 On the centrality of the doctrine of taste in eighteenth-century moral philosophies, see Howard Caygill, *Art of Judgement* (Oxford: Basil Blackwell 1989), 38–102.

37 William Wordsworth, preface to the 2nd edition of the *Lyrical Ballads* (1802), in *Wordsworth's Literary Criticism*, ed. W.J.B. Owen (London: Routledge and Kegan Paul 1974), 80–1.

38 Eagleton, *Ideology of the Aesthetic*, 65.

39 Francis Meres, *Palladis Tamia, Wits Treasury* (London 1598), 281–2.

40 Dryden heads Walter Jackson Bate's list of European authors who feel pressured to differentiate themselves from the literary achievement of the past, in *The Burden of the Past and the English Poet* (New York: Norton 1970), 26–31. For Harold Bloom, anxiety is the condition of all writing though it is particularly pronounced for English poets writing in a post-Miltonic universe. The theories of Bate and Bloom have provoked wide and not always favourable responses. Among those that deal specifically with Dryden are Maximillian E. Novak: "Never was there a poet who felt less directly the 'burden of the past' than Dryden" ("Johnson, Dryden, and the Wild Vicissitudes of Taste," in *The Unknown Samuel Johnson*, ed. John J. Burke, Jr and Donald Kay [Madison: University of Wisconsin Press 1983], 63); and Roger Sale: "In all this [Dryden's attitude toward the literary past] what one is most aware of is self-consciousness, a sense that one must always be comparing oneself to the past, weighing virtues and faults, making one's own way by doing better what the previous age has done ill, of doing what it had left undone. But I have no sense that Dryden was crippled in all this" (*Literary Inheritance* [Amherst: University of Massachusetts Press 1984], 61). That Dryden could entertain both attitudes at once might seem an unacceptably paradoxical proposition, yet Dryden was far more willing than most to tolerate paradox.

41 Dennis, *Critical Works*, 1:410.

41 Dennis, *Critical Works*, 1:410.

42 Dennis, *Critical Works*, 1:410.

43 Elizabeth Elstob, *The Rudiments of Grammar for the English-Saxon Tongue* (London 1715), iii.

44 Fredric Jameson, *Marxism and Form* (Princeton, N.J.: Princeton University Press 1971), 333–4.

45 Susan Staves, "Pope's Refinement," *The Eighteenth Century: Theory and Interpretation* 29 (1988): 153.

46 For more on how stylistic value was distinguished from the valuable exchange of knowledge, see my "Copyright and the Invention of Tradition," *Eighteenth-Century Studies* 26 (1992): 1–27.

47 The altering of Shakespeare's plays begun during the Restoration may have been undertaken in response not just to problems with the text, its length, or the composition of the acting companies, but to immediate economic and legal circumstances. In particular, Davenant, as has often been noted, promoted Shakespearean adaptations within his theatre in order to compete with Killigrew's rival company, which had secured the rights to many pre-1642 plays, including those of Beaumont and Fletcher, whose comparative modernity ensured that their popularity eclipsed Shakespeare's well into the eighteenth century. Gary Taylor rehearses the standard argument in *Reinventing Shakespeare* (Oxford: Oxford University Press 1989), 13–16. I consider the declining status of these "new-modellings" in my sixth chapter.

48 Frank Kermode, "Dryden: A Poet's Poet," *The Listener* (30 May 1957), 878. Kermode's view is seconded by Earl Miner, who says that Dryden "was the first to conceive of Chaucer as a classic" ("Chaucer in Dryden's *Fables*," in *Studies in Criticism and Aesthetics, 1660–1800*, ed. Howard Anderson and John S. Shea [Minneapolis: University of Minnesota Press 1967], 71).

49 George Sewell, pref. to vol. 7 of Pope's edition of Shakespeare's *Works*, in *Shakespeare: The Critical Heritage 1623–1801*, ed. Brian W. Vickers, 6 vols. (London: Routledge and Kegan Paul 1974–81), 2:419. Pope had nothing to do with this seventh volume, which was merely Sewell's reprint of an earlier spurious "Volume Seven" from Rowe's edition.

50 On the New Rhetoric, and the importation into English of the term "belles-lettres," see Wilbur Samuel Howell, *Eighteenth-Century British Logic and Rhetoric* (Princeton, N.J.: Princeton University Press 1971).

51 Among the several discussions of Dryden's comparativism are Hume, *Dryden's Criticism*, 51–8; Calvin S. Brown, "John Dryden as Comparativist," *Comparative Literature* 10 (1973): 112–24; Earl Miner, "The Poetics of the Critical Act: Dryden's Dealings with Rivals and Predecessors," in *Evidence in Literary Scholarship*, ed. René Wellek and Alvaro Ribeiro (Oxford: Clarendon Press 1979), 45–62; and the contributions to

Literary Transmission and Authority: Dryden and Other Writers, ed. Earl Miner and Jennifer Brady (Cambridge: Cambridge University Press 1993).

52 George Sewell, *A New Collection of Original Poems* (London 1720), 82.

53 Dennis, *Critical Works*, 2:395.

54 Thomas Wilkes, *A General View of the Stage* (London 1759), 19.

55 Ralph Cohen contends that "the concept of an 'age' remains one of the most provocative of Dryden's contributions to literary history" ("John Dryden's Literary Criticism," *New Homage to John Dryden*, ed. Alan Roper [Los Angeles: William Andrews Clark Memorial Library 1983], 70). See also Achsah Guibbory's chapter on Dryden's conceptions of literary history in *The Map of Time: Seventeenth-Century English Literature and Ideas of Pattern in History* (Urbana: University of Illinois Press 1986).

56 John Ellis, *The Theory of Literary Criticism* (Berkeley: University of California Press 1974), 44. Emphasis in original.

57 Joseph Addison, *A Discourse on Ancient and Modern Learning*, in *Miscellaneous Works*, ed. A.C. Guthkelch, 2 vols. (London: G. Bell and Sons 1914), 2:451. Emphasis in original.

58 Frank Kermode, *The Classic*, 2nd ed. (Cambridge, Mass.: Harvard University Press 1983), 74. Addison would press the point further in *Spectator* 273, where he noted that the gulfs of time had made the characters in the *Iliad* and *Aeneid* seem as "Strangers, or indifferent Persons" to English readers. References, by essay number, are to Donald F. Bond's edition of *The Spectator*, 5 vols. (Oxford: Clarendon Press 1965).

59 Addison, *A Discourse on Ancient and Modern Learning*, 2:449–50.

60 One exception was in support of neo-Boethian commonplaces of the kind Edward Phillips called on to justify his canon-making in the preface to his *Theatrum Poetarum* (London 1675): "some [writers] deserve Fame & have it, others neither have nor deserve it, some have it, not deserving, others though deserving yet totally miss it, or have it not equal to their deserts" (sig. *4$_r$).

61 Dryden, pref. to William Walsh, *A Dialogue Concerning Women* (1691), in *The Critical Opinions of John Dryden: A Dictionary*, ed. John M. Aden (Nashville, Tenn.: Vanderbilt University Press 1963), 275; pref. to St Evremond, *Miscellaneous Essays* (1692), in *Critical Opinions*, 269. For other examples, see Christopher Ricks, "Allusion: The Poet as Heir," *Studies in the Eighteenth Century III*, ed. R.G. Brissenden and J.C. Eade (Toronto: University of Toronto Press 1976), 230. On Dryden's use of paternal metaphors in constructing his own poetic identity, see Jennifer Brady, "Dryden and Negotiations of Literary Succession and Precession," in Miner and Brady, ed., *Literary Transmission and Authority*, 27–

54; and Ian Donaldson, "Fathers and Sons: Jonson, Dryden, and *Mac-Flecknoe*," *Southern Review* 18 (1985): 314–27.

62 David Hume, *Essays Moral, Political, and Literary*, ed. Eugene F. Miller, 2nd ed. (Indianapolis, Ind.: Liberty Classics 1987), 246–7, 237. Hume's liberalism, much like our own, chafed at the evident moral shortcomings of many long-established classics: "The want of humanity and of decency, so conspicuous in the characters drawn by several of the ancient poets, even sometimes by *Homer* and the *Greek* tragedians, diminishes considerably the merit of their noble performances, and gives modern authors an advantage over them" (246).

63 Samuel Johnson, *The Lives of the English Poets*, ed. George Birkbeck Hill, 3 vols. (Oxford: Clarendon Press 1905), 1:411.

64 Joseph Priestley, *A Course of Lectures on Oratory and Criticism* (London 1777), 115.

65 Giles Gunn, "Rorty's *Novum Organum*," *Raritan* 10 (Summer 1990): 103.

CHAPTER FIVE

1 Charles Gildon, *Miscellaneous Letters and Essays, on Several Subjects* (London 1694), 86. The event had previously been mentioned in passing by Dryden in the *Essay of Dramatic Poesy*, and later repeated by Rowe in his biography of Shakespeare (1709).

2 John Evelyn, letter to Samuel Pepys, 12 August 1689, *Diary and Correspondence*, ed. William Bray, 2nd ed., 4 vols. (London 1887), 3:310. On the Royal Society's plans, see O.F. Emerson, "John Dryden and a British Academy," *Proceedings of the British Academy* 10 (1921): 45–58. On eighteenth-century proposals for an academy, see G.L. Anderson, "Charles Gildon's Total Academy," *Journal of the History of Ideas* 16 (1955): 247–51; and James G. Basker, "Minim and the Great Cham: Smollett and Johnson on the Prospect of an English Academy," in *The Age of Johnson*, ed. James Engell (Cambridge, Mass.: Harvard University Press 1984), 137–61.

3 John Wilmot, Earl of Rochester, "An Allusion to Horace," *Poems*, ed. Keith Walker (Oxford: Shakespeare Head Press 1984), 102.

4 Matthew Pilkington, *Poems on Several Occasions* (London 1731), 101.

5 William Bullein, *A Dialogue against the Fever Pestilence* (London 1564; rev. 1578), ed. Mark W. Bullen and A.H. Bullen (London 1888), 16–17. See also Richard Robinson, *The Rewarde of Wickednesse* (London 1574), sig. P4$_v$-Q3$_v$; and I.C., *A poore Knight his Pallace of private pleasures* (London 1579), sig. Ciij$_v$.

6 "Jemmy Copywell" [William Wotyx], "A Familiar Epistle from the Shades below," *Gentleman's Magazine*, vol. 30 (March 1760): 146.

7 On the history of the office, see Edmund Kemper Broadus, *The Laure-ateship* (Oxford: Clarendon Press 1921).

8 "An Elegy Upon the Death of Sr. William Davenant" (1668), in *A Little Ark*, ed. G. Thorn-Darry (London: Dobell 1921), 87.

9 Richard Flecknoe, "Sir William D'avenant's Voyage to the Other World" (1668?), in *Theatre Miscellany*, ed. A.K. Croston (Oxford: Lut-trell Society 1953), 64.

10 Thomas Gray, letter to William Mason (19 December 1757), *Correspon-dence*, ed. Paget Toynbee *et al.*, 2nd ed., 3 vols. (Oxford: Clarendon Press 1971), 2:545.

11 Alexander Pope, *Poems*, Twickenham ed., ed. John Butt *et al.*, 11 vols. (London: Methuen 1939–69), 5:415.

12 Trajano Boccalini, *Ragguagli di Parnaso*, trans. Henry Cary, Earl of Mon-mouth (1656), cited in Philip H. Gray, "Suckling's *A Sessions of the Poets* as a Ballad: Boccalini's 'Influence' Examined," *Studies in Philology* 36 (1939): 61.

13 Sir John Suckling, *Works*, ed. Thomas Clayton, 2 vols. (Oxford: Claren-don Press 1971), 1:76. Michael P. Parker suggests that, in attempting to disparage his rivals with his poem, Suckling was betraying his anxi-ety about his own poetic talents. See "'All are not born (Sir) to the Bay': 'Jack' Suckling, 'Tom' Carew and the Making of a Poet," *English Literary Renaissance* 12 (1982): 341–68.

14 According to one contemporary report, "The Wits" was "sung to the King when he was in *New Forest*" in the late summer of 1637, as quoted in Parker, "All are not born," 361.

15 Suckling uses the phrase at least twice in his writings, in *Aglaura* (1638) and in a letter of uncertain date. These are apparently the first recorded usages of the phrase in English. See Parker, "All are not born," 366 and note.

16 Andrew Marvell, *Poems and Letters*, ed. H.M. Margoliouth *et al.*, 3rd ed., 2 vols. (Oxford: Clarendon Press 1971), 1:96. Howard Erskine-Hill makes the argument for distinguishing Marvell's views from his fictive Jonson's. See *The Augustan Idea in English Literature* (London: Edward Arnold 1983), 190–4.

17 "The Tryal of Skill" (1704), in *Poems on Affairs of State*, ed. George deF. Lord *et al.*, 7 vols. (New Haven, Conn.: Yale University Press 1963–75), 6:697.

18 Daniel Kenrick, *A New Session of the Poets* (London 1700), 9; Matthew Coppinger, "A Session of the Poets," in *Poems on Affairs of State ... Part III* (London, 1698), 310. For an example of an attack on Dryden, see *A Journal From Parnassus* (*c.* 1688), ed. Hugh MacDonald (London: Dobell 1937).

19 Habermas's idea of a "public sphere" first becoming operative in the coffee houses of the early eighteenth century has been popularized by Terry Eagleton in *The Function of Criticism* (London: Verso 1984), and by Peter Stallybrass and Allon White in *The Politics and Poetics of Transgression* (Ithaca, N.Y.: Cornell University Press 1986), though it has not been universally endorsed. Dustin Griffin has argued that the historical evidence for such a sphere is ambiguous; see "Fictions of Eighteenth-Century Authorship," *Essays in Criticism* 43 (1993): 181–94. See also Neil Saccamano, "The Consolations of Ambivalence: Habermas and the Public Sphere," *MLN* 106 (1991), 685–98. Whether an actual public sphere can be said to have emerged during the period is less significant, it seems to me, than how it was felt at the time that critical discourse was becoming more public and the process of canon-making more open and inclusive.

20 *The Session of the Poets, Holden at the Foot of Parnassus-Hill* (London 1696), 3.

21 "The Lovers' Session" (1687), in *Court Satires of the Restoration*, ed. John Harold Wilson (Columbus: Ohio State University Press 1976), 184–5.

22 *A Journal from Parnassus*, ed. MacDonald, 28.

23 John Sheffield, Duke of Buckinghamshire, "The Election of a Poet Laureat in MDCCXIX" (1719), in *Works of the English Poets*, ed. Alexander Chalmers, 21 vols. (London 1810), 10:98–9.

24 See, for example, "A new Session of the Poets, for the Year 1730," *Gentleman's Magazine*, vol. 1 (February 1731): 71–2.

25 *Gray's-Inn Journal*, no. 39 (22 June 1754), rptd. as 86 (8 June 1754) in the 1756 collected edition of the *Journal*, ed. Arthur Murphy, 2 vols. (London 1756), 2:212–3.

26 "A Session of the Poets" (1676), rptd. as appendix 1 in Rochester, *Poems*, 133–5.

27 Coppinger, "A Session of the Poets," 305.

28 "The Oxford Laureat," in *Miscellanies over Claret*, no. 1 (London 1697), 6–19. Henry Birkhead, the scholar who bequeathed his estate and livings in order to establish the Oxford chair, may have have acted out of personal spite: his last will, written three years before his death in 1696, specifically instructed his executors to "give all my lands tenements and hereditaments whatsoever" to the university, saving only a shilling for one "Jane Stevenson whom I have formerly called and written to as my wife to save her credit in the world though I was never married to her nor betrothed to her," and who, Birkhead declared, "has been extream false and many wayes injurious to me." It appears, however, that the income from Birkhead's leases was insufficient to endow a chair, which was instituted only later, in 1708, after the university had sold the estate. See J.W. Mackail, "Henry Birkhead and the

Foundation of the Oxford Chair of Poetry," in *Studies in Humanism* (London: Longmans, Green 1938), 169–185.

29 *Gray's-Inn Journal*, 2:216–17.

30 *Visits from the Shades, Part II* (London 1704), 85.

31 John Lacy, *The Steelieds, or, The tryal of wit* (London 1714), 53.

32 Charles Gildon (?), *The Battle of the Authors Lately Fought in Covent-Garden* (London 1720), 27. Gildon's Apollo is not entirely unequitable, since he condemns one of the polite losers "to have his Eyes pick'd out by the *Pen* of the vilest *Ballad-maker* in *Town.*"

33 Girolamo Briani, "A Continuation of the Advices," in John Hughes's translation of Trajano Boccalini's *Advices from Parnassus* (London 1706), 451.

34 *A Journal from Parnassus*, ed. MacDonald, 26.

35 *The Session of the Poets, Holden at the Foot of Parnassus-Hill*, 43, 49.

36 Anne Finch, Countess of Winchilsea, *Poems*, ed. Myra Reynolds (Chicago: University of Chicago Press 1903), 94.

37 Charles Hanbury Williams, "To Mrs. Bindon," in *A Collection of Poems*, ed. Robert Dodsley, 5th ed., 6 vols. (London 1758), 5:156.

38 Robert Folkenflik, "The Artist as Hero in the Eighteenth Century," *Yearbook of English Studies*, vol. 12 (1982), 93. See also Michael West, "Dryden and the Disintegration of Renaissance Heroic Ideals," *Costerus* 7 (1973): 193–222.

39 Numerous critics have pointed out how Dryden's poem may be an oblique commentary on Charles II's poor record of patronage. See, for instance, Erskine-Hill, *Augustan Idea in English Literature*, 222–3, and Laura Brown, "The Ideology of Restoration Poetic Form: John Dryden," *PMLA* 97 (1982): 401. Line references for *Mac Flecknoe* are to the California edition of Dryden's *Works*, ed. Edward Niles Hooker *et al.* (Berkeley: University of California Press 1956—in progress), 2:54–60.

40 Book and line references to *The Dunciad* are to the edition of 1743. Thomas Woodman sees Pope's *Dunciad* as announcing the end of the laureate tradition. See "'Wanting nothing but the Laurel': Pope and the Idea of the Laureate Poet," in *Pope: New Contexts*, ed. David Fairer (New York: Harvester Wheatsheaf 1990), 45–58.

41 Andreas Huyssen, *After the Great Divide: Modernism, Mass Culture, Postmodernism* (Bloomington: Indiana University Press 1986), 47.

42 Catherine Ingrassia, "Women Writing/Writing Women: Pope, Dulness, and 'Feminization' in the *Dunciad*," *Eighteenth-Century Life* 14 (1990): 55. Later in the century, with the complete erasure of the laureate ideal, opposition to the print market could itself be devalued as effeminate. See Linda Zionkowski, "Gray, the Marketplace, and the Masculine Poet," *Criticism* 35 (1993): 589–608.

43 Oliver Goldsmith, *An History of England* (1764), in *Collected Works*, ed. Arthur Friedman, 5 vols. (Oxford: Clarendon Press 1966), 5:311n.

44 Because women poets were precluded from obtaining a classical education, they were discouraged from writing in the "higher" and more rigorous genres of epic, panegyric, and the like. As a result, "the *Lyric*," according to Gildon, was "a Poem in which ... the *Ladies* have excell'd"; see *The Complete Art of Poetry*, 2 vols. (London 1718), 1:172. Douglas Lane Patey discusses this aspect of cultural feminization, and its later male appropriation, in his valuable essay "'Aesthetics' and the Rise of Lyric in the Eighteenth Century," *Studies in English Literature* 33 (1993): 587–608.

45 On Burke's resistance to the feminization of culture, see David Simpson, *Romanticism, Nationalism, and the Revolt Against Theory* (Chicago: University of Chicago Press 1993), 126–42. Nancy Armstrong proposed the case for the feminization of culture in the eighteenth century in her *Desire and Domestic Fiction: A Political History of the Novel* (Oxford: Oxford University Press 1987), 3–27, as did Terry Lovell in *Consuming Fiction* (London: Verso 1987), 36–45.

46 Huyssen, *After the Great Divide*, 45.

47 Dorothy Mermin suggests that the poets' renunciations of social ambitions were debilitating in going "smoothly with the grain of social expectation, not interestingly against it"; see "Women Becoming Poets: Katherine Philips, Aphra Behn, Anne Finch," *ELH* 57 (1990): 349. In an immediate sense, this is no doubt true, though their gestures anticipate how later eighteenth-century male poets, such as Gray and Cowper, would make such renunciation an aspect of their self-definition.

48 The standard account of the retirement theme in Pope's later work remains Maynard Mack's *The Garden and the City* (Toronto: University of Toronto Press 1969). In a seminal essay, G.K. Hunter contrasted Horace's serene sense of withdrawal to Pope's barely concealed resentment: under the "fine classical façade" of the Imitations of Horace, Pope spoke rather from the point of view of "the injured Byronic sensibility of the individual" ("The 'Romanticism' of Pope's Horace," *Essays in Criticism* 10 [1960]: 403).

49 For this argument, see Kristina Straub, "Indecent Liberties with a Poet: Audience and the Metaphor of Rape in Killigrew's 'Upon the saying that my verses' and Pope's *Arbuthnot*," *Tulsa Studies in Women's Literature* 6 (1987): 27–45.

50 Walter J. Ong, *The Presence of the Word* (New Haven, Conn.: Yale University Press 1967), 252.

51 For this argument, see Manuel Schonhorn, "Pope's *Epistle to Augustus*: Notes Toward a Mythology," in *Pope: Recent Essays*, ed. Maynard Mack and James A. Winn (Hamden, Conn.: Archon Books 1980), 548–9.

52 Pope himself appears in such a procession before "wise AUGUSTUS," in James Ralph's coronation ode, *The Muses' Address to the King* (London 1728): "lo! the living *Bards*, / A num'rous crowd! approach P[ope], T[homso]n, Y[oung], / Great E[us]d[e]n, the joy of ev'ry muse! / An hundred more .... / O lend a favourable ear, / Illustrious GEORGE! / And, as the greatest, be the best of *kings* ... / So shall [the poets'] names again revive" (pp. 18–20).

53 Brean S. Hammond, *Pope* (Atlantic Highlands, N.J.: Humanities Press 1986), 93. Emphasis in original.

54 Anthony Ashley Cooper, Earl of Shaftesbury, *Characteristics of Men, Manners, Opinions, Times*, ed. John M. Robertson, 2 vols. (Gloucester, Mass.: Peter Smith 1963), 1:214.

55 Howard Caygill makes the point in relation to aesthetic and moral philosophies of the period, in *Art of Judgement* (Oxford: Basil Blackwell 1989), 100–2.

56 Margaret Anne Doody, *The Daring Muse* (Cambridge: Cambridge University Press 1985), 168.

57 Popular defences of women from the period often put forward the essentialist claim that women were blessed with a spontaneous creativity, which could only be impaired were women to submit this natural eloquence to the conventional laws of poetry. Women, according to one such treatise, "express neatly, and in order, what they conceive: Their words cost them nothing; they begin, and go on at their pleasure, and when they have their liberty, their fancy supplies them always with inexhaustible liberality" (François Poulain de la Barre, *The Woman as Good as the Man: Or, the Equallity of Both Sexes*, trans. A.L. [London 1677], 31). On how such essentializing helped to perpetuate a double standard for women's poetry, see Germaine Greer, *Slip-Shod Sybils: Recognition, Rejection and the Woman Poet* (Penguin 1995), 45–7.

58 John Dryden, *Of Dramatick Poesy and Other Critical Essays*, ed. George Watson, 2 vols. (London: Dent/Everyman 1962), 2:272.

59 The phrase "Muse of Pain" is David B. Morris's, from *Alexander Pope: The Genius of Sense* (Cambridge, Mass.: Harvard University Press 1984), 214. Though Morris deals splendidly with the violent nature of Pope's satire in the Epistle, he does not relate Pope's "individuation of pain" to the poet's own expressions of distress. On the role of physical deformity in Pope's self-definition, see Dennis Todd, *Imagining Monsters: Miscreations of the Self in Eighteenth-Century England* (Chicago: University of Chicago Press 1995), 217–68, and more generally, Helen Deutsch, *Resemblance and Disgrace: Alexander Pope and the Deformation of Culture* (Cambridge, Mass.: Harvard University Press 1996). Deutsch considers Pope in terms of cultural feminization, including its manifestations in the poet's assertions of compulsive sincerity. Yet, whereas Deutsch

examines these assertions as part of what she sees as Pope's desire for self-possession, I argue that they should be understood as responses to altered conditions for English poetry in general.

60 Leopold Damrosch, Jr has noted that Pope often used sexual metaphors to describe the burdens of artistic creation. He cites, in particular, a bitter passage from a letter Pope had written to the aspiring poet Judith Cowper: "You (Madam) are in your honeymoon of poetry; you have seen only the smiles and enjoyed the caresses of Apollo. Nothing is so pleasant to a muse as the first children of the imagination; but when once she comes to find it mere conjugal duty, and the care of her numerous progeny daily grows upon her, 'tis all a sour tax for past pleasure" (Pope, *Correspondence*, ed. George Sherburn, 5 vols. [Oxford: Clarendon Press 1956], 1:209, as quoted in Damrosch, *The Imaginative World of Alexander Pope* [Berkeley: University of California Press, 1987], 133).

61 Finch, *Poems*, 7.

62 On how women's "feeblenesses" became equated with expressions of sincerity in the fiction of the period, see Janet Todd, *Sensibility: An Introduction* (London: Methuen 1986), 78–81.

63 Of Pope's reworking of Horace's original, Rebecca Ferguson writes that "the compulsion to compose satire is represented as a spontaneous emotional force – 'my Head and Heart thus flowing thro' my Quill' – and also again as a distinctively masculine form of energy" (*The Unbalanced Mind: Pope and the Rule of Passion* [Philadelphia: University of Pennsylvania Press 1986], 149). G. Douglas Atkins argues that the *Epistle to Arbuthnot* dramatizes Pope's own feminization as the "sexual object" of the hacks who seek him out; see *Quests of Difference: Reading Pope's Poems* (Lexington: University of Kentucky Press 1986), 134–46.

64 Carole Fabricant, "Pope's Moral, Political, and Cultural Combat," *The Eighteenth Century: Theory and Interpretation* 29 (1988): 168–9.

65 Hammond, *Pope*, 129.

66 Joseph Warton, *An Essay on the Genius and Writings of Pope*, vol. 1 (London 1756), iv.

67 Edward Young, *Conjectures on Original Composition. In A Letter to the Author of Sir Charles Grandison*, 2nd ed. (London 1759), 25–6, 50, 30. Emphases in original.

68 If male writers of the period disparaged Pope as "effeminate" while ignoring his defence of the poet's compulsion, women poets were not averse to asserting their natural eloquence in Popeian terms. Turning down an invitation to write for the *Monthly Review*, Mary Jones offered a disclaimer that seemed to wed gender essentialism with an unmistakable echo from the *Epistle to Arbuthnot*: "All I ever did in ye poetic

Fields was spontaneous, or by mere accident – I sought not ye Numbers, but ye Birds, & ye Numbers *came*" (letter to Ralph Griffiths, 16 March 1761, cited in Roger Lonsdale, ed., *Eighteenth-Century Women Poets: An Oxford Anthology* [Oxford: Oxford University Press 1989], 156).

69 Pierre Bourdieu, *The Field of Cultural Production*, ed. Randal Johnson (New York: Columbia University Press 1993), 187.

70 Ben Jonson, *Works*, ed. C.H. Herford, Percy Simpson, and Evelyn Simpson, 11 vols. (Oxford: Clarendon Press 1925–52), 4:33.

71 Samuel Johnson, *Lives of the English Poets*, ed. George Birkbeck Hill, 3 vols. (Oxford: Clarendon Press 1905), 3:251.

72 The Abbé Batteux, in *Les Beaux-Arts réduits à un même principe* (1746), was evidently the first to invoke the phrase "Poësie pure," which he used to designate works of the imagination in verse. See D.J. Mossop, *Pure Poetry: Studies in French Poetic Theory and Practice, 1746 to 1945* (Oxford: Clarendon Press 1971), 32–3. On the English adaptation of the phrase, and its relation to the reorganization of knowledge in the later eighteenth century, see Patey, "'Aesthetics' and the Rise of the Lyric" (n.44 above).

73 This is the argument of Howard Weinbrot's *Britannia's Issue: The Rise of British Literature from Dryden to Ossian* (Cambridge: Cambridge University Press 1993). J.C.D. Clark also sees the rise of the vernacular canon as helping to displace an "Anglo-Latin tradition," though he insists that "humanist classicism ... lasted for longer, and was more powerful, than historians or literary scholars have generally allowed" (*Samuel Johnson: Literature, Religion and English Cultural Politics from the Restoration to Romanticism* [Cambridge: Cambridge University Press 1994], 2).

74 Citing examples of "sublimity of expression," Lowth observed that "whoever will attend with any diligence to the poetry of the Hebrews, will find that examples of this kind almost perpetually occur, and much more frequently, than could be endured in the poetry of the Greeks and Romans, or even in our own" (*Lectures on the Sacred Poetry of the Hebrews*, 2 vols. [London 1753; trans. 1787], 1:329).

75 J.G.A. Pocock, *Virtue, Commerce, And History: Essays on Political Thought and History, Chiefly in the Eighteenth Century* (Cambridge: Cambridge University Press 1985), 37–50 (quote at 49).

76 "The discourse of civic humanism," John Barrell suggests, "was the most authoritative fantasy of masculinity in early eighteenth-century Britain," and since it emphasized economic independence and masculine autonomy for the citizen, civic humanism helped to intensify the cultural gendering of commercial activity as feminine: the citizen could be "effeminated as much by submission to 'female charms' as by the urge to acquire and spend" ("'The Dangerous Goddess': Masculinity,

Prestige, and the Aesthetic in Early Eighteenth-Century Britain," in *The Birth of Pandora and the Division of Knowledge* [Philadelphia: University of Pennsylvania Press 1992]: 64–5).

77 This is not to suggest that cultural capital was not operative in a pre-capitalist economy. Clearly any author had to demonstrated special competences, rhetorical skills, and classical learning to achieve distinction as a cultural producer, but such an accummulation of cultural capital was not treated as an end in itself. Rather, the author was expected to use these skills to further the circulation of symbolic capital within a larger moral economy.

78 "A work of art," Bourdieu writes, "has meaning and interest only for someone who possesses the cultural competence, that is, the code, into which it is encoded" (*Distinction*, trans. Richard Nice [London: Routledge and Kegan Paul 1984], 2). My definition of cultural capital is based on Randal Johnson's summary paraphrase in his introduction to *The Field of Cultural Production*, 7.

79 Young, *Conjectures*, 27–8.

80 Young, *Conjectures*, 28. Young's account of the poetic compulsion allows for the possibility of outside stimuli but stresses its unpredictability, even to the poet of genius: "That a man may be scarce less ignorant of his own powers, than an oyster of its pearl, or a rock of its diamond; that he may possess dormant, unsuspected abilities, till awakened by loud calls, or stung by striking emergencies, is evident from the sudden eruption of some men, out of perfect obscurity, into publick admiration, on the strong impulse of some animating occasion; not more to the world's great surprize, than their own" (50).

81 William Wordsworth, preface to the 2nd edition of the *Lyrical Ballads* (1802), in *Wordsworth's Literary Criticism*, ed. W.J.B. Owen (London: Routledge and Kegan Paul 1974), 72.

82 Pocock, *Virtue, Commerce, and History*, 114.

83 Wordsworth, *Wordsworth's Literary Criticism*, 72. Bourdieu and Jean-Claude Passeron define symbolic violence as "the imposition of a cultural arbitrary by an arbitrary power"; this imposition may include the work of various pedagogical agencies or cultural institutions, as well as what they call the "discontinuous and extraordinary actions of symbolic violence like those of the prophet, the intellectual 'creator' or the sorcerer" (*Reproduction in Education, Society and Culture*, trans Richard Nice, 2nd ed. [London: Sage Publications 1990], 5, 31). On eighteenth-century attempts to locate the source of genius in providence or nature, see Ken Frieden, *Genius and Monologue* (Ithaca, N.Y.: Cornell University Press 1985).

84 As Bourdieu suggests, the evolution of the cultural field towards a greater autonomy is "accompanied by a greater *reflexivity*" in which

producers and consumers must increasingly demonstrate a knowledge of its history in order to participate within it. Even those poets who are designated as "naifs" are increasingly consecrated in terms of their "paradoxical relationship with history's legacy" (*The Rules of Art: Genesis and Structure of the Literary Field*, trans. Susan Emanuel [Stanford, Calif.: Stanford University Press 1996], 242–4).

85 *The Poems of Mr Gray, to which are refixed Memoirs of his Life and Writing*, ed. William Mason, 2 vols. (York 1775), 2:91, quoted in Folkenflik, "The Artist as Hero," 97. In this essay, Folkenflik shows how, in representations of the poet, "the English were for a change in the avant-garde" over the course of the eighteenth century, going from the Augustan poet-hero of ethical purpose to the isolated, anti-political bard of Gray's ode (92).

86 Richard Hurd, *Works*, 8 vols. (London 1811; rptd., New York: AMS Press 1967), 1:104. Emphases in original.

87 Warton, *Essay on the Genius and Writings of Pope*, v.

88 Warton, *An Essay on the Genius and Writings of Pope*, vol. 2 (London 1782), 478–9. I discuss Warton's canonic rankings in more detail in my final chapter.

89 Young, *Conjectures*, 5–6, 45.

90 Thomas Gray, *Correspondence*, ed. Paget Toynbee *et al.*, 2nd ed., 3 vols. (Oxford: Clarendon Press 1971), 1:296. On Gray's authorial self-definition in relation to the book market, see Linda Zionkowski, "Bridging the Gulf Between: The Poet and the Audience in the Work of Gray," *ELH* 58 (1991): 331–50. In another article, Zionkowski examines how similar claims for the transcendent value of writing could yet inform arguments made in defence of commercial authorship. In *The Case of Authors by Profession or Trade* (London 1758), James Ralph, one of Pope's dunces, insisted that "the Writer who serves himself and the Public together, has a good a Right to the Product in Money of his Abilities, as the Landholder to his Rent, or the Money-jobber to his interest." Authors who refused to recognize their own economic interests, Ralph defiantly declared, were "Dupes of [their] own delusions." And yet, possibly because copyright was being debated in the law courts at this time, Ralph could also abide by the metaphysical belief that the writer's "Accomplishments and Abilities are the Patents of *God Almighty* for Place Precedency" over other professions. See Zionkowski, "Territorial Disputes in the Republic of Letters: Canon Formation and the Literary Profession," *The Eighteenth Century: Theory and Interpretation* 31 (1990): 3–22.

91 The passage was added after the original 1782 edition of Warton's second volume of the *Essay*. I quote from the version that appears in the corrected 5th edition, 2 vols. (London 1806), 2:402. I consider Warton's criteria for canonicity in my final chapter.

92 William Duff, *An Essay on Original Genius* (London 1767), 292.

93 Bourdieu, *Distinction*, 31. Bourdieu elsewhere suggests that "those 'inventions' of Romanticism – the representation of culture as a kind of superior reality, irreducible to the vulgar demands of economics, and the ideology of the free, disinterested 'creation' founded on the spontaneity of innate inspiration – appear to be just so many reactions to the pressures of an anonymous market" (*The Field of Cultural Production*, 114).

94 John Sitter makes the case for this poetic "flight from history" in *Literary Loneliness in Mid-Eighteenth-Century England* (Ithaca, N.Y.: Cornell University Press 1982), 77–103. William C. Dowling has since proposed a revision of Sitter's thesis, wherein the poetic revival at mid-century reflected a change from the Augustans' "retrospective radicalism" to a modern notion of historical progressivism ("Ideology and the Flight from History in Eighteenth-Century Poetry," in *The Profession of Eighteenth-Century Literature: Reflections on an Institution*, ed. Leo Damrosch [Madison: University of Wisconsin Press 1992], 135–53). Dowling's argument anticipates mine in several respects, including the use of Pocock's intellectual history to suggest how the generational shift from the Augustans to their successors involved differing responses to new economic realities. Yet, whereas he sees this contest of ideologies as involving an epistemological shift in perceptions of history, I am following Bourdieu in proposing that the rejection of classicism reflects a complex historical realignment of the fields of activity, a realignment necessitated by those new material realities.

95 Lowth, in *Lectures on the Sacred Poetry of the Hebrews*, 1:308.

96 Wordsworth, *Wordsworth's Literary Criticism*, 71.

CHAPTER 6

1 Bernard le Bouvier de Fontenelle, *Digression sur les Anciens et les Modernes* (1688), appended to later editions of his *Entretiens sur la Plurality des Mondes* (orig. 1686), ed. Robert Shackelton (Oxford: Clarendon Press 1955), 174 (translation mine).

2 *An Essay on Wit* (London 1748), 18.

3 Saint-Evremond, *Miscellaneous Essays* (London 1692), 213; Jonathan Swift, *Prose Works*, 14 vols., ed. Herbert Davis (Oxford: Shakespeare Head Press 1939–68), 4:217; John Oldmixon, ed., *The Life and Posthumous Works of Arthur Maynwaring* (London 1715), 4. On how certain disciplines of learning came to be viewed as "polite," see Lawrence Klein, "The Third Earl of Shaftesbury and the Progress of Politeness," *Eighteenth-Century Studies* 18 (1984/5): 186–214.

4 Anthony Ashley Cooper, Earl of Shaftesbury, *Characteristics of Men, Manners, Opinions, Times*, ed. John M. Robertson, 2 vols. (Gloucester, Mass.: Peter Smith 1963), 2:257.

5 References, by essay number, are to Donald F. Bond's edition of *The Spectator*, 5 vols. (Oxford: Clarendon Press 1965).

6 Neil Saccamano, "The Consolations of Ambivalence: Habermas and the Public Sphere," *MLN* 106 (1991): 695. On the *Spectator* and the formation of a reading public, see Michael G. Ketcham, *Transparent Designs: Reading, Performance, and Form in the* Spectator *Papers* (Athens: University of Georgia Press 1985).

7 On the early academic study of English literature, see D.J. Palmer, *The Rise of English Studies* (London: Oxford University Press 1965).

8 Samuel Johnson, *Lives of the English Poets*, ed. George Birkbeck Hill, 3 vols. (Oxford: Clarendon Press 1905), 2:146–7.

9 On the early eighteenth-century aestheticization of Milton's poetics, see Leslie E. Moore, *Beautiful Sublime: The Making of* Paradise Lost, *1701–1734* (Stanford, Calif.: Stanford University Press 1990).

10 Addison's efforts were likely part of a larger marketing strategy to introduce *Paradise Lost* to a broad audience, since the appearance of the Milton papers coincided with Tonson's publication of the poem in relatively cheap, smaller-sized editions, with the papers eventually being reprinted as prefaces to these editions. See Moore, *Beautiful Sublime*, 7, and Lillian D. Bloom, "Addison's Popular Aesthetic: The Rhetoric of the *Paradise Lost* Papers," in *The Author in his Work*, ed. Louis L. Martz and Aubrey Williams (New Haven, Conn.: Yale University Press 1978), 266.

11 Patrick Daly, Jr suggests that Addison decided to extend his series to eighteen numbers only after the sixth paper, when it "dawned on Addison the journalist that he could get much more mileage out of Milton's epic" by borrowing heavily from Patrick Hume's 1695 commentary on the poem ("Patrick Hume and the Making of Addison's *Paradise Lost* Papers," *Milton Studies* 31 [1994]: 182).

12 Robert L. Montgomery writes of how much Addison's view of the reading process eliminates any rhetorical function: "Figurative speech is not employed in the service of persuasion; the vividness and presence of verbally mediated objects are not avenues to thought or truth. They are there simply to be enjoyed" (*Terms of Response: Language and Audience in Seventeenth- and Eighteenth-Century Theory* [University Park: Pennsylvania State University Press 1992], 84).

13 Many critics have discussed Addison's role in the formation of the aesthetic experience. See, in particular, William H. Youngren, "Addison and the Birth of Eighteenth-Century Aesthetics," *Modern Philology* 79

(1982): 267–83, and Neil Saccamano, "The Sublime Force of Words in Addison's 'Pleasures,'" *ELH* 58 (1991): 83–106.

14 That Addison's misrecognition of his own authority altered the operative assumptions within critical discourse is testified by how eagerly modern scholars perpetuate this misrecognition in praising Addison's achievement: "Addison's originality," Leopold Damrosch, Jr writes, "lies in his conviction that the reader is more important than the prosecutor or judge, and should not let himself be bullied by authority. It is not simply as a pose that Addison appears as the reader's companion rather than his master" ("The Significance of Addison's Criticism," *Studies in English Literature* 19 [1979]: 423).

15 Voltaire, "Milton," from *An Essay Upon the Civil Wars of France* (1727), in *Milton: The Critical Heritage*, ed. John T. Shawcross (London: Routledge and Kegan Paul 1970), 255.

16 Theophilus Cibber, *Lives of the Poets* (London 1753), 5:196n.

17 By mid-century, this circle of belief was so widely prevalent that a critic like Joseph Warton could misrecognize how Milton's canonicity, which the Milton industry had established, could by then legitimate the industry: "If we consider the high rank which MILTON has deservedly obtained among our few English classics, we cannot wonder at the multitude of commentaries and criticisms of which he has been the subject." By then, Milton had become an author whose value was considered inexhaustible, open to ever new critical discoveries: "Among innumerable beauties in the PARADISE LOST, I think the most transcendant is the speech of Satan at the beginning of the ninth book ... and yet Mr. ADDISON has passed it over, unpraised and unnoticed" (*The Adventurer*, 23 October 1753, no. 101 in coll. ed., 2 vols. [London 1754], 181, 186).

18 See J.A.W. Bennett, "The Early Fame of Gavin Douglas's *Eneados*," *Modern Language Notes* 61 (1946): 83–8.

19 James Greenwood, ed. *The Virgin Muse* (London 1717), sigs. A3$_{r–v}$. Greenwood's selections consisted primarily of light and devotional verse by Waller, Denham, Roscommon, Prior, Watts, and Katherine Philips, though he also included notable extracts from *Paradise Lost* and Dryden's *Fables*.

20 Ian Michael, *The Teaching of English: From the Sixteenth Century to 1870* (Cambridge: Cambridge University Press 1987), 171. Schoolmasters since Richard Mulcaster in the 1580s had been advocating the teaching of the English language, and a few encouraged the reading of English texts. In *Logonomia anglica* (1619), an English grammar though written in Latin, Alexander Gill offered a number of selections from contemporary English poets and suggested that religious instruction might better be conducted in the vernacular. As Franklin E. Court

notes, Gill "appears to have been the first actually to use a textbook to promote the idea that written works in English could be used in the classroom to propagate religious principles and improve conduct" (*Institutionalizing English Literature: The Culture and Politics of Literary Study, 1750–1900* [Stanford, Calif.: Stanford University Press 1992], 11–12).

21 On the opposition to traditional classical education during the period, see Penelope Wilson, "Classical Poetry and the Eighteenth-Century Reader," in *Books and their Readers in Eighteenth-Century England*, ed. Isabel Rivers (Leicester, U.K.: Leicester University Press 1982), 72–5.

22 Benjamin Franklin, "Sketch of an English School," *Complete Works*, 3 vols. (London 1806), 2:370–8.

23 James Barclay, *A Treatise on Education* (Edinburgh 1743), 64.

24 Ann Fisher, *The Pleasing Instructor* (London 1756), x–xi. Emphases in original.

25 James Buchanan, *The First Six Books of Milton's Paradise Lost Rendered into Grammatical Construction* (Edinburgh 1773), title page and 1.

26 *Proposals for an Amendment of School-Instruction* (London 1772), 11. Michael (*Teaching of English*, 205) attributes this work to "J. Butler" without providing evidence for the ascription.

27 William Milns, *The Well-bred Scholar, or Practical Essays on the Best Methods of Improving the Taste, and Assisting the Exertions of Youth in their Literary Pursuits*, 2nd ed. (New York 1797), 17.

28 Maria Edgeworth and Richard Lovell Edgeworth, *Practical Education*, 2 vols. (London 1798), 1:367, as cited in Michael, *Teaching of English*, 209; Richard Lovell Edgeworth, *Poetry Explained for the Use of Young People* (London 1802), and Maria Edgeworth and Richard Lovell Edgeworth, *Readings on Poetry* (London 1816).

29 Vicesimus Knox, "On Novel Reading," essay 18, *Essays, Moral and Literary*, 2 vols. (London 1779), 2:190.

30 On the gendering of reading practices, see Peter de Bolla, *The Discourse of the Sublime* (Oxford: Basil Blackwell 1989), 252–78.

31 William Jackson, *Thirty Letters on various Subjects*, 3rd ed. (London 1795), 16, cited in De Bolla, *Discourse of the Sublime*, 268n.78.

32 Some educators, like the Edgeworths, believed that students prescribed relatively undemanding works would approach their education "with as much eagerness, and with more rational curiosity, than is usually shown by students who are nourished with the hardest fare, and chained to unceasing labour" (*Moral Tales* [London 1801], pref., cited in Michael, *Teaching of English*, 208–9).

33 Michael (*Teaching of English*, 196–8) tabulates the frequency of these authors' appearances among nineteen anthologies published between 1771 and 1801: Pope leads with twelve appearances, followed by

Thomson (eleven), Cowper (seven), Shakespeare (six), Addison and Milton (five each), and Elizabeth Carter and others (four apiece).

34 Oliver Goldsmith, pref. to *The Beauties of English Poetry* (1767), in *Collected Works*, ed. Arthur Friedman, 5 vols. (Oxford: Clarendon Press 1966), 5:318.

35 *Critical Review* (June 1767), quoted in Goldsmith, *Collected Works*, 5:317n.1. On the boom in literary anthologies, and how it affected contemporary perceptions of the canon, see Thomas F. Bonnell, "Bookselling and Canon-Making: The Trade Rivalry over the English Poets, 1776–1783," in *Studies in Eighteenth-Century Culture*, vol. 19, ed. Leslie Ellen Brown and Patricia Craddock (East Lansing, Mich.: Colleagues Press 1989), 53–69.

36 Barbara M. Benedict, *Making the Modern Reader: Cultural Mediation in Early Modern Literary Anthologies* (Princeton, N.J.: Princeton University Press 1996), 212.

37 *Sentimental Beauties and Moral Delineations from the Writings of the celebrated Dr. Blair, and other much admired authors* (London 1782), title page.

38 Joshua Collins, *A Practical Guide to Parents and Guardians, in the right choice and use of books*, 2nd ed. (London 1802), cited in Michael, *Teaching of English*, 211–12.

39 John Clarke, *An Essay upon Study* (London 1731), 194. Emphasis in original.

40 James Buchanan, *A Plan of an English Grammar-School Education* (Edinburgh 1770), 116.

41 Franklin E. Court makes much of Smith's efforts at including English literature in the university curriculum and at initiating "an attitude toward English literary study that taught that truly 'great' writers, by virtue of their sterling characters, reinforce the natural moral authority that claimed to be the theoretical base of free-market capitalism" (*Institutionalizing English Literature*, 28). Yet, while it is true that Smith's lectures made extensive reference to English writers, this "attitude" had really more to do with the traditional rhetorical principle of *bonus orator, bonus vir* even if it was being applied in defence of capitalist relations.

42 Hugh Blair, *Lectures on Rhetoric and Belles Lettres*, 2 vols. (London 1783), 1:4–5.

43 Wilbur Samuel Howell, *Eighteenth-Century British Logic and Rhetoric* (Princeton, N.J.: Princeton University Press 1971), 535.

44 Blair, *Lectures on Rhetoric and Belles Lettres*, 1:10.

45 Blair, *Lectures on Rhetoric and Belles Lettres*, 1: 9–10, 12–13.

46 George Chapman, *A Treatise on Education*, 3rd ed. (London 1784), 197–9.

47 Northrop Frye, *Anatomy of Criticism* (Princeton, N.J.: Princeton University Press 1957), 17.

48 Brian Vickers, *Returning to Shakespeare* (London: Routledge 1989), 229.

49 Margreta de Grazia, *Shakespeare Verbatim: The Reproduction of Authenticity and the 1790 Apparatus* (Oxford: Clarendon Press 1991). For an overview of eighteenth-century theories of editorial revision, see Grace Ioppolo, *Revising Shakespeare* (Cambridge, Mass.: Harvard University Press 1991), 19–31.

50 Edward Young, *Conjectures on Original Composition. In A Letter to the Author of Sir Charles Grandison*, 2nd ed. (London 1759), 80. Emphasis in original. I have elsewhere noted that one of the consequences of the copyright debate was an increased critical emphasis on an author's style as the determining criterion for value, and this emphasis clearly influenced the movement towards textual authenticity. See "Copyright and the Invention of Tradition," *Eighteenth-Century Studies* 26 (1992): 1–27.

51 Lewis Theobald, pref. to *The Tragedy of King Richard II* (London 1720; first performed 1719), cited in *Shakespeare: The Critical Heritage, 1623–1800* (hereafter *SCH*), ed. Brian Vickers, 6 vols. (London: Routledge and Kegan Paul, 1974–81), 2:352. Also worth noting is Theobald's 1727 play *Double Falshood*, which was purported to be his adaptation of an unpublished tragicomedy by Shakespeare and Fletcher.

52 Ian Ousby surveys the various efforts throughout the century to transform Stratford into a tourist attraction in *The Englishman's England* (Cambridge: Cambridge University Press 1990), 33–57.

53 Michael Dobson, *The Making of the National Poet: Shakespeare, Adaptation and Authorship, 1660–1769* (Oxford: Clarendon Press, 1992) 14. Dobson suggests that the movement towards an authentic Shakespearean text was part of a larger effort to appropriate his works on behalf on "what became the dominant, nationalist ideology of mid-eighteenth century England" (12). Dobson's claim has been recently seconded by Robert D. Hume, who writes that "eighteenth-century audiences finally got around to appreciating the greatness of Shakespeare" only once his plays had begun to be staged "as celebrations of British monarchy and British power" ("Before the Bard: 'Shakespeare' in Early Eighteenth-Century London," *ELH* 64 [1997]: 66–7). As an argument about the phenomenal rise of Bardolatry during the period, there is no doubt some justice to this claim. Yet, as I have already suggested in relation to other arguments about how canon-making is primarily motivated by nationalist sentiment, there is no necessary connection between the prevalence of such sentiments and the particular way in which literary works may come to be treated as canonical. Dobson and Hume, it seems to me, do not provide a plausible explanation as to how a rising

tide of nationalist ideology during the eighteenth century should have necessarily led to a drive among critics and editors towards textual authenticity. If anything, nationalist ideology in and of itself was the impetus for much of the continued updating of Shakespeare's text that occurred in response to events like the Seven Years' War. National-ism may have contributed to Shakespeare being transformed into the Bard, but the increased attention paid to determining an authentic Shakespearean text was chiefly propelled by another set of ideological values, which were cultural rather than political in nature. These values are suggested by Hume himself when he maintains that Bardola-try has been sustained into the twentieth century by "widespread, gen-erally mandatory indoctrination in schools" (67–8). This claim seems to me applicable as much to the eighteenth century as to our own: the drive towards textual authenticity, I am proposing in this chapter, repre-sented an attempt by critics, editors, and finally educators to assert their authority as cultural experts, to vaunt this expertise as a desirable form of social capital, and to position themselves in a position of privi-lege within a new and hierarchical domain of culture.

54 Henry Fielding, *The Historical Register For the Year 1736* and *Eurydice Hissed* (London 1737), III, ll. 129–31, in Regents Restoration Drama Series, ed. William W. Appleton (Lincoln, Nebr.: University of Nebraska 1967), 44. Fielding may have been the author of an essay from the *Craftsman* (no. 574) that satirized the political cynicism of the Licensing Act. In the paper, "Cibber" recommends himself to the ministry as political censor and adaptor of such works as *King John*, *Richard II*, and Jonson's *Sejanus* because, he claims, "the *late Act, for restraining the Stage*, will not answer the Purpose intended by it, unless there be some Regulation of *old plays*, as well as *new ones*" (*New Essays by Henry Fielding*, ed. Martin Battestin [Charlottesville: University of Vir-ginia Press 1989], 234).

55 On these later adaptations, see Jonathan Bate, *Shakespearean Constitutions: Politics, Theatre, Criticism 1730–1830* (Oxford: Clarendon Press 1989).

56 See George Winchester Stone, Jr, ed., *The London Stage 1660–1800* (*Part Four: 1747–1776*) (Carbondale: Southern Illinois University Press 1962), 1:clxxii. Eliza Haywood was perhaps the first to recognize that the commercial monopoly of the patent theatres made for an attenu-ated repertory bounded by tradition. "If the eye," she pleaded with the managers, "could be satisfied with seeing, or the ear with hearing always the same things over and over repeated, it must be owned there are many old plays, which the best of our modern poets would not per-haps be able to excel; but nature delights in variety, and though it would be unjust and ungrateful to strip the laurels from the brows of *Shakespear, Johnson, Beaumont* and *Fletcher, Dryden, Otway, Lee, Congreve,*

and several other deservedly admired authors, to adorn those who shall succeed them, yet we love to see a genius the growth of our own times, and might find sufficient trophies for the merits of such, without any injury to their predecessors" (*The Female Spectator*, 2nd col. ed., 4 vols. [London 1748], 2:73).

57 *A Letter to Colley Cibber* (London 1745), cited in *SCH*, 3:157.

58 John Hill, *The Actor: A Treatise on the Art of Playing* (London 1750), cited in *SCH*, 3:373.

59 William Warburton, pref. to his edition of *The Works of Shakespeare* (London 1747), cited in *SCH*, 3:225.

60 Vickers, "Introduction," *SCH*, 4:24.

61 MacNamara Morgan, *A Letter to Miss Nossiter Occasioned by Her First Appearance on the Stage* (London 1753), cited in *SCH*, 4:53.

62 Arthur Murphy, in *Gray's-Inn Journal* (19 January 1754), cited in *SCH*, 4:105. Murphy was no doubt obliquely mocking Warburton's edition.

63 George Steevens, review of Garrick's adaptation of *Hamlet*, in *General Evening Post* (17–19 December 1772), cited in *SCH*, 5:472.

64 Goldsmith, "An Enquiry into the Present State of Polite Learning in Europe" (1759), in *Collected Works*, 1:325.

65 Theophilus Cibber, *Two Dissertations on Theatrical Subjects* (London 1756), cited in *SCH*, 4:252.

66 William Warburton, ed., *The Works of Shakespeare*, 8 vols. (London 1747), 1:viii–xv.

67 Simon Jarvis interprets claims like Warburton's as signalling an increasing professionalization of intellectual labour and a widening class division between gentlemanly amateurs and working editors; see *Scholars and Gentlemen: Shakespearian Textual Criticism and Representations of Scholarly Labour, 1725–1765* (Oxford: Clarendon Press 1995). Jarvis does not, however, consider how this professionalization helped to alter prevalent notions of what made Shakespeare's works canonical.

68 Vickers, "Introduction," *SCH*, 5:21. Vickers cites as a typical example a letter to *The Gentleman's Magazine* for May 1765 that begins: "While almost every body is making emendations, annotations, or illustrations, of some part or other of *Shakespeare* ... give me leave to take this opportunity of throwing one mite into the treasury."

69 William Dodd, *The Beauties of Shakespeare*, 2 vols. (London 1752), cited in *SCH*, 3:465,468.

70 Samuel Johnson, *Proposals For Printing, by Subscription, The Dramatick Works of William Shakespeare* (1756), in *Works*, ed. A.T. Hazen *et al.* (New Haven, Conn.: Yale University Press 1958—in progress), 7:55-7.

71 Steevens, preface to his revision of Johnson's edition of Shakespeare (London 1773), cited in *SCH*, 5:515. For additional examples of such addresses to the reader, see De Grazia, *Shakespeare Verbatim*, 68–9.

72 Steevens, proposal for his edition of Shakespeare (London 1766), cited in *SCH*, 5:251. Such appeals for collaboration did not usually extend, however, to other editors, from whose work every new edition had to be distinguished in order to justify its entry into an already crowded market. Common to all notable editions of the period were lengthy rehearsals of previous editors' errors and failings, rehearsals that arguably functioned to deflect attention from the commercial interests that lay behind the introduction of any new edition. Johnson, in his preface, characteristically admitted that "every editor has an interest to suppress" the work of his predecessors, however valuable their contributions (*Works*, 7:95).

73 David Hume, *The History of Great Britain*, vol. 1 (Edinburgh 1754), cited in *SCH*, 4:173.

74 Such prejudice often led critics, well before Lamb, to elevate reading above playgoing. Addison's remarks on staging made it clear that he believed audiences experienced tragedy more fully when treated like readers: "A good Poet will give the Reader a more lively idea of an Army or a Battel in a Description, than if he actually saw them drawn up in Squadrons and Battalions, or engaged in the Confusion of a Fight. Our Minds should be opened to great Conceptions, and inflamed with glorious Sentiments, by what the Actor speaks, more than by what he appears" (*S* 42).

75 Adam Smith, *The Theory of Moral Sentiments*, ed. D.D. Raphael and A.L. Macfie (Oxford: Clarendon Press 1976), 21. On Smith's use of the theatrical metaphor, see Jonas Barish, *The Anti-Theatrical Prejudice* (Berkeley: University of California Press 1981), 243–55; David Marshall, *The Figure of the Theater* (New York: Columbia University Press 1986), 167–92; John Mullan, *Sentiment and Sociability* (Oxford: Clarendon Press 1988), 44–50.

76 Certainly, by the time Burke was defending the sociable illusions of the theater against the rationalism of the French revolutionaries, the metaphor's associations with an aristocratic and paternalistic order had become apparent. See Julie Carlson, "Impositions of Form: Romantic Antitheatricalism and the Case against Particular Women," *ELH* 60 (1993): 149–79.

77 For a stimulating discussion of walking metaphors and their prevalence in liberal thinking, see Celeste Langan, *Romantic Vagrancy: Wordsworth and the Simulation of Freedom* (Cambridge: Cambridge University Press 1995).

78 Unsigned essay, *Oxford Magazine*, iii (1769), cited in *SCH*, 5:362.

79 George Steevens, "Observations on the plays altered from Shakespeare," *St. James's Chronicle*, no. 2809 (13–16 March 1779), cited in *SCH*, 6:207. Censuring the managers for playing it safe was a common

tactic among critics of the alterations, as evidenced by Richardson's famous charge to Garrick, in the postscript to *Clarissa*, for not having "the courage to try the Public Taste" by reviving the original *King Lear* (cited in *SCH*, 3:326).

80 Colley Cibber, preface to his adaptation of *Richard III* (London 1700), cited in *SCH*, 2:102.

81 Johnson, *Lives of the Poets*, 3:441. Of Johnson's use of the figure in the Preface to *Shakespeare*, Robert DeMaria, Jr remarks that he "makes the common reader, as he is purified by time, generalized, abstracted, the real test of literature and the authorization of Shakespeare's greatness" ("Samuel Johnson and the Reading Revolution," *Eighteenth-Century Life*, vol. 16 [1992], 93). DeMaria offers the argument that Johnson resisted a change that seemed to occur during the eighteenth century from "intensive" reading (passionate yet confined to a narrow selection of texts) to "extensive" (wide-ranging yet less engaged with each text). Lawrence Lipking suggests that the evidence for this reading revolution is ambiguous; see "Inventing the Common Reader: Samuel Johnson and the Canon," in *Interpretation and Cultural History*, ed. Joan H. Pittock and Andrew Wear (New York: St Martin's Press 1991), 153–74. My argument has less to do with the precise method of reading than with the increasing idealization of reading in the latter half of the period. Johnson may be for Lipking "the Hero as Reader" (160), but such a characterization, I suggest, would not have been possible had it not been for this change in how reading was valued.

82 George Colman, "Critical Reflections on the Old *English* Dramatic Writers," in *Dramatic Works of Philip Massinger*, ed. Thomas Coxeter, 4 vols. (London 1761), 1:2–4. On the frequent anthologizing of Restoration drama after the repeal of perpetual copyright, see Brian Corman, "What is the Canon of English Drama, 1660–1737?" *Eighteenth-Century Studies* 26 (1992/3): 307–21.

83 Johnson, *Works*, 7:111.

84 Edmund Malone, preface to his edition of Shakespeare (London 1790), cited in *SCH*, 6:523.

85 Richard Farmer, *An Essay on the Learning of Shakespeare* (Cambridge 1767), cited in *SCH*, 5:278.

86 Johnson, *Works*, 7:60–1.

87 Alvin C. Kibel, "The Canonical Text," *Dædalus* 112 (1983): 239–41. Emphases in original. As Kibel notes, "anyone proposing to discuss the works of Plato, St. Mark, Rousseau, or Freud had better know them by direct acquaintance, not by hearsay" (239).

88 Thomas Seward, preface to his edition of Beaumont and Fletcher's *Works* (London 1750), cited in *SCH*, 3:384.

89 Vickers ("Introduction," *SCH*, 6:47–58) offers a brief summary of some of the issues at stake in determining an "accurate" text among competing editions like Capell's and Steevens's.

90 See Vickers, "The Emergence of Character Criticism, 1774–1800," in *Returning to Shakespeare*, 197–211. Jean I. Marsden suggests that the psychologism of later eighteenth-century Shakespearean criticism reflected changed assumptions about the role of the critic, who increasingly saw himself "an individual reader, not a social spokesman." This "growing emphasis on the individual," Marsden adds, "most affected the study of Shakespeare in the emphasis on the reader and the validation of individual response rather than the earlier emphasis on consensus (as seen, for example, in Dryden's *Essay of Dramatick Poesy*)." See "The Individual Reader and the Canonized Text: Shakespeare Criticism after Johnson," *Eighteenth-Century Life* 17 [1993]: 63. Marsden does not, however, discuss this change in relation to the debates between editors and adaptors over the meaning of Shakespeare's text.

91 Malone, cited in *SCH*, 6:523.

92 Martin Sherlock, *A Fragment on Shakespeare*, trans. from the Italian (London 1786; orig. Naples 1779), cited in *SCH*, 6:436.

93 *Farrago. Containing Essays, Moral, Philosophical, Political, and Historical*, 2 vols. (London 1792), cited in *SCH*, 6:573–4.

94 Steevens, preface to his edition of Shakespeare (London 1793), cited in *SCH*, 6:578, 584.

95 Tony Bennett, *Outside Literature* (London: Routledge 1990), 280. Bennett is paraphrasing Ian Hunter's argument in *Culture and Government: The Emergence of Modern Literary Education* (London: Macmillan 1988), 214.

96 Pierre Bourdieu, *The Rules of Art: Genesis and Structure of the Literary Field*, trans. Susan Emanuel (Stanford, Calif.: Stanford University Press 1996), 305. Emphases in original. Bourdieu remarks, in one of his more prolix sentences: "One cannot get out of the enchanted circle of *legenda* producing the *modus legendi* which reproduces [texts] as objects worthy of being read, and read as timeless objects of a purely aesthetic delectation, without taking that circle as object within two sorts of inquiry: on the one hand, a history of the progressive invention of pure reading, a mode of apprehending works which is partly linked with the autonomization of the field of literary production and the corresponding appearance of works demanding to be read (or reread) in themselves and for themselves; on the other hand, a history of the process of canonization which has led to the constitution of a corpus of canonic works whose value the education system tends continually to reproduce by producing aware consumers (which means converted ones) as well as sacralizing commentaries" (*Rules of Art*, 304).

97 Jonathan Arac notes the correlation in Romantic idealizations of
Shakespeare between a suitably isolated mode of reading and "the loss,
or abandonment, of a decent public world of politics." See "The
Media of Sublimity: Johnson and Lamb on *King Lear*," *Studies in Romanticism* 26 (1987): 209–20 (quote at 218).

98 Thomas Dale, *An Introductory Lecture Delivered in the University of London*
(London 1828), quoted in Gary Taylor, *Reinventing Shakespeare*
(Oxford: Oxford University Press 1989), 194. On English studies at
University College, see Franklin E. Court, *Institutionalizing English Literature*, chap. 2. Much of the same process I have been surveying in later
eighteenth-century England would be repeated in the next century in
the United States, as Lawrence W. Levine has shown in *Highbrow/
Lowbrow: The Emergence of Cultural Hierarchy in America* (Cambridge,
Mass.: Harvard University Press 1988), chap. 1. Originally considered
popular entertainment, Shakespeare was gradually made a "highbrow"
author whose works were considered to be above the ordinary American playgoer's comprehension and required the special ability of professional experts to elucidate. Levine quotes James Russell Lowell, who
presided at one time over the Modern Language Association, on how
the Shakespearan text could serve as prime justification for making
the study of English literature an academic discipline: "I never open
my Shakespeare but I find myself wishing that there might be profes-
sorships established for the expounding of his works as there used to
be for those of Dante in Italy" (72).

99 Vickers, *Returning to Shakespeare*, 231.

CHAPTER SEVEN

1 Ernst Robert Curtius began the modern examination of canon-
formation in *European Literature and the Latin Middle Ages*, trans. Willard
R. Trask (New York: Harper and Row, 1963), 256–72. Jan Gorak has
since provided a fuller account of the term's various usages in *The
Making of the Modern Canon: Genesis and Crisis of a Literary Idea*
(London: Athlone 1991), 9–88. Douglas Lane Patey provides a good
summary account of the relation between canon-formation and the
discourse of aesthetics in "The Eighteenth Century Invents the
Canon," *Modern Language Studies* 18 (1988): 17–37.

2 René Wellek, *The Rise of English Literary History* (Chapel Hill: University
of North Carolina Press 1941), 1.

3 Lawrence Lipking, *The Ordering of the Arts in Eighteenth-Century England*
(Princeton, N.J.: Princeton University Press 1970), 328–9.

4 Wellek, *Rise of English Literary History*, 134.

5 David Hume, "Of the Standard of Taste," *Essays Moral, Political, and Literary,* ed. Eugene F. Miller, rev. ed. (Indianapolis, Ind.: Liberty Classics 1987), 227.

6 "No serious discussion," Steven Connor writes, "of the question of value can proceed very far without encountering one form or another of the conflict between absolute and relative value, a conflict traditionally polarized by those who, on the one hand, believe in the need for, and possibility of, norms and values which are unconditional, objective and absolute, and those who, on the other, accept the unmasterable historicity, heterogeneity and cultural relativity of all values." And yet, as Connor observes, these positions are mutually implicated, for, "as well as contradicting each other, each side of the argument also requires, confirms and regenerates the other" (*Theory and Cultural Value* [Oxford: Basil Blackwell 1992], 1).

7 Though the entry of the novel into the general literary canon would not be secured until much later, eighteenth-century novelists defined the terms for this entry by vaunting the moral value of their activity at the expense of the popular forms that had first established the conventions of prose fiction. See William B. Warner, "The Elevation of the Novel in England: Hegemony and Literary History," *ELH* 59 (1992): 577–96.

8 Oliver Goldsmith, "An Account of the Augustan Age in England," *The Bee,* no. 8, and "An Enquiry into the Present State of Polite Learning," in *Complete Works,* ed. Arthur Friedman, 5 vols. (Oxford: Clarendon Press 1966), 1:498, 318. On eighteenth-century ideas of poetic refinement and decline, see René Wellek, "The Price of Progress in Eighteenth-Century Reflections on Literature," *Studies on Voltaire and the Eighteenth Century* 155 (1976): 2265–84; and James Engell, *Forming the Critical Mind: Dryden to Coleridge* (Cambridge, Mass.: Harvard University Press 1989), 44–75.

9 Elijah Fenton, "An Epistle to Mr. Southerne, from Kent, January 28, 1710/11," in *Works of the English Poets,* ed. Alexander Chalmers, 21 vols. (London 1810), 10:399.

10 "W.Z.," "Parallel between the French and English Writers, Part II," *The Universal Museum and Complete Magazine* (October 1765), 527.

11 The scale has been reproduced by James M. Osborn in "Joseph Spence's 'Collections Relating to The Lives of the Poets,'" *Harvard Library Bulletin* 16 (1968): 132.

12 "The Ballance of Poets," *The Museum: or, the Literary and Historical Register,* ed. Robert Dodsley, 19 (6 December 1745), rpt. in collected ed., 3 vols. (London 1746), 2:165–9; "The Poetical Scale," *The Literary Magazine* (January 1758): 6–8. Roger de Piles's "Balance des Peintres" is

translated in Elizabeth Gilmore Holt, ed., *Literary Sources of Art History* (Princeton, N.J.: Princeton University Press 1947), 414–16.

13 Samuel Johnson, *Rambler* 92, in *Works*, ed. A.T. Hazen *et al.* (New Haven, Conn.: Yale University Press 1958–in progress), 4:122.

14 Hume, *Essays Moral, Political, and Literary*, 231.

15 Foucault notes that one of the main functions of the "author" is to provide a principle of coherence (*Language, Counter-Memory, Practice*, ed. Donald F. Bouchard [Ithaca, N.Y.: Cornell University Press 1977], 123–8). The unsigned essay from *The British Magazine*, "An Essay on the Merits of Shakespear and Corneille," was the first in a series of comparative estimates of authors "calculated to promote critical knowledge" and to provide "a considerable insight into human nature, as the characters of men may be as fully collected from their writings as from personal acquaintance and conversation" ("Considerations on the Similitude of Genius Between Horace, Boileau and Pope," 1 [August 1760]).

16 Wordsworth attributes the thought to Coleridge in his letter to Lady Beaumont of 21 May 1807, but he repeats the maxim without attribution in the 1815 "Essay, Supplementary to the Preface." I quote the original version, from *Wordsworth's Literary Criticism*, ed. W.J.B. Owen (London: Routledge and Kegan Paul 1974), 115.

17 Citing Wittgenstein's critique of foundationalist reasoning as his inspiration, Bourdieu uses the phrase "rules of the game" to suggest how categories of taste possess an "extreme vagueness and flexibility" which "makes them completely resistant to essentialist definition" (*The Rules of Art: Genesis and Structure of the Literary Field*, trans. Susan Emanuel [Stanford, Calif.: Stanford University Press 1996], 296).

18 Bourdieu adds that the "spectator deprived of this historic competence is doomed to the indifference of one who does not have the means to make differentiations" (*Rules of Art*, 248).

19 Joseph Warton, *An Essay on the Genius and Writings of Pope*, vol. 1 (London 1756), xi–xii; vol. 2 (London 1782), 477, 480.

20 Samuel Johnson, *The Lives of the English Poets*, ed. George Birkbeck Hill, 3 vols. (Oxford: Clarendon Press 1905), 3:251. In *The Ordering of the Arts*, 364–6, Lipking takes Warton to task for his "weakness for tautology."

21 Warton, *Essay on the Genius and Writings of Pope*, 1:xi–xii, 5, 203. Warton's critical anxieties were also evident in the revisions he made to his original rankings of authors in subsequent editions of the first volume. Evidence suggests that Warton slavishly followed the suggestions of reviewers, who could not understand how he could have originally classed Otway and Lee alongside Spenser, Shakespeare, and Milton in

the first rank. Presumably, Warton had ranked these playwrights highly because tragedy had long been grouped with epic and the great ode as the higher poetry in traditional hierarchies of genres. That Warton's reviewers failed to appreciate this, and that Warton had to alter the normative underpinnings of his hierarchy in order to accommodate his revisions, suggest how notions of canonicity based on genre had by this time lost considerable normative force. On Warton's revised classifications, see Hoyt Trowbridge, *From Dryden to Jane Austen* (Albuquerque: University of New Mexico Press 1977), 157–60.

22 Warton, *Essay on the Genius and Writings of Pope*, 2:477, 241–2.

23 Warton, *Essay on the Genius and Writings of Pope*, 5th ed. corr., 2 vols. (London 1806), 2:402. The passage was added in editions subsequent to the original 1782 issue of volume 2.

24 Warton, *Essay on the Genius and Writings of Pope*, vol. 2 (London 1782), 480.

25 For a recent defence of this liberal humanist position, which views critical evaluation as best conducted through such open-ended treatments, see S.L. Goldberg, *Agents and Lives* (Cambridge: Cambridge University Press 1993), 223–52.

26 See my remarks in chapter 5 on Warton and cultural capital.

27 Joseph Spence, *Observations, Anecdotes, and Characters of Books and Men*, ed. James M. Osborn, 2 vols. (Oxford: Clarendon Press 1966), 1:178. Pope's classification of poets first appeared in Owen Ruffhead's *Life of Alexander Pope* (London 1769), 425.

28 James M. Osborn, "The First History of English Poetry," in *Pope and His Contemporaries*, ed. James L. Clifford and Louis A. Landa (Oxford: Clarendon Press 1949), 230–50.

29 Gray described his plan in a letter to Warton (15 April 1770), *Correspondence*, ed. Paget Toynbee *et al.*, 2nd ed., 3 vols. (Oxford: Clarendon Press 1971), 3:1122–5.

30 Thomas Warton, pref. to *History of English Poetry*, 3 vols. (London 1774–81; vol. 4, incomplete, was added in 1790), 1:v.

31 Warton, *History*, 2:463.

32 Lipking, *Ordering of the Arts*, 375. Pat Rogers suggests that Lipking overstates his criticism of Warton. See "Thomas Warton and the Waxing of the Middle Ages," in *Medieval Literature and Antiquities*, ed. Myra Stokes and T.L. Burton (Cambridge, U.K.: D.S. Brewer 1987), 175–86. Warton claims that the "peculiar merit" of histories like his own lies in their "faithfully recording the features" of the literary past (*History*, 1:ii).

33 Warton, *History*, 2:31 (Gower and Chaucer); 3:12 (Petrarch); 2:219 (Hawes); 3:29 (Wyatt).

34 Warton, *History*, 3:490, 497.

35 Warton, *History*, 1:i–ii.

36 Warton, *History*, 2:341.

37 Thomas Warton, *Observations on the Fairy queen of Spenser*, 2nd. ed., 2 vols. (London 1762; New York: Haskell House 1969), 1:15.

38 Warton, *Observations*, 1:15.

39 Warton, *Observations*, 2:87.

40 In a stimulating argument that complements my earlier remarks on how Milton and Shakespeare came to be valued for the inexhaustibility of their meaning, Jonathan Brody Kramnick analyses the terms Warton used to canonize Spenser as an author whose works were valuable precisely because of the alterity and difficulty they presented for modern readers. Relying much as I do on Bourdieu's categories, Kramnick demonstrates how Warton enshrined Spenser alongside Milton and Shakespeare as the central figures in a restricted culture that could be prized for its "relative autonomy from the ruck of commerce" ("The Cultural Logic of Late Feudalism: Placing Spenser in the Eighteenth Century," *ELH* 63 [1996]: 871–92). I would add, however, that this restricted culture nonetheless allowed for a *relatively* more plural canon than had previously been the case in English criticism. Engrossed in an imaginative experience that freed them from outside obligations, Warton's ideal readers could overcome their presentist complacencies and familiarize themselves not just with the sublime masters of English poetry but with diverse and challenging authors from all centuries.

41 Warton, *History*, 1:ii.

42 Vicesimus Knox, Essay 39: "On the Old English Poets," in *Essays, Moral and Literary*, 2 vols. (London 1779), 1:298. Joseph M.P. Donatelli has suggested that Warton's narrative in his initial volume is "remarkably similar in form and content to a work of fiction" ("The Medieval Fictions of Thomas Warton and Thomas Percy," *University of Toronto Quarterly* 60 [1991]: 439).

43 Warton, *History*, 2:462–3.

44 Warton, *Observations*, 2:268.

45 Warton, *History*, 1:ii.

46 Warton, *History*, 3:464.

47 Johnson, *A Dictionary of the English Language*, 2 vols. (London 1755), 1:5. Recent critics have tended to see the *Dictionary* as instituting a modern configuration of the canon, yet their arguments seem based on problematic historical assumptions. "From the time of its appearance until the middle of the present century," Alvin Kernan has claimed of Johnson's work, "it was generally taken for granted by a print society that language is ruled by its professional writers, particularly its major literary figures, who make language their chief study,

maintain its length, expand the range of possibilities, create new words and meanings, rework the tropes, and in the end are the ultimate authorities on wordcraft" (*The Death of Literature* [New Haven, Conn.: Yale University Press 1990], 159–60). Such a view of writers would have been taken for granted well before Johnson, it being a central premise of rhetoricist thinking, but Kernan has ignored this fact in order to make his nostalgic lapsarian narrative seem to culminate definitively in a contemporary post-print age. Kernan is revising remarks he first presented in *Printing Technology, Letters and Samuel Johnson* (Princeton, N.J.: Princeton University Press 1987), where he maintained that the *Dictionary* "established as fact the primary source of the aura of the literary text over the last two centuries, its special proprietary relationship to language" (198). If it is true that print intensified this aura, this would seem to reverse what Benjamin believed were the effects of mechanical reproduction; it is just as likely, however, that print reduced the aura that written works possessed for a pre-print age (or for the manuscript culture of the Renaissance courtiers) and objectified language for ready consumption by a reader removed from scenes of social interaction. More tempered is Pat Rogers's suggestion in his Past Masters volume on Johnson (Oxford: Oxford University Press 1993) that Johnson's "citation in bulk of earlier writers helped to define a canon of English classical authors for the first time" (71). Yet the canon affirmed in the *Dictionary* is very much the producers' canon of a rhetorical culture, with theologians and philosophers being cited as much as literary authors.

48 Johnson, *Works*, 7:60.

49 Johnson, from the review of Jenyns's *Inquiry into … Evil*, in *Literary Magazine*, nos. xiii–xv, (April–July 1757), 2:302 in the collected edition of the periodical.

50 Thomas Reinert has suggested that many features of Johnson's writing, such as his lengthy lists of examples, "are organized strictly according to rhetorical force" but are framed by Johnson's probabilistic thinking, which allows for a wide range of contingencies within the conceptual category of the "human," a category that is for Johnson both absolute and intractably complex (*Regulating Confusion: Samuel Johnson and the Crowd* [Durham, N.C.: Duke University Press 1996], 130).

51 Fredric V. Bogel has described how Johnson seems to undercut his own authority as author by displaying its arbitrariness: "Johnson does not surrender authority, but he redefines and demystifies it. He shows that the magisterial absoluteness which often functions as the very image of authority – that 'state of solemn elevated abstraction' which Boswell had inferred from Johnson's writings and which had grown in his fancy 'into a kind of mysterious veneration' – depends on, is

produced from, is often but a special case of all that it is taken to transcend: labor, rhetoric, artifice, textuality, self-division, histrionic energy, and, not least, the ambition to display magisterial absoluteness" (*The Dream of My Brother: An Essay on Johnson's Authority* [Victoria, B.C.: English Literary Studies 1990], 67). While Johnson may advertise this arbitrariness in a variety of ways, the device is highly conventional; the claim for "magisterial absoluteness" of the author-figure may be the more recent gesture.

52 Johnson, *Works*, 2:424–9.

53 Robert DeMaria, Jr, "Johnson's Form of Evaluation," *Studies in English Literature* 19 (1979): 511. This is not quite the same argument that Leopold Damrosch, Jr proposes in trying to account for Johnson's evaluative inconsistencies, which Damrosch relates to Johnson's refusal to work according to a systematic set of rules: "The usual reason for his real or apparent self-contradictions is his admirable effort to respond fully to specific works, and to take account of elements in his response that may not agree with his response at other times to works that look similar. Consistency may be of the first importance for a philosopher, but it is not always a virtue in a critic" (*The Uses of Johnson's Criticism* [Charlottesville: University Press of Virginia 1976], 21–2). Yet Johnson's inconsistencies, one could argue, only seem so from the objectivist perspective of method, and can equally be seen as divergent modes of rhetorical valuation. For an argument that treats Johnson's writing by opposition and complication as part of a larger rhetorical tradition of thought, see James Boyd White, "Teaching a Language of Morality: Johnson's *Rambler* Essays," in *When Words Lose Their Meaning* (Chicago; University of Chicago Press 1984), 138–62.

54 Johnson, "Prologue Spoken at the Opening of the Theatre in Drury-Lane, 1747" (l. 48), *Works*, 6:89.

55 Lawrence Lipking claims that Johnson was interested in "history" but loathed "historicism" ("What Was It Like To Be Johnson?" in *The Age of Johnson* 1, ed. Paul J. Korshin [New York: AMS Press 1987], 57n.21). Johnson may not have subscribed to a strong version of historicism, but then very few in his age would have. In any case, a strong historicism, like an absolute relativism, may be a logically untenable position.

56 Johnson, *Lives* 1:410.

57 Johnson, *Lives*, 1:1. Specific examples of such gestures from the *Lives* include Sheffield ("a poet of no vulgar rank," 2:174), Mallet ("cannot be placed in any high class," 3:410), and Tickell ("cannot be refused a high place among the minor poets," 2:311).

58 Johnson, *Lives*, 1:412.

59 Lipking goes on: "Yet this analysis omits what Johnson himself considered the point of knowing the self: to close the gap between the self

and the other, between the unique, solitary person and all other persons or between the interests of the soul and the interests of God, until the individual becomes identified with the universal" ("What Was It Like To Be Johnson?," 50–1).

60 See the section on Jonson in chapter 2 and the references there to articles by Thomas M. Greene and Stanley Fish.

61 Johnson, *Works*, 7:61; *Lives*, 1:457.

62 Johnson, *Lives*, 1:457, 3:223.

63 Johnson, *Lives*, 1:418.

64 Johnson, *Works*, 7:67.

65 Johnson, *Lives*, 1:183. Stephen Fix offers a fine explication of what Johnson meant by this idea. See "Johnson and the 'Duty' of Reading *Paradise Lost*," *ELH* 52 (1985): 649–71.

66 Johnson, *Lives*, 2:125.

67 Johnson, *Works*, 7:71, 339. G.F. Parker presents the most persuasive version of this argument in *Johnson's Shakespeare* (Oxford: Clarendon Press 1989), 15–28.

68 James Boswell, *The Life of Samuel Johnson, LL.D.*, ed. George Birkbeck Hill, rev. by L.F. Powell, 6 vols. (Oxford: Clarendon Press 1934–50; corr., 1964), 2:238.

69 Johnson, *Lives*, 1:302.

70 Johnson, *Works*, 7:60–1.

71 Johnson, *Works*, 7:61. Paul Alkon considers Johnson's use of the figure in "Johnson and Time Criticism," *Modern Philology* 85 (1988): 543–57. For a brief summary of the problems involved in observing a set term for canonicity, see Michael Tanner, "The Test of Time," *The Critical Review* 28 (1986): 3–17.

72 Johnson, *Lives*, 3:104.

73 On the test of time and Johnson's defence of copyright, see my "Copyright and the Invention of Tradition," *Eighteenth-Century Studies* 26 (1992): 19–20.

74 Johnson, *Lives*, 1:375, 144, 49.

75 Johnson, *Rambler* 203, in *Works*, 5:295.

76 Johnson, *Lives*, 1:23.

77 Johnson, *Lives*, 3:441.

78 Robert DeMaria, Jr, *The Life of Samuel Johnson* (Oxford: Basil Blackwell 1993), 293. See also Clarence Tracy, "Johnson and the Common Reader," *Dalhousie Review* 57 (1977): 405–23. Tracy writes that Johnson's negative definitions leave the common reader "a little bloodless" yet at the same time transform him into a transcendent figure: "When one has stripped away from a real person his layers of acquired knowledge and experience, his particular manners and customs, his race, age, and sex, his personal and ideological commitments, and all

his other similar wrappings, what is there left of him? What was left for Johnson was the basic man who was so much the preoccupation of seventeenth and eighteenth century thinkers, man deprived of innate ideas, of traditions, and of superficial differences owing to time, place, and culture, man, in short, reduced to the level on which all men's minds work alike. The advantage possessed by the concept of the common reader was universality" (410). In effect, what the modern reader achieves by rising above his own provincialism through an act of the imagination, Johnson's common reader achieves through a process of willful self-denial.

79 Hugh Blair, *Lectures on Rhetoric and Belles Lettres*, 2 vols. (London 1783), 1:10.

80 Johnson, *Lives*, 1:411.

81 Johnson, *Works*, 7:3, 91.

82 John Dryden, *Of Dramatick Poesy and Other Critical Essays*, ed. George Watson, 2 vols. (London: Dent/Everyman's Library 1962), 1:246; *Lives*, 1:18.

83 Johnson, *Works*, 7:71.

84 Johnson, *Lives*, 1:421.

85 Johnson, *Works*, 7:81; *Lives*, 3:240.

86 Johnson, review of Joseph Warton's *An Essay on the Writings and Genius of Pope*, from *The Literary Magazine*, no. 1 (15 April–15 May 1756), in *Samuel Johnson: Oxford Authors*, ed. Donald Greene (Oxford: Oxford University Press 1984), 489.

87 Johnson, *Lives*, 3:242–4.

88 Johnson, *Lives*, 3:251, 2:230.

89 The full passage reads: "This easy and safe conveyance of meaning it was Swift's desire to attain, and for having attained he deserves praise, though perhaps not the highest praise. For purposes merely didactick, when something is to be told that was not known before, it is the best mode, but against that inattention by which known truths are suffered to lie neglected it makes no provision; it instructs, but does not persuade" (Johnson, *Lives*, 3:52).

90 Johnson, *Rambler* 136, in *Works*, 4:359; *Rambler* 104, in *Works* 4:192.

91 On Johnson's "rigorous economy of praise," see James Eli Adams, "The Economies of Authorship: Imagination and Trade in Johnson's *Dryden*," *Studies in English Literature* 30 (1990): 467–86.

92 Johnson, *Lives*, 3:438; *Idler* 85, in *Works* 2:266.

93 Johnson, *Lives*, 1:454.

94 Johnson, *Lives*, 3:104, 3:234, 1:170; *Works*, 7:61.

95 Johnson, *Lives*, 3:222; *Works*, 7:81; *Rasselas*, ch. 10, *Works*, 16:45; *Lives*, 1:398–9.

96 Johnson, *Lives*, 1:2.

97 Johnson, *Adventurer* 137, in *Works*, 2:490; Boswell, *Life*, 2:350–1.

98 John Hawkins, *The Life of Samuel Johnson, LL.D.*, ed. Bertram H. Davis (New York: Macmillan 1961), 108–9.

99 *Adventurer* 138, in *Works* 2:496.

100 Boswell, *Life*, 3:110. On Bell's edition and the challenge of Johnson's, see Thomas F. Bonnell, "Bookselling and Canon-Making: The Trade Rivalry over the English Poets, 1776–1783," in *Studies in Eighteenth-Century Culture* 19, ed. Leslie Ellen Brown and Patricia Craddock (East Lansing, Mich.: Colleagues Press 1989), 53–69.

101 Johnson, *Lives*, 2:16. On Johnson and authority, see Bogel, *The Dream of My Brother*, and James Gray, "*Auctor et Auctoritas*: Dr. Johnson's Views on the Authority of Authorship," *English Studies in Canada* 12 (1986): 269–84.

102 Boswell, *Life*, 4:35n.3.

103 Johnson, *Lives*, 1:181, 1:7, 3:324, 3:301.

104 Johnson, *Lives*, 3:417. J.C.D. Clark has presented the most extended and controversial detection of a political agenda in the criticism. See *Samuel Johnson: Literature, Religion, and English Cultural Politics from the Restoration to Romanticism* (Cambridge: Cambridge University Press 1994).

105 Johnson, *Lives*, 2:41, 174–5.

106 Johnson, *Adventurer* 115, in *Works* 2:457; *Works*, 7:71.

107 Johnson, "Prologue Spoken at the Opening of the Theatre in Drury-Lane, 1747," l. 54, in *Works* 6:89; *Lives*, 3:220, 1:xxvi.

108 Johnson, *Idler* 59, in *Works* 2:184. Emphasis added.

109 Johnson, *Lives*, 1:180; *Rambler* 208, in *Works* 5:319; *Works*, 7:65.

110 Johnson, *Lives*, 3:442; *Works*, 7:67.

111 Johnson, *Lives*, 3:248. DeMaria relates this passage to Johnson's common reader: "To have perception without principles is something that Johnson might admit to be humanly impossible, even in his most empirical mood. Yet as a figure of perfection, Johnson's common reader has neither principles of criticism nor learning, and in these deficiencies finds power ... As he did in the Preface to Shakespeare and some other earlier writings, Johnson does not in the *Lives* work hard to forge an apotheosis of the common reader as an allegorical representative of the judgment of time. He creates instead a reader who is pure perception" (*Life of Samuel Johnson*, 292–3).

112 Johnson, *Works*, 7:112.

113 Johnson, *Lives*, 1:381, 2:64.

114 Johnson, *Idler* 85, in *Works*, 2:266; *Idler* 59, in *Works*, 2:183.

115 As ever, Johnson could complicate this thought with what seemed like a relativizing gesture. Of works of antiquity, he wrote: "If in books thus made venerable by the uniform attestation of successive ages, any

passages shall appear unworthy of that praise which they have formerly received; let us not immediately determine, that they owed their reputation to dulness or bigotry; but suspect at least that our ancestors had some reasons for their opinions, and that our ignorance of those reasons makes us differ from them" (*Adventurer* 58, in *Works*, 2:372). Johnson did not speculate on whether those reasons might be caused by extrinsic interests or by a divergent understanding of absolute value, and so this claim about the moderns differing from the ancients retains its unresolved ambiguity.

116 Johnson, *Idler* 59, in *Works*, 2:183.

117 Johnson, *Works*, 7:61; *Lives* 3:238.

EPILOGUE

1 Michel Foucault, *The Order of Things* (New York: Vintage 1973), 300. See also René Wellek, "What is Literature?" in *What Is Literature?* ed. Paul Hernadi (Bloomington: Indiana University Press 1978), 16–23; Raymond Williams, *Marxism and Literature* (Oxford: Oxford University Press 1977), 45–54; and Clifford Siskin, *The Historicity of Romantic Discourse* (New York: Oxford University Press 1988), 84–93.

Recently, Richard Terry has contested the standard claim that the increased prevalence in the later eighteenth century of the word "literature" as a term for a body of "creative writings" ought to be read as evidence that the canon of English literature began to be formed only during this period. (See his "The Eighteenth-Century Invention of English Literature: A Truism Revisited," *British Journal for Eighteenth-Century Studies* 19 [1996]: 47–62, and "Literature, Aesthetics, and Canonicity in the Eighteenth Century," *Eighteenth-Century Life* 21 [1997]: 80–101. See also the replies to the latter essay by Thomas P. Miller and Clifford Siskin in the same issue of the journal; further replies, as well as Terry's response, are expected to appear in the November 1997 issue of the journal.) In support of his claim that canon-formation was occurring prior to the eighteenth century, Terry has relied upon some of my previously published research, yet his conclusions are dramatically at odds with those that I present here and in an earlier summary essay, "The Emergence of 'Literature': Making and Reading the English Canon in the Eighteenth Century," *ELH* 63 (1996): 397–422. Terry maintains that the idea of creative writings, or what is now called "literature," had existed for centuries before the idea began to be designated by this term. Moreover, he suggests that canon-making was altered during the eighteenth century only in two, relatively minor ways: by the rise of an antiquarian "spirit" that opened the canon up to pre-Chaucerian writings, and by the schematizing of literary history into a procession of "schools" (97–8). Though I am in general agreement with Terry's view that the old rhetorical category of "poetry" once occupied much of the same conceptual space that is now denoted by "literature," I believe that he greatly oversimplifies the significance of this change and of the rise of literary history and other critical practices during the eighteenth century. His error is in assuming that both the canon and the works that were deemed canonical were valued *for the same reasons* during the early modern period through to the early nineteenth century. It is my contention that the change from "poetry" to "literature" reflected a much broader normative change wherein consumption gradually displaced production as the central emphasis within canon-making.

2 Aristotle, *Poetics* 1.6–7, trans. M.E. Hubbard, in *Ancient Literary Criticism*, ed. D.A. Russell and M. Winterbottom (Oxford: Clarendon Press 1972), 91. Editorial interpolations are the translator's.

3 Sir Philip Sidney, *The Defence of Poesie*, Ponsonby ed. (London 1595), sig. C2$_v$.

4 John Dennis, *Critical Works*, ed. Edward Niles Hooker, 2 vols. (Baltimore, Md.: Johns Hopkins Press 1939–43), 2:35.

5 Francis Bacon, *Of the proficience and advancement of Learning, divine and humane* (London 1605), sig. A3$_v$.

6 John Clarke, *An Essay upon Study* (London 1731), 5–6.

7 Samuel Johnson, *The Lives of the English Poets*, ed. George Birkbeck Hill, 3 vols. (Oxford: Clarendon Press 1905), 1:143–4.

8 James Boswell, *The Life of Samuel Johnson, LL.D.*, ed. G.B. Hill, rev. L.F. Powell, 6 vols. (Oxford: Clarendon Press 1934–50; with corrections, 1964), 1:57.

9 Boswell, *Life*, 3:332–3.

10 Wellek, "What Is Literature?" 19.

11 Johnson, *Works*, ed. A.T. Hazen *et al.* (New Haven, Conn.: Yale University Press 1958—in progress), 7:61.

12 "Preface," *The Cases of the Appellants and Respondents in the Cause of Literary Property, Before the House of Lords* (London 1774), in *The Literary Property Debate: Six Tracts, 1764–1774*, ed. Stephen Parks (New York: Garland 1975), sig. a$_v$.

13 Isaac D'Israeli, *Miscellanies; or, Literary Recreations* (London 1796), vii, xxi.

14 Vicesimus Knox, Essay 39: "Of the Old English Poets," in *Essays, Moral and Literary*, 2 vols. (London 1779), 1:298.

15 Knox, Essay 124: "On the Influence of Politics, as a Subject of Conversation, on the Taste of Literature," in *Essays, Moral and Literary*, 14th ed., 2 vols. (London 1795), 2:171. Knox varied the selection of essays throughout the multiple editions of his collection. This essay began to appear only in later editions.

16 Wordsworth, with whom we associate the inaugural demarcation of poetry from science, situated this demarcation at the end of a long line of similar "exclusions" which the reader could trace within "the revolutions, not of literature alone, but likewise of society itself." By the act of writing verse, Wordsworth explains, the poet "not only apprizes the Reader that certain classes of ideas and expressions will be found in his book, but that others will be carefully excluded. This exponent or symbol held forth by metrical language must in different eras of literature have excited very different expectations: for example, in the age of Catullus, Terence and Lucretius, and that of Statius or Claudian; and in our own country, in the age of Shakespeare and Beaumont and Fletcher, and that of Donne and Cowley, or Dryden, or Pope" ("Preface" to the 2nd Edition of the *Lyrical Ballads* [1802], in *Wordsworth's Literary Criticism*, ed. W.J.B. Owen [London: Routledge and Kegan Paul 1974], 70).

17 David Bromwich, "The Invention of Literature," in *A Choice of Inheritance* (Cambridge, Mass.: Harvard University Press 1989), 19.

18 William Godwin, Essay 15: "Of Choice in Reading," in *The Enquirer: Reflections on Education, Manners and Literature* (London 1797), 135.

19 Archibald Alison, *Essays on the Nature and Principles of Taste* (Edinburgh 1790), 10–13.

20 William Wordsworth, "Essay, Supplementary to the Preface" (1815), in *Wordsworth's Literary Criticism*, 210–14.

21 Michel Foucault, *Language, Counter-Memory, Practice*, ed. Donald F. Bouchard (Ithaca, N.Y.: Cornell University Press 1977), 73.

Index